Arab Responses to Fascism and Nazism

Arab Responses to Fascism and Nazism

Attraction and Repulsion

EDITED BY ISRAEL GERSHONI

University of Texas Press ◢◣ *Austin*

First paperback edition, 2015

Requests for permission to reproduce material from this work should be sent to:
Permissions
　　University of Texas Press
　　P.O. Box 7819
　　Austin, TX 78713-7819
　　http://utpress.utexas.edu/index.php/rp-form

♾ The paper used in this book meets the minimum requirements of ANSI/NISO
Z39.48-1992 (R1997) (Permanence of Paper).

Library of Congress Cataloging-in-Publication Data
Arab responses to fascism and Nazism : attraction and repulsion / edited by
Israel Gershoni. — First edition.
　　p.　　cm.
　　Includes bibliographical references and index.
　　ISBN 978-0-292-75745-5 (cloth : alk. paper)
　　ISBN 978-1-4773-0757-1 (paperback)
1. Arab countries—Politics and government—20th century.　2. Fascism—Arab
countries.　3. National socialism—Arab countries.　4. Political culture—Arab
countries.　5. World War, 1939–1945—Political aspects—Arab countries.
I. Gershoni, I., author, editor of compilation.
　　DS63.A64　2014
　　320.53′30917492709044—dc23
　　　　　　　　　　　　　　　　　　　　　　　　　　　　　　　2013038483

doi:10.7560/757455

Contents

Preface

The subject of Arab responses to Fascism and Nazism, particularly Egyptian responses, has guided my scholarship over the past two decades. I have attempted to understand how Egyptians perceived totalitarian regimes and positioned themselves vis-à-vis these forces. The further I delved into the subject, the more I discovered that the literature suffers from gaping lacunas and outdated methods and approaches. Upon realizing that many other scholars share my feelings toward the state of the research, I initiated and convened a workshop entitled "Arab Responses to Fascism and Nazism, 1933–1945: Reappraisals and New Directions" at Tel Aviv University and the Open University. The event took place at the end of May 2010. Renowned scholars worldwide submitted papers that suggested a profound rethinking and reappraisal of the Arab responses to Fascism and Nazism and charted a path for future research. They revised established narratives and commonly held paradigms.

I open the collection with a review essay in which I critically survey the historiographical literature produced by Middle Eastern scholars on the subject of Arab responses to Fascism and Nazism. I suggest that alongside a persisting established narrative, a new revised narrative is emerging. The historiographical review introduces and situates the volume's articles that contribute to this nascent narrative.

The articles collected in this book focus on **Syria, Lebanon, Palestine, Iraq,** and **Egypt** as well as the broader Arab Middle East. The rationale for this selection rests upon the assumption that these countries were major arenas for Fascist and Nazi activities and Arab responses, although it is true that North African countries were also an important arena. However, because the countries of the *Mashrek* received considerably more attention in Middle Eastern studies and because the conference papers that focused on the North African arena are published elsewhere,[1] this volume gives priority to the former.

Götz Nordbruch demonstrates how the Syrian and Lebanese encounters with Nazism and Fascism in the 1930s gave rise to internal debates and arguments in the public sphere regarding fundamental issues such as nationalism, ethnicity, religion, gender, class, social order, the political system, and political culture. He shows how fascination with Fascist models coexisted alongside ardent rejection of Fascism and the reassertion of humanist and enlightened values concerning individual rights and political liberties. Meir Zamir focuses on the Syrian and Lebanese political elites' assessment of wartime developments, highlighting how influential political leaders anticipated an Allied success despite both resounding German victories in the battlefields and their control of Syria and Lebanon via the Vichy regime. They secretly contacted senior British officials in the region in order to secure their countries' independence in the event of a Nazi-Fascist defeat. Their efforts to collaborate with Great Britain suggest that local leaders perceived it as the hegemonic power in the Middle East that would ultimately emerge victorious. Eyal Zisser examines individual and collective memories of prominent Syrian intellectuals and political leaders. He counters the commonly held claim that they tend to remember their admiration for Nazism and Hitler from their youth and their will to collaborate with them against French colonial rule. Examining a substantial corpus of memoirs, he clearly demonstrates that many agents of memory vehemently rejected the Nazi option, its totalitarian and racist worldview, and its expansionist ambitions. Some demonstrated empathy for the persecuted Jews of Nazi Germany.

René Wildangel revisits the question of collaboration between Palestinian leaders and the Nazi regime. He shows that al-Hajj Amin al-Husayni, the foremost leader of the Palestinian national movement who participated in the Nazi war efforts and Jewish genocide, was not necessarily the exclusive representative of the broader Palestinian public and national movement. Although Husayni's positions undoubtedly reflected those of important segments of Palestinian society, Wildangel sheds light on other Palestinian voices that rejected Fascism and Nazism's racist anti-Semitic ideology and policies. Many Palestinians viewed support for these totalitarian regimes as counterproductive and inconsonant with Palestinian interests. Despite the struggle against Zionism and the British Mandate, in the complicated reality of the worldwide struggle between Fascism and democracy, they backed the latter. Mustafa Kabha examines Palestinian attitudes to the Spanish Civil War, which stood at the center of Europe's crisis in the 1930s. He concludes that alongside support for Franco and the monarchists, there were many voices in the Palestinian press identified with the Republicans and supported their cause.

A prevailing assumption in the historiographical literature locates Iraq as a country with strong pro-Nazi tendencies and policies in the 1930s. Iraq's posture culminated in Rashid 'Ali al-Kaylani's anti-British, pro-Nazi revolt in the spring of 1941. Orit Bashkin suggests that there were other forces and voices. She provides a new reading of interwar Iraq through a systematic examination of anti-Fascist, anti-Nazi intellectuals, journalists, public figures, and organizations. She brings the prominence of these antitotalitarian forces into sharp focus, uncovering their principled struggles for liberal, pluralistic, and democratic values as they were expressed in the public sphere. The fact that Jewish Iraqi intellectuals were highly active in the Iraqi press and other print media strengthened Iraqi anti-Nazism.

Egypt was not only the political leader of the Arab world, but also the largest producer of print culture and thereby the most critical shaper of Arab public opinion. In addition, during the war, Egypt became the Middle East's war front. Owing to these reasons, the Egyptian positions—the monarchy, the governments, the army, and broader civil society—vis-à-vis Fascism and Nazism versus democracy is of utmost importance to this volume and the entire topic. As was the case in other Arab countries and colonial struggles, Egyptians reached the conclusion that these totalitarian forces were more vicious imperialist powers that endangered Egypt and the Arab world, despite their potential utility as "the enemy of my enemy is my friend." James Jankowski examines the methods by which the British officials assessed Egyptian public opinion and the Egyptian government's position toward the unfolding of wartime events, particularly during the critical years, 1939–1942. He convincingly argues that the frequent British tracking of Egyptian positions suggested that in principle, Egyptian governments and Egyptian public opinion were in favor of the British and opposed to subversive activities that would undermine the British status in Egypt and the Middle East. Jankowski reveals that the British were not impressed with what they perceived as the limited impact of Nazi propaganda in Egypt. However, as Rommel and the German army appeared to gain the upper hand in the North African battlefields, particularly during 1941–1942, Ambassador Miles Lampson and other British officials feared that in anticipation of an Allied defeat, Egyptians tended to show more support for the Axis. According to the British, the anti-British stance of ultranationalist forces in Egypt reinforced this tendency temporarily; the strong Wafd government and the sweeping British triumph in al-'Alamayn swung the pendulum back in the favor of the Allies. In his final analysis, Jankowski claims that according to British reports (and some American reports), "the threat of internal subversion never reached critical proportions." Rami Ginat provides innovative analysis of the development of Egyptian communism and the major role played by Jews. He shows how the communist option became most alluring when Egyptian activists, including Jews, weighed it against the threat of Fascism, Nazism, and anti-Semitism. Part of Egyptian communism's evolution and its ascendance during the war was inextricably connected to the struggle that was waged against Fascism by Egyptians in general and Egyptian Jews in particular. They confronted the Fascist danger and its totalitarianism, racist chauvinism, Jew hatred, and imperialism with socialist principles of equality, liberty, humanism, and universalism. Israel Gershoni examines the attitudes of Egyptian intellectuals toward Hitler and Nazism in the late 1930s and the beginning of the war. Analyzing the positions of a prominent intellectual, Ahmad Hasan al-Zayyat, and his popular periodical, *al-Risala*, he highlights a prevailing current of vehement rejection of Nazism. Zayyat opposed Nazism as a totalitarian doctrine and practice, as a racist set of policies, and particularly as a new pernicious version of European imperialism that in particular would endanger all "small nations," including Egypt and the Arab countries. Esther Webman examines early attitudes toward the Holocaust in the Egyptian press. She clearly shows that immediately after World War II, Egyptians were empathetic and sometimes even sympathetic to the fate of the Jews and their genocide. She demonstrates that the Egyptian press devoted a high degree of attention to the horrors that occurred in Europe and detailed the events and pictures of the Holocaust. This expression of empathy for the Jewish tragedy faded with the growing reverberations of the conflict between Jews and Arabs in Palestine. Webman documents how Egyptian intellectuals' and publicists' empathy gave way to anti-Semitic positions as their identification with the Palestinians and their rejection of Zionism increased.

The final chapter on Arab responses serves as a microcosm of Arab encounters with Fascism, Nazism, and liberal democracy. Haggai Erlich displays the opinions of two prominent publicists active in Egypt and Syria. He juxtaposes the moral attack of Muhammad Lutfi Jum'a against the racism and imperialism of Fascist Italy, particularly in the context of Italy's annexation of Ethiopia, with Zabiyan al-Kaylani's justification for Mussolini's war in Ethiopia and support for Fascist influence in the

Middle East and Africa. For Kaylani, Fascist Italy was a natural ally for the Arabs in their anticolonial struggle against the British and French. For Lutfi Jumʻa, Fascism represented the most dangerous imperial enemy of the Arabs and the East.

This collection is an attempt to articulate the new contours of an emerging revised narrative. Without ignoring the findings and conclusions that generations of scholars have put forth, the contributors have revisited the subject of Arab responses to Fascism and Nazism from new angles. I have no pretensions that this volume will bring the historiography of this topic to its close. Conversely, it is my hope that it will spawn further research and provide a new platform by which to develop new understandings of this subject, which is complex yet critical to the modern history of the Arab Middle East as well as to Middle Eastern studies.

Acknowledgments

This volume is the result of an international workshop, "Arab Responses to Fascism and Nazism, 1933–1945: Reappraisals and New Directions," held at Tel Aviv University and the Open University of Israel in May 2010. I am indebted to the Israel Science Foundation of the Israel Academy of Sciences and Humanities, which was generous enough to support this project. In addition, I would like to thank Tel Aviv University's Department of Middle Eastern and African History, dean of humanities, rector, and president; the Open University of Israel; and the Kaplan Chair for Egyptian History for their generosity, effort, and support for this workshop.

For their insightful and critical contributions, my gratitude goes to the authors of the volume and to the other participants in the workshop: Nir Arielli, Anna Baldinetti, Martin Cueppers, Yoav DiCapua, Joel Gordon, Sonja Hegesy, Jeffrey Herf, Meir Litvak, Eve Troutt Powell, Mona Russell, Keith David Watenpaugh, and Peter Wien. I would like to extend my appreciation to all of them for their dedication and commitment to this important event.

The workshop and the book benefited greatly from the meticulous work of my assistants, Rachel Kantz Feder, Ari Heistein, Ran Levy, and Lisa Ratz. Their incessant efforts in seeing this project through are highly appreciated. The final stages of the editing and revising processes were completed during my year (2011–2012) as a member at the School of Historical Studies at the Institute for Advanced Study in Princeton. The intellectually stimulating atmosphere at the institute and the insightful feedback that I received from the other members helped me to reconceive issues and themes and to rewrite the introduction. I am deeply indebted to the staff at the School of Historical Studies for their efforts to help me complete this project.

The book has also benefited greatly from the professional guidance and help of Jim Burr. Without his devotion to the project and his fruitful suggestions, this volume could have never come to light. Also, we would like to thank Leslie Tingle, Annette Wenda, and the editorial staff at the University of Texas Press. Their tireless efforts to improve upon our work were incredibly valuable and helpful.

Israel Gershoni

Arab Responses to Fascism and Nazism

Introduction: An Analysis of Arab Responses to Fascism and Nazism in Middle Eastern Studies

ISRAEL GERSHONI

Arab responses to Fascism and Nazism during the interwar era and World War II have preoccupied scholars of the Middle East since the early 1950s. A basic assumption that underpinned ongoing scholarly curiosity was that Arab contacts and experiences with Fascist Italy and Nazi Germany definitively influenced individuals and groups in the Arab Middle East from 1933 to 1945. These totalitarian influences were understood to have penetrated Arab politics, society, and culture, leaving behind an indelible authoritarian legacy. At the core of this assumption stands the claim that radical political forces and organizations that emerged in the 1930s and 1940s under heavy Nazi and Fascist inspiration refashioned the Arab Middle Eastern world in the 1950s and 1960s. Thus, throughout the years, scholars who adopted this master narrative have endeavored to recover the motivations of Arab actors' attitudes toward Fascism and Nazism during the 1930s and the war. They attempted to answer the following questions: How were these two authoritarian powers received by Arab individuals, organizations, movements, and governments? What ideological and practical positions did Arab forces adopt vis-à-vis the Axis during the war, particularly when the Axis was on the verge of occupying the Middle East and ending French and British colonial rule? What were their motivations for adopting these positions? How did their experiences with Germany and Italy contribute to their rise to power in the 1950s and 1960s?

Since George Kirk's classic work, *The Middle East in the War* (1952),[1] these questions (and variations thereof) have remained on the agenda of Middle Eastern studies. Three central historical contexts that developed in the Arab Middle East after World War II have fueled the longevity of this academic curiosity. The first context is the Arab decolonization struggles that culminated in the 1950s and 1960s and then evolved into a general anti-Western and anti-American antagonism. The military republican regimes that led fierce national liberation projects invented collective memories after achieving independence. These official formulations of national memory projected a retrospective understanding of their own roots and political and ideological positions and activities dating back to the 1930s and early 1940s.

In their narration of memory, the new revolutionary leaders and spokespersons depicted the wartime era as the founding cornerstone of their worldview that triggered later subversive revolutionary activity. They claimed that through their collaboration with Nazi Germany and Fascist Italy, "their heroic deeds" during the war aimed to rescue their countries from France and Britain. Through these historical narratives, they legitimized their coups d'état against the ancient regimes. In this retrospective self-narrative, revolutionary leaders contrasted themselves to the old national elites in Syria, Egypt, and Iraq, whom they portrayed as corrupt opportunists and collaborators with French or British colonialism. These old elites demonstrated their utter incompetence in the decolonization struggles, unlike the young revolutionaries who represented an authentic young and dynamic national force whose unabated struggle and commitment to independence ultimately prevailed. Even during the war, when their societies were severely repressed by massive foreign military presence, censorship, and martial law, the revolutionary leaders persevered in their anticolonial resistance. Hence, they were the credible representatives of the national struggle for liberation.

Usually, these young military men did not claim to have been ardent Nazis or Fascists; rather, they explained their pro-Axis sympathy and activity through the strategy of "the enemy of my enemy is my friend." Because they perceived these totalitarian regimes as partners in their liberation and international powers that would help them end French and British colonialism in the Middle East, they supported or collaborated (or both) with Mussolini and Hitler. In the 1950s and 1960s, these new Arab leaders crafted their revolutionary narrative of decolonization and disseminated it in their memoir literature and in official government texts.[2] Their memoir literature, an integral part of the official revolutionary ideology and propaganda, evinced an unmistakable impression of significant Arab support for Fascism and Nazism during the interwar period and World War II. As will be shown, this narrative also seeped into academic research in Middle Eastern studies.

A salient example is the scholarly treatment of Anwar al-Sadat's memoir, *Asrar al-Thawra al-Misriyya* (1957) as a historical document that proves Egypt's concrete support for Rommel and Hitler and fierce anti-British sentiment during the war. Because Jamal 'Abd al-Nasir, the Egyptian president at the time, wrote an enthusiastic introduction that defined the memoir as an "authoritative source" for understanding the history of "our blessed revolution," it became a historical identity marker of the July 1952 revolution.[3]

Many scholars accepted Sadat's translated memoirs, *Revolt on the Nile* (1957), as a historical record of "history as it actually was" and employed it as an authentic representation of the roots of the revolutions that swept the Arab world in the postwar era. Like the memoirs' authors, they located these roots in the Fascist and Nazi-inspired organizations and underground cells that operated in the Middle East in the 1930s and 1940s. They found that these organizations adopted Fascist-inspired practices, patterns of organization, modes of operation, and worldviews. The insights from these revolutionary narratives and memoirs undoubtedly pervade studies that deal with the new regimes' genesis and the course of their assumption of power.

The protracted conflict between Arabs and Jews constitutes the second context that has influenced the historiography of Arab responses to Fascism and Nazism. This context's relevance—at times more implicit than explicit—stems from the relations between Zionists and Arabs before the Israeli state's establishment in 1948. The development of Arab-Israeli hostilities, and particularly the 1967 war, gave new life to the impact of this context. In the "war of narratives," which has transpired on both an official and an unofficial level, all parties have exchanged accusations that equate the other's worldview and behavior with Nazism.

The grand mufti of Jerusalem al-Hajj Amin al-Husayni and his active involvement in the Jewish genocide have figured prominently in Israeli efforts to prove the tangible collaboration between the "Arab world" and Nazis. Here, it is imperative to distinguish between "official" and academic efforts. Although scholars are certainly more cautious in depicting the Husayni and Arab-Nazi collaboration, sometimes their work mirrors the generalization that indicts Arabs at large as active supporters or sympathizers with Nazism. The Arab-Israeli conflict's escalation and its redefinition as the Palestinian-Israeli conflict reinforced this mutual demonization. On the Israeli-Jewish side, it has triggered an emphasis on Holocaust denial and extensive, sometimes disproportionate, study of the intimate Nazi-mufti collaboration that is embodied by Husayni's unabashed enthusiasm for Nazi anti-Semitism and his historical role in the atrocities.

For the Arab-Palestinian part, many Arab spokespersons have accused Israel of adopting Nazi-style racism against Palestinians and Arabs. These charges have inspired scholars and historians to prove Israel's Nazi-like racism, resulting in a substantial literature on the subject. Also, just as the evolution of the Arab-Israeli conflict to the Palestinian-Israeli conflict led to further developments on the Jewish-Israeli side, it also produced new allegations on the Palestinian-Arab side. It has given rise to the claim that Israel cynically manipulates the Holocaust as a self-defensive mechanism in order to justify atrocities against Palestinians.[4]

The impact of this politicization on studies concerning Arab responses to Fascism and Nazism can be elusive and difficult to detect, but nonetheless is present in the literature to varying degrees. That is not to say that the authors of studies examined in this historiographical survey explored Arab responses to Nazism and Fascism with impure motives. Rather, in many different senses, it is difficult to escape the conflict's shadow that looms in the background. The present author is no exception to the influence of this context.

The third context concerns the tragic terrorist attacks of September 11, 2001. Following this event, a new academic and pseudoacademic literature has emerged with the explicit goal of tracing the historical roots of global Islamic jihadism to Arab-Muslim collaboration with Nazis during the 1930s and World War II. Here, students of this topic posit a new historical argument according to which contemporary Islamist Jew hatred and anti-Semitism first formed against the backdrop of interactions between Muslim-Arab organizations, movements, and individuals and Nazi Germany. According to proponents of this view, radical Nazi anti-Semitism was transmitted to the Arab world through these radical Islamist organizations and individuals. Therefore, a historical understanding of current violent Islamic jihadism's essence and its anti-Semitism necessarily involves the reconstruction of Muslim-Arab collaboration with Nazism, which in their view produced shared militant anti-Semitic ideology and practices. Thus, the presence of new violent Islamic radicalism has once again redirected scholarly attention to Arab responses to totalitarian ideologies and policies.[5]

In some senses, it is understandable and almost unavoidable that these three contexts have perpetuated scholarly interest in this topic. However, it is imperative to be attentive to the distinct pitfalls in studying this topic through the retrospective and anachronistic prism of these postwar contexts. The residual Arab decolonizing struggles, the Arab-Israeli and later Palestinian-Israeli conflict, and the attacks of September 11, 2001, are historical developments that emerged in the postwar era and were not necessarily related to Arab responses to Fascism and Nazism in the 1930s and 1940s. Historians and other observers, captive to later narratives and memories, are not always cautious enough to neutralize and isolate the contexts' impact in order to reach and explain the historical reality of Arab responses.

This chapter seeks to critically survey the historiographical literature concerning Arab responses and attitudes to Fascism and Nazism produced by scholars of Middle Eastern studies. It endeavors to demonstrate that until fairly recently, the subject of reception has been dominated almost exclusively by a specific narration that focused on aspects of pro-Fascist, pro-Nazi, pro-Axis Arab attitudes, policies, and collaborations. After expounding this narrative from its inception, through its crystallization, and to its institutionalization, this review hopes to display the new approaches and directions of research that seek to revise and supplement scholarly understanding of Arab encounters with Fascism and Nazism.

The Formation and Conventionalization of a Narrative: Hirszowicz's Legacy

The first wave of systematic research on this topic emerged in the 1950s and early 1960s. The opening of some Western archives, the extensive usage of German archives captured by the Allies, and the selective inclusion of Arabic memoirs enabled historians to conduct research based on primary sources for the first time.[6] Lukasz Hirszowicz's pioneering work, *The Third Reich and the Arab East*, which extensively incorporated German archival material, broke the ground in this respect. The importance of his work lies not only in the comprehensive scope of his study and innovative usage of German sources, but also in its establishment of an enduring conceptual framework. The main contours of his framework were reproduced by subsequent scholars and formed a master narrative of the topic.

Hirszowicz systematically recorded Nazi Germany's activities in the Middle East in the 1930s and during the war. In addition to his commendable reconstruction of Germany's and Italy's conflicting intentions, ambitions, and interventionist strategies in the "Arab East," Hirszowicz also studied Arab reactions to these policies, despite his rather limited usage of Arabic. He described the Arab world's response in general and treated each Arab country individually, placing emphasis on Iraq, Syria, Lebanon, Egypt, and Palestine. His work concentrated on the responses of those Arab governments, forces, organizations, and individual politicians and army officers that sympathized or collaborated with the Third Reich.[7]

Hirszowicz's discussion of pro-Ally forces and individuals is marginal at best. In his depiction, the Arab actors who counted were the pro-Nazi, pro-Fascist, or semi-Fascist organizations and movements. This included the following: in Palestine, Amin al-Husayni and his cohorts in the Palestinian national movement; in Iraq, the Futuwwa; in Syria and Lebanon, Antun Sa'ada's Syrian Social Nationalist Party; and in Egypt, "the Fascist organization" Young Egypt (Misr al-Fatah, known as "the so-called Green Shirts of Ahmed Husein"), and to some extent, the Muslim Brothers. He generalized that "the appearance of these groups reflected a wider phenomenon, namely the growing disillusionment with the policies of the Western powers and the ideals of parliamentary democracy they professed."[8] He also presented the worldview and activities of Shakib Arslan, senior army officers and radical politicians in Iraq led by Rashid 'Ali al-Kaylani, Egyptian politicians such as 'Ali Mahir, 'Abd al-Rahman 'Azzam, 'Aziz 'Ali al-Misri, and "the conspiratorial group of nationalist army officers," namely, pro-Axis junior officers such as Anwar al-Sadat.

Hirszowicz described these actors as sympathizers or imitators of totalitarian ideas and practices and later as collaborators with the Axis. Yet he recognized that they were motivated by a multitude of factors. He ascribed to them the view that Fascist authoritarian forms of government and political culture were alternatives to decaying liberal democracy,[9] but admitted that the determinant impetus of those "Arab nationalist" forces was their ardent resistance to British and French rule. Their belief that Nazi Germany and Fascist Italy would support the aspirations of Arab nationalism and help them throw off the yoke of colonial rule motivated their conduct. Hirszowicz also observed that Nazi racist anti-Semitism and persecution and extermination of Jews in Germany encouraged many pro-Palestinian Arab nationalists to express sympathy or support for Hitler and Nazi Germany.[10]

In Hirszowicz's narration, Arab backing for the Axis significantly increased in the early years of the war, when "owing to the Axis victories, British and French prestige continued to decline among the Arabs."[11] In this context, he devoted sizable sections of his book to the pro-Nazi and anti-British Kaylani coup d'état in Iraq, which he perceived as an embodiment of the general Arab desire to liberate the Arab world through cooperation with the Axis forces. Consequently, Amin al-Husayni's participation in this coup d'état and eventually his collaboration with Italian and German war efforts were also interpreted as an expression of broad Arab alignment with Nazi Germany. Although Hirszowicz was not the first to expose the intimate mufti-Nazi collaboration, he was the first to firmly root it within the general Arab political milieu.[12]

Having established the framework for widespread Arab will to align with Nazism and Fascism, Hirszowicz attributed a number of incidents to this greater objective. He was the first academic to brandish documentation of King Faruq's attempt to establish contact with Nazi Germany through his brother-in-law, Yusif Dhu al-Faqqar Pasha, the Egyptian ambassador in Tehran.[13] In this vein, he also portrayed 'Aziz 'Ali al-Misri's "abortive flight" to Iraq as evidence of a broad expression of the Egyptian army's motivations and sentiments, particularly among the subversive young officers.[14] In a more salient example, he found that at the end of January and beginning of February 1942, in addition to the severe domestic governmental crisis, "German victories in Cyrenaica and the British and American defeats in the Far East exerted a tremendous influence on popular opinion in [Egyptian] towns. In demonstrations, calls of admiration for Rommel were sounded."[15] Therefore, he averred that Rommel's invasion of Egypt in the spring and summer of 1942 and the Afrika Korps' conquest of al-'Alamayn were welcomed by substantial Egyptian actors and popular opinion.[16]

To be fair, Hirszowicz skillfully exposed the plentiful constraints that hindered the Third Reich's aspirations in the Arab Middle East and precluded efficacious Arab-Axis collaboration. He detailed "Kaylani's defeat"[17] and the Allies' triumph in conquering Lebanon and Syria and noted the fact that Ahmad Mahir, the leader of the Sa'adist majority party of the Egyptian Parliament, was pro-British and even called for Egypt to declare war on Germany and Italy.[18] Moreover, he chronicled the German and Italian failures to mobilize the "pro-British Wafd," whose "well-known enmity to the Axis"[19] was pivotal to the British cause, particularly in the critical moments of the summer and fall of 1942.[20] Hirszowicz also discussed Rommel's defeat in late-autumn 1942, "the Axis rout in Egypt," and the final expulsion of the Axis forces from Tunisia and North Africa in May 1943.[21] Although he accepted some of Sadat's "stories," he disqualified his tale about "German-Egyptian connections," which supposedly resumed in the summer of 1942. Using German material, he proved "the breaking off of contacts" between Germans and Egyptians and aptly demonstrated that the Wafd government was determined to sever any remnants of former ties.[22]

Hirszowicz regarded Nazi racism as the principal reason for the failure of German-Arab cooperation. He observed German leaders' and officials' "contemptuous attitude to the Arabs, aversion to their character and political behaviour, disbelief in their state-forming capacity and their loyalty as allies."[23] In his final analysis, he posited that the "extremist Arab nationalist politicians'" fundamental assumption that the war presented a great opportunity to bring about their liberation and independence "was an illusory occasion which no responsible politician should have relied upon." In a candid value judgment, he wrote, "Their ties with the Axis brought the Arabs nothing positive. They, in fact, can consider themselves lucky in not experiencing the lot of the European countries in one form or another under German or Italian domination during World War II."[24] Thus, in this pioneering study, Hirszowicz concluded that the Arab-German nexus was essentially stillborn due to Nazi Germany's misunderstandings and miscalculations, Fascist Italy's manifest incompetence, the Allies' military superiority, and no less the misconduct of the Arab nationalists and their false illusions.

In his narrative, Hirszowicz neglected to consider the possibility that the Allies' Middle Eastern victories were even tangentially related to the anti-Fascist and anti-Nazi sentiments that were prevalent in Arab publics. Parties, governments, and broader sectors of civil society in official and nonofficial levels espoused anti-Fascism and anti-Nazism. During the war, many of these actors identified with and supported the Allies. For these Arab forces, "the enemy of my enemy" was simply not an option because they clearly understood that Nazi Germany and Fascist Italy represented a new European ultraimperialism that was more oppressive and vicious than the old forms embodied by Britain and France. These forces and voices cultivated a sympathetic and supportive environment that was conducive to Allied victories in the Middle East. Hirszowicz's otherwise impressive work does not award any space to the abundant rejections of Nazism and Fascism. Although *The Third Reich and the Arab East* lacks a critical dimension of the story, its narrativistic legacy has been enduring.

Eliezer Be'eri's book *Army Officers in Arab Politics and Society* is a salient example of subsequent scholarship that uncritically reasserted Hirszowicz's narrative and its contours. Whereas Hirszowicz dealt with sundry aspects of the Arab-Axis connection, Be'eri exclusively focused on the relationship between Arab army officers and Fascism and Nazism. The importance of his work stems from the fact that he was the first to conduct a comprehensive study of the genesis of the army officers who assumed power in the late 1940s to 1960s in Syria, Egypt, and Iraq.[25] These radical officers usurped power through military coups d'état in the 1950s and 1960s and dismantled the old monarchist and republican parliamentary regimes, implanting a new authoritarian political culture. Be'eri pinpointed their beginnings in the subversive political movements in the 1930s and during the war and argued that the formation process arose under the distinct inspiration of Fascism and Nazism.[26] He invoked the Egyptian and Iraqi cases in order not only to construct the connection between the officers' origins and the Fascist nature of their new regimes, but also to emphasize what he viewed as a widespread Arab phenomenon, albeit with local particularism.

Be'eri assumed that the confluence of Iraqi Arab nationalism and Nazism was a central factor in Rashid 'Ali al-Kaylani's military uprising, which produced a formative model and legacy for regimes that later emerged in Iraq and in other Arab countries.[27] Therefore, his discussion of Iraq centered on Rashid 'Ali al-Kaylani and other senior pro-Nazi officers and politicians such as Salah al-Din Sabbagh, Naji Shawkat, and Yunis Sab'awi (the translator of *Mein Kampf*), who fomented an anti-British military coup d'état in the spring of 1941.[28] He found that the combination of these officers' and politicians' aspiration to rescue Iraq from British colonial rule through alignment with Nazi Germany led to the connection between Kaylani's entourage and Amin al-Husayni.[29] Furthermore, the "Iraqi insurrectionists of 1958 and 1963 . . . stressed that their movement was the successor to the uprising of 1941 and its pinnacle of triumph."[30]

As for the Egyptian case, Be'eri meticulously analyzed the worldviews and activities of the young officers who were impressed by German power. Given Jamal 'Abd al-Nasir and Anwar al-Sadat's membership in Misr al-Fatah (Young Egypt) and the Muslim Brothers, respectively, he identified an ideological affinity between the officers and totalitarianism. In his characterization, Young Egypt "promoted secular Egyptian chauvinism under the direct influence and imitation of Italian Fascism and German Nazis," and the Muslim Brothers "fostered a mystic Islamic zealotry together with an extremist nationalism, hatred of the imperialist nations — primarily England — and a hostility to every progressive western cultural influence."[31] Nevertheless, he contended that the young officers expressed sympathy and admiration for Nazi Germany largely because of German military successes in the beginning of the war and because of their hope to liberate Egypt.

Like Hirszowicz, Be'eri pointed out that the ultranationalist anti-British senior officer 'Aziz 'Ali al-Misri became these junior officers' role model when he attempted to defect from Egypt in the spring of 1941 and reach Rommel's army (in contrast to Hirszowicz's claim, which stated that he tried to reach Iraq). Therefore, the junior officers established "an underground organization of officers" within the Egyptian army. They aimed to foment a pro-German coup d'état in order to "take over the country and join the Germans in the fight against the common enemy." They viewed Rommel as a liberating force and were determined to help him conquer Egypt and oust the British.[32]

In detailing the formation of this "pro-German underground," Be'eri mainly relied on Sadat's memoirs, which led him to conclude, "There is no doubt at all that an underground organization of officers did exist." Perhaps also owing to his acceptance of Sadat's narration, he also determined that the junior officers operated in a context of widespread pro-Nazi sentiment. He wrote that when Rommel reached al-'Alamayn, the "Nazi supporters in Egypt prepared for his coming. Swastikas were to be seen in many places."[33] Given this environment, the reader can more reasonably accept the claim that the pro-Nazi officers' activities reflected a widespread phenomenon.

Yet Be'eri vitiated the strength of his assertion when he recognized that these attempts embarrassingly failed. Misri's and Sadat's attempts to contact Rommel were fruitless and ended with their own arrests and imprisonments. Be'eri himself candidly observed that in "the memories of Anwar Sadat . . . truth and fantasy intermingle[d],"[34] but nonetheless he employed them as a record of hard facts in the absence of other evidence. He wrote, "The unavailing endeavors of a number of officers testify to their passionate support of Hitler and their confidence in his victory. In the history of the war, these adventures were only marginal events. But their importance in the antecedents of Nasser's Egypt is great."[35] Thus, it appears as though even Be'eri understood that in Egypt, the idea of a pro-Axis coup d'état remained the aspiration of only a handful of army officers.

Be'eri was convinced that the war constituted the ideological and operational milieu from which the Free Officers movement emanated. For him, Nasir's book *The Philosophy of the Revolution* carried the same importance for Egypt as *Mein Kampf* for Germany: it started as a neglected text, but eventually served as the platform of a radical revolutionary regime.[36] In his analysis, the Egyptian and Iraqi revolutionary regimes of the 1950s and 1960s continuously received ideological and political capital from the Arab-Nazi collaboration during World War II. The seminal failure of this collaboration did not preclude this episode from serving as the basis for revolutionary leaders' claims to legitimacy. Nor did it factor into Be'eri's assessment. For him, Arab leaders' anti-British sentiment and their desire to exterminate Israel further reinforced their affinity and sympathy for Nazism.[37] He regarded the asylum granted by Nasir's regime to Nazi war criminals, propagandists, and scientists as a direct continuation of Nasir's and other officers' admiration for Hitler and Nazi Germany, which "continued into the 1960's."[38]

Be'eri was not interested in what prevented fruitful Arab-Axis cooperation. Consequently, his arduous search for origins and continuity came at the expense of his utter neglect of Arab anti-Nazi and anti-Fascist voices and activities. Like Hirszowicz, he did not consider the possibility that these forces could have played at least some role in the manifest failures of Kaylani, Misri, Sadat, and others. Whereas Hirszowicz at least peripherally acknowledged them, they are nonexistent in *Army Officers in Arab Politics and Society*.

In the 1960s, historians such as Haim, Lewis, Tillmann, Abdel-Malek, and Kedourie expanded upon similar themes raised by Hirszowicz and Be'eri. Although most of them did not employ Hirszowicz's and Be'eri's works directly (some were published before their translations), they produced and reproduced evidence and conclusions that fall within the confines of Hirszowicz's and Be'eri's narrativistic framework. Some highlighted Arab nationalism's (in its Pan-Arab stage) essential ideological affinity to Fascist and Nazi totalitarianism, and others explained Arab nationalists' support for Germany and Italy as a means to expel Britain and France.[39] Some explored the Arab-Palestinian rebellion of 1936–1939, the escalation in the Arab-Jewish conflict, and later the establishment of the state of Israel, which was seen to have invigorated Arab support for Fascism and Nazism after the Axis defeat. These historians also devoted attention to Kaylani's, Husayni's, and Arslan's pivotal roles in forming the Arab-Nazi nexus and regarded their positions as an embodiment of wider Arab public opinion.[40]

Although Robert Melka's dissertation received less attention than these prominent historians' works, it is the most comprehensive English-language study of this wave of scholarship. It aptly encapsulated the general thrust of the historians' studies and the manner in which they depicted the Arab-Axis relationship. He demonstrated that the Allied victory dashed the hopes of the Arab nationalists who sought to exploit Germany's and Italy's Middle Eastern ambitions in their quest to "achieve independence and unity."[41] He also perceptively observed that "many Arabs, nevertheless, did look to Germany to help them against the Zionist Jews, the British, and the French. No contradictions in German policy could alter the fact that Adolf Hitler, the leading actor on the stage of international politics in the 1930's, was also the only world figure to denounce British policy in Palestine."[42]

Melka's description of the impediments to Nazi-Arab collaboration was perhaps more nuanced than that of his predecessors and contemporaries. He found that although many saw the benefits of cooperating with the Axis, there were others who recognized "the true face of Axis imperialism . . . [and] a more accommodating British attitude towards Arab nationalism, which caused Arabs to turn an increasingly deaf ear to the appeals of Rashid Ali and the Mufti." He also acknowledged that Italy's propaganda efforts to "win Arab confidence" failed due to Arab "distrust" and that many regarded Axis imperialism as more threatening and daunting than that of Britain and France.[43] In line with Hirszowicz, Melka similarly concluded, "The Arabs may have come to some realization of the deeper cleavage between their culture and the Nazi ideology."[44] In other words, they understood that Nazi theory of the Aryan superiority was predicated on the Semites' inferiority.[45]

Although some of the studies produced in the 1960s conveyed awareness of the Fascist-Nazi-Arab alliance's categorical failure, Melka and these other historians assumed that it resulted from the Axis's incompetence and particularly the Allies' military triumph and ability to co-opt some of the Arab leaders and governments. Consequently, Melka and these historians entirely neglected anti-Fascist and anti-Nazi sentiment in the Arab public spheres. Hence, they did not even consider the direct or indirect impact of Arab anti-Fascist attitudes on the Allied victory.

The Institutionalization of the Narrative: Further Developments from the 1970s Onward

Since the 1970s, Middle Eastern studies has continued to reinforce and at times rejuvenate the established narrative. Scholars who dealt with the general history of the Arab Middle East or with specific countries in the interwar era and the 1940s were captivated by the influences of Fascism and Nazism on Arab societies, cultures, and polities. Other scholars who treated this period as a formative era for the evolution of the Arab Middle East in the second half of the twentieth century were seemingly compelled to address the Arab connection to Fascism and Nazism. These scholars' unprecedented access to British, French, American, Italian, German, and Israeli archives and the growing usage of Arabic printed sources allowed them to expand the breadth of the discussion. Developments in source availability evidently contributed to the production of more narrow focuses on individual countries.

As for Iraq, scholars underscore the rivalry between the pro-British Hashemite camp and a variety of radical and pro-Nazi forces that challenged the political establishment. They focus on the ideological lure of Nazism for this network of individuals and groups. From a political and strategic perspective, scholars reinforce the notion that Nazi Germany appeared to be the only power capable of challenging British colonial hegemony in Iraq and in the Arab Middle East. Rashid 'Ali al-Kaylani's pro-Nazi coup d'état, in April-May 1941, is presented as evidence of strong support for Nazi Germany among the Iraqi-Arab military elite, especially younger officers who sought to liberate their country from the yoke of British colonialism. In a similar vein, Sami Shawkat's fascination with the winning combination of patriotism, militarism, and physical education in Nazi schools has received thorough treatment, particularly due to his role in Iraqi education and politics. The activities of the paramilitary youth organization al-Futuwwa are considered a manifestation of Nazi youth-indoctrination practices, and speeches supporting Nazism delivered in Baghdad's Pan-Arab al-Muthanna Club are perceived as reflecting popular support for Nazi Germany among the Iraqi *effendiyya*.[46]

In the cases of Syria and Lebanon, studies that analyze the processes of political radicalization in the 1930s often highlight pro-Fascist and pro-Nazi tendencies among various newly created nationalist organizations. These tendencies are thought to have manifested themselves particularly in the mushrooming of new radical youth organizations such as the League of National Action, the Lion Cubs of Arabism, the Syrian Social Nationalist Party led by Antun Sa'ada, the Arab Club, the Steel Shirts, the early Ba'ath movement, and various radical Islamic organizations. Scholars hold that in Lebanon, the White Shirts, the Najjada, and the Phalanges/Kata'ib led by Pierre Gemayel were inspired by Nazi or Fascist ideology and forms of organization.[47]

Concerning Palestine, studies elaborate upon the established narrative that focuses on the pro-Nazi ideas and activities of the exiled mufti al-

Hajj Amin al-Husayni. After his participation in Kaylani's abortive 1941 coup d'état in Iraq, Husayni fled to Nazi Germany and actively assisted the German war effort. Although he was the leader of the Palestinian national movement, the conventional narrative identifies him as the representative of Arab opinion at large. In the literature, the mufti's activities are portrayed as a reflection of official and unofficial Arab politics even in the postwar years.[48]

Studies that deal with the broader Arab region follow the same historiographic line. They tend to emphasize the great allure that Nazism held for various official and nonofficial Arab groups, organizations, parties, and young military officers. They explain their motives and describe their ideology and patterns of behavior as imitations of Fascist and Nazi ideas and actions.[49] For example, Martin Kramer's pioneering work, *Islam Assembled*, examined Arabs' and Muslims' efforts to convene Islamic congresses from the late nineteenth century until the middle of the twentieth. In his final chapter, "Congresses of Collaboration: Islam and the Axis, 1938-1945,"[50] Kramer discussed the designs and motivations of "leading Muslim activists to side with the Axis powers, and attempts to organize wider Muslim opinion in support of Axis war aims."[51] As many before him, his major protagonist is Amin al-Husayni, who in his view reflected a substantial current of "Muslim cosmopolitans and the congresses they had championed."[52] For him, aside from the mufti, the activities of Shakib Arslan, Rashid 'Ali al-Kaylani, and Shaykh Muhammad Mustafa al-Maraghi reinforced the Islamic and Arab will to sympathize and collaborate with the Axis.[53]

Egypt figured prominently in this later stage of the historiography. Owing to this country's prominence in the region in the 1930s and intense involvement in the war, scholars have focused on Egypt as a key to understanding Arab responses in this period. More generally, Middle Eastern studies has always treated Egyptian history as the critical front due to its pivotal political, social, and cultural leadership role in the Arab Middle East and its centrality in major historical shifts. Therefore, it is reasonable that the historiography of Arab responses allots weightier emphasis to Egyptian experiences, thereby warranting additional attention in this survey.

Many studies on the history of modern Egypt describe the socioeconomic, political, and cultural processes of the 1930s. They highlight the decline of liberalism (the "crisis of liberalism"), the "failure of the democratic liberal experiment," the ideological and political nationalist radicalization, the emergence of traditionalist forms of Islam, and the intellectual shift to Islamic subjects. Scholars aver that the cumulative result of these trends produced a growing fascination with Fascist-inspired authoritarianism.[54]

Other studies, focusing on extraparliamentary movements and organizations, underline the process of political radicalization propelled by the Young Egypt's Green Shirts (Misr al-Fatah), the Wafd Blue Shirts, the Muslim Brothers, Pan-Arab organizations, and radical student bodies.[55] Studies that relate directly to World War II tend to concentrate on political leaders, events, and processes. In investigating the war, discernible historiographic focus centers on the conflict between King Faruq, the British, and the Wafd. These studies of political history award attention to the following: the pro-Axis inclinations of the 'Ali Mahir government (1939–1940); palace sympathy for the Axis powers; the famous ultimatum issued by British ambassador Miles Lampson (Lord Killearn) on February 4, 1942, that resulted in Britain's imposition of a Wafdist government on the king; and the pro-Nazi activities of Egyptian army officers (such as the young Anwar al-Sadat) inspired by 'Aziz 'Ali al-Misri.[56]

P. J. Vatikiotis's works indelibly reshaped the historiographical narrative at hand due to his authoritative status in the history of modern Egypt. In his work *The Modern History of Egypt*, which became the seminal reference book for scholars and students, he opened his chapter "The Failure of Liberalism and the Reaction against Europe, 1930–1950" as follows:

> When there arose in Europe powers which advocated ideologies and implemented policies directed against the constitutional democracies, the effect of their confrontation echoed beyond the continent. The temporarily successful challenge Fascism and Nazism presented to the Western European democracies undermined constitutional government as a model for emulation by non-European societies. When this confrontation led to a Second World War, Europe's direct influence upon Egypt eventually came to an end. The echo in Egypt was quite resounding. It was reflected in the rapid appearance of new social and political groups which, despite their different leadership, shared a belief in violence—the use of force for the attainment of political ends.[57]

In his later work *Nasser and His Generation*, Vatikiotis reconstructed the intellectual and political origins of Jamal 'Abd al-Nasir and his generation, reproducing the similar motifs and themes. Nasir's early ideological and political formation was precipitated by the spirit of the time in which "the great democracies were being seriously challenged by Fascism and Nazism in Europe, and their prestige was at a low ebb."[58] In Fascist or semi-Fascist organizations, such as Young Egypt and the Muslim Brothers, Nasir and his cohorts found a natural platform from which to express and practice their radicalized worldviews. These organizations (Nasir himself was a member of Young Egypt, and Sadat was a member of the Muslim Brothers) were the hotbed for their future revolutionary political agendas. Thus, in describing Nasir's political roots, Vatikiotis institutionalized the trope that Nasir and his generation's modus operandi is incomprehensible without the recognition of Fascist and Nazi heavy inspiration (similar to the formation of the Ba'ath in Syria and Iraq). Moreover, for him this influence is the key to understanding the republican authoritarian regime that the revolutionaries established in the 1950s and 1960s, their worldview, their policies, and their modes of operation.[59] In this fashion, Vatikiotis asserts that the Free Officers, particularly Nasir in his *Philosophy of Revolution*, did not set forth a clear-cut philosophy. "Their political ideas were blurred by religious faith and the confused admixture of Islamic-Fascist notions."[60] One should add that other important introductory books on the history of modern Egypt, such as Sayyid-Marsot's popular *A Short History of Modern Egypt*, reiterated the fact that many Egyptians "believed that the presence of the Germans might be used as a lever with which to drive out the British from Egypt once and for all." Rommel's campaign and his military successes engendered "the people's adulation of him."[61]

Arabic-language studies produced by Egyptians have added a unique dimension to Egyptian historiography on the subject. Leading historians 'Abd al-'Azim Ramadan, Muhammad Anis, 'Asim al-Dasuqi, and Wajih 'Atiq, who all focused on foreign and domestic political history, have provided new perspectives by framing the issue differently from conventional Western historiography. They underscore the Wafd's pro-Allied and anti-Fascist stance and the immense Egyptian contribution to the Allies' war effort, but also expose additional evidence for Egyptian-Axis collaboration.

Ramadan explains the Wafd's liberal positions within the context of "the struggle between democracy and autocracy [Fascism] in Egypt," equating political and ideological rivalries in Egypt with "the great global struggle between democracy and fascism."[62] He explains that King Faruq and his political allies "identified and sympathized with the Axis and waited for the opportunity to attack the democratic camp." The palace assumed that winning this struggle would enable it to achieve "absolute rule" in Egypt.[63]

Ramadan presents King Faruq, the palace, and its political allies led by 'Ali Mahir as "Fascist autocratic forces." He also defines the extraparliamentary movements and organizations such as the Muslim Brothers and Young Egypt as "Fascist organizations," which together with the palace constituted the "Fascist autocratic threat" during the years 1937–1945.[64] It appears that in order to defend and rehabilitate the Wafd—apparently a major objective—Ramadan inappropriately associates monarchal autocratic proclivities with Fascism. Because he projects the worldwide struggle between Fascism and democracy on the Egyptian political scene, he crudely defines the entire anti-Wafd camp as "Fascist," without any theoretical or documentary justification.

Ramadan defines the Wafd as "the democratic force," which was representative of the majority of the Egyptian people and their legitimate national and civil aspirations. This understanding of the Wafd's character challenges the commonly held anti-Wafdist revolutionary interpretation that originated in the Free Officers' self-narratives. He views the Wafd as an essentially anti-Nazi and anti-Fascist power that courageously stood against the "Fascist wave," which threatened to engulf Egypt. For him, the Wafd was the guardian of the 1923 Constitution and of a genuine and open parliamentary democracy. He highlights the Wafd's struggle against the pro-Axis palace and its supporters who tried to violate the constitution and dissolve the parliamentary system. Thus, despite the Wafd's historical anti-British struggle for independence, during the war it sided with the British in order to save Egypt from Fascist rule.[65]

Ramadan examines the concrete historical dilemma that confronted Egyptians during the early years of the war. He sympathetically explains the Wafd's policy in the moment of crisis on February 4, 1942, when the king—faced with the famous British ultimatum—unwillingly appointed Mustafa al-Nahhas as the prime minister of a pure Wafdist government. Later, the Free Officers interpreted this incident as the legitimizing cornerstone of their July 1952 Revolution. The officers claimed that at this moment of national crisis, given the Wafd's crude collaboration with the colonial power, the party was devoid of legitimacy and the right to lead the national movement. Earlier Egyptian historiography also viciously attacked the Wafd for this shameful collaboration. Concomitantly, Western historiography identified this pivotal moment as the catalyst of the Wafd's demise.

Yet in his industrious examination and convincing analysis, Ramadan justifies the Wafd's actions through his rigorous contextualization of its critical decision and policy. The Wafd neutralized the domestic pro-Axis

"Fascist" forces allied with the palace and restored the democratic constitutional process through elections in March 1942.[66] The Wafd sided with the British because the triumph of Fascism would imply the end of the Wafd, the end of the constitution, and the destruction of the democratic camp in Egypt. "Therefore, the Wafd's interest in fascism's defeat was a matter of life and death."[67]

Ramadan claims that after the February 4 incident, and despite the harsh criticism leveled against the Wafd by the palace and the rest of the parliamentary parties, "all this didn't in any way affect the masses that received the Wafd's return to power and the end of the crisis with enormous enthusiasm and open arms."[68] For him, even after this incident, the Wafd remained popular in the Egyptian public and was therefore able to play a role in holding off the Nazi German onslaught in North Africa en route to Egypt. Thus, according to Ramadan, in the context of early-February 1942, the Wafd's position toward Nazi Germany was appropriate for Egypt's national interests.[69]

Muhammad Anis also dedicated a study to the momentous episode of early February 1942, in which he defends the Wafd's policy. Although for a while Anis was the leading co-opted historian for the Nasserite regime, his conclusions contradict those of young Sadat. For Anis, during the years 1937–1942, the Wafd struggled against the palace's attempts to undermine the parliamentary government and to constitute an autocratic form of government that would lend expression to the king's pro-Fascist proclivities. Anis is fully aware of what he regards as the Wafd's "opportunism," but holds that "it represented the majority of the Egyptian people." Thus, in his view, by the end of 1941, British authorities reached the conclusion that in order to defend Egypt, Britain had "a strong need" to install a Wafd government, which would represent the will of the majority.[70]

'Asim al-Dasuqi's impressive work on Egypt in the Second World War is not far from Ramadan's and Anis's interpretations. He has analyzed the variety of Egyptian political forces' and parties' attitudes to the war, the Allies, and the Axis. He provides in-depth analysis of the positions of the palace; the parliamentary parties, particularly the Wafd; the Liberal Constitutionalists; the Sa'adists, the two-house parliament; and the various governments, namely, those of 'Ali Mahir, Hasan Sabri, Husayn Sirri, and Mustafa al-Nahhas. He does not hide the fact that the palace and some of the king's allies supported Germany and the Axis. However, Dasuqi details the worldviews and behavior of the Sa'adist Party that publicly supported Egypt's declaration of war against the Axis.[71] Dasuqi also focuses on the Wafd's pro-British stance, tending to defend the Wafd's views and strategies in the war, including their position in early February 1942. He highlights the Wafd's support for the constitution, democracy, and parliamentary government as well as its essentially anti-Axis stance[72] and details the activities of other organizations and individuals who supported the British war effort.[73]

Dasuqi's study reveals the hitherto neglected practical support that Egypt supplied to the British and Allied war efforts. His work uncovers the critical logistical, economic, and intelligence aid that Egyptians provided to the Allies. He demonstrates that even if Egypt officially remained neutral, its practical support was of utmost importance to the Allies' victory in the battle for North Africa in 1942–1943.[74] "During the Second World War Egypt became the strategic basis, the main center for military actions, and the major arena for political maneuvers associated with the war and its results."[75] Therefore, Dasuqi concludes, perhaps with a degree of exaggeration, that without Egypt's support, the defeat of the Axis would have been inconceivable.

Although these important interpretations that bring Egypt's role in fighting the Axis into sharp focus are invaluable contributions, they too neglect the role played by the public sphere and print media and miss the broad landscape of anti-Fascist and anti-Nazi public voices and opinions. They fail to understand that a vibrant democratic public discourse lent expression and legitimacy to the Wafd and the Sa'adists' anti-Axis policies. Whether due to the lack of a better alternative or a genuine anti-Fascist democratic worldview, this public was instrumental in bolstering the Wafd, the Sa'adist, and other pro-British forces in Egyptian politics in the critical moments of the early years of the war.

In the early 1990s, Wajih 'Atiq returned to the traditional narrative, emphasizing wartime Egyptian collaboration with the Axis. In two books that study King Faruq's connections with Nazi Germany and a few Egyptian officers' attempt to collaborate with the Axis during the war, 'Atiq has reproduced the skeleton of the well-established narrative initiated by Hirszowicz and developed by Be'eri.[76] The basic premise of 'Atiq's two studies is that "the general Egyptian feelings during the Second World War were imbued with a clear cut animosity towards Britain and its rule in Egypt."[77]

In obvious contrast to Ramadan and Dasuqi, 'Atiq employs "the enemy of my enemy" syndrome to explain Egyptian sympathy and collaboration with Nazi Germany. He asserts that the Wafd and the older national forces' inability to achieve full Egyptian independence motivated the young king and an entire generation of militant young officers to try to succeed where the Wafd failed. Using German archival material and Arabic Egyptian memoirs, 'Atiq reconstructs Faruq's efforts to contact the Germans during the war and supply Nazi Germany with intelligence relevant to its ambitions in the Middle East. Elaborating on Hirszowicz's findings, he details the king's attempt to initiate negotiations with Nazi Germany through his brother-in-law Dhu al-Faqqar, the Egyptian ambassador in Tehran in 1941–1942. 'Atiq admits that these efforts did not come to fruition and that later contacts between Faruq and Nazi Germany also amounted to nothing.[78]

'Atiq's second book describes the activities "of that handful of officers" who tried to defect from Egypt in order to join Rommel and the Axis campaign in North Africa. Like those before him, he reexamines 'Aziz 'Ali al-Misri's abortive attempt to defect in the spring of 1941. He presents a network of connections between Misri and Nazi officials and military officers, thereby determining that Misri "was the arch enemy of the English" and "a close friend of the Germans."

More important, 'Atiq finds that Misri's worldview and subversive activities were venerated by young Egyptian officers, who held him as a "pioneering model" for their operations during the war. Beyond the support of these army officers, 'Atiq believes that Misri and 'Abd al-Mun'im 'Abd al-Ra'uf (the pilot who attempted to fly him from Egypt) "were supported by some leaders of Young Egypt and the Nationalist Party."[79] He claims that after Misri was captured and tried in a public court, his popularity rose within Egyptian popular opinion.[80]

Later in his book, 'Atiq describes copycat incidents in which two junior air force officers, Ahmad Sa'udi and Muhammad Radwan, sought to defect to Rommel's line in the summer of 1942.[81] While Sa'udi's plane was mysteriously brought down, Radwan reached the Afrika Korps units in Libya and was taken to Berlin for further investigation.[82] However, 'Atiq admits that "from an intelligence/military point of view," Radwan "did not bring anything productive to the Germans."[83] Thus, although he provides new evidence of collaboration, in the final analysis, 'Atiq's narration is also a story of a series of failed episodes. Like in previous works that display this narrative, Sadat's memoir commands presence in 'Atiq's reproduction of earlier portrayals and leads him to conclude that the palace's and the army officers' strategic thinking were representative of the Egyptian people's pro-Axis sentiment. 'Atiq ignores the solid findings and thoughtful conclusions of 'Anis, Ramadan, and Dasuqi. In 'Atiq's sometimes dramatic and sensational portrayal, one gets the impression that nearly all

Egyptians were "collaborators," "sympathizers," or "identifiers" with Nazi Germany.[84]

During the 1980s, Francis Nicosia and Stefan Wild contributed to the historiographical debate through their work in new German archival material and Arab print media, which produced more nuanced interpretations. Yet, in many respects, they too articulate familiar themes of the now institutionalized narrative. Both of these scholars explore Nazi Germany's interests and policies in the Middle East. Nicosia emphasizes the "ideological and strategic incompatibility" between Arab nationalism and National Socialist Germany. "Hitler was not willing to commit Germany to Arab independence," due to his racist *weltanschauung*, his commitment to maintain the status quo of the post–World War I Middle East (i.e., not to harm Britain's interests in the region), and later his desire to secure Italian interests in the Mediterranean and Middle East.[85] In Nicosia's analysis, it was thus Germany's lack of interest in Arab nationalist ambitions that was responsible for "wasted opportunities" and the fact that "Germany failed to utilize Arab hostility toward Britain and France."[86]

Wild concentrates on the modes through which the Arab Middle East received National Socialism's ideas and practices. Building on previous themes, he shows that authoritarian ideas and patterns of organization embedded in National Socialism were assimilated by several organizations and parties: the early Ba'ath (particularly Sami al-Jundi), the Syrian Social Nationalist Party led by Sa'ada in Syria, the Kata'ib in Lebanon, Young Egypt in Egypt, and the Futuwwa in Iraq. Wild finds that for many of these organizations, National Socialism in Germany provided "a model for the swift development of a society towards an economically developed, politically united and militarily strong state under a charismatic leader." Moreover, the National Socialist leaders were "a natural ally of the Arab countries which were trying to liberate themselves from colonial structures imposed on them by England and France."[87] Finally, the anti-Semitic and anti-Jewish ideology and policy of Nazi Germany were additional sources of attraction for Arab nationalists who struggled against increasing Jewish colonization of Palestine.[88]

Like others, Wild identifies the obstacles and constraints to Arab-German relations—most important, the Germans' inconsistent and hesitant support for the Arab right to self-determination. The Nazi theory of race further impeded the development of a genuine alliance. Thus, accepting Nicosia's terminology, Wild concludes, "Before and during World War II, Arab nationalism and National-Socialist Germany were an example of 'ideological and strategic incompatibility.'" Consequently, "there was never a National-Socialist movement of any significance in the Arab world."[89]

Despite Nicosia's and Wild's substantial contributions, they too fail to reconstruct the diversity of Arab public spheres. In tracing reception, Wild examines various Arabic translations of *Mein Kampf* (most of which were partial and flawed), assuming that the need for translations presupposed Arab interest and reception of its ideas. However, he does not consider that many translations of popular European anti-Hitler texts simultaneously appeared in all major Arab capitals. Hermann Rauschning's *Hitler Speaks: A Series of Political Conversations with Adolf Hitler on His Real Aims* is an important example.[90] Wild does not take into account the possibility that many Arabs explicitly rejected ideas, practices, and institutions central to German National Socialism. Almost condescendingly (though unconsciously), these two scholars discuss National Socialism's incompatibility with Arab nationalism, as if Arabs themselves, particularly Egyptians, were not the first to articulate the gulf between the two nationalisms in real time. Indeed, various Arab intellectuals and publicists identified the intractable problems and discordant worldviews and tried to disassociate themselves from Fascism and Nazism.

Bernard Lewis's studies on Arab responses to Nazism and Fascism are particularly acclaimed, as his unique sensibilities regarding the complex historical relations provide new depth. In his book *Semites and Anti-Semites: An Inquiry into Conflict and Prejudice* he uncovers new German, British, and American archival source material and skillfully synthesizes its contents with Arabic sources. A main chapter in the book, "The Nazis and the Palestine Question," addresses the complicated network of ties between a few Arab political leaders and intellectuals and Nazi Germany.[91] Lewis maintains, "The close and at times active relationship that developed between Nazi Germany and sections of the Arab leadership, in the years from 1933-1945, was due not to a German attempt to win over the Arabs, but rather to a series of Arab approaches to the Germans."[92] Unsurprisingly, the hero of these Arab approaches was the mufti of Jerusalem, al-Hajj Amin al-Husayni, whom Lewis defines as the "principal architect of the wartime alliance between German Nazism, Italian fascism, and Arab nationalism."[93]

Lewis's renewed emphasis on the mufti is justified in light of fresh evidence concerning his collaboration with National Socialism, including its program of the Jewish genocide. However, he also equates the mufti's activities with the prevailing Arab attitude. The crux of the chapter focuses on the mufti's incessant efforts to mobilize Nazi Germany for the Arab-Palestinian struggle against the British, the Zionists, and Jews in general. Lewis underscores the imbalance in the relationship between the Nazis and the mufti. Al-Hajj Amin al-Husayni did everything in order to get closer to the Third Reich, but the "Axis powers were unwilling to commit themselves publicly, or for that matter, even privately, to full support for the mufti's pan-Arab and pan-Islamic projects, or even to grant him the full personal recognition which he sought as the Führer of the whole Arab nation."[94]

Lewis, loyal to the well-established narrative, presents the ideology and activities of a variety of radical and paramilitary organizations as manifestations of Arab-Nazi collaboration. Beyond the enemy-of-the-enemy syndrome, Lewis holds that organizations such as Young Egypt, "obviously Nazi in form," borrowed "its racism and anti-Semitism" and its "viciously anti-Jewish propaganda" directly from "Nazi philosophy."[95] Moreover, during the war, the mufti was not alone: "While the mufti and his associates were at work in Germany, there were many in the Arab lands of the Middle East and North Africa who were at least in sympathy with the same cause, and sometimes active on its behalf."[96]

In order to prove the strong pro-Nazi tendencies, Lewis examines Kaylani's pro-Axis activity and the sympathy demonstrated by the young founders of the Ba'ath toward the coup d'état in Iraq. He heavily quotes from Syrian Sami al-Jundi, who professed his total identification with and deep admiration for Nazism, its power, its theory of race, and its anti-Semitism.[97] In Egypt, again, it was Faruq and his entourage, the 'Ali Mahir government, 'Aziz 'Ali al-Misri, and other army officers associated with Young Egypt. All of them strove to promote a German victory in the war and anticipated a British defeat. Lewis assumes that these diverse Arab pro-Nazi radical forces authentically represented mainstream political and ideological currents in the Arab world.[98]

Typical of contributors to the institutionalized narrative, Lewis adopts the Sadat memoirs, with all of its shortcomings. For him, these memoirs serve as a documentary record of the overwhelming pro-German "mood of the young officers in Egypt" in the early years of the war. Beyond viewing the Nazis as the enemy of their enemy, Sadat and the officers conveyed their ideological affinity to Nazi Germany as a military superpower and to its authoritarian political culture. Like Be'eri, Lewis accepts the purported continuum between Sadat's politically driven memoir about his pro-Axis activity during the war and his later sympathy for Hitler and Nazism in the 1950s.[99]

Lewis's usage of *Revolt on the Nile* is consonant with those before him who treated it as an empirical mirror of "history as it actually was." He utterly ignores Allen Wingate's cautionary note in the preface. The publisher's decisive warning that fell on deaf ears is worth quoting at length. Wingate correctly observed that Sadat's memoirs is

> a document which is inevitably biased, because it is the work of a man who took a leading part in the Egyptian Revolution under President Nasser, was twice imprisoned for his subversive activities against the British, was, until last year, a Minister in Nasser's Cabinet, and remains today Nasser's confidant and the editor of the leading Egyptian daily newspaper, *Al Goumhourya*. For this reason, whatever he has to say is obviously something which the British public should be enabled to read, however violently they may disagree not only with his views but with his account of historical events.

Wingate clearly understood that this text, published in the mid-1950s, was a biased interpretation of events that transpired during the war that served the contemporary political exigencies.[100] Thus, unfortunately, otherwise serious scholars and eminent historians accepted Sadat's assertions, which Wingate thought would be "violently" objectionable for the English-speaking public.

Later, Lewis penned an epilogue for Uriel Dann's important collection, *The Great Powers in the Middle East, 1919–1939*, in which he slightly modified his approach. Still, he reiterated that it was the Arabs who were "wooing" the Nazis and not vice versa. He also emphasized, "What emerged with surprising clarity was that, at least for the period up to the outbreak of the war in 1939, the nature and magnitude of that threat [Nazi Germany and Fascist Italy] had been greatly exaggerated." Mussolini "could hardly be regarded as a serious contender, while Hitler, for both political and ideological motives, refrained from giving to Arab nationalism the encouragement which was often attributed to him, both by Arabs and others."[101]

Lewis differentiated between political and strategic cooperation and German and Italian influence on Arab ideology and political culture, although he viewed them both as integral dimensions of the Arab-Axis connection. From a strategic point of view, "the greatest service the Middle East rendered to the West was the provision of base and support facilities for the war against the Axis."[102] As for ideology, Lewis determined that the Axis's pervasive impact on the political culture of Arab states stemmed from their strain of totalitarian nationalism that was more conducive to conditions in the Middle East. In his view, Nazi Germany and Fascist Italy's

> new pattern of thought and of social and political organization had a double appeal—first because it was opposed to the dominant West . . . and second because the ideologies and ideas that were being offered corresponded in many ways much more closely to both the realities and traditions of the region. In countries of uncertain territorial definition and of changing national identity, ethnic nationalism of the Middle European kind was more readily understandable than patriotism of the West European kind, defined by country and political allegiance; radical and authoritarian ideologies had greater appeal than the liberal and libertarian ideas of the West. Similarly, communal and collective identities and rights made better sense than the more individualistic formulation of the West, which at this particular point seems irrelevant and inappropriate.[103]

Thus, whereas Lewis's new approach was more nuanced than his initial treatment of the subject, he nevertheless remained well within the contours of the institutionalized narrative. Given his exclusive focus on pro-Nazi and pro-Axis individuals and forces, he too failed to explain who or what stood behind "the greatest service the Middle East rendered to the West" and "the provision of base and support facilities for support against the Axis." Consequently, the reader is left to ponder what seems to be a contradiction: on the one hand, Arab intellectuals, political leaders, and movements were avidly pro-Axis, while, on the other, the Arab Middle East's operational support was a central factor in the Allies' triumph. Lewis and other contributors simply do not pose the logical question: is it possible that anti-Nazi and anti-Axis governments and civil publics that supported the Allied war effort—for a plethora of reasons—played at least some role in the fate of the war in the Middle East?

In this middle stage of the historiographical debate, most scholars reproduced and reinforced the contours of the established narrative of Arab responses to Fascism and Nazism. Despite their industrious efforts to provide a fresh and thorough understanding of the twentieth-century Arab Middle East and despite their new evidence and nuanced interpretations, ultimately their work served to further institutionalize the narrative.

The Impact of September 11, 2001

The tragic terrorist attacks of September 11, 2001, sparked a new wave of interest in Arab and Muslim responses to Fascism and Nazism. The desire to comprehend the essence and historical roots of the new phenomenon of the violent global jihadist movement motivated scholars and other observers to return to the 1930s and World War II for answers. This new academic and pseudoacademic literature has produced a central thesis that characterizes global jihadism as a type of "Islamofascism," born from the Nazi-Arab collaboration in the years 1933–1945. In many cases, proponents of this view equate the Jew hatred and anti-Semitism present in the worldviews of jihadists with the murderous Nazi racism and anti-Semitism of the 1930s and 1940s. In order to establish this historical and ideological continuum, scholars have reasserted and radicalized the now institutionalized narrative. In fact, many of these studies do the narrative a serious injustice by severely distorting its facts and conclusions.[104]

Matthias Küntzel's well-received and highly acclaimed *Jihad and Jew-Hatred: Islam, Nazism, and the Roots of 9/11* aptly reflects the nature of the literature that was produced in the wake of the September 11 attacks. Selectively relying on academic contributions to the established narrative, Küntzel locates contemporary radical Islamism in the historical context of Arabs' and Muslims' interactions with Nazism and Hitler. Predictably, his catalysts are the mufti and the Palestinian national movement, Hasan al-Banna, and the Muslim Brothers of Egypt, all of whose intimate ties with Nazi Germany and its radical and violent anti-Semitism constitute the historical source of today's Islamic jihadism, and thereby the roots of September 11, 2001.[105] Küntzel explains, "My book demonstrates that al-Qa'ida and the other Islamist groups are guided by an antisemitic ideology that was transferred to the Islamic world in the Nazi period. It shows that the Nazis' paranoid worldview and the 'fictional reality' that drove their actions rule the minds of the Islamist terrorists and determine their policies today."[106]

What were the channels of this transmission? For Küntzel, the answer is to be found in the historic alliance between Banna and the Muslim Brothers and the mufti and the Palestinian national movement. The "Muslim Brothers were inspired . . . by European fascism of [the] 1930s" and in a more concrete way by Nazism.[107] The movement was an early manifestation of the radical jihadist Islam imbued by the reverberations of European Nazism and Fascism. Küntzel identifies the proof in their ideology; patterns of organization and operation; veneration and total submission to a strong authoritarian leader; glorification of the cult of martyrdom, "the Art of Death"; and, more important, essential hatred for Jews and Judaism.[108]

According to Küntzel, in the late 1930s, the Muslim Brothers' determined struggle on behalf of the Palestinians brought them closer to the mufti and the Palestinian national movement. Through guilt by association, Küntzel indicts Banna for his connections to the mufti, the infamous collaborator with Nazis. For him, Banna's bond with the mufti, which was based on the Muslim Brothers' support for the Palestinian cause, automatically associated him with Nazi crimes. In many instances, the Brothers' avid support for the Palestinian revolt against Zionism translated into attacks against Egyptian Jews, resembling an "anti-Jewish jihad."[109] Hence, Küntzel contends that the Brothers' anti-Semitism was appropriated directly from Nazi anti-Semitism and its persecution of Jews in Europe. However, this topic was thoroughly studied by the best scholars in the field years before Küntzel and September 11, 2001, and no one found that the Muslim Brothers' anti-Zionist and anti-Jewish attitudes were appropriated from Nazism.[110]

Küntzel claims that during the war, the Muslim Brothers were involved in pro-Axis subversive activities in Egypt. They distributed *Mein Kampf* and "collaborated with the Third Reich's Egyptian agents and at the start of 1941. . . . The Brotherhood's paramilitary wing offered the Nazis their support with not just a few of these activists being recruited by the German secret services."[111] In other words, the Muslim Brothers actively aided the Nazi agents in their effort to undermine British rule and pave the way for the Nazi conquest of Egypt. His evidence for this claim is problematic, to say the least.[112]

Furthermore, Küntzel vitiates his own argument by raising the common theme of the enemy-of-my-enemy syndrome. Again, qualified scholars who investigated the Muslim Brothers' positions during the war never found any solid basis for such an assertion. The reader senses that perhaps the author himself is not fully committed to his accusation that the Muslim Brothers possessed an affinity for and collaboration with Nazism, when pondering Küntzel's disclaimer: "However, it would be wrong to characterize the Muslim Brothers as ardent followers of the Nazis. The Brotherhood rejected the Nazis' race policies and German supremacist nationalism, since both were at odds with their concept of the umma as the universal Islamic brotherhood. Moreover, al-Banna was far too religious a man to accept a non-Muslim leader such as Hitler as his model."[113] This disclaimer illuminates the holes in Küntzel's findings and thesis and leaves the reader perplexed. It seems that in order to prove that the Muslim Brothers were the main channel of transmission of Nazi ideology to the Arab-Islamic world, the precursors of current global jihadism, and thereby constituted the roots of 9/11, Küntzel should have provided ample evidence that is more convincing. In the absence of concrete historical evidence, his attempt to define global jihadism's roots in the Muslim Brothers' purported collaboration with Nazis via the mufti seems to be at best a stretch, and at worst a forced, ideologically driven association.

Toward Revising the Established Narrative

Many of the studies covered throughout this survey have contributed invaluably to our understanding of Arab encounters with Nazism and Fascism. Their centrality to scholarly understanding of this era is not in question. They thoroughly recover the Arab modes of sympathy, identification, and collaboration with Fascist Italy, Nazi Germany, and the Axis. Their emphasis on the mufti's collaboration with the Nazis is undeniably justified in light of his active support for the Axis war efforts and his participation in the Nazi program for Jewish genocide. Nevertheless, it is clear that the established narrative's presentation of the subject is one-dimensional and reductionist and lacks historical proportion. Even if the narrative underscores the utter failure of the Arab-Nazi nexus, its exclusive focus on pro-Nazi and pro-Axis forces, movements, and organizations is only part of the story.

None of these studies relates to the broader intellectual and political landscape constituted by Arab public spheres. The studies evade an inherent defect that the narrative contains: If so many Arab forces were pro-Axis and pro-Nazi, then why did the Nazi-Arab project collapse, and how did the Allies secure such a resounding triumph in the Middle East as early as November 1942? Is it possible that the Axis defeat and the "incompatibility" between Nazi Germany and Arab nationalism also derived from widespread Arab anti-Nazism and anti-Axis positions?

A new picture began to take form when a few revisionist historians freed themselves from the paradigm of sympathy and collaboration and reframed the question. They asked, were there Arab individuals and forces that rejected Nazism and Fascism? Without underestimating those pro-Axis and pro-Nazi forces that operated in the Middle East in 1933–1945, the new narration showed that there was a multitude of other Arab voices. Only by recovering and analyzing these alternate voices and attitudes can one accurately portray this period and produce a deeper understanding of Arab responses to Fascism and Nazism.

Ami Ayalon's pioneering article "Egyptian Intellectuals versus Fascism and Nazism in the 1930s" was the first attempt to investigate Egyptian encounters with Fascism and Nazism from this new angle. Interestingly enough, his article appeared in Dann's edited volume for which Lewis wrote the epilogue. The few Egyptian intellectuals and activists that Ayalon sampled were sufficient to seriously problematize the institutionalized narrative and begin to erode the conventional perception of a monolithic Arab reaction. Most of the Egyptians examined in his brief article unquestioningly supported liberal democracy and Britain.[114] Analyzing "widespread disapproval of the totalitarian call among broad circles of the Egyptian intellectual elite"[115] in the 1930s, Ayalon asserts that "as the war broke out, a wave of strong denunciations of Germany and Italy swept through the pages of numerous Egyptian publications. Admittedly, they were printed under the open eye of the British and under strict censorship regulations. But their harsh language no doubt reflected real hostility toward Hitler and Mussolini."[116] He concludes, "Parliamentary democracy, despite the discredit it had recently incurred, continued to enjoy much of its former support among the Egyptian intellectual elite. The voices of democracy's champions were louder than those of its critics who were fascinated by the Fürher and the Duce. . . . Most of them . . . remained dedicated to the democratic idea, with its implied liberties and rights, and were prepared to defend it at all times against the perils of totalitarianism."[117]

In the same edited volume, I analyze the anti-Western *weltanschauung* of the Muslim Brothers. Based on their writings, I demonstrate that the Muslim Brothers viewed Nazi Germany and Fascist Italy as chauvinist-aligned powers, genuine representatives of European, nationalistic, racist, and imperialist attacks on Islam and the East. The Muslim Brothers therefore concluded that they should be rejected as models for emulation.[118] In the late 1990s, in a much lengthier and comprehensive work on Egyptian encounters with Fascism and Nazism during the interwar era, I molded the new approach by deconstructing many of the old contours. I showed that mainstream Egyptian politicians, intellectuals, and publics criticized Fascism and Mussolini, particularly in the context of the Ethiopian war in the middle of the 1930s, while other voices expressed opposition to the racist theories of Nazi Germany. I found that those attitudes that were identified due to their enthusiasm for Nazism were overwhelmingly eclipsed by anti-Nazi voices and positions.[119]

This revisionist tendency gained momentum in the first decade of the 2000s. Contributors to the newest wave of scholarly discourse pose the following questions: What role did these newly discovered alternate voices play in thwarting the widespread introduction and impact of Fascist and Nazi ideas and practices? To what extent, if at all, did Arab intellectual and political support for democracy and the Allies factor into the defeat of Italy and Germany in the Middle Eastern arena?

Recent studies reflect two important developments in scholarship on the topic. The first underscores the shortcomings and disservices to our understanding created by the careless application of the labels "Fascist" and "Nazi" in the documentation of Fascism's and Nazism's influence on Arab individuals and organizations (particularly in greater Syria).[120] The second embodies a more substantial current that entrenches the problematization of the established narrative. Using a much richer scope of Arabic sources and considering the subject from a more internally positioned Arab location, these new studies reconstruct robust local public discourses and demonstrate that the global importance of Nazi Germany triggered lively public debates on crucial issues such as democracy versus dictatorship, liberalism versus authoritarianism, and pluralism versus totalitarianism. Their discussions of racism gave rise to controversial debates about the very concept of the nation, the status of ethnic and religious minorities among an Arab-Islamic majority, as well as the relationship between the individual and his assumed primordial community. By carefully analyzing public discourses, these studies reconstruct mainstream voices that supported liberal democracy and rejected Fascist and Nazi totalitarianism and imperialism.

Studies by Peter Wien and Orit Bashkin have challenged the established narrative by demonstrating that the scholarly focus on pro-Nazi and pro-Fascist forces obscures many liberal and democratic spokespersons that were present in Iraqi public spheres and the print media.[121] For Syria and Lebanon, recent studies by Götz Nordbruch, Manfred Sing, and Eyal Zisser underscore the uninterrupted power of liberal and democratic forces both on the political level and within civil society. Support for the French model of parliamentary government and a commitment to a representative, constitutional system are shown to have persisted in both Lebanon and Syria throughout the interwar years.[122] René Wildangel and Mustafa Kabha have thoroughly perused the Palestinian press, demonstrating the widespread anti-Fascist and anti-Nazi sentiments among Palestinians.[123] In a full book, James Jankowski and I have emphasized the role of public spheres and print media in constituting anti-Nazi and anti-Fascist positions and support for liberal democracy in Egypt. By analyzing tens of newspapers, magazines, and periodicals, we give voice to mainstream intellectual and political forces' commitment to liberalism, the 1923 Constitution, and parliamentary democracy in Egypt. These protagonists provided the vast support for the hegemonic parliamentary forces: the Wafd, the Saʿadi, and the Liberal Constitutionalist Parties, as well as other liberal democratic politicians who supported Britain and the Allies during the war.[124]

The endeavor to problematize and revise this institutionalized narrative is in the making. The described body of new scholarship suggests that this effort is already in a rudimentary stage. To be sure, elements from the established narrative still endure. Jeffrey Herf's recent work on Nazi propaganda in the Middle East adds a new and distinctive dimension to our understanding of German attitudes and policies toward the Arab world. He thoroughly investigates the project of Nazi propaganda for the Arab world, showing how the Palestinian issue was a dominant theme of Nazi propaganda. By highlighting British support for Zionism and consequent disavowal of the Palestinian cause, the Nazi messages were framed specifically in order to appeal to Arab anticolonial and anti-Zionist sentiments and, according to Herf, penetrated Arab opinion and promoted collaboration.[125]

However, it is clear that the emerging narrative brings at least four new interrelated observations to the fore of the debate on Arab encounters with Fascism and Nazism. The first is that accurate comprehension of Arab responses requires in-depth research on public spheres and public opinions. The second observation is that the preliminary studies covered in this survey as well as those in the present volume have already revealed the discernible presence of anti-Fascist and anti-Nazi voices and forces. The third observation is that upon reconstructing these antitotalitarian forces, appropriate historic proportion is given to the constellation of pro-Fascist and pro-Nazi organizations and their activities. By highlighting the anti-Fascist attitudes, the new narrative introduces proper balance to the subject of Arab responses. Finally, the emerging narrative seriously problematizes the axiomatic "enemy of my enemy is my friend." Further academic investigation is imperative to determine the extent to which the scholarship that constitutes the emerging narrative can translate into a full-fledged revisionist narrative. It is my hope that the new evidence and proposed methods of investigation suggested in this collection will advance the project of revision so critical to Middle Eastern studies today.

PART I

SYRIA AND LEBANON

CHAPTER 1

A Challenge to the Local Order: Reactions to Nazism in the Syrian and Lebanese Press

GÖTZ NORDBRUCH

The Lebanese and Syrian public closely followed developments in National Socialist Germany. Nazism, as a political regime and an ideology,
was a regular topic in local debates; it was scrutinized for signposts with
potential directions for future reform and the local political culture in
countries under French mandate. As in other countries in this region, the
fascination was widespread for modernization projects that promised to
rebuild the future of the nation. Nazism in Germany was one of a number
of potential models; Fascism in Italy, Kemalism in Turkey, Communism
in Soviet Russia, and the authoritarian modernization of Iran were other
trajectories followed with great interest.

This chapter aims to reconstruct Lebanese and Syrian encounters with
National Socialism, as reflected in the local press. Responses to Nazism
were not limited to superficial or sporadic discussions about major events
and key policies implemented by the Nazi regime. Instead, events and
developments in Germany were reported in detail, echoing a persistent
interest in Nazi German politics and ideological claims. The following
analysis of news reports in the daily press and commentaries in cultural
magazines illustrates the context of these encounters in local political culture. Both apologetic and critical perspectives on Nazism reflected the
ongoing transformations of local societies. In addition, this chapter argues that the confrontation with Nazism provided the catalyst for intense
debates about the future of the Syrian and Lebanese states and societies.
In many respects, developments in Germany and Nazi Germany's ideological claims served as a basis for sharp criticism of authoritarian rule
and radical nationalist and expansionist visions. Throughout the 1930s and
1940s, Nazism was a starting point for public deliberation about the future
of society and the social order, often echoing controversial and contra-

dictory interpretations and positions. The concerns and questions raised in these debates often closely resembled those that have marked Western intellectual publics in the years before and after the First World War.

The war did not spare the Levantine regions of Lebanon and Syria; the devastating events left deep marks within the collective memory.[1] Facing up to the new realities after the breakup of the Ottoman Empire and the abolition of the caliphate in 1924, local populations had to adapt to changed regional and international contexts. Conflicting messages from the imperial powers contributed to the ongoing political antagonisms and intellectual debates. Social, economic, and political change had been ongoing for decades in most parts of the late Ottoman Empire, and the intellectual answers to these challenges reverberated in emerging political and religious movements calling for restoration, reform, or revolution. The quest for a collective identity, questions about the relationship between the individual and the community, and disputes about the role of religion as a factor influencing identity and politics again came to the fore during these years.[2]

These conflicts and the controversies over the composition of the future order were not restricted to political institutions and interventions in the form of strikes, demonstrations, and public protests; they also involved the shaping of public discourses and forming public imageries of cultural, religious, and political concepts. Reflecting the emergence of mass politics, the urban public had gained importance as a battlefield for political authority and cultural legitimacy. The increasing number of newspapers and magazines that were published not only in major cities, but also in several provincial towns echoed a growing public awareness of the central challenges during these years.[3] They not only provided information about local, regional, and international developments, but also offered daily comments and analyses of cultural and philosophical questions. Despite serious obstacles posed by a lack of funding and administrative censorship, the press thus voiced the attitudes of an increasingly politicized public; it provided a channel for airing public reflections and conflicts about the future political order.[4]

The Nazi Regime through Levantine Eyes, 1933–1936

Prior to Hitler's takeover in January 1933, Arab readers were already closely following the ascent of Nazism. In 1925 Marshal Hindenburg's election as successor to Social Democrat Friedrich Ebert as president of the Weimar Republic was considered an indication of the increasing influence of militarist and radical nationalist currents.[5] Yet revisionist tendencies within the German political spectrum were not necessarily perceived as a threat to peace; in many circles, they were seen as a consistent objection to an unjust postwar regional order laid down by the victorious powers in the aftermath of the First World War. From this perspective, the German situation paralleled the fate of countries now under French mandate rule.

Hitler's nomination as Reich chancellor was of immediate interest for the political milieus in the French mandates of Lebanon and Syria. For most observers, the question of democracy was closely linked to the problem of gaining national independence from French rule. The principle of the people's sovereignty was thus limited neither to mechanisms of internal decision-making processes nor to the balancing of social and political interests. In the context of French mandate rule, democracy was tantamount to independence from foreign domination.

However, opposition to French rule was not necessarily related to calls for individual rights and political freedoms. The priority of various nationalist voices was not political pluralism, but national unity against outside aggression. In this regard, the coverage of the Röhm affair in June–July 1934, in which major critics from within the Nazi movement were executed, was particularly striking. Referring to the political tensions within the National Socialist movement, the nationalist activist and member of the National Bloc Munir al-'Ajlani published an article for *al-Qabas* in which he openly expressed respect for Hitler's determination and the resolute submission of his critics. Apparently by executing his opponents, according to this view, Hitler in fact prevented a civil war:

> Hitler "did his duty towards Germany by killing a gang of people, saving his country from bloody revolts that might have led to tens of thousands of victims. It might have weakened the belief of the Germans and threatened their firm will. The result could have been that all of Germany would have been thrown into the claws of anarchy."[6]

In 'Ajlani's view, a repressive but firm leader who was acting in the interest of the nation appeared as a legitimate ruler. Such perception echoed the self-image of Nazism as a modernizing movement that was to revolutionize the established order. Similar to Fascism in Italy and Kemalism in Turkey, the National Socialist movement was complemented by prominent nationalist voices as breaking with outdated social structures and traditional powers. In this regard, its turn to violence against the opposition was interpreted as a precondition to its successful transformation of society.

This position did not go unchallenged, with many authors openly questioning the brutality of the German regime and its repression against intellectual and political opponents. Mishal Zakkur, the editor of the Lebanese magazine *al-Ma'rid*, offered some of the most outspoken criticism of authoritarian rule, considering the new German regime as one of its most brutal expressions. For him, the persecution of German Jews was part of a strategy to "distract the public from a revolt against the rule of tyranny" that had been established since Hitler's rise to power.[7]

Reports about developments in Germany were generally not restricted to news about the repression of political opposition. Nazi racial theories and the resulting racial hierarchies were noted in the Lebanese and Syrian public as formative aspects of the rise of the National Socialist movement. Under the French mandate, and even earlier under Ottoman rule, struggles over definitions of community and delimitations of its boundaries had been central to political debates. Addressing issues related to questions of identity and of ethnic and religious minorities, Nazi politics touched the core of an ongoing formation process of communal loyalties in the Levant. As in Europe and the United States, scientific theories about the genetic constitution and the evolution of life stirred controversial debates in the Arab–Muslim world.[8] Yet the racial hierarchy and the ambivalent position of "Arabs" or "Orientals" in National Socialist ideology appeared problematic even to those observers who held favorable views of the nationalist "German revolution." This became most visible in local approaches to Hitler's programmatic text *Mein Kampf*. In January 1934, the daily *al-Nida'* — a Lebanese newspaper of explicit Arab nationalist orientation — featured daily serializations of an Arab translation of the book. As one of the first Arab translations from *Mein Kampf*, these extracts gave detailed insights into Hitler's thoughts and politics.[9] Barely covering his fascination for Hitler and his political program, the translator voiced the hope that the reader might choose "the best and the most suitable"[10] from the premises expressed in *Mein Kampf*.

The translation of the book and its positive introduction inevitably raised concerns. Reacting to criticism voiced by readers, Kazim al-Sulh, the editor of *al-Nida'*, commented on the publication and, in an editorial note, clarified his paper's position. While refuting Hitler's racial theories, he insisted on a supposed message that could be derived from Hitler's arguments. In light of Germany's postwar history and Hitler's personal life, Sulh declared:

> *Mein Kampf* is thus the plan of a man and a nation that resemble the life of our youth and our nation at their beginnings. My intention was that our youth and our nation would become acquainted with the renaissance of this man and this nation, so that they will learn from their examples in the next phase of their life. We do not think that this plan contains any unexpected plots of aggressions against other peoples—aggressions that are not preceded by an aggression [against Germany]. . . . But if there is something in Hitler's book that is deviating from this "plan," this is not according to our intention. [Such deviation] cannot be supported and adopted by men who know that others also have a national dignity and human emotions.[11]

In the Levantine context, questions of national identity were linked to the status of ethnic and religious minorities. The issue of minorities also influenced local perceptions of Europe and European politics. The central notion in Nazi ideology of an enmity toward Jews and Judaism had been noted even before the National Socialist rise to power. At the beginning of the 1930s, newspapers already characterized the expressions of anti-Jewish hostility as a basic tenet of Nazism.[12] Reports about the introduction of discriminatory laws and the boycott of Jewish businesses frequently reflected the worsening situation in Germany. Anti-Jewish resentment was not unknown in Levantine societies. Classical Christian anti-Judaism and the ambiguous depictions of the Jews in Islamic traditions noticeably echoed in reactions to the anti-Semitic measures implemented in Germany.[13] Such resentments surfaced in reactions to a possible settlement of German Jewish refugees in the mandates. Already by the summer of 1933, the increasing number of exiled Jews who were looking for refuge had turned into a problem, which directly involved daily politics in Lebanon and Syria. Given the socioeconomic context, the possibility of an influx of German Jews—similar to a potential settlement of Assyrian refugees from Iraq—polarized the different public views. For some observers, the immigration of Jews to Syria and Lebanon risked creating a community apart, unable or unwilling to integrate into their new social surroundings and thus posing a threat to national loyalty.[14]

These discourses about preservation of the community were often tied to longing for a national revival. In Arab nationalist ideologies, the youth was perceived as a driving force for the reemergence from a state of decay and submission. The formation of youth movements in various European countries, but also in Turkey, Russia, China, and Japan, had stimulated local debates about the role of the youth within society. The press played an important role in fostering this development. For many commentators, the organization of the youth was perceived as a necessity to develop society and to step up the nationalist struggle. *Al-Qabas*, for instance, explicitly called on the youth to unify its ranks in an attempt to overcome the current state of weakness:

> Arab Youth! Let your eternal slogan be: We shall be strong! . . . We are not wrong if we say that the current age is the age of power. Whoever wants to survive and to triumph in life—as an individual or as a nation—has to be strong. Strong in every aspect of intellectual, cultural and material life.[15]

The editor of the Aleppine journal *al-Hadith* addressed this question in a similar way. In an article based on a speech held at an event organized by Muslim scouts in Beirut, Sami al-Kayyali pointed to the experiences of youth organizations in Europe as potential forces of social renewal.[16]

Similarly, the situation of women in various European countries was frequently covered in local newspapers and magazines and scrutinized for potential lessons—National Socialist Germany being no exception.[17] Questions about wearing the veil, woman suffrage, and the status of women had increasingly attracted attention since the final years of the Ottoman Empire. During the earliest phases of the emerging women's movement, these questions had already explicitly been placed in the context of a struggle for a revival of the nation. The success of Nazism stimulated reflections about the appropriate balance of gender relations in society. Similar to its glorification of the youth, National Socialist gender policies were considered as proof for the modernizing vision of the Nazi regime. As in the cases of Fascism, Kemalism, and Bolshevism, the importance attached to these relations in National Socialist declarations echoed in the views of the local public. An article written by a French journalist about the different role models of women in Nazi Germany and Bolshevist Russia appeared in Arabic in several local newspapers.[18] Comparing the relative freedom of women's life in Russia to the National Socialist limitation of women's role to motherhood, the respective status and situations of women highlighted two fundamentally different conceptions of society. The declared goal of such references to the experiences of other societies was to render visible the variety of social concepts and to discuss their relevance for possible reforms in Syria and Lebanon.[19] These reports frequently addressed the state of morality and culture. The safeguarding of the family and of morality and order was a major concern of nationalist movements. Yet from the perspective of Lebanese and Syrian commentators, the experiences of Western societies were ambivalent; in some cases, they were perceived as illustrations of failures and degenerations that were to be prevented. Stressing the ambivalent character of Europe as a role model for Arab societies, the editor of *al-Nida'*, Kazim al-Sulh, explicitly highlighted the experience of women in European societies—and Nazi Germany again featured as one of the experiences to draw on:

> While we are beginning to live a nationalist life—[a life of] nationalism that we are trying to build on the basis of modern science and modern civilization—we should take care not to commit the mistakes of the civilized nations, only to regret them later and to retract. We should instead directly take up only those things that were adopted by young nations that arose in modern times, such as Czechoslovakia, Germany, and Italy. We should prepare the women, the educated as well as the uneducated ones, for their particular roles, which were given to them by nature. This would be of no harm for them, as both man's leisure and income will be for her and for him—even more so, if man and woman are two partners forming together a well advanced national family. This is what the modern patriotic nationalists are calling for, in this country as elsewhere.[20]

Nazism figured prominently in these quests for orientation, as reflected in the local press. Yet fascination with Hitler's rule and his resolute drive for a revival of the nation did not remain unchallenged. From early on, the interest in National Socialist ideas and visions, which was sparked within local discourses, was followed by other voices with considerable concern.

Echoes of the Crisis in Europe, 1936–1939

The years preceding the Second World War brought the developments in Europe even closer to the local political context. No political movement could avoid following events in central Europe and inquiring into their potential impact on the Mediterranean. Strategic and ideological and, equally, ethnic and religious affiliations had drawn most political actors into the regional arena in the Levant, and in many cases, local politics presented an explicit international message.

The situation of the Syrian Communist Party (CP) was no exception. Since its formation in the mid-1920s, its politics and ideological concerns were tightly bound to wider international considerations. International alliances, for this party, were not only strategically necessary, but served as ideologically based associations in a universally shared struggle against the existing order. The position adopted by the Seventh Conference of the Comintern in 1935 added to this orientation. The shift of priorities from class struggle to a struggle against imperialism and Fascism necessarily implied an international outlook.[21] Communist reaction to the Spanish Civil War reflected this approach. In a personal account that was published in the intellectual and CP-affiliated magazine *al-Tali'a*, an anonymous participant in the war, who had fought in the International Brigades, pointedly stated: "I defended Arab freedom at the front in Madrid."[22] In the Syrian and Lebanese context, the struggle against Fascism called for an alliance with the Popular Front in France. Although the CP was aware that the Popular Front provided no guarantees for Syrian and Lebanese independence, the increasing influence of European Fascist powers in the Arab world made a change of priorities necessary. Instead of immediate independence, the defense of the very existence of bourgeois democracy in Europe had turned into a priority.

This reformulation of its priorities also echoed in various efforts to enhance the party's public outreach. In addition to the publication of the clandestine newspaper *Nidal al-Sha'b* and the takeover of the renowned monthly cultural magazine *al-Duhur*,[23] the organization of strikes and demonstrations added to the popularity of its activities—and further shifted its political priorities to questions of Arab independence, national unity, and Palestine. Over the past few years, the CP had substantially extended its public basis. With its increased membership from only several hundred in 1933 to more than three thousand in 1939,[24] the party had established itself as an influential political force. Whereas the creation of the monthly cultural magazine *al-Tali'a* had widened the party's outreach into socialist and liberal nationalist spectrums, the licensing of the daily *Sawt al-Sha'b* in May 1937 finally allowed for regular interventions into broader public debates.[25] The creation of the League against Nazism and Fascism in Syria and Lebanon was part of these efforts. In May 1939, Beirut witnessed one of the most outstanding public statements against Fascism and Nazism and in support of European democratic forces in the prewar years. The Syrian-Lebanese Conference against Fascism that was organized by the League against Nazism and Fascism on May 6–7, 1939, successfully highlighted a prevailing mood of French–Syrian and French–Lebanese partnership. The impact of the conference was furthered by the reproduction of the speeches in the May edition of the journal *al-Tariq*. On behalf of the preparatory committee of the conference, the Lebanese intellectual and activist Ra'if Khuri outlined the context of the meeting and the urgency of a united stand. Addressing the audience, Khuri declared:

> Our relations . . . with the democratic states were no love affair; but whatever our problem with these countries, we do not want fascism to intervene in our affairs, letting its imperialist claws dig themselves into our region. . . . Our conference shows that we are a people that is confident in democracy and its strength. We believe in cooperation with democracies and democrats. Our people knows that neutrality is a joke in a struggle between fascism and democracy, for fascism will not let them stay neutral. It is aware that it is impossible to gain fascism's friendship by staying aside, for fascism is no friend of small and weak peoples. Finally, our people is confident that the noble and beautiful face of democracy that is shining on us through the flame of the great French Revolution will not be defaced by false democrats, neither here nor there. Our slogan is: we are part of the democratic front![26]

The democratic option, which was forcefully defended in the name of the anti-Fascist league, continued to shape the agitation of these circles, coming to an unexpected end only with the Nazi–Soviet pact of August 1939.

Yet interest and concern over developments in Germany were not confined to leftist milieus. Various monographs and numerous magazines and journals that were published in the years preceding the Second World War offer an insight into the elaborate reconstructions and assessments of contemporary German ideology. Interest in the essence of Nazism and its relevance for the Arab world was most visible in urban educated strata. Given their predominance and direct involvement in political life, these milieus deeply influenced strategies and visions pursued by political forces. Magazines such as *al-Tali'a*, *al-'Urwa al-Wuthqa*, *al-Hadith*, *al-Amali*, *al-'Irfan*, and *al-Tamaddun al-Islami*—which were often closely related to activist cultural circles and clubs—explicitly aimed at direct intervention in society.

Given the prospect of independence following the signing of a treaty with France, the quest for philosophical foundations of an Arab revival had become ever more pressing. Similar experiences in other contexts appeared as potential stimuli for Lebanese and Syrian society. The Damascene teachers magazine *Majallat al-Mu'allimin wa-l-Mu'allimat*, which was coedited by the renowned intellectuals Jamil Saliba and Kamil 'Ayyad,[27] illustrated such a search for outside inspiration. Dedicated to the development of national education, the magazine offered comparative approaches to teaching, socialization, and methods of instruction. Already in late 1935, the magazine had published an article, explicitly drawing on the experiences of other nations' revival. Germany, here, was one example, as it had witnessed an "inner revolution aiming at ending the past age and to follow new ways of life."[28] The image of an "inner revolution" that was to be inspired in the hearts of the next generations reflected a prevailing mood in Syria and Lebanon themselves; change was not only about a new political order, but also about a revolution of values and traditions that could be brought about by an education that would suit the needs and challenges of the nation. The call for an authentic "national education" thus in these years became a frequent issue in the various cultural journals.

As in past years, articles continued to be published about the Hitler Youth and its role and links within German society;[29] interest, however, had become much broader, questioning the so-called educational reason for paramilitary organization and the role of the youth—these "soldiers of war and guardians of peace"[30]—within a nation's struggle for revival. Such calls implied an education that would not be limited to the elites, but would be directed to an entire generation, thus serving as the nation's fundament in the future.

In this context, the interest shown by contemporary Syrian and Lebanese writers in "fin de siècle" Europe and European thinkers is striking.[31] Prior to the outbreak of the Second World War, intellectuals turned to the writings of Friedrich Nietzsche, Gustave Le Bon, and Victor Hugo. Whereas these authors had already attracted much interest in past decades, their thoughts again appeared topical to ongoing events and challenges. Nietzsche's concept of the *Übermensch*, for instance, lay at the core of several articles in the recently founded cultural weekly magazine *al-Amali*.[32] Interest was further promoted by an Arab translation of Nietzsche's *Thus Spoke Zarathustra* that was published by Filiks Faris in 1938;[33] recent conservative and *kulturpessimistische* reinterpretations of Nietzsche's "philosophy of strength,"[34] which had become popular in Europe, echoed in local intellectual debates.[35] Nietzsche's critique of the state of morality in European societies provided answers that were considered relevant for the Arab context as well.[36] Whereas Faris himself remained critical of some aspects of Nietzsche's philosophy—albeit endorsing its main tenets—others were more enthusiastic. Writing in a review of Faris's translation, Khalil Hindawi declared:

> For a long generation, this book will remain one of the best that has been translated into Arabic, for it is a book of its people, it is owned by a nation that is at one with its psyche and at one with its personality. This translation closes a big void in Arab literature, and it will have a strong influence on the next generation.[37]

The journal *al-Amali*, in which this review had appeared, was edited by 'Umar Farrukh, who had studied in Leipzig during the mid-1930s. His esteem for German romantic thought was not limited to nineteenth-century thinkers, but extended to its *völkisch* expressions in the twentieth century.[38] Farrukh, too, perceived Nietzsche as relevant for Arab societies. According to Farrukh, Nietzsche

> believed in nothing, only in something that was emanating from the spirit of the people and that was practised by the people, something that adds to the absolute strength of the spiritual and cultural might for struggle.[39]

The second half of the 1930s witnessed a noticeable development of Arab nationalist thought. In the Syrian and Lebanese contexts, the works of Edmond Rabbath, Antun Sa'ada, and Qustantin Zurayq were important expressions of increasing intellectual sophistication and diversity. Racial theories formulated by Arthur de Gobineau and Houston Stewart Chamberlain, which had inspired National Socialist ideologists, rarely reverberated in Arab nationalist discourses in their original forms; their theories' premises were generally rejected. Yet although race appeared scientifically questionable as a biological concept of a distinct and pure communal entity, essentialized definitions of community based on suprahistorical traits nevertheless furnished alternative concepts that allowed the determination of communal boundaries. The theories of the French medical doctor and social psychologist Gustave Le Bon, for instance, who had attracted much attention for his positive depiction of Arab civilization, figured as a prominent point of reference among Syrian and Lebanese thinkers.[40] Racialized imagery was also present in other contexts. Since the establishment of the French mandate, the presence of Senegalese soldiers as part of the French army had provoked additional resentments against the occupying power. The image of these soldiers as a particular threat to Arab women resembled the imagery that had marked European scholarship and public opinion about people of African origins.[41]

In these debates about communal identities, the question of the nation, of its origins and constituents, was closely related to questions of rule, the balance of power, and the relations between the individual and its community. The evolving conflict opposing the Axis powers, on the one hand, and Britain and France, on the other, substantiated the need to take up a position in a possible global confrontation between dictatorial and democratic regimes. From a nationalist perspective, the legitimacy of leadership appeared much more as a function of its ability to protect the nation. Consequently, the perception of Nazism and Italian Fascism was based on their national credentials; as Shakib Arslan, a prominent nationalist voice and activist, put it:

> Hitler's reputation in the Muslim world is due to all that he has done for Germany—a country that, due to him, has regained its global standing and that has realized more than it had hoped for. This is an undeniable fact, and it is not limited to the Orient.[42]

Other observers, who highlighted the "national compassion"[43] guiding the politics of European dictators, with Hitler being the most prominent, voiced similar views.

However, such views were widely contested. In light of frequent reports about the suppression of political opposition and the repression of intellectuals, academics, and artists in Germany, the defense of individual rights and freedoms had turned into an important feature of the coverage of developments under Nazi rule. The most outspoken circles to call for a democratic order were among those affiliated with the League against Nazism and Fascism and the magazine *al-Tal'ia*.[44] For those parties concerned, the prospect of the war only added to the urgency of their challenge.

At War with Nazism, 1939–1945

The effects of the outbreak of war in September 1939 were not restricted to the European continent, for events had an immediate impact on the

Arab Middle East as well. As mandate powers, France and Britain had, since the summer of 1939, imposed severe measures to ensure they maintained their grip on their respective mandates. Economically as much as strategically, mandate Lebanon and Syria were cornerstones of the French empire. Intensive efforts were thus made to rally public opinion in support of the struggle of the Allies against the *puissances totalitaires*. Whereas the dissolution of political parties and organizations reflected an attempt to prevent any opposition from within by force, propaganda was another means to distract the public from existing or prospective sympathies for the German regime. Since the end of April 1939, Germany had taken an active role in the *guerre des ondes* between Britain and France, on the one hand, and Italy, on the other.[45] Already in December 1937, during a visit to Berlin, the head of the radical nationalist Arab Club in Damascus, Sa'id Fattah al-Imam, had drawn the attention of German officials to the potential effects of German Arabic broadcasts. Yet from a German perspective, an active involvement in the "war of propaganda" appeared undesirable, as it risked being interpreted as an anti-British gesture.[46] It was only in late 1938 that such reservations were to be watered down, resulting in an Arabic-language program on Radio Berlin-Zeesen that aimed at weakening France's stand with the public.[47]

The French Service de la Presse et de la Propagande had put on a program to counter the impact of such propaganda. Since early November, the French authorities in Damascus had organized a daily screening of French- and Arabic-language news updates in the local cinemas. With reduced prices for students, the events were aimed at a younger educated audience, but they also included special arrangements for broader, often illiterate, segments of society.[48] In addition, a series of public conferences was organized that was intended to provide a forum for intellectuals, potentially supporting the Allies' cause. Although not all talks reflected a clear message that was to be exploited for the French cause, a French-sponsored cultural program facilitated the highlighting of French goodwill toward local history and traditions. The same strategy was pursued by Arab translations of articles from the French press.[49] Such efforts were not in vain. Together with strict censorship, French propaganda encouraged explicit expressions of support for the democratic states. In this sense, the Beirut paper *Lisan al-Hal* depicted the stand taken by the Arab–Islamic world in the following terms:

> We do not recognize any German right to influence us. Since the
> beginning of the war, the Arab-Muslim world deliberately placed itself

amongst the democracies. This position is not only dictated by the cultural ties that continue to exist between the Arab–Islamic East and the Western democratic powers; in addition and above all, this position is due to the fact that Islam always followed the maxim of the French Revolution: "freedom, equality, fraternity," and because the prophet himself has been the real apostle of democracy.[50]

Assumed affinities between Islamic traditions and European democracies were also central to articles appearing in cultural magazines. Reproducing a speech that had been broadcast earlier on French Radio Orient under the title "Democracy and the Arabs," the Aleppine magazine *al-Hadith* explicitly called on the Arab world to join the battle against Nazism for its own ends. In his talk, Salah al-Asir concluded that democracy was the very message of the East:

> Oh, children of true democracy, the fragrance of the eastern soil . . . wants to come over the world yet again. You are invited to fulfill the message of the East, the message of democracy. Who other than you is more advantageous for this heritage, who other than you is more suited [to fulfill its message] and to guarantee its success?[51]

Al-'Irfan, a magazine of predominantly Shia affiliation published in Sa'ida, expressed similar opinions. In an editorial entitled "The War, the Arabs, and Islam," the editor stressed the Islamic roots of Arab desires for the victory of democracy.[52]

From a different perspective, the threat of Nazism was addressed by the satirical journal *al-Dabbur*. Since the spring of 1939, the Beirut journal had frequently covered the events in Europe and their repercussions in the region. Already by May, the front cover of the weekly featured the terrifying sketch of a soldier's head with the faces of Hitler and Mussolini superimposed over the eyes, thus alluding to the danger posed by both figures.[53] Various other cartoons and illustrations published throughout the summer again focused on this motif. Writing a week after France's declaration of war and the related measures adopted by the French high commissioner, *al-Dabbur* emphasized the need for Lebanese solidarity with France, justifying France's strict administrative steps as being in "preparation for the case of emergency, and to prevent any surprises that might occur in future."[54] Support for France and its British ally, however, was not unquestioned. Contacts and affinities to Germany that had in the past been entertained by the relevant personalities in press and politics survived both French administrative repressions and Germany's war against its neighbors.

The occupation of Damascus and Beirut by British and Free French troops in July 1941 had put an end to a brief period of Vichy influence in the Levant. The defeat of the Vichy-led administration marked a significant setback for German outreach in the region. The changing international balance of power also impacted the local political scenery. Whereas several parties, which had shaped Syrian and Lebanese public opinion in the prewar years, now resurfaced in an atmosphere of diminishing political repression, new organizations were formed that gave voice to previously marginal or nonexistent views. The emergence of the Ba'th movement and the merging of various Islamist groups into the nucleus of the future Muslim Brotherhood were visible expressions of such changes. A new wave of recently founded newspapers and magazines mirrored such transformations. In Lebanon as in Syria, new sets of political cleavages and ideological discontent came to the fore.

While fears about Communism prevailed among the authorities, by mid-August the Free French administration agreed to release most members of the Communist Party who had remained imprisoned under Vichy rule in the Lebanese Prison des Sables, thus paving the way for an immediate restructuring of the party under the leadership of Khalid Bakdash and Faraj Allah al-Hilu.[55] The re-publication of the party's newspaper, *Sawt al-Sha'b*, in January 1942 provided an important forum; as a core topic of Communist agitation, the call for anti-Fascist opposition was central to the newspaper's editorial line.[56] Writing in the first edition after its relaunch, Bakdash declared:

> The extermination of Nazism has become the highest goal of human kind. It has become our, the Arab people, highest national goal, and we proceed towards it with all the others and we reach out our hands to all others [to achieve this goal].[57]

Reflecting the urgent need to mobilize public opinion and to confront the impact of Fascist propaganda, one of the reestablished anti-Fascist league's first decisions after the fall of Vichy in the mandates included the creation of a journal to inform the public about the ideological context of the war. The first edition of the magazine *al-Tariq* was released on December 20, 1941—its cover showing a man smashing a huge swastika with an ax.[58] The journal's political outlook echoed that of its precursor, *al-Tali'a*, calling for cooperation of a broader political spectrum unified for the single cause of anti-Fascist struggle.[59]

In light of growing frustrations among the local population about the continuation of French rule, France needed all expressions of anti-Fascist opposition that could be mustered. At the turn of the year in 1942–1943, any prolonging of the past approach of French politics had become increasingly untenable. The German defeat at al-'Alamayn in November 1942 and Stalingrad in January 1943 was publicly perceived as a major turning point of the war. While the German Wehrmacht was in retreat in Eastern Europe, Operation Torch, the British- and U.S.-led invasion of North Africa in November 1942, pushed back Axis troops from their last bastion in Tunisia. Coverage of these developments in the local Arab press was extensive. The landing of the Allies in Sicily and the ensuing dismissal of Mussolini on July 25, 1943, further reduced the influence of both European Axis powers. Given these events, the chances were slim of a German takeover of any of the Middle Eastern territories under Allied control. By the autumn of 1943, the French administration noted with relief a significant decline of Axis activities in the region.

Yet the summer 1943 elections in Syria and Lebanon and the ensuing conflicts with the French authorities proved crucial for the future of the two Levantine societies. Once again, France only reluctantly agreed to a shift of its policies toward the local population. The transfer of powers from the French authorities to the national governments, which progressively expanded from a formal takeover of the "common interests" to include all administrative fields, changed the popular perception of the parliament and administration. In the past, state institutions had long been perceived as instruments of French control; now, political offices potentially allowed the expression of popular will. Political battles thus ever more transcended informal politics and increasingly involved state institutions as well. Referring to these developments in late 1943, Elizabeth Thompson concludes:

> The 1943 elections were to be more than a vote for or against the French: They became a referendum on the postcolonial civic order. The expansion of welfare and liberalization of the political arena had mobilized opposing parties in a rivalry to capture control of the now-powerful state, each seeking to implement radically different visions of citizens' relationship to the state.[60]

With Germany on the retreat and independence from French rule appearing ever more realistic, German Nazism increasingly lost appeal. The decline of Nazism as a potential reference was best exemplified in the monthly journal *al-Adib*. Published in Beirut by Albert Adib, the journal offered a forum for broad circles of intellectuals. Jibran Tuwayni, again, was one of these voices. Writing in the first issue of the journal in January 1942 about the necessity to support the democratic states against dictatorship, Tuwayni justified his call for democratic rule with long-standing ties linking Arab civilization with democratic ideals:

> The Arab is endowed by nature with [the tradition] of consultation, be it as a Bedouin or in a state of civilization. If some Arab states have at a certain point in history deviated into tyranny, this was due to a penetration and a takeover of control of the state by foreign influences.[61]

Such a portrayal of democracy as the core of Arab heritage was not new. Whereas this image had in the past often been applied in confrontations with the mandate power, now the defense of democracy as an authentic tradition had increasingly gained importance as an argument in inner-Arab controversies as well. Despite significant ideological differences that shaped the contributions to the journal *al-Adib*—with authors ranging from Qustantin Zurayq and Edmond Rabbath to Iliyas Abu Shabka, Qadri Qala'aji, 'Umar Fakhuri, and Ra'if Khuri—the spectrum of views was framed by an agreement about the importance of individual rights as a cornerstone of the civic order. In addition to detailed discussions of the totalitarian and racist foundations of Nazism, the journal provided substantial arguments in defense of humanism and human rights. In an article, Jamil Saliba, a functionary in the Syrian Ministry of Education, explicitly highlighted the need to focus on the individual as the basis of society: "Democracy, humanism and liberty are the general principles on which we must build our national education."[62] Another issue that was repeatedly addressed within the pages of *al-Adib* was the question of racial theories and their link to imperialism and colonial rule.[63]

The Beirut journal *al-Tariq* shared many of the views articulated in *al-Adib*. As an outlet of the League against Nazism and Fascism, however, its ideological stance was much more determined. In addition to the extensive refutations of the basic premises of National Socialist ideology, the journal vehemently pushed for debates about the foundations of democratic and parliamentarian rule.[64] This defense of the ideas of liberty, equality, and fraternity was not limited to a critique of Nazism and Fascism as European phenomena, but explicitly intended to confront anti-democratic and anti-liberal forces at home. Several contributions were dedicated to interventions in local debates and disputes. This included, for instance, a sharp critique of the Syrian Nationalist Party that was authorized by the Lebanese Ministry of Interior to restart its activities. In the summer of 1944, the anti-Fascist league and the Communist newspaper *Sawt al-Sha'b* started a campaign against the party, focusing on the danger of Fascist ideologies for local political culture. "Down with fascism and its agents, and long live the free, independent and democratic Lebanon"[65] was the conclusion of an open letter addressed to Prime Minister Riad al-Sulh.

While parts of the public eagerly followed Allied successes in Europe, reactions to their advance in France were not necessarily enthusiastic.[66] In the spring of 1945, restrained optimism was characteristic of Syrian and Lebanese public opinion. Despite considerable conflicts that had confronted the various, often antagonist, movements and organizations, neither of these dominated or monopolized political decisions. Intellectually, the situation was similar. While radical nationalist ideologies of various shades were paralleled by Islamic populism as strong popular forces calling for a revival of imagined communities of the past, the implementation of social and political rights was at the center of other actors eager to push for internal reform and international integration. In this context, the option of Nazi Germany as a potential partner and point of reference gradually disappeared. Major sections of the public considered integration into an Allied-sponsored postwar international order worth a try; such integration, it was argued, could ensure national independence, but would advance social and political progress in Syria and Lebanon as well. Here, the prospect of the San Francisco Conference from April until June 1945 on the postwar order fostered expectations that the end of the war would finally lead to unconditional independence and self-determination. Drawing on the deception surrounding the conference of Versailles in 1919, the participation of Lebanon and Syria at the conference provided hope that the Arab world would now be spared the frustrations that had marked the aftermath of the First World War. An editorial for the Damascene daily *al-Kifah* made this expectation explicit. It is to be hoped, the author declared,

> that the San Francisco Conference will gather in a different atmosphere than the one in Versailles. [It is to be hoped] that this conference will

open the doors to the Arabs, and will tell them: enter in peace and participate—without any limitations and without any conditions—in its work. Sit on the carpet [table] as an equal to the great and small states. From this day on, there will be no arbitrary rule [by outside powers], no monopolization of power, no preference [to any state] and no competition. The smallest states will have the same rights as the largest ones, and both have the same right in negotiations and votes.[67]

Similar expectations were raised throughout the preceding months and following the end of the war in Europe.[68] Explicitly linking the new international order to the future of local political culture, the young Lebanese politician Kamal Jumblatt called for a "new type of democracy"[69] in a study published in a French Orientalist journal. His idea of this "new democracy" was that it would reflect the experience of the Allied war against the Axis.

Conclusion

The expectations related to the end of the war and the defeat of Nazism did not prevail for long. News of the Soviet army's encirclement of Berlin in late April 1945 had been met with public manifestations of joy and relief, echoing the hopes for a new dawn that would allow for profound social and political changes.

French politics frustrated any hope for an immediate release of the two mandates and complete independence. The arrival of more French troops in Beirut in early May sparked serious concerns about the prospects for a rapid French withdrawal from the region. Reports from Algeria, where on May 9 the French army had massacred Algerian demonstrators calling for independence, added to the suspicious view of French intentions locally, thus deepening fears that France would maintain its mandate rule even after the cessation of hostilities. The violent confrontations between protesters and the French army in Syria in late May 1945 and French cannon attacks against the parliament and government buildings further highlighted the ambivalences of Allied politics toward the region.

The reluctance of France to grant independence and sovereignty had shaped local responses to Nazism over the previous decade. Although calls for democratic rule and political rights and freedoms were an important part of local political debates, the mandate status obstructed the emergence of a political system that would have matched the public quest for political participation. Throughout the 1930s and early 1940s, the confrontation with Nazism triggered intense controversies about the appropriate postcolonial civic order; in this context, the political systems of France and the Allied powers long remained important points of reference for political circles that called for political and social reforms. In public discourses, these systems stood for explicit alternatives to the authoritarian and radical nationalist visions promoted by Nazi Germany, exemplified in the image of the two opposing camps—democracy against dictatorship—that confronted each other in the war. While the defeat of Nazi Germany in May 1945 proved those voices, which had scrutinized National Socialist politics and ideology for potential lessons, to be wrong, the persistent colonial ambitions of the French seriously harmed those who had taken the side of the Allies. Speaking on May 9, 1945, the Lebanese president, Bishara al-Khuri, described the day of the German capitulation as the outset of "a world ruled by freedom, security and justice."[70] In light of the postwar events in the region, disillusionment about the Allied camp and the political ideals it purported to represent was thus even greater.

CHAPTER 2

Against the Tide: The Secret Alliance between the Syrian National Bloc Leaders and Great Britain, 1941–1942

MEIR ZAMIR

On December 15, 1940, Nuri al-Sa'id, former Iraqi prime minister and now foreign minister, sent a letter to the prime minister, Rashid Ali al-Gailani, who headed the pro-German camp, following the escalating tension between Iraq and Great Britain. Referring to the mood that had prevailed in the summer after the German Blitzkrieg in Western Europe, he noted:

> The fall of France put fear among the Iraqi people as well as among other nations, so much so that they began to seek solutions to ensure its very existence. The situation reached a stage that some of its leaders came to the conclusion that the British Empire was about to collapse, that Iraq would remain without a protector and that a solution had to be found to save the country from destruction. But today, nearly six months after the fall of France, the events show that it is not easy to break up the British Empire. Britain has been able to survive in a way that few expected. The outcome of the war lay in the hands of providence, but the events show that despite France's capitulation, the British Empire can stand alone against the Axis powers, and that its defeat is not certain, as some people assumed last summer.[1]

Nuri al-Sa'id, a staunch supporter of Great Britain, wrote the letter after the Luftwaffe's defeat in the Battle of Britain and Hitler's subsequent decision to abort Operation Sea Lion to invade the British Isles, and after the victories of the British army, commanded by General Archibald Wavell, over the Italian armies in Greece and Libya. But his warning fell on deaf ears, and Rashid Ali al-Gailani, with German military aid sent via French Vichy in Syria and Lebanon, led his country to a confrontation with Great Britain that ended with the latter's reoccupation of Iraq and the escape of Rashid Ali and the mufti Amin al-Husaini to Berlin. His warning was, however, heeded by three Arab nationalist leaders in Syria and Lebanon—Shukri al-Quwatli, Jamil Mardam, and Riad al-Sulh. The three secretly negotiated deals with British officials in the Middle East in 1941 and early 1942 that would help them attain power and eventually gain their countries' independence from France—Sulh in Lebanon in November 1943 and Quwatli and Mardam in Syria in May 1945.[2]

The aim of this chapter is to examine the motives that led three committed Arab nationalists to secretly collaborate with Great Britain, although a British victory was far from certain. They acted against the stand of the general population and public in Syria and Lebanon, most of whom were greatly impressed by the rapid successes of Nazi Germany. Their policies also differed from those of leaders in Iraq, Egypt, and Palestine, who were either pro-German or advocated neutrality. Another aim is to highlight Britain's extensive use of covert action and secret diplomacy in the Middle East during the war to co-opt top local leaders into collaborating with it.[3]

The chapter is limited to the period from March 1941 to September 1942. In the second half of 1940, following the fall of France, there had been considerable uncertainty in the Arab world regarding Great Britain's fate. Only at the beginning of 1941, when it became clear, as Nuri al-Sa'id noted, that Great Britain was not about to give in, did the British option become a reality. The victory in al-'Alamayn and Operation Torch in North Africa, which removed the direct German military threat in the Middle East, prompted many Arab politicians to jump on the British bandwagon. It should be noted that Sulh and Mardam had contacted British agents even before the British-Gaullist occupation of Syria and Lebanon in July 1941 (Operation Exporter). The occupation, which created practically an Anglo-French condominium in the Levant, strengthened the local leaders' willingness to collaborate with Great Britain, whether for national, political, or personal goals. In fact, Quwatli negotiated with the British officials mainly after July 1941, and in April 1942, while a British victory in the Middle East was still far from certain, he concluded a secret agreement with Nuri al-Sa'id, well aware that Great Britain was behind it. Indeed, in the summer of 1942, there was deep concern that Germany was about to occupy the Middle East by pincer attacks by Rommel's Afrika Korps in Egypt from the west and from the Caucasus in the north after the invading German forces overcame the Soviet stronghold in Stalingrad.[4]

Details of the three nationalist leaders' collaboration are revealed in secret British documents obtained by the French military intelligence from the British Legation in Beirut (Spears Mission) in the summer of 1944. I was able to trace only a small number of documents on their co-operation with the British in 1941–1942; there are many more documents pertaining to 1943–1945, from which more can be learned of its nature. Additional documents from French, British, and Israeli archives provide further details of the circumstances in which the three reached secret deals with the colonial power that only a few years previously had suppressed their brethren in Palestine and was now seeking to impose its will in Iraq and Egypt.[5]

The three leaders, however, also collaborated with Axis agents, especially in the months after the fall of France, when it was widely believed that Germany would overrun Britain. French documents from Vichy and Free France provide details of Quwatli's and Sulh's cooperation with three German envoys—Rudolf Roser, Werner Otto von Hentig, and Rudolf Rahn—who operated in Syria and Lebanon from August 1940 until June 1941. Mardam was less involved, as he had been forced to flee to Baghdad in October 1940. British sources also confirm that Quwatli and Sulh were in touch with Axis agents. The former was in fact included in a list prepared before Operation Exporter by the British and the Free French secret agencies of Syrian and Lebanese pro-German sympathizers who were to be arrested in the event of public disorder. Quwatli and Sulh had also tacitly collaborated with the German emissaries in organizing assistance and volunteers for Rashid Ali's coup in Baghdad. Reports by the Sûreté Générale under Vichy and later under the Free French often referred to Sulh's collaboration with German agents and the fact that he received money from them. In a survey prepared by the Sûreté Générale in June 1942 of the activities of German agents in Syria and Lebanon under Vichy, Sulh was described as one of the main collaborators of Roser, an Abwehr officer. Details are also given of Mardam's ties with members of the Italian Armistice Commission that arrived in Beirut in August 1940 and the Italian consul's visit to his home, although he was also visited by the British consul general. Mardam later denied cooperating with Axis agents, claiming that he had criticized the Italian consul for his country's invasion of Albania in April 1939, telling him that "the Muslims would never regard the dictator of Rome as a protector, but as an enemy."[6]

A word of caution is necessary. Not all those who met with German agents or received money from them were active collaborators with Nazi Germany. Even in the French documents, Quwatli and Sulh were portrayed as pro-Axis and Germanophiles rather than as members of a fifth column. Moreover, the French regarded Quwatli, Sulh, and Mardam as adversaries and thus highlighted their support of the Axis powers. Indeed, Sami al-Sulh was nominated as prime minister by General Georges Catroux in August 1942, although he had actively collaborated with Roser more so than his cousin Riad al-Sulh. The latter's candidacy, which had been promoted by the British, was turned down because of his known anti-French stance and his close ties with the Spears Mission.[7]

Describing the mood among the general population and the political leaders in Syria and Lebanon after the outbreak of the war in Europe, Hourani maintains that in their eyes, "there was nothing to choose between the oppression exercised in the name of democracy and that exercised in the name of Fascism."[8] All three were veterans of the First World War, and their stance was influenced by their experiences during Faysal's Arab government in Damascus. They, like other Arab nationalists, remembered well the upheaval brought about by the previous war and anxiously awaited the outcome of this one. Their attitude was shaped by national as well as personal considerations. Although apprehensive of its outcome, they hoped it would help them realize their national goals of independence and unity. Nevertheless, shortly after the outbreak of the war, Sulh declared his loyalty and that of the Muslim community in Lebanon to France, while Mardam sought to mend relations with its high commissioner, Gabriel Puaux. This is understandable if one takes into account that at the time, there were three divisions, with one hundred thousand troops commanded by General Maxim Weygand, stationed in Syria and Lebanon as an expeditionary corps to the Balkans. The nationalists, like many others in the region, assumed that this war too would be long and protracted. France's defeat within six weeks and its humiliating Armistice agreement signed by Marshal Philippe Petain's government with Hitler on June 22, 1940, and with Italy a few days later, therefore came as a shock. The decision by the three to collaborate with Great Britain, albeit in secret, evolved from two major events: France's capitulation and the occupation of Syria and Lebanon by the British army together with the Free French forces.[9]

The initial reaction of the Arab nationalists in Syria and Lebanon to the fall of France was disbelief and panic accompanied by satisfaction and contempt of the much-hated mandatory power's humiliating surrender to the Germans. They detested France, which had reneged on its 1936 treaty in which it pledged to grant Syria independence and unity and ceded part of its territory—Alexandretta—to Turkey. The Syrian Arab nationalists, however, were more concerned with the immediate threat to their country brought about by France's capitulation than with the opportunities offered by the new situation. There were fear and uncertainty with regard to the power that would fill the vacuum. Threats to Syria's independence and territorial integrity came from other European powers as well as from neighboring states. As part of Mussolini's agreement with Hitler, Italy was to have a dominant position in North Africa and the Middle East, including in Syria and Lebanon. For the nationalists, the prospect of Italy, another Catholic Christian power known for its anti-Muslim stance, replacing the defeated France, was far from reassuring. The close ties established by Italian diplomats with the Maronite Church and their support for an independent Christian Lebanon reinforced the nationalists' mistrust. A possible British occupation of their countries was therefore openly debated. Some, such as followers of 'Abd al-Rahman Shahbandar, the leader of the pro-Hashemite party and the hero of the 1925 revolt, stressed the advantages of such an occupation for Syria, especially for its economy. But National Bloc leaders feared that it might enable Great Britain to implement its old plan to incorporate their country in a Hashemite federation and install either 'Abdullah, the amir of Transjordan, or Abdul-Illah, the Iraqi regent, on the Syrian throne. They knew that Great Britain was attempting to lure Turkey into the Allies' camp and were concerned that once again Syria would pay a territorial price in Aleppo and the Jazira. Concern was also voiced by Iraqi leaders regarding Turkey's claims over Mosul. Besides, the military situation in Europe was still far from certain, and it was unclear whether Great Britain would win this war.[10]

Hardly had the ink dried on France's capitulation agreement when Syria became the arena for a struggle for control between the Hashemites and the House of Sa'ud. With the French stumbling block about to be removed, the door to Arab unity was opened. In early July, Nuri al-Sa'id arrived in Damascus to promote an Iraqi-Syrian union, bringing a message from Ankara that Turkey would not attack Syria. 'Abdullah's emissaries stepped up their efforts among the Druze in Jabal Druze, the Bedouin tribes in the Syria desert, as well as Syrian politicians to enlist support for the amir's candidacy for the Syrian throne. 'Abdullah was further encouraged by the campaign by Shahbandar and his followers for a Hashemite Greater Syria. Sheikh Yusuf Yasin, Ibn Sa'ud's top political adviser, had also come to Damascus to foil the Hashemite plans and seek support for the nomination of Prince Faysal, Ibn Sa'ud's son, to the Syrian throne. Yasin met with Quwatli, who was known to have close ties with the Saudi king, as well as with other Syrian dignitaries, and handed out money to politicians and journalists. Some French officials expressed preference for a Saudi prince, arguing that a Hashemite king would place the mandated territories under British hegemony, whereas under a Saudi prince France would retain some of its influence in Syria and Lebanon.[11]

Shahbandar's assassination in early July highlighted the intense struggle for Syria that emerged after the fall of France. The High Commission and Shahbandar's family accused three National Bloc leaders (Jamil Mardam, Lutfi al-Haffar, and Sa'adallah al-Jabiri) of being involved in the crime. Quwatli, who had been sought for questioning, found refuge in the Saudi consulate in Damascus after French police tried to arrest him. Although in January 1941 a special court formed by the High Commission exonerated Mardam, Haffar, and Jabiri of personal involvement in the murder, the charges against the National Bloc leadership undermined its reputation and seriously hindered its political activities. It also altered the balance of power between Quwatli and Mardam, the two main contenders for leadership of the bloc, as the latter had to flee to Baghdad in October, where he was to remain until early 1941, traveling occasionally to Cairo. In his absence, Quwatli emerged as the main nationalist leader. Paradoxically, both he and Mardam, who since the 1930s had opposed Shahbandar's attempt to incorporate Syria in a Hashemite Greater Syrian federation, would, under British pressure, secretly endorse such a scheme.[12]

The demoralization within the High Commission and the French army in the Levant, the arrival of the Italian Armistice Commission to supervise the disarming of the French forces, the intensifying activities of German agents, and especially the sea and land blockade imposed by Britain brought the war closer to the people of Syria and Lebanon. For the next two years, the two countries would become an arena for an intense propaganda war involving regional and foreign powers. On one level, the Hashemites competed with the Saudis for Syrian support; on another level, the Vichyists and the Gaullists struggled to gain control over the mandated territories; and on yet another level, the Allies fought the Axis powers for the hearts and minds of the general public. Germany's military victories in the first two years of the war in Western and Eastern Europe, in the Balkans, and in the Western Desert enhanced its prestige among the Arab Muslims throughout the Middle East. Radio Berlin in Arabic, which focused its attacks on Britain's policies in the region, was extremely popular in Syria and Lebanon, the only countries in the Middle East where German agents were able to operate freely and establish direct ties with the local leaders. The Metropole Hotel in Beirut became a center for German activities, and Roser and von Hentig traveled throughout the mandated territories meeting with local politicians and dignitaries. Reports by the Sûreté Générale under Vichy and later Free France provided details of these activities, including lists of political leaders, dignitaries, and journalists whom they met or to whom they handed out money. Another German propaganda tactic was the public screenings of films of their sweeping military victories in Western Europe, including France.[13]

The German propaganda also focused on provoking the Arab Muslims, especially the younger generation, against Great Britain, while stressing the tyrannical nature of its colonial rule.[14] It highlighted Britain's efforts to prevent the Arabs from gaining true independence, its policy of divide and rule, its support for the Jews against the Arabs in Palestine, and its exploitation of the region's natural resources, especially oil. In contrast, after defeating Britain, the Germans claimed, the Axis powers would ensure that the Arab Muslims in the Middle East would enjoy genuine independence and unity.

Pamphlets scattered by their airplanes over the main cities in Syria and Lebanon in 1942–1943 provide an opportunity to examine the Axis propaganda tactics.[15] Some of the recurring themes were:

1. The military superiority of the Axis powers. For example, a twenty-four-page pamphlet that was dropped over Damascus on July 1, 1942, contained photographs portraying the naval and aerial superiority of the German weapons over those of the Allies. It also included photos of the British aircraft carrier the *Ark Royal*, which was sunk near Gibraltar by a German submarine, as well as of the *Hood*, the largest battleship of the British fleet, sunk by the *Bismarck* in the Atlantic Ocean.

2. British collaboration with the Bolsheviks and the Jews against the Arabs and Muslims. One of the pamphlets accused Britain of collaborating with the Bolsheviks in taking over Iran and exploiting its oil, disregarding its Muslim population. It also claimed that the British were violating the honor of Muslim women. Another leaflet (Italian) promised that the advancing Axis armies would liberate the Arab Muslims and throw the British and the Jews into the sea.

3. Economic warfare. One of the leaflets warned against the use of worthless British bank notes. Another, written in colloquial Arabic, used Goha, a well-liked clown in Arab popular culture, to encourage acts of sabotage:

Pille, anglais, pille,

Le pétrole de Ferdaca, de Suez et de Mosoul

L'intelligent Goha mettre le feu, la nuit, au pétrole

Et tes bateaux s'immobiliseront sur l'eau comme des poissons

crevés . . . . La malédiction de Dieu est sur toi, anglais!

La malédiction de Dieu est sur toi!

Tu nous fais goûter, depuis des années, l'amertume de la souffrance,

Comme tu as fait souffrir autrefois nos aieux,

Retourne à ton pays lointain,

Peut-être, le Seigneur te pardonnera-t'il tes crimes et tes méfaits.[16]

4. Several Italian pamphlets included photographs of Mussolini or the mufti Amin al-Husaini, the latter aimed at negating British propaganda that portrayed fascist Italy as anti-Muslim. Some of the pamphlets were addressed to "The Syrians, from the Taurus Mountains to Egypt."[17]

British and Free-French sources admitted that the German propaganda was effective, at least until the end of 1942. Indeed, it had a major impact on the British officials in the region, who were driven to take drastic countermeasures to ensure Arab support. But in the first year of the war, after their military retreat, the British had difficulty contending with it. Their ability to operate in Syria and Lebanon was limited, as in the aftermath of the fall of France the Vichy authorities there had ceased to collaborate. Vichy's success in imposing its authority over pro–Free French officials and officers in the mandated territories and the blockade imposed by the British themselves severed the ties between Syria and Lebanon and their neighboring countries. The intelligence vacuum was filled partly by the Hagana's intelligence organization (Shay), whose own agents in the Levant provided information to the British. In addition to dropping leaflets on the main cities and smuggling in hundreds of thousands of pamphlets from Palestine, until the summer of 1941 the British used mainly radio broadcasts in Arabic (BBC, Radio Jerusalem, and Radio Haifa) in their propaganda war against the Axis powers in Syria and Lebanon.[18]

Britain's position improved drastically after the occupation of Syria and Lebanon in July 1941. British and Free French security agencies imposed tight security, and pro-Axis sympathizers fled to Turkey, were imprisoned, or were placed under surveillance. British political officers posted throughout the mandated territories maintained close contacts with national and local leaders. British secret agencies used various tactics to entice local leaders to collaborate. Owners of newspapers and journalists were bribed, and tight censorship was imposed. Posters were affixed to walls on the cities' main streets, and mobile cinema vans screened pro-Ally films to large crowds. An ingenious method developed by the Ministry of War Information and used initially in Egypt and Iraq in 1941 was the spreading of oral propaganda through existing social networks, thus exploiting the Arabs' propensity to spread rumors. Security in Syria and Lebanon improved after the British succeeded in deciphering the Abwehr's coded communications in Turkey in December 1941. A British document in the autumn of 1942 claimed, justifiably, that in the propaganda war against the Axis in Syria and Lebanon, Britain had the upper hand.[19]

The importance of the propaganda war for gaining the hearts and minds of the Arab Muslim masses in the Middle East notwithstanding, the main struggle between the Allies and the Axis powers was for the support of the political leadership in the Arab world. The Germans' successes in this field came in the first two years of the war and, paradoxically, in the countries under British rule—Rashid Ali in Iraq; the mufti Amin al-Husaini, now exiled in Iraq; and Ali Mahir and Aziz al-Masri in Egypt. Only a few Syrian and Lebanese leaders wholeheartedly allied themselves with the Axis powers, most notably Shekib Arslan, who since the 1920s had been active in Europe. His influence on the national and political level, however, was limited due to his Druze origins. Although prominent Syrian National Bloc leaders met with German agents and received money from them, they remained at a distance; they were too sophisticated to be exploited by one European power against another. In fact, they used such rivalry to their own advantage.

All three leaders discussed in this chapter understood that the destiny of their peoples and countries, as well as their own political futures, depended on which of the warring European powers they sided with. It was imperative that they choose the power that would win and impose its postwar settlement over the region. With the defeat of France, the mandatory power, they enjoyed greater freedom of action than leaders of the neighboring Arab states that remained under British rule. They had three options: to maintain neutrality until it became clear which side would win the war; to negotiate, overtly or covertly, with both sides and thus gain time until the military situation became clearer; or to ally themselves, either openly or secretly, with one side.

Until July 1941, they pursued the second option, but after the British occupation of Syria and Lebanon, they allied themselves wholeheartedly with Great Britain, aiming to obtain its assistance in ending the French mandate and thereby gain their independence and national unity. In the early stages of the war, neither the Axis nor the Allies were at liberty to help them. Germany ascribed much importance to its ties with Vichy, acknowledging its authority over France's overseas colonies, including Syria and Lebanon. It also recognized Italy's preeminence in the Mediterranean and the Middle East. Neither remaining under the authority of the much-hated and now defeated France nor being ruled by Fascist Italy was an adequate solution. But Great Britain also had its constraints, as it endorsed General de Gaulle's claims over Syria and Lebanon after their liberation from Vichy. Yet the three collaborated with Great Britain, despite its military setbacks in the Middle East in 1941–1942, and negotiated secret deals with its agents in the region.[20]

The first to take the initiative were Riad al-Sulh and Jamil Mardam, followed by Shukri al-Quwatli. Their decisions resulted from their readings of the situation on regional, national, and political levels:

1. After Britain had established its control, albeit not formally, over Syria and Lebanon in July 1941, they needed its support to realize their national and political goals—the end of French rule, independence and national sovereignty, restoration of Syrian unity, and rise to power.
2. Despite the Lyttelton–de Gaulle agreement in which Great Britain had recognized Free France's predominant position in Syria and Lebanon, British officials, especially General Edward Spears, the most senior British representative in Syria and Lebanon, let the National Bloc leaders understand, albeit discretely, that given the choice between supporting Free France or the Arab nationalists in Syria and Lebanon, Great Britain would ultimately choose the Arabs, but only after the war in Europe ended, as it needed de Gaulle's collaboration to liberate France.[21]
3. Britain, in contrast to Nazi Germany, had publicly undertaken to help the Arabs realize their national aspirations, both in Anthony Eden's well-known Mansion House statement (May 29, 1941) and in Catroux's declaration, guaranteed by the British government, on the eve of the invasion of Syria and Lebanon (June 8, 1941). Syria's independence as declared by Catroux in September 1941 may have been limited, but Britain demonstrated its willingness to confront Free France on their behalf.[22]
4. Already in March 1941 Catroux had noted that the Syrian Arab nationalists were inclined to side with Britain and not with Germany,

as "Britain was in the Middle East, while Germany was far away in Europe." This comment became even more valid after July 1941. Besides, the Syrian politicians were well acquainted with the British policies in the region and the men who were implementing it. If Germany, nevertheless, won the war in Europe and occupied the Middle East, they could always negotiate an agreement with it.[23]

5. All neighboring Arab states were either under direct or indirect British rule, and their leaders were collaborating with Great Britain. The National Bloc leaders could therefore not pursue a policy that contradicted the positions of the Hashemites, Ibn Saʿud, or King Faruq.

6. The suppression of Rashid Ali's coup d'état had served as a valuable lesson on two levels: it demonstrated the high price that local leaders had to pay for their active involvement in the war between the Axis and the Allies and Great Britain's resolve to use force against any Arab regime that endangered its vital interests in the region. Great Britain also showed its support for those who remained loyal.

7. The British diplomats and high-ranking officers with whom the Syrian leaders negotiated were far more professional and held more senior positions than the German agents in Syria and Lebanon. They were well acquainted with the regional politics and employed overt as well as covert diplomacy to gain the leaders' cooperation. They also used their trusted allies, such as Nuri al-Saʿid, and later Mustafa al-Nahhas, to entice the Syrian politicians to collaborate with them.

An important issue frequently overlooked by historians, and whose critical role emerges in the British and Syrian documents, was Britain's use of covert action and secret diplomacy during the war in the Middle East to ensure the collaboration of political elites. Such tactics were employed alongside traditional diplomacy and military force. Traditional diplomacy was limited by its very nature, especially in Iraq and Egypt, whose independence Great Britain had formally recognized, or where such diplomacy was constrained by the presence of other powers (Free France in Syria and Lebanon and the United States in Saudi Arabia). Military force as a means of control also had its drawbacks, as it required the allocation of troops who were needed on other fronts such as in the Western Desert or in Europe. Besides, military force exacted a heavy political price, as it antagonized the local political leadership as well as public opinion. This was clearly illustrated in the suppression of the Rashid Ali coup d'état and in the forcing of King Faruq to appoint Mustafa al-Nahhas as prime minister. Secret diplomacy and covert action, on the other hand, provided flexibility, and, indeed, British undercover agents and diplomats made extensive use of such tactics in their foreign policy in the region. This was to continue even after the war.[24]

An examination of Britain's covert activities during the war to secure its control over the Middle East is beyond the scope of this chapter. It suffices to say that it was partly based on co-opting prominent Arab leaders by gathering intelligence on each one. Diverse methods were used to ensure collaboration, including political and financial bribery, extortion, and other means of pressure. Such methods were used to secure the collaboration of Quwatli, Mardam, and Sulh. Their cooperation enabled the three to have their cake and eat it too. Publicly, they emerged as national heroes who had liberated their countries from the hated colonial power, while in secret they had yielded to yet another colonial power in return for its help in getting rid of the former.

Riad al-Sulh was the first to initiate secret talks with British diplomats. In early March 1941 he met a British agent, and on March 14 he sent a letter to Geoffrey Furlonge, a diplomat in the British consulate in Beirut, offering to collaborate in order to reach an "entente that will save us from this hell." He also exchanged messages with Nuri al-Sa'id via the Iraqi consulate in Beirut, while he was also engaged in discussions with Roser and von Hentig.[25]

An intriguing question to which there is no clear answer is whether Quwatli was involved behind the scenes in Sulh's negotiations with the British diplomats and Nuri al-Sa'id. There are certain indications that strengthen such an assumption. Quwatli was close to Sulh ideologically (both were originally from the Istiqlal Party), and they shared a deep hatred of the French. Furthermore, Sulh's father-in-law, Sa'adallah al-Jabiri, with whom he was coordinating his political activities (Jabiri was at the time in exile in Baghdad), was also Quwatli's close political ally. Secret British and Syrian documents from 1943–1945 disclose that Sulh coordinated his policies toward the British and the French with Quwatli and Jabiri and that the British used him as a go-between. French sources claim that Quwatli had considered fleeing to Turkey on the eve of the military campaign, but at the last minute decided, for unknown reasons, to remain in Damascus. As for Mardam, French sources indicate that while in exile in Baghdad, he established close ties with British officials and received money from the British embassy. In this case too, Nuri al-Sa'id was involved.[26]

On the eve of the invasion of Syria and Lebanon, the British and the

Free French stepped up their efforts to win the Arab nationalists' support, despite the latter's collaboration with the Axis powers. Quwatli's success in March and April in organizing popular anti-French demonstrations protesting against the economic hardships enhanced his prestige. Moreover, the Rashid Ali rebellion aroused deep anti-British sentiment throughout the Arab world, especially in Damascus and Beirut. This further highlighted the importance of securing the cooperation of the Arab nationalists in the two Levant states, many of whose leaders had assisted the rebels in Iraq. This was the main goal of General Catroux's declaration on June 8 undertaking to grant independence to Syria and Lebanon. Spears was even more convinced of the need to ensure the cooperation of the nationalists in Syria following rumors at the end of May that General Henri Dentz, the high commissioner and commander of the Vichy forces, might withdraw his troops from Syria to Lebanon. For his part, Catroux, who was well acquainted with the nationalists' politics after having served as head of military intelligence in the High Commission in the late 1920s and early 1930s, initiated a letter from de Gaulle to Mardam on June 6, urging him to collaborate with Free France. In fact, Mardam was one of the few National Bloc politicians invited to a reception for Syrian dignitaries held by de Gaulle in Damascus a day after the occupation of the city. However, Mardam and other nationalist leaders had no intention of concluding a treaty with a movement claiming to represent a declining power that could jeopardize their independence and national sovereignty.[27]

With the conclusion of the military operation, the National Bloc leaders made clear to British officials their preference for a British rather than a Free French administration for the duration of the war. But Great Britain, which recognized de Gaulle as the sole representative of France, was unprepared at that stage to formally administer Syria and Lebanon, as laid down in the Lyttelton–de Gaulle agreement. Nevertheless, British diplomats and officers in the region had no doubts regarding the policy that ought to be implemented once the war was over. Even before the invasion, Spears wrote to Churchill stressing that Britain's interests in the Arab world would compel it to favor the Arabs in Syria, who were demanding national sovereignty and an end to the French mandate, rather than de Gaulle's Free France, which was seeking to restore France's influence in the mandated territories. Most of the British diplomats and high-ranking officers shared such views. Spears's main concern in the coming months, therefore, was to prevent public protests against the lack of basic commodities, like those that had taken place the previous spring. He had been warned that the nationalists might seize this opportunity to enhance their prestige, as Quwatli had done in March. He thus embarked upon forming an efficient economic organization that would ensure the supply of basic commodities and placate the nationalists. He and other British agents reassured the National Bloc leaders, who were concerned that Great Britain once again would go back on its word as it had done after the First World War, that this time Britain would keep its word. Meanwhile, Spears urged them to reject Catroux's offer for independence and power in return for their endorsement of the 1936 treaty.[28]

Despite the British assurances, the nationalists had ample reason for concern. Britain's military situation was far from encouraging, especially after the fall of Singapore in February 1942. Locally, the economic situation continued to deteriorate, and basic commodities remained in short supply. On the political level, they were once again distanced from power after Catroux's nomination of their rival Taj a-Din al-Hasani as president and Hasan al-Hakim from Shahbandar's party as prime minister, a move they saw as Free France's intention to revert to its prewar policies. The independence for Syria that Catroux declared in September was far from what they had been promised in the Allies' declaration on the eve of the invasion. Although Great Britain recognized Syria's and Lebanon's independence, the United States, Iraq, Egypt, and Saudi Arabia did not. It was therefore understandable that their leaders, including Sulh and Mardam, appealed to the British officials to keep their promises.[29]

After the German offensive in the Soviet Union came to a standstill in the winter of 1941 and the United States joined the war against the Axis powers following Pearl Harbor, the Arab nationalists came to believe that Great Britain could win the war. Subsequently, Quwatli, Mardam, and Sulh stepped up their efforts to obtain British support. Talks were held discreetly with Spears and other British officials, as well as with Nuri al-Sa'id's emissaries, especially Tahsin al-Kadri, the consul general in Beirut. Eliyahu Sasson, who was then in Damascus and met with National Bloc leaders with whom he was personally acquainted, reported on the rapprochement between the nationalists and the British and the Hashemites. He provided details of Mardam's visit to Cairo in January 1942 where, far from the eyes of the French, he met with senior British diplomats and military and intelligence officers, including Lampson and two top British intelligence agents — Brigadier Iltyde Clayton and Walter Smart. For his part, Quwatli sent emissaries to Spears to convince him that his collaboration with the Germans had been merely a passing episode and that now he was eager to cooperate with Great Britain.[30]

Shukri al-Quwatli was the one with whom the British chose to collaborate. Evidently, his anti-British record and previous collaboration with the Germans did not affect their decision. He was an obvious choice, as since the spring of 1941 he had established himself as a dominant nationalist leader with considerable prestige among the general public in Syria. The British preferred him over his rival Mardam, who was much discredited for his failure in the 1936–1939 treaty negotiations with the French and the assassination of Shahbandar. Moreover, Mardam was known for his opportunism and continued to maintain good relations with Catroux. Nonetheless, Quwatli had some drawbacks: his strong opposition to the Hashemites and his close ties with Ibn Sa'ud. But to win British support, Quwatli was evidently willing to forego, at least for the meantime, his hostility toward the Hashemites.[31]

At the end of December 1941, Quwatli departed for Iraq and Saudi Arabia. His visit was described as a pilgrimage to the holy cities of Mecca and Medina, but it had been prepared by Furlonge to enable him to hold talks with British officials and Nuri al-Sa'id. While in Saudi Arabia, he met with the British consul in Jedda, who reported Quwatli's declaration:

No Arab of reliability can possibly wish for German victory. Germans by their treatment of Europeans had taught the Arabs what they might expect if they came under the influence of those people, who had none of the characteristics necessary for the guidance of others. He said the only hope of the Arabs lay in Britain, and one has only to compare Iraq and Syria to see what he meant. He was not happy about the conditions in Syria, but understood that Britain could not stop the war merely in order to put things straight and was prepared to await the end of the war when His Majesty's Government, he was confident, would see that the assurances given were fully implemented. He thought that a German defeat would solve the only problem standing in the way of complete agreement between British and the Arabs, for the Jews from Germany and Central Europe would flock back when their countries were freed from Nazi tyranny.

It is of course impossible to form useful judgment after half hours conversation, but I am inclined to agree with Ibn Saud that whatever he may have felt or done in the past, Shukri al-Quwatli now realizes, firstly, that the Germans are not going to win this war, and secondly, that it would be entirely against Arab interests that they should win.[32]

Quwatli remained in Baghdad for almost nine months as a guest of the Iraqi government. Nuri al-Sa'id used Quwatli's close ties with Ibn Sa'ud to send him twice to Riyadh with messages to the Saudi king. The content of those messages is unclear, but they might have been part of the Iraqi prime minister's efforts to convince Ibn Saʿud that his plan for an Iraqi-Syrian union was not aimed against the House of Saʿud. While in Baghdad, Quwatli met with Kinahan Cornwallis, the British ambassador there, who strongly supported the incorporation of Syria in a Hashemite federation. The issue of Quwatli's standing was raised with Nuri al-Saʿid during the visit of Oliver Lyttelton, the minister of state, to Baghdad in January 1942. On March 6, Catroux was surprised to receive a letter from Eden requesting that Quwatli be allowed to return to Damascus. The personal intervention of the British foreign minister on behalf of a known anti-French Syrian Arab nationalist politician who had collaborated with Nazi Germany must have seemed rather unusual to Catroux, who was unaware at the time of Quwatli's secret deal with the British and the Hashemites. He replied that it would be undesirable to allow him to return to the mandated territories at that stage, but in light of Eden's special request, he would be willing to authorize his return. Quwatli, however, remained in Baghdad and returned to Damascus only in September 1942.[33]

On April 25, 1942, Quwatli concluded a secret agreement with Nuri al-Saʿid undertaking to collaborate with Iraq. Although Great Britain was not party to the agreement, British diplomats had in fact initiated it, and Cornwallis sent a copy of it to Spears in Beirut. The agreement comprised eighteen articles that laid the foundation for Iraqi-Syrian collaboration. Its main focus was Quwatli's agreement that Syria, after obtaining independence from France, would become part of an Arab federation under the Hashemites. There was no reference to what he would receive in return, but in a conversation three years later with a colleague, he recounted that the British had promised to oust France from Syria and Lebanon and ensure his election as president. The British, he noted, kept both promises. The agreement testified to the lengths to which Quwatli, a sworn opponent of the Hashemites, would go to gain British and Hashemite support for ending French rule and securing for himself the Syrian presidency.

An analysis of the agreement is beyond the scope of this article, but Article 7(a) should be noted:

> Great Britain, which is the largest global Power dominating the Near
> East, is not a hostile obstacle to the Arabs, because the interests of the
> Arabs necessitate a true friendship and staunch loyalty with regard
> to this Power; and if the Arabs do not gain its friendship of their own

accord, the circumstances and events will force them to submit to it by force, which must be avoided by all means.[34]

This statement should be viewed in the context of the events that had taken place two months previously in Egypt, when the British forced King Faruq to appoint their ally Mustafa al-Nahhas as prime minister. That incident demonstrates once again that Great Britain would not allow any Arab leader in the Middle East to act against its interests while it was at war with the Axis powers. Moreover, the dissolution of the Egyptian Parliament, the holding of elections, and the return of the Wafd party to power were further proof that Great Britain knew how to reward its allies.[35]

With Nuri al-Sa'id backing his rival, Mardam sought the support of the new Egyptian prime minister in an effort to persuade the British and the Free French to adopt the Egyptian precedent and hold elections that would enable his return to power. In June, accompanied by Beshara al-Khuri, he traveled to Cairo, where he met Nahhas and British officials. But his activities backfired. His claim that he had received British endorsement of his nomination as prime minister strained Spears's relations with Catroux and led the British to temporarily disavow him. His appointment as foreign minister in Sa'adallah Jabiri's government in August 1943, after Quwatli's election as president, marked his success in restoring British confidence in him.[36]

On August 4, 1942, as Rommel's Afrika Korps was advancing in Egypt, Syrian and Lebanese nationalists met in Sofar in Lebanon to discuss Syrian unity. At the meeting, attended by Mardam, Jabiri declared:

Nous tenons actuellement l'occasion de revendiquer l'Unité syrienne. Nous aurons ainsi une indépendence véritable et la sécurité pour l'avenir car, si les alliés remportent la victoire nous resterons indépendants, si l'Axe remporte la victoire, nous trouvant indépendants ils nous laisseront en cet état.[37]

Jabiri's statement was actually only partly correct. Apart from a short period after the fall of France, his colleagues—Quwatli, Mardam, and Sulh—collaborated with Great Britain. In retrospect, their gamble on a British victory and their secret cooperation with Great Britain enabled them to realize their national aspirations as well as their personal political ambitions. Great Britain indeed won the war and after forcing France out of Syria and Lebanon established itself as the dominant power in the

Middle East. Germany, in the end, was never considered as an alternative by the Syrian National Bloc leaders. But its military offensives against Great Britain in the Middle East and its propaganda pressured the British to do their utmost to gain the collaboration of the Arab nationalist leaders in Syria and Lebanon. But it came at a price: the Syrians had to acquiesce to the British conditions—integration in a regional federation under British-Hashemite hegemony—in return for their support in ending France's rule. In the final analysis, the Syrian nationalists were not as successful, as some historians claim, in furthering their national goals by exploiting Britain's rivalry, first with Germany and then with Free France. Great Britain remained in control all along.[38]

Memoirs Do Not Deceive: Syrians Confront Fascism and Nazism— as Reflected in the Memoirs of Syrian Political Leaders and Intellectuals

EYAL ZISSER

Nassuh Babil (1905–1986) was one of Syria's leading journalists during the first years of the country's independence. He was the owner and editor of Damascus's leading daily newspaper in those days, *al-Ayyam*, which he purchased in 1932. He also served as chairman of the Association of Syrian Journalists from 1943 until 1963, when the Ba'th Party carried out its coup d'état. Babil also tried his hand at politics. He linked up at first with 'Abd al-Rahman Shahbandar, leader of the People's Party, and after Shahbandar was assassinated in 1940, he drew close to Shukri al-Quwatli, one of the prominent leaders of the National Bloc (*al-Kutla al-Wataniyya*).[1]

In 1987, after Babil's death, his memoirs were published under the title *Sihafa wa Siyasa: Suriyya fi al-Qarn al-'Ishrin* (Journalism and politics: Syria in the twentieth century). In this book, written from the distance of a generation, Babil surveyed the path he had taken in his public and political activity from the 1920s to the 1960s, casting light on what was happening in Syria during one of the most gripping periods in the country's history. Light is also cast on the issue at the center of this study, the response of Syrian public opinion to the challenge of Nazism and Fascism during the 1930s and 1940s as reflected in the backward-looking memoirs of Syrian leaders, intellectuals, and journalists. Or perhaps the question should be phrased somewhat differently: what was the image of those years that the Syrian writers of memoirs seek to reconstruct, and how did they want people to remember the way in which the Syrian public responded to Nazism and Fascism?

In this regard, the chapter in Babil's memoirs dealing with the outbreak of World War II is of particular interest. There he notes that the outbreak of the war and its course aroused great interest among the Syrian public.

The victories reaped by Hitler became the talk of the day, and it seems as if many Syrians welcomed them. This happened as a way of expressing their anger against France and England, and even as a way of showing their desire to take revenge against those empires for the policies they adopted after World War I that alienated them from the Arabs. Nevertheless, the educated stratum of Syrian society viewed with worry what might happen if the Axis powers—Germany and Italy—actually won the war. Among this class the concern was clearly evident that Syria and Lebanon might be handed over to Italy, in accord with a secret agreement between the two Axis powers on how to divide up the spheres of influence between them.[2] Babil thus testifies to the existence on the Syrian street of a mood of satisfaction over the victories Nazi Germany achieved at the beginning of World War II. At the same time, however, he shows that there was a sense of reservation, and even concern, especially among the Syrian elite of those days, over the possible implications of a German victory for the future of Syria and Lebanon.

Evidence of these attitudes is also to be found in the memoirs of the Syrian politician and longtime minister of defense during the Hafiz al-Asad era, Mustafa Talas (b. 1932). Talas was just a young boy in the days of World War II, a pupil in the school in his village of al-Rustan near the town of Hims. Talas's book of memoirs, *Mir'at Hayati* (The story of my life), published in Damascus in 1992, is clearly marked by a tone of self-justification after the event. This is what he has to say there:

> I shall not hide from the reader that people's hearts and feelings were inclined toward the Nazis at that time. We all hoped that Germany would be victorious, and we also hoped that with this victory it would free us from the scourge of French imperialism. The military victories achieved by the German army on the various battle fronts aroused in us a feeling of identification and pride as well. After all, the significance of the class struggle had not yet become sufficiently clear in Syria of those days. At the same time, the reality on the ground taught that the wealthy favored the American side and the allies of the United States, while the poor favored the party of Adolf Hitler. We even hoped, as I have already noted, that it would succeed in extricating us from the jaws of the British occupation.

Talas adds: "I would receive the information on the events of the war from the daily newspaper that my cousin, Muhammad Salah Isma'il, would bring to my village, al-Rustan. I would read it to my 'fallahin' brothers without hiding my enthusiasm over the Germans' victories and belittling the value of the achievements of the English and Americans."[3]

In his memoirs, Talas cites another reason for the sympathy toward Germany, as follows: "The blows (that Hitler) brought down on the heads of the Jews, the saboteurs who carried out acts of sabotage against Germany, and inside Germany—Jews whom Hitler called, 'a fifth column'— these blows gave us satisfaction and relief, because the Zionists are the historical enemies of the Arabs, and there was already someone who said that the enemy of my enemy is my friend."[4] Reading this, it is impossible to escape the impression that these lines in Talas's memoirs represent views adopted many years after the period under discussion, since until that time, as Talas notes elsewhere in his book, he had never met any Jews, not even Syrian Jews. And indeed, in his mature years Talas adopted views that bordered on being clearly anti-Semitic, like those that found expression in his book *Fatir Sahyun* (The matzah of Zion), where he discusses the use Jews allegedly make of blood in their religious rituals.[5] On the other hand, apart from the lines cited above, in Talas's memoirs Jews are not mentioned at all until the point when the Arab-Israeli conflict begins to influence his life. This was after he was drafted into the army in 1952, or perhaps a little before this, when he joined the Ba'th Party, near the time of its founding in April 1947.

Babil's and Talas's accounts join a long series of memoirs published in recent decades by Syrian statesmen and intellectuals, dealing with the lives of their authors and also, in fact, with the course of events in Syria in the 1930s, 1940s, and 1950s—formative years in the history of the Syrian state. Such memoirs can be valuable historical sources, although they present a number of methodological and other challenges. This is because most are written with hindsight and wisdom after the fact, often many years after the events being described, and, what is most significant, with a clear agenda, the main aim of which, usually, is to rewrite history in a way that is self-serving for the author and often for purposes of glorifying his image or justifying the path he followed. Still, insofar as they need to be addressed with great caution, memoirs are almost no different from any other historical source. The memoirs now available can serve as a rich resource for any research aimed at reexamining existing historical assumptions, and at better understanding the development of Syria's history in its formative and critical years.

Additionally, however, it is important to emphasize again and again that these memoirs enable us to learn how the writers sought to reconstruct the memory of those years with the passage of time. Thus, we are obliged to ask on what did each writer base his effort to construct a historical memory that does not necessarily reflect what really happened in Syria in the 1920s and 1930s, but rather reflects the moods and events of the period in which the authors were writing? The memoirs in question, we note, were published at different times, although most came out in recent decades, during the rule of the Ba'th Party in Syria.

This study is devoted to an examination of the various responses within Syrian public opinion toward the ideas of Nazism and Fascism and toward the German or Italian options in World War II. This topic has already been dealt with in a systematic and pathbreaking manner by Götz Nordbruch in his book *Nazism in Syria and Lebanon*.[6] This study thus seeks to add another tier to the structure erected by Nordbruch. It proposes to do so by means of an examination of the corpus of memoirs published in recent decades by Syrian politicians and intellectuals who held prominent positions in Syria's political life during the 1930s and 1940s. It should come as no surprise that an investigation of this material reveals a much more complex picture than the one known until now of the public debate in Syria at that time, and especially of what was being said on the Syrian street, but also among the intellectuals and political leaders, in regard to Germany, Italy, Nazism, and Fascism.

Syria: The Struggle That Never Ends

During the first years of its independence, and even before that, Syria found itself trapped in a stormy spiral of struggle, rebellion, and coups d'état. A main element in the turmoil was the question of what path the state should take and, of course, the issue of who would rule it.

At first there was the struggle of the Syrian population, led by the National Bloc, the Syrian national movement of those years, against the French mandate authorities. Their aim was to achieve full independence from the French, but as an interim aim to achieve a greater degree of integration of the Syrians in the administration of the country. To be more precise, the leaders of the National Bloc, most of whom came from the traditional urban elite of the notable families, wanted to ensure their role in the administration of the Syrian state the French were establishing. Next there was a struggle within the Syrian elite for influence and dominance. Other factions joined the fray, trying to pave their way into the center of the political arena, factions from outside the elite, made up of politicians and intellectuals from the urban Sunni community in Syria.

Finally, and most important, there was the struggle of the members of the minorities and of the geographical periphery of Syria to integrate into the state structure and its administration, and, later, even to rule it.[7]

Against the background of these struggles and the weakness that characterized Syria during the 1920s, and even more during the 1930s, there were signs of a radicalization of the Syrian political arena. In retrospect, this radicalization was like a fire in a field of dry grass, and ultimately it spread to all of Syria. As noted, it was a direct result of the struggle for power among the various social and political factions in the country, and it should be seen as an expression of the frustration felt by the various groups, or, alternatively, as a convenient platform they could ride in paving their way to the center of the political arena and, later, to the highest echelons. It is no wonder that historical research tends, with hindsight, to represent the Syrian historical narrative as one whose end is known in advance, that is, Syria is portrayed as a state inevitably doomed to fall into radicalism, whether nationalist radicalism (the Ba'th Party) or, alternatively, Islamic radicalism (the Muslim Brothers).

One of the first expressions of this radicalization of the Syrian state was the appearance during the 1930s of semimilitaristic groups with radical worldviews. Among them may be mentioned the Iron Shirts (al-Qumsan al-Hadidiyya), the White Badge (al-Shara al-Bayda' or L'insigne Blanc), the League of National Action ('Usbat al-'Amal al-Qawmi), and the PPS, the Syrian Nationalist Party, which began as a secret organization. In addition, in Lebanon there were the Najada and the Phalange movements. These groups prepared the ground for the appearance of radical political parties in Syria from the mid-1940s onward, parties such as the already mentioned PPS, the Ba'th, the Communists, and, finally, the Muslim Brotherhood movement.

The three radical political parties, more than the youth movements and the semimilitaristic groups of the 1930s, appealed to the same target populations and managed to strike roots there, that is, they attracted members of the minority communities, Sunni villagers and residents of the periphery, and Syrian youths from the middle class in the big cities. Each of the radical parties offered these different social groups an answer to the identity crisis they faced that would encompass them all, whether it was a Syrian (that is, Greater Syria) identity such as the Syrian Nationalist Party offered, an Arab identity such as the Ba'th Party offered, or a cosmopolitan identity such as the Communist Party offered. In any case, the identities being offered were not confined to the Syrian state and its territory as determined by the French mandate authorities during the 1920s.[8]

It goes without saying that the character of the PPS has been the focus of scholarly debate ever since its founding at the beginning of the 1930s, and certainly since the 1940s, when it became a significant political power in Syria and Lebanon. The PPS is discussed more than any other political party active in the Syrian lands in those days, with the main question being whether the PPS was a Fascist party that drew its inspiration from Nazi Germany or if it perhaps had other roots, for example, nationalistic views encountered by Antun Saʻada during the time he spent in Brazil. At the same time, it has often been claimed that the Baʻth Party members were influenced by Fascist ideas during the first stages of the party's development. However, studies of the ideological roots of the party's founders, Michel ʻAflaq and Salah al-Din al-Bitar, trace their views back to national and socialist ideas developed in Western Europe, and especially France, at the beginning of the twentieth century.[9]

In any case, it should be mentioned that the research of the intellectual and the political debate in Syria during the first half of the twentieth century is still in its infancy. Despite the significant contribution made by thinkers and writers from the Syrian lands (Bilad al-Sham) to Arab cultural revival (the *nahda*) (Butrus al-Bustani, for example) to the development of Arab nationalism (ʻAbd al-Rahman al-Kawakibi) and Islamic modernism (Rashid Rida), academic research at some point lost interest in the Syrian lands, as if the intellectual and ideological developments there had come to an end all of a sudden. Thus, there were no sequels to the books by Albert Hourani, *Arabic Thought in the Liberal Age, 1798–1939*; David Commins, *Islamic Reform, Politics, and Social Change in Late Ottoman Syria*; Marwan R. Buheiry's edited *Intellectual Life in the Arab East, 1890–1939*; and others.[10]

Only in the 1960s did scholars turn their attention once more to Syria, but their studies were clearly influenced by the political events that took place, and mainly by the radicalism in this region during the first half of the twentieth century. Indeed, since it seemed quite clear that Syria was destined to fall under the rule of the Baʻth regime, a regime governed by army officers with a radical hue to their thinking and a commitment to the ideology of the Baʻth Party, it seemed as if any ideological developments and debates that might have taken place in Syria about alternatives to this ideology were futile and consequently of little or no importance or interest to scholarly research. Therefore, little or no attention was devoted to this dimension in Syrian political and ideological life. Furthermore, almost no genuine research or scholarly attention was devoted to the question of the trends in Syrian society regarding radical ideologies, including, of course, Fascism and Nazism, during the 1930s and 1940s. At best, the inadequate, from a scholarly point of view, assumption prevailed that whatever was true of Egypt, the "elder sister," was also true of Syria, as if the latter had no distinctive society, worldview, or, especially, will of its own. In addition, scholars tended to assume that there was a clear continuity between the Syrian lands of the eighteenth, nineteenth, and twentieth centuries, or at least the first half of the twentieth century. It also assumed that the key to the developments in Syria should be sought among the elite of notables that had ruled up to the twentieth century. The studies of Syria published up to the 1970s and 1980s served only to fortify this approach. Thus, one finds among this academic literature mainly works dealing with Syrian-French relations, or, to be more precise, French policy toward Syria, and especially toward the notable families, and mainly that part of it residing in Damascus.[11]

Again, in all this academic literature, there was no discussion of how people in the Levant, and in Syria in particular, reacted to Fascism and Nazism and whether totalitarianism was adopted or rejected by the population. In studies devoted to political developments in Syria in that period, it appeared merely as a negligible footnote, as if the great events taking place around the Levant and, in fact, even touching upon it had nothing to do with it, as if those events did not evoke any attention, interest, or responses among the populations residing there.

Because in practice there was no real political connections or contacts between the political and social forces active in Syria and the Axis powers, Nazi Germany in particular, and as it is doubtful whether Nazism was really a source of inspiration for any of the thinkers and founders of Syria's radical movements or the movement that eventually took power in Syria, the Ba'th, the discussion of the issue became charged and employed mainly for political ends. Thus, for example, efforts were made, mainly by the French, but after their departure, also by the opponents of the PPS, to prove that it was a movement that developed right out of the teachings of Nazism. In another example, since the 1970s and 1980s there has been a clear tendency to portray the Ba'th movement as having at its root anti-Semitic and Fascist principles. True, those making such claims do not do so in serious scholarly works, but rather in other frameworks, like blogs and comments on news websites.[12]

One of the first scholars who sought to confront the issue of the face of Syrian society in these years, without necessarily focusing on the elite of notables and its political maneuvering, was Keith Watenpaugh, in his book *Being Modern in the Middle East: Revolution, Nationalism, Colonialism, and the Arab Middle Class*. Watenpaugh sums up this phenomenon of radicalization very accurately:

> Yet unlike these more obviously fascist groups, the formation of the Iron Shirts and the White Badge in Aleppo, while representing a successful interpolation of the language of fascist paramilitary organization, carried with it little engagement with the rather amorphous ideological dimensions of fascism. Rather, the limited incorporation of fascist forms in the mid-1930s brings into relief the changing nature of the communal and class aspects of violence in the cities of the post-Ottoman Eastern Mediterranean. The specific impulse to use these forms grew from the desire of a traditional elite masquerading as nationalists to contain forces and groups increasingly outside of the locus of its control; while simultaneously, the plastic nature of such forms provided an emergent middle-class minority with the means to demarcate the terms of its identity, gain momentarily a measure of power within the urban milieu, and dissent from dominant forms of Arabism and Syrian citizenship. . . .
>
> More significantly, the fascist interlude points to a critical moment of urban dissonance in the city's architectures of community. Those who saw themselves as modern, the elite, and middle-class elements of these movements—nationalist or otherwise—drew legitimacy from mimicking European, primarily German and Italian, models, as closely as possible—and thereby indicating that being fascist had become for some evidence of being modern. At the same time, by locating these groups within colonial resistance to or collaboration with the French presence, this chapter can eschew what Robert Paxton labels "the 'bestiary' approach" to the comparative study of fascism.[13]

Beside Watenpaugh's work, we should mention once more Götz Nordbruch's pathbreaking book *Nazism in Syria and Lebanon* (2008). By using the published memoirs dealing with the period under discussion, one can add an additional tier to the structure erected by Nordbruch and also investigate what can be learned from the manner in which the authors, leading Syrian political and public figures, try to fashion the way in which that period is remembered.

The several memoirs published by Syrian politicians and intellectuals in recent decades seek to revivify the memory of the first half of the twentieth century and the period up to the Ba'th coup d'état in 1963. These memoirs have obvious limitations for the researcher. The picture they present is often influenced by the "spirit of the present times" (zeitgeist), as we saw in the case of Mustafa Talas, and the authors' knowledge of how Syria's history developed following the times being portrayed certainly influenced and contributed to molding the picture they present. Nevertheless, these memoirs can serve as a rich resource for researchers wanting to test already existing historical assumptions and, alternatively, to reinterpret important chapters in the history of modern Syria.

Sami al-Jundi: Exception of a Representative Case?

A Google search using the words *Nazism in Syria* or *Fascism in Syria* calls up a large number of links that include the name Sami al-Jundi. Indeed, it is customary to use a quotation from Sami al-Jundi's memoirs, *Al-B'ath*, published in Beirut in 1969, as a basis for the claim that sympathy for Nazism and a tendency to adopt its views took root in the Syrian expanse. There Jundi testifies that his comrades read "Nietzsche's *Thus Spoke Zarathustra*, Fichte's *Addresses to the German Nation*, H. S. Chamberlain's *The Foundations of the Nineteenth Century*. They were the first who thought about translating [Hitler's] *Mein Kampf.* . . . Whoever has lived through this period in Damascus will have noticed the inclination of the Arab people toward Nazism. Nazism was the force that took revenge for them. The defeated naturally admire the victorious. We, however, were of a different school."[14] Note that those who view Jundi as testifying to the inclination toward Nazism end the quote from his memoirs just at this point. However, a more thorough investigation of the memoirs reveals something entirely different. Thus, for example, Jundi writes: "Whoever lived in those days in Damascus could understand the Arabs' attraction to Nazism and to the power and energy that found expression in the Nazi revolution. For the defeated loves the victor as he is, but we were a camp (mazhab) and belonged to two separate camps, and whoever reads the principles of the National Party, which became the principles of the Arab Ba'th, without going into them deeply, will make a mistake."[15]

Sami al-Jundi (1921–1995) was one of the Ba'th Party's most prominent leaders during its early years. He studied dentistry at the University of Damascus, graduating in 1944. During his studies, he met Zaki al-Arsuzi, one of the founders or at least one of the first to develop the ideas of the Ba'th during the period before its formal founding. Jundi himself is counted among the party's founding members from its inception in 1947. He broke into the highest echelons following the establishment of the United Arab Republic (UAR) in 1958, when he was appointed UAR minister of information and propaganda. After the Ba'th Party took power in Syria in March 1963, Jundi held a number of ministerial positions, including minister of information and minister of national guidance and culture. Earlier, in May 1963, he was even commissioned with forming a government, but in this he failed. In October 1964, Jundi was sent to serve as Syrian ambassador to France. He held this position until Hafiz al-Asad came to power in 1970, at which point Jundi resigned and left political life. He wandered first to Beirut and then, in 1981, returned to Syria, where he went back to working as a dentist. It goes without saying that Sami al-Jundi was a son of the Ismaili Jundi family that held a prominent position in the political life of Syria during the second half of the 1960s, after the neo-Ba'th coup d'état. His cousin 'Abd al-Karim al-Jundi served as the powerful minister of information who also ruled over Syria's internal security apparatus, until he committed suicide in 1968, against the background of the power struggles then raging among the members of the highest echelon. 'Abd al-Karim's rivals were the members of the group of Alawite officers led by Salah Jadid and Hafiz al-Asad. Sami's brother Khalid al-Jundi headed the Syrian General Federation of Workers' Unions.[16]

As noted above, it is customary to base the claim that Fascist and Nazi views spread in the Syrian expanse on the quotation from Sami al-Jundi's memoirs in which he states how he and his companions manifested an interest in those ideas. However, a deeper and more comprehensive look into Jundi's memoirs gives a somewhat different impression, a picture of soul-searching, searching for self, and wavering between identities. Such uncertainty and seeking were more characteristic of the Syrian youth of those years than a commitment to the Fascist worldview. Jundi himself testifies to this in his memoirs:

> The youth joined together seeking deliverance and salvation, and this in the face of a difficult international situation, and an even more difficult local situation. The negotiations over the signing of a French-Syrian contract ended in disappointment. The province [of Alexandretta] was taken [from Syria], and the world war broke out, and all this in a situation in which the Arab world was comparable to a map without any content, as if it were a matter of a living creature without any flesh on it. Against this background, local party organizations sprang up, all preaching Arab nationalism, most even holding a socialist point of view, but in most cases they were not more than small groups. After all, getting organized in an organization appeared to be a national and human necessity, as part of the struggle in a collective form and as a proof of existence.[17]

As noted, more than anything else, Jundi's words indicate his marginality and the marginality of his ideas in the Syrian expanse, and his anomalousness. And so he testifies, among other things:

> In this period, it will be remembered, we felt upon ourselves, in the society in which we lived, the difficult isolation, and it was the result of the fact that we rebelled against all the values of the past and turned into enemies of all custom and accepted behavior. We accused every faith and religion of heresy, and we sought struggle and confrontation. We fought against the society and decreed the destruction of the old, of the wisdom of the past, of the institutions, and in this respect, we were like babies who regress in time to the stage of infancy, more and more as the years pass. . . . We became committed to struggling against anything that was different from us, without distinguishing between traitor and loyalist, The differences between [our political rivals] we viewed as an expression of tribalism, as if the future Arab state had no possibility of existence without the destruction of the past. We acted with absolute determination and violence that often blinded us. We accused others of heresy. We were idealists. . . The teacher (Arsuzi) would speak with us a lot about the Messiah, and in my opinion he was influenced by Nietzsche's book, *The Birth of Greek Tragedy*, and saw in the Jahiliyya his supreme ideal and the golden age of the Arabs. He was a man of refusal and rejection, and we went along with him.[18]

However, it would seem that not only a critical reading of Jundi's memoirs is required here. The memoirs of other figures from that period need to be read and analyzed as well. This is because Jundi reflects only a small and marginal segment of Syrian society at the time, as he himself testifies in his book. The fact that the segment of which he was part was destined in future years to make its way into the highest echelons of the country does not negate the importance at the time of the other parts of the society. In this connection, in general, among the memoirs available to us, we should distinguish between those written by figures who belonged to the leadership and political and intellectual elite of the time, such as Nassuh Babil, on the one hand, and young people, like Sami al-Jundi, who were just taking their first steps toward the highest echelons, on the other hand.

The issue here is not just the difference in age but in fact two separate worlds. On the one side was the traditional elite based upon the notable Sunni families from the big cities who had played a leading role in the political and social life of the Syrian expanse for hundreds of years and who continued to lead Syria in the framework of the National Bloc until the Ba'th coup d'état in 1963. On the other side were the young men who arose from the margins of Syrian society, led by figures from the rural areas and the periphery, and members of the minority communities who came from the local elite in their home areas (as Hanna Batatu noted in his book *Syria's Peasantry, the Descendants of Its Lesser Rural Notables, and Their Politics*). These men gained political power and influence on the national level in the framework of the radical political parties then active, and they were destined eventually, after 1963, to rule the country.[19]

Thus, the Syrian elites, made up of the old-time notables identified with the National Bloc, which occupied the center of the political stage in Syria during those years, were in time pushed aside and their place taken by circles from the margins of the society. Nevertheless, in the period under consideration, these elites were a significant force in Syrian public affairs, and it is clear that they mostly distanced themselves from Fascist ideas and Nazism. Rather, they showed a commitment in principle to the democratic and liberal tradition, as can be seen from the path they followed and the worldview they expressed, and this at a time when the marginal factors were showing an interest in Fascism and Nazism, as Sami al-Jundi testifies in his memoirs.

As mentioned, Nassuh Babil was an important actor in Syrian social and political life of that time. This was, first, because of his connections with two of the most prominent, and certainly among the most colorful, figures in Syrian politics of the 1920s and 1930s. One of them was 'Abd al-Rahman Shahbandar, and the other was Shukri al-Quwatli, with whom Babil became close after Shahbandar's assassination in 1940. Quwatli was one of the leading members of the nationalistic faction in the Syrian National Bloc and eventually became the first president of independent Syria. If there was a leading faction in Syrian society and a particular tendency that gained predominance in the country's political life in those years, then their main representatives and spokesmen were these two figures, Shahbandar and Quwatli, along with their close associate Babil. The second reason is that Babil was the father of the modern Syrian press. This made him a personage of great interest for students of Syrian history, as someone who represents not only the atmosphere prevailing among the Syrian public in general, but also the atmosphere that found expression in the Syrian press of that period. As noted above, from 1932 Babil was the owner and editor of Damascus's leading daily newspaper in those days, *al-Ayyam*, which initially served as a mouthpiece for Shahbandar and his views. After Quwatli's election as president of Syria in 1943, Babil became, with Quwatli's blessing and patronage, chairman of the Association of Syrian Journalists. Babil held this position persistently, despite all the ups and downs experienced by Syria over the years, until the Ba'th coup d'état in 1963. During these years, Babil controlled all of Syria's leading press organs, including, besides *al-Ayyam, Alif Ba al-Shaam* and *al-Qabas*.[20]

As noted above, Babil testifies in his memoirs that there was a populistic atmosphere on the Syrian street, an atmosphere of satisfaction, even if superficial, over the victories achieved by Nazi Germany at the beginning of World War II. However, at the same time, he notes that there was an atmosphere of reservation, and even concern, especially among the circles of the Syrian elite, regarding the possible repercussions of the German victories on the futures of Syria and Lebanon.

It is, thus, appropriate at this point to cite once again the words Nassuh Babil used when summing up his memoirs:

> The outbreak of the war and its course aroused great interest among the Syrian public. The victories reaped by Hitler became the talk of the day, and it seems as if many Syrians welcomed them. This happened as a way of expressing their anger against France and England, and even as a way of showing their desire to take revenge against those states for the policies they adopted after World War I that alienated them from the Arabs. Nevertheless, the educated stratum of Syrian society viewed with worry what might happen if the Axis powers—Germany and Italy—actually won the war. Among this class the concern was clearly evident that Syria and Lebanon might be handed over to Italy, in accord with a secret agreement between the two Axis powers on how to divide up the spheres of influence between them.[21]

Khalid al-'Azm (1903–1965) was a member of the traditional Syrian elite and one of Syria's most important political leaders. He held major governmental positions during the first half of the twentieth century. His memoirs present us with another representative example. His father, Fawzi Pasha al-'Azm, served as minister of the Aqwqaf of the Ottoman Empire during the reign of Sultan Abdul Hamid II. Khalid al-'Azm studied law at the University of Damascus and graduated in 1923. He belonged to the National Bloc and was known for his close ties with Shukri al-Quwatli. Later, however, the two parted ways, and in 1955 they even competed for the presidency of the Syrian Republic, with Quwatli winning the race. Most of the time from the first parliamentary elections in Syria in 1943, with the country still under the French mandate, until 1963, 'Azm was elected to the Chamber of Representatives. He also held a number of ministerial positions, occupying the post of prime minister in the periods 1950–1951 and 1962–1963. He was serving at the time of the Ba'th coup d'état, in the wake of which he fled to Lebanon, where he died in poverty on November 18, 1965.[22]

Khalid al-'Azm's memoirs, written during his exile in Lebanon and published in 1973, became one of the most important sources for learning about the history of Syria in those years. Insofar as the question we are examining is concerned, it is somewhat surprising to discover that the issue of relations with Germany and Nazism does not occupy a central place in 'Azm's book. He was not an intellectual or ideologist, but a man of action whose worldview was formulated during the 1920s and 1930s in the shadow of the French mandate, and, in light of the memoirs, it appears that his views were colored, both positively and negatively, by influences from the period of Ottoman rule as well. Still, 'Azm's remark that he felt esteem and respect for Germany, but also the need to be cautious and reserved in relation to it, is quite interesting. This is what he wrote in his memoirs, when summing up the results of World War II and explaining its background and the reasons it broke out:

> President Roosevelt involved the U.S. in World War II in order to destroy Germany, after Hitler began to advance and develop it and turn it into a superior and proud world power. To reach his goal, Roosevelt invested all his energy and enlisted all the world powers. He promised the Zionists aid in order to get their help, and simultaneously also made a pact with Communism, by which he was able to enlist two hundred million Russians on his side. Roosevelt also reached understandings with the imperialist powers, and was even clever enough to impose his will on them, and by doing this he in fact turned Britain and France into victims of his policy.
>
> However, the result of this policy of Roosevelt was that Russia conquered a large part of the territory of Germany and also took control over Czechoslovakia, Hungary, Poland, Rumania, Bulgaria, and Yugoslavia. The communist idea ruled over them, which led to the division of the European continent into two parts and the establishment of the Iron Curtain. . . . Roosevelt's policy thus led to the spread of communism all over the world, and thus raised a new enemy for the U.S., stronger and more dangerous than the German enemy. For the only thing Hitler sought was to strengthen Germany and turn it into a world power, and to return to its hands the German colonies that it had lost, and to open

the world markets to its products . . . at a time when communism wanted to rule the whole world by virtue of its social philosophy. However, in contrast to Hitler, communism seeks to rule the world and impose its social philosophy. . . . Thus, the Americans did not understand that the war against Germany only strengthened the Soviet Union. They came to their senses only after the war ended, and so they turned immediately to the reconstruction of Germany and began to struggle with the Soviets.[23]

It is doubtful that 'Azm had such insights during the war years themselves. However, two points emerge and stand out from his words: first, a basic, if superficial, sympathy for the German effort and, second, an emphatically critical and even disapproving stance toward the United States, which, incidentally, 'Azm accused of being responsible for his political fall inside Syria. In the 1950s, 'Azm changed his tune toward the USSR and even came to be called "the red prince," because he preached drawing near to and collaborating with the Soviets. 'Azm's motives here were a combination of political opportunism and his understanding and assessment of the regional situation. The manner in which he understood the period of the Cold War and the Arab-Israeli conflict was no doubt reached rather late, and there is little doubt that his views on these matters influenced his views on World War II. What is most important and most instructive for the purposes of the present study is the fact that the issue of how Syrians related to Germany, Nazism, Italy, and Fascism in the 1930s and 1940s, including the war years, receives no real treatment or serious mention in 'Azm's memoirs. This absence of treatment undoubtedly results from the fact that the issue had no relevance or real interest for the author.

In contrast to Khalid al-'Azm, the memoirs of 'Adil Arslan (1882–1954) give prominent expression to the author's reservations about Nazi Germany's violent and totalitarian way. 'Adil Arslan was born in Mount Lebanon to a notable Druze family. His better-known brother Shakib Arslan (1869–1946), chose a path different from that of most of the members of his generation and his colleagues and sided with the Axis powers during World War II. After the fall of the Ottoman Empire, 'Adil Arslan abandoned his obligation to the empire and went over to the side of the Hashemite family. He was appointed adviser to King Faysal and the king's prime minister, Rida Pasha al-Rikabi. After the conquest of Syria, Arslan fled, at first to Amman, and from there to Cairo. In 1924 he established the Syrian-Lebanese Congress and served as its head while working from Geneva. In 1936, after receiving a pardon from the French, Arslan returned to Syria and joined the ranks of the National Bloc. He served as ambassador to Ankara from 1937 until 1939, when the embassy in the Turkish capital was closed following the French-sanctioned annexation of Alexandretta to Turkey. In the Syrian parliamentary elections of 1943, Arslan was elected to the Chamber of Deputies. In 1949 he linked up with Husni al-Za'im, who carried out a military coup d'état in March of that year and appointed him foreign minister. However, Arslan resigned a month later, after Za'im asked him to meet with the Israeli foreign minister, Moshe Sharett. He then moved to Beirut and remained there until his death, keeping himself detached from Syrian political life.[24]

'Adil Arslan's memoirs express curiosity, interest, esteem, and sometimes even admiration for the German experiment, but beside these thoughts one also finds caution and reservations, and more than once even aversion and abhorrence toward the boundlessness of German ambition and the murderousness of Hitlerism. These emotions were felt by this son of a notable family, a member of the Syrian expansive elite, and a man who grew up in the Ottoman Empire and received his education there. To illustrate these points, one might cite a number of passages from 'Adil Arslan's memoirs.

In his diary entry for June 10, 1934, regarding Hitler's Jewish policy, Arslan writes that "one of the results of Hitler's policy is that the Zionist gang succeeded in sending thousands of German Jews to Palestine. For prior to this, Zionism had failed to convince these Jews to immigrate to Palestine."[25]

In his diary entry for June 30, 1934, regarding the Röhm plot, Arslan writes:

Today Hitler violently exterminated several of his supporters in Munich. He flew there early in the morning, broke into their homes while they were sleeping, pointed a gun at their heads, and when they awoke and surrendered without protest, he gave orders to liquidate them. The Führer even demanded that their leader (Röhm) shoot himself. He was given a pistol, but when he refused to commit suicide, Hitler entered his room and shot him, along with several of his [Röhm's] loyalists and supporters. In the room neighboring Röhm's they found the Breslau SA commander Edmund Heines in bed with a young male. Those two were also killed. The whole world was surprised to hear the reports about this surprising massacre. Various explanations of it were given, but Hitler himself explained to the German nation that these Hitlerites had organized a plot against him and come into contact with a foreign government, an allusion to France. A deed such as this can be perpetrated only in a place where the leader seeks to rule with an iron fist and pays no attention to anyone but himself, and no one is able to stand in his way as he acts to reach his goal. There were those who thought that following the event, a revolution against Hitler would break out in Germany, but it would seem that the German people accepted Hitler's explanations and gave him their support.[26]

During the second half of the 1930s, 'Adil Arslan was quite active in the realm of foreign policy, mainly in connection with Italy, which had become a close ally of Hitler. In his diary entry for June 16, 1935, Arslan writes:

Hitler claims that he prefers that Italy win the war in Ethiopia, out of concern that its defeat in the struggle will arouse the African peoples to rebel and rise up against the white peoples. Many in Europe believe him in this claim. But I think that Hitler is interested in Italy ruling a new colony, for the following reasons: First, so that Italy will become absorbed in dealing with it, which in turn will enable him [Hitler] to advance his interests in Austria. Second, in order to exploit the Italian victory in order to obtain colonies for himself. I am concerned, in this regard, that in light of the European hunger for new colonies, no more colonies will be left for distribution among these greedy gluttons, except for the Arab states, which will become a target for them.[27]

Arslan's insights into Nazi Germany's swallowing up of Czechoslovakia are very interesting and instructive. In his diary entry for March 16, 1939, he writes:

The oppressed became the oppressor. Hitler obliterated Czechoslovakia's independence. Czechia [that is, the Sudetenland], became a kind of German district under Germany's protection (a protectorate), and in fact there is no different between it and Germany's other districts, apart from the fact that its language is not German, at least for the time being. Slovakia also became an independent state under German protection. Meanwhile, Hungary took over the Ruthenian Ukraine region. I must admit that I had some special sympathy for Germany, because I viewed them as a distinguished people, and in the past I thought that their humiliation (after World War I) was a kind of crime and betrayal. But now, after they have become strong and powerful, they have begun to attack peaceful nations. Even if Hitler succeeds in his path and his policy, still, every person of conscience must feel discomfort from, and even disapproval of Hitler's deeds, and the matter will even cause serious damage to Germany, because all of Europe will become tense and stand on its guard, and in the end will come out against the German people, which does not really seek such a confrontation. I am also afraid that Hitler's course will force the democratic governments to try to appease the eastern states, and of course, these developments will have repercussions in the Arab states, and especially in Syria.[28]

In his diary entry for August 23, 1939, Arslan addresses the signing of the Ribbentrop-Molotov Non-Aggression Pact. He writes:

The echoes of the explosion Russia and Germany set off are still resounding all over the world, and certainly in Turkey and Rumania. . . . There are those who try to calm Turkey with the assertion that if war breaks out, the Russians, in accord with their obligations, will supply fuel to Germany. For otherwise, the Germans would be forced to seek fuel in Rumania, and later in Iraq as well, and this by means of Turkey taking control or by an effort to force it to take control and rule for them over the sources of the oil in Iraq in order to export it to Germany.[29]

Finally, at the end of the war, in a surprisingly candid passage, Arslan notes the efforts of the grand mufti of Jerusalem to reach a German-Arab understanding. In his diary entry for May 21, 1945, Arslan writes:

The Mufti of Jerusalem, Hajj Amin al-Husayni, went to Germany. He did this because he thinks that Britain and the U.S. will not back away from their support of Zionism. He knows that Britain will continue to support Zionism to a certain extent, while the U.S. will support it all the way until the establishment of a Jewish state in Palestine and Trans-Jordan. The Mufti therefore thought that no one except Germany could save Palestine from Zionism. He therefore thought that it was incumbent upon him as President of the Supreme Muslim Council and as the most important Palestinian leader, and perhaps even as someone who saw himself as the representative of all the Arabs. . . . It is possible that he imagines to himself that the German government maintains a viewpoint that favors friendship with the Arab nation, and also, that the hostility of Hitler's Germany to the Jews was enough in itself to turn Hitler into a friend of the Arabs. . . . But the truth is that Germany is attached to Italy by a contractual tie, and in this framework it is obligated to turn

Palestine into a zone of Italian influence. Therefore, if Italy gets its hands on Palestine, it might expel all the Jews from Palestine, but it will send in their place millions of Italian emigrants, and in any case, the Arabs in Palestine will find themselves confronting a great danger, and in fact, not only they, but all the Arabs. But Hajj Amin does not understand anything about European foreign policy and he believes the German propaganda. And still, it is impossible to blame the Arabs of Palestine for the deeds of the Mufti. After all, they have been in distress since 1936 right up until today, and they are seeking deliverance.[30]

We can find similar views expressed in the memoirs of Akram al-Hawrani (1912–1996), one of Syria's most important political figures in the 1940s and 1950s. His memoirs were published in five volumes by Madbuli Publishers in Cairo, shortly before Hawrani's death in 1996. His political opportunism and his many sharp shifts of position were a reflection of the vicissitudes of fate that affected Syria in those years, from the PPS to the National Bloc to the Ba'th Party. Hawrani's manner of political action also signified the beginning of populist politics in Syria, with politicians appealing to the lower classes and the peasantry, whose votes elected Hawrani to the parliament and defeated his rivals. His political behavior also signified the transformation of the officers corps into a key factor in Syria, for he was the first to penetrate the ranks of the officers in an effort to win their hearts.

Hawrani was born in Hama into a notable family of modest circumstances. His father lost the race for a place in the Ottoman Parliament in the 1908 elections. Hawrani studied law at the University of Damascus, but chose to become a politician. He joined the PPS in 1938 and in 1941 volunteered to go to Iraq to help Rashid 'Ali al-Kaylani. Later, in 1948, he also volunteered to help the Army of Salvation forces of Fawzi al-Qawiqji fighting against the emerging state of Israel. In 1943 Hawrani was elected to the Syrian Parliament on the National Bloc list. However, he quickly turned against the bloc's leaders. In 1949 he joined Husni al-Za'im, after Za'im had carried out, in March of that year, the first military coup d'état in the history of the Syrian state. However, he soon turned his support from Za'im to Sami al-Hinnawi, who overthrew Za'im, and then from Hinnawi to Adib al-Shishakli, Syria's military dictator from 1951 to 1954. After a short time, Hawrani also turned against Shishakli. In 1954 he joined Michel 'Aflaq and Salah al-Din al-Bitar, who together established the Ba'th Party. During the period of the UAR, Hawrani served as chairman of the UAR Parliament and afterward as vice president. In the end, however, he came out against Nasir and supported Syria's withdrawal from the UAR in September 1961. He severed his ties with the Ba'th, left Syria for Iraq, and finally died in exile in Amman at the age of eighty-four.[31]

Surprisingly, or perhaps not so surprisingly, the issues of Nazism and the German option did not occupy a significant place in Akram Hawrani's memoirs. An almost isolated mention of these questions can be found in the chapter dealing with the author's joining the Syrian Nationalist Party in the mid-1930s. He testifies thus:

> The dictatorial behavior of Antoun Sa'ada and the concentration of all the leadership authority in his hands, which resembled very much what was happening in the Nazi Party in Germany, did not arouse any special objections among the public, because the Nazi Party aroused interest among the public, which even showed sympathy for Hitlerite Germany because of the fact that it was the enemy of Britain, France, and the Zionist movement. However, it is important to emphasize that this was not the case in regard to Italian fascism. It was hated, because it represented the Italy of Mussolini, the enemy of the Arabs and the imperialist enslaver of Libya and Ethiopia, a detested and despicable enslaver like no other.[32]

One can elaborate on this point by looking at the differences between the Syrians' attitudes toward the British and the French, as these attitudes emerge from the memoirs, and the difference between the Syrians' attitudes toward those two powers and their attitudes toward the Germans and the Italians. Initially, the Syrian elite held a positive attitude toward Britain, as an ally that had helped it a great deal vis-à-vis the French. After all, France, and not Britain, had been the conquering power, and it had sought to hinder Syria's move toward independence, in contrast to the way the British had behaved in Iraq and Egypt. Hostility toward Britain on account of the question of Palestine was indeed already felt at this period, but the transformation of Britain into the enemy of mankind and the Arabs would come only later, in the 1950s, as a result of the 1948 war and the Suez crisis.

France, on the other hand, was perceived as a conquering power. But here too it is important to note the nuances. It became clear to everyone that France's power was in decline from the beginning of the 1930s and that it was in the process of reconsidering its role in Syria. Testimony to this may be found in France's momentary preparedness to sign the Syrian-French Treaty of 1936. By 1940 it was clear to everyone that France's days in Syria were numbered. Indeed, from 1941 Britain became the conquering power and as such enjoyed close relations and fruitful cooperation with the elites in Syria and Lebanon.[33]

From this perspective, Britain and France were both "the devil we know and are used to." Italy, in contrast, was perceived as a real threat, especially against the background of its conduct in Libya and Ethiopia. As for Germany, it seems that the elite in Syria did not have much trust in that power, assuming it would ultimately hand the Middle East over to Italy. It also turns out, contrary to the accepted supposition, that people in the Levant had no great admiration or respect for the way in which Hitler imposed his rule over Germany or the means he used to govern there.

Conclusion

We have reviewed a number of memoirs that represent or reflect the face of Syria's political elite in the 1930s and 1940s, and perhaps even more, in the years that followed. In this regard, it is important to emphasize that the reader detects in these memoirs a patent effort to address not necessarily the members of the generation that experienced the events of the 1930s and 1940s in Syria, but rather the members of the following generations, the people for whom the 1950s and 1960s were their formative years. The memoirs under consideration were written in light of the events of the 1950s and 1960s: the 1948 war, the rise of Pan-Arab nationalism and Nasserism, the chaos in Syria, and, finally, the retreat of the imperialist forces and the decline of imperialism. They reflect an Arab world in whose political discourse Britain and France were the enemy, sympathy for Germany was not an attitude that anyone felt needed to be condemned outright and absolutely, and the Arab-Israeli conflict was casting its shadow over the way in which the past was perceived and portrayed. All these factors must be taken into consideration. Additionally, however, it is interesting to discover that despite all this, one still finds a sober view of the world emerging from the memoirs. The atmosphere they portray shows clearly that the mainstream among the Syrian elite and the Syrian public in general of the 1930s and 1940s was not deceived by the Nazis' victories or the imagined glitter of the Nazi movement. On the contrary, these people showed a preference for stability and continuity and a rather liberal and softened conception of government. They did not want a dictatorial regime dominated by one person that forced itself on the body politic. From this point of view, the voice heard from the memoirs is one that should find expression in the scholarly discussion, which until now has virtually ignored it.

Several conclusions may be drawn from the image these memoirs reveal of the issues of Nazism and Fascism, Germany and Italy. First, in general, the memoirs set out to portray what was happening on a daily basis in Syria. This being so, it is impossible not to gain the impression that the attention given by the authors to the issues of interest in this study was much more marginal and negligible than one might have expected. We may conclude that those issues were not grasped as urgent or particularly relevant to the political agenda of the Syrian elite of those days. The situation on the ground undoubtedly contributed to this circumstance. Syria was ruled by the French and, from June 1941, by a French government under British supervision. Apart from a small segment on the very margins, Germany did not interest the elite very much. It was much more involved in trying to enlist the British to support them in their political struggle against the French.

Second, it is important to note that in all the memoirs, there is a definite rejection, even if often based on hindsight and wisdom after the fact, of the Nazi option—of the Nazi ideology and worldview, of Nazi totalitarianism and tyranny, of the type of relationship that existed between the leader and his regime and the people, and of the type of international relations with its neighbors conducted by Nazi Germany. The authors also portray a rejection of the option of political collaboration or even of associating with Germany and relying on it for the purpose of promoting Arab interests.

This situation is self-evident insofar as the political elite of those years is concerned. As Philip S. Khoury in his *Syria and the French Mandate* and Elizabeth F. Thompson in her *Colonial Citizens: Republican Rights, Paternal Privilege, and Gender in French Syria and Lebanon* have shown in their book-length studies,[34] these elites were anchored in a Western and liberal worldview. But this is also true of those who on the face of it seemed to be captivated by sympathy to Germany, such as Mustafa Talas or Sami al-Jundi. These figures, in retrospect, undertook to give excuses and explain their deeds or political tendencies of those earlier days and showed that they took no pride in them.

Third, it is clear that the attitude of the Syrian public toward Germany and Italy was formulated in the shadow of the struggle for independence from French rule. This struggle was the main issue occupying the Syrians and Lebanese in those years. Insofar as a positive attitude was taken toward Germany, it was definitely and explicitly the direct consequence of the confrontation with the French and the disappointment with the British. Still, it would seem that the Syrian elites clearly preferred the British. For them, cooperation with the British was a more practical matter than establishing ties with Germany. However, it would also seem that the authors of the memoirs published in recent decades, members of the old Syrian elite, wanted to conceal just this point. Therefore, they made the effort, especially from the 1950s onward, to reconstruct a historical narrative whose main point is that they distanced themselves from Britain and, in this framework, showed sympathy for Nazi Germany's battle against Britain and France.

Fourth, it cannot be denied that the Jewish question, that is, Germany's treatment of the Jews, occupies a certain place in the memoirs of some of the authors. However, it is not clear whether these instances are an echo of authentic thoughts from those early days or, perhaps, as seems more likely, a reflection of attitudes that took root later, in the wake of the eruption of the Arab-Israel conflict at the end of the 1940s and onward. In not a few instances, it is possible to determine that the author is claiming viciously anti-Semitic views that he actually began to identify with later, under the influence of the Arab-Israel conflict. It should be mentioned, however, that Jamil Mardam, in his well-known letter of 1937, represented more closely the attitude of the ruling Syrian elite of those years than the writers just referred to. In that letter, Mardam expressed his identification and empathy with the Jews of Germany who were being persecuted by the Nazis.[35]

Fifth, Italy and, consequently, Italian Fascism were viewed in a completely negative light and as a real threat, perhaps even worse than the French presence. This negative view resulted from Italy's image as the enslaver of Libya and Ethiopia. Many of the memoir authors also express a lack of trust in Nazi Germany, since it was perceived as such a close ally of Italy that it might hand over the Middle East region to that state.

Sixth, it should be emphasized that the memoirs draw a distinction between the attitude toward Germany and Hitler in the 1930s and up to the outbreak of World War II and the attitude toward them afterward, especially after their true face became clear. To be sure, the German experiment of the 1930s, especially the developments in the realms of nationalist ideology, political organization, and political order, aroused a great deal of interest among the Syrian public. At the same time, Germany prompted reservations among the educated Syrian public. It found German radicalism and Nazi totalitarianism rather disturbing. In general, on the whole, the reader of the memoirs of the period will find it difficult to get away from the feeling that the way Syrians related to Nazism was superficial and opportunistic, a kind of cynical and cold politics.

Two important questions arise at this point: How central were the issues of Fascism and Nazism to the public debate in Syria of those years? What place did they hold on the public agenda? It may very well be that the effort to turn these issues into major ones when portraying the period stems from the discussion in the Egyptian context, which, of course, does have implications for the Syrian context. It may also stem from the effort to project a marginal phenomenon on to the mainstream of Syrian public opinion. In any case, it is very important to add and emphasize that the efforts to shape anew the way the period under discussion is remembered were made in the shadow of events that happened later, including the struggle for Syria (as described by Patrick Seale in his book *The Struggle for Syria*), the Arab-Israeli conflict, and the Cold War, all of which engendered deep hostility toward the West.

It is perhaps appropriate to end by turning to Khayriyya Qasimiyya's book *Al-Ra'il al-'Aarabi al-Awwal: Hayat wa Awraq Nabih wa 'Adil al-'Azma* [The first Arab vanguard: The lives and papers of Nabih and 'Adil al-'Azma], published by Riad el-Rayyes in London in 1991. This book joins another work she wrote, or, to be more precise, edited, containing the memoirs of Fawzi al-Qawiqji. In both cases, we have an example of the editor reconstructing a historical memory. Qasimiyya served for many years as chair of the History Department of the University of Damascus, and she is perhaps the best-known Syrian historian in the world.

Nabih al-'Azma (1886–1971) was born into a prominent and famous Damascus family. He studied at the Military Academy of Istanbul, graduating in 1907. He served in the Ottoman army during World War I and, after it ended, joined the ranks of King Faysal in Damascus. After Faysal's fall, 'Azma moved to Transjordan and joined King 'Abdullah. Under British pressure, 'Azma left 'Abdullah's ranks and during the 1930s lived for some time in Palestine. At the end of the 1930s, he returned to Damascus, where he joined the National Bloc. In 1940 he was arrested by the French, and after his release in 1941 he moved to Turkey, where he remained until 1946, the year Syria gained independence.[36]

In the collection of documents of Nabih al-'Azma and his brother 'Adel edited by Khayriyya Qasimiyya, the editor cites Nabih's summary of the situation in July 1943, and on the basis of this summary she reconstructs a memory of the past consisting of a struggle against the British and the French, while collaborating, in a qualified and cautious manner, and without any enthusiasm, and especially without any illusions, with the Axis.

The struggle is portrayed as having failed because, in the end, Germany proved that it was not much better than the French, and especially than the British, who also promised to assist in the establishment of Syrian independence.

'Azma is speaking about how relations between the Arabs and the Germans had developed since the end of World War I and in the shadow of the Syrian, and, indeed, the Pan-Arab, struggle against British and French imperialism:

> The Arabs preceded Germany and turned to it even before Germany turned to them. They were natural and loyal allies to whomever could help them remove the yoke of the imperialist occupation, consolidate their racial unity, and ensure their freedom and independence. Therefore, it was quite natural that they identified themselves with Germany in its struggle against its enemies. But they made this conditional on someone promising them their future and even being a guarantor of this future. However, the more they waited, the greater became their frustration and disappointment in light of the news items that reached them from Rome and Berlin. This was because what was being offered to Rashid Ali al-Kilani and the Mufti was no different from what had been offered by the British and the French, and because the conduct [of Germany and Italy] was no different from that of [Britain and France], who were known for their hostility to the idea of Arab unity. We can see from Germany's answers that it seeks to build itself up using the discord among the Arabs, and that it seeks to postpone to a distant and obscure future the giving of a clear answer, exactly as the British did in 1915 when they gave the Arabs promises that were, in spite of everything, much stronger and much more tangible than anything heard until today from Berlin and Rome.[37]

PART II

PALESTINE

More than the Mufti: Other Arab-Palestinian Voices on Nazi Germany, 1933–1945, and Their Postwar Narrations

RENÉ WILDANGEL

The Mufti Phenomena

The story of the "grand mufti," al-Hajj Amin al-Husayni, is the most famous—or infamous—example of Arab collaboration with Nazi Germany. Various historians have shown the extent of Husayni's pro-Nazi and anti-Semitic activities in Germany and the Balkans during the war. He is regularly referred to as a symbol of an alleged "natural" Arab or Islamic inclination toward Nazism and anti-Semitism. In the highly politicized debate on Islamist terrorism and the roots of the Middle East conflict, the mufti is mentioned by some as proof of either anti-Semitic notions in Islamic tradition or extremist Arab nationalist ideology, and thus he is portrayed as the archetype of Palestinian radicalism. Others try to minimize his collaboration or depict it as part of an anticolonialist struggle reflected in the slogan "The enemy of my enemy is my friend."

By the 1920s and 1930s, Husayni had become the leader of an Arab revolt against rapidly increasing Jewish immigration into mandatory Palestine. The establishment of a Jewish state was unacceptable for Arab Palestinians, who considered their land an inseparable part of the Arab homeland. Authors like Matthias Küntzel, a German, argue that the "so called 'Arab revolt' in Palestine . . . was in fact the first Islamist revolt against Jews and modern life." Arab violent protest is explained as essentially inspired by anti-Semitism.[1] But Arab Palestinians turned to violence not because they were collective anti-Semites, but for concrete political reasons vis-à-vis an increasingly determined, economically and militarily capable, and powerful Zionist movement.

The Arab national movement formulated its sharp rejection of a Jewish state long before the dawn of National Socialist rule with its anti-Jewish laws and racist agenda. Arabs fighting Jews in the 1920s and 1930s had less to do with Germany, the rise of totalitarianism, and anti-Semitism in Europe than with post–First World War politics and the aspirations of an Arab national movement in the quasi-colonial situation of the mandate. Popular resistance and violent attacks were sparked by the reality of the Balfour Declaration and the Zionist movement's efforts to speed up Jewish immigration, and not by the fictions in the *Protocols of the Elders of Zion* or Nazi anti-Semitism. It was the German persecution of the Jews in Central Europe that accelerated Jewish immigration to Palestine in the late 1930s, which increased Arab opposition to immigration at a critical moment.

This was the time when mostly Christian Arabs and missionaries had imported Western anti-Semitism from Europe. But mass reception of anti-Semitic literature materialized as a side effect of the escalating Israeli-Palestinian conflict only after 1948, leading up to today's deplorable situation of an almost enveloping presence of anti-Semitic literature and stereotypes in the Muslim world.[2] However, it clearly was not Arab or Islamic anti-Semitism that produced the Israeli-Palestinian conflict, as some authors imply. Rather, the conflict fatally inflated the use of anti-Semitic stereotypes and propaganda in the wider Arab and Islamic world.

Arabs fighting Jews in Palestine was a sad but inevitable reality given the historical circumstances (i.e., the fatefully divisive policy of the British mandate) and the mind-set of the two national movements. So, too, was Jews fighting Arabs, with militant excesses stemming from the ideology of revisionist Zionism and its leader, Zeev Jabotinsky, who flirted with Fascist Italy. Husayni clearly went further, promoting anti-Semitism by seeking refuge in Germany during the war and actively taking part in their inhuman and genocidal war efforts.

Although Husayni was expelled from mandate Palestine as early as 1937 as the leader of a violent revolt, his collaboration story dominates the historical account of Arab Palestinian society in the 1930s and 1940s. In fact, there is no aspect of Arab Palestinian history that has been so intensively studied and written about as the mufti.[3] Less attention has been paid to alternative views and experiences of Arab Palestinian society and the diversity and ambiguities in its relationship with the British mandate power.[4] As others have noted, the *Encyclopedia of the Holocaust* includes a biographical entry on Husayni that exceeds even the entries of the leaders of the Third Reich.[5] Dan Diner points out, "Some marginal, and, regarding the relevant historical events rather insignificant, collaboration activities of Arab Nationalists with the German Nazis were given the status of their own branch of research to obligate the Arab side, at least, on the historical legitimization of the state of Israel."[6]

This "branch of research" on Husayni, and especially the numerous popular scholarly accounts, contributed to the image of a somewhat natural affinity of "the Palestinians" with Nazism or even impugned a collective Arab responsibility for the Holocaust. This image affects the ongoing conflict in the Middle East, which is fought not only with tanks and Qassam rockets, but also with vigorous attempts to dominate historical discourses and gain historical legitimacy. A national movement that willingly cooperated with Hitler's murderous apparatus loses all of its moral and political legitimacy. Arab unawareness, postwar authoritarianism, and the inability to find a critical historical perspective beyond the narratives of the national liberation movements have contributed to a completely other-directed narrative. Robert Satloff had a telling experience while researching his book *Among the Righteous* about Arab responses to the Holocaust.[7] Although Satloff was able to find stories of Arabs who saved Jews from the Nazis (which resulted in the candidacy of the first Arab, Khaled Abd al-Wahab, to be recognized as a "Righteous of the Nations" in Yad Vashem), relatives were reluctant to talk about this part of their family histories[8] because they did not want to be associated with these remarkable acts—an indication of how the ongoing conflict in the Middle East has shaped Arab memory and pushed aside many historical experiences.

Simon Wiesenthal, the Eichmann Trial, and the Invention of "Islamofascism"

No regional perception of Nazism and Fascism has been as vigorously loaded with postwar politics as the Palestinian Arab situation. The Israeli-Arab conflict provides an impressive case study on how competing political discourses are shaped and how strategies of delegitimizing and demonizing "the other" evolve. Thus, the Arab connection with National Socialism became a popular paradigm of accusation—from the Eichmann trial to the term *Islamofascism*—a tendentious reading of history that has created a powerful narrative with obvious political implications. As Jeffrey Herf points out in his recent study *Nazi Propaganda for the Arab World*, "The issue of the impact of Fascism and Nazism on the Middle East and its aftereffects has become inseparable from contemporary political controversies about anti-Semitism, radical Islam, 'Islamofascism' and international terrorism since the attacks of September 11, 2001."[9] This politicization, of course, is a challenge to any historian working on these subjects.

In addition to the political dimension, many studies on Arab Palestinian attitudes in the 1930s and 1940s lack Arab sources and present outsiders' views. A quote from George Antonius's book *The Arab Awakening* (1938) shows an earlier tradition of disregarding voices of the Arab Palestinian community in mandate Palestine:

> Even such sources as the Arabic Press of Palestine, which provide a valuable body of comment on the operation of the mandate as it effects the Arab population, are not used. Petitions and memoranda drawn up in Arabic have to be submitted at Geneva in translation. It requires more than mere transposition to turn good Arabic into readable English or French, and the Arabs of Palestine are so notoriously unskilled in the art of presenting their case in a foreign language that the rendering is usually a travesty.[10]

Instead of drawing on a large number of sources, studies on the topic sometimes reproduce a narrow translated corpus of quotations and anecdotes or limit themselves to the story of the "mufti"[11] to illustrate the image of the "Arab-Nazi-Nexus," as Robert Wistrich has called it. Wistrich presents the diary entry of a Syrian Ba'athist to illustrate how "anti-Semitic and anti-British feelings (which anticipated some of the anti-Americanism rampant today) created a powerful sense of affinity between German Nazis and Arab nationalists in Egypt, Syria and Iraq."[12]

The political dimension of this issue became obvious during the Eichmann trial. Israeli prime minister David Ben-Gurion hoped to raise the "connection of [the Nazi-Perpetrators] with different Arabic rulers." Hannah Arendt commented in her account *Eichmann in Jerusalem* that the motivation was not the urge to expose collaboration and collaborators, but the need to establish the narrative of this "Arab-Nazi-Nexus"—while the Israeli government refrained from blaming its new political ally, West Germany, where, meanwhile, numerous Nazi dignitaries had managed to start new careers. "For us a decent German," in the words of David Ben-Gurion, "although he belongs to the same nation that twenty years ago helped to murder millions of Jews, is a decent human being." "Decent Arabs," Arendt wrote, were not mentioned.[13]

Especially after the trauma of the Yom Kippur war in 1973, some nearly forgotten existential fears returned to Israel. When the first Likud government, led by Menachim Begin, took power in 1977, it amplified the reference to the collective nightmare of Arabs as the "new Nazis," an image that was now of inflationary use — even if it inevitably led to a banalization of the Nazis' own crimes.[14] Linking Yasser Arafat to the grand mufti (in this context often falsely referred to as his nephew), thus put him in an anti-Semitic tradition and made a strong instrument to discredit (legitimate) Arab aspirations.

After 9/11 a new term was introduced into the debate: *Islamofascism*.[15] Whereas an academic debate on structural similarities between Fascist and Islamic extreme political ideologies could add to defining and understanding totalitarianism (as comparative studies on Fascist-Nazi and Communist-Stalinist ideology have in the past), the term was created and used mainly as an ideological weapon. It soon became an inseparable part of the fatal "war-on-terror" logic. Demonizing Saddam Hussein as the new Hitler and linking him to the "tradition" of the mufti was a powerful way to ideologically prepare for the invasion of Iraq. In this context, U.S. president George W. Bush embraced the term *Islamofascism*,[16] while his successor, Barack Obama, quickly dropped it in concert with his attempts to repair relations with the wider Arab-Muslim world. Recently, Ernst Nolte — the scandalous protagonist of the 1980s historical dispute in Germany on totalitarianism, who linked the origin of Auschwitz to the Soviet gulags — tried to revive the paradigm.[17] But Nolte's confused book was so full of Islamic stereotypes and anti-Semitism that it was consistently dismissed.

On the other hand, several studies have recently attempted to take another look at Arab encounters with National Socialism and Fascism. They use a large number of original sources, including everyday experiences or marginalized voices, and try to reconstruct a more precise and complex picture of the range of Arab perspectives. Why, such projects ask, are Arabs and Muslims in retrospect seen as "natural allies" for National Socialism and Fascism, if those ideologies' core racist values classified Arabs as racially inferior "non-Aryans"? How did Arabs react to Mussolini, the self-declared "defender of Islam," who led brutal colonial wars against Muslims? What were the different motives for collaboration? What about other forgotten experiences, such as those of hundreds of thousands of Muslim and Arab colonial soldiers, who were recruited to fight the European war against the Nazis? And what about Arab intellectuals or socialists, who had a different perspective on the rise of the extremist right in Europe, but who also fostered their own expectations and hopes for the future in the Middle East?[18]

I will raise a similar range of questions, based on Arabic, Hebrew, and British sources from the 1930s and 1940s.[19] I would like to stress that presenting these alternative voices does in no way negate the mufti's or other Arabs' collaboration, which is well known. I intend neither to defend nor to diminish contemporary Arab sympathy toward Hitler and Nazism, or, even less so, to make light of today's fatal dissemination of anti-Semitism in the Muslim world. Instead, I will try to rewrite some forgotten or underexposed Arab Palestinian experiences into the history of the mandate era and to revise a one-dimensional picture of Arab sympathy for the Nazis and their ideology in Palestine.

Arab Palestinian Society and Nazi Rule in Germany, 1933–1939: Social Change

The years after 1929 were a time of rising unrest and conflict in Palestine, and also a time of unprecedented change within Arab society. These changes stemmed from a combination of internal and external developments closely connected to the ambiguous effects in Palestine of British policy, which oppressed and controlled the Arab movement's political formation while accelerating a modernization process with far-reaching consequences. The rapidly increasing Arab population[20] was going through a massive urbanization and industrialization process, which sped up during the war years. Arab education improved during the mandate, though resources far from met demand. Secondary-school training was enforced, and the number of male schools increased from 283 to 398 in towns and 254 to 354 in the countryside, whereas female schools rose from 33 to 80. The census of 1931 noted a literacy rate of 20 percent among the Arab community in Palestine (14 percent Muslims and 58 percent Christians), whereas in 1947 it had grown to 27 percent (21 percent Muslims and 75 percent Christians).[21] Considering that current news reports, i.e., the newspapers, were read in public, a significantly higher percentage of Arabs in rural areas also had access to printed news information. In the 1930s, radio broadcasting became more important. The technical modernization process in Palestine had changed the communication landscape through the 1920s and 1930s with improved printing facilities, a telephone system, and a broadcasting service, developments that also transformed the role of the recipients as readers, listeners, and consumers of all kinds of information.[22] This coincided with the ascent of a younger generation, who formed a group of professional lawyers, administration officials, and

businessmen who were partly educated in the West or in Western institutions and who played an important role in shaping Palestinian public
opinion beyond the old boundaries of family and clan legitimacy.

Arab Newspapers

Growing Jewish immigration, Arab land sales, economic decline, and
opposition to the policies of the mandate politicized the populace and led
to the founding of new Arab parties in Palestine. Increasingly, the discourse in a more vibrant and professional Arab press shaped public opinion and the political consciousness of Arab Palestinians.[23] Thirty-eight
newspapers employed 253 journalists in the 1930s.[24] Most newspapers in
the 1930s were connected to the newly established political parties. *Al-
Jami‘a al-‘Arabiyya* was close to the mufti's party, while *al-Liwa* served as
its mouthpiece. *Al-Jami‘a al-Islamiyya*, edited by Sheikh Sulayman al-Taji
al-Faruqi, was opposed to the mufti. The Arab Christian daily *Filastin* was
owned by ‘Isa al-‘Isa and edited by Yusuf Hanna and reached a remarkable daily circulation of nine thousand. *Filastin*, like the other traditional
Christian paper, *al-Karmil*, edited by Najib Nassar, was generally closer
to the biggest opposition bloc (*al-mu‘arada*) against Amin al-Husayni,
and was dominated by the Nashashibi family. *Al-Sirat al-Mustaqim*, edited
by ‘Abdullah al-Qalqili, supported the same faction. Ibrahim al-Shanti's
al-Difa‘, close to the Pan-Arabic Istiqlal Party, was one of the most professional newspapers and raised its circulation up to thirteen thousand
in 1946.[25] Apart from those publications, a small number of magazines
and other publications were available. The rising demand for the dailies
was remarkable. Papers became more professional, making use of news
agencies and translations from the European press and using their own
correspondents.

The growing, more unified opposition posed a threat to the mandate
authorities, which introduced stricter censorship and media control. During the violent period of 1936–1939, several Palestinian newspapers were
closed or temporarily suspended, provoking protest by their readers.
During the outbreak of violence between April and October 1936, Arab
newspapers were suspended on thirty-four occasions. However, even the
most nationalistic papers with the most radical rhetoric against the British
mandate power did not automatically lean toward Fascism or Nazism,
although many sympathetic articles appeared in the 1930s.[26]

However, since the dawning of Hitler's *Machtergreifung*, parts of the
Arab press had underlined the incompatibility of Arab and German inter-

ests, pointing out that Hitler's anti-Jewish policies in the 1930s were directed toward Jewish emigration and the expulsion of Jewish citizens from the territories under German control. To this end, the Haavara Agreement, which facilitated transfer of Jewish capital from Europe to Palestine, was signed in 1933. The Arab newspapers discussed the agreement[27] and were well aware of the negative impact that the German expulsion policy would have on the Arab community. This was highlighted by *al-Jami'a al-Islamiyya*:

> Hitler's victory is a dangerous development for the Arabs in Palestine; his plans regarding the Jews are well known. He will not hesitate to realize these plans and we will witness waves of refuges to [Palestine]. The German Jews are rich industrials and they will be the first, who will take the land from our hands.[28]

Arab newspapers in Palestine covered all aspects of Nazi rule in Germany. Articles on Hitler were driven by curiosity about his character and often exhibited a blatant sympathy during the 1930s. Often, parallels were drawn between Germany after the Treaty of Versailles and the Arab Palestinians under the mandate.[29]

However, from its early stages, Hitler's ascent was linked to a rising fear of a new war. The Arab newspaper *al-Difa'* published an article in 1936 that stated: "There will be no peace in Europe until the spirit of the Swastika, ruling Germany today, will be overcome."[30] Newspapers like *Filastin* extensively covered Germany's new armament policy. As early as 1934, the newspaper warned, "Europe will see no peace if it will not keep distance from the spirit of the swastika [*ruh al-swastika*] that dominates Germany today. . . . [Hitlerism] is an ideology full of disrespect of all peoples; it glorifies the German, and therein lies a danger."[31] Between February and April 1935, the newspaper *al-Jami'a al-Islamiyya* printed a forty-five-part series with the title "Hitler and the Jews." The author was identified as a lecturer at London's King's College, and the newspaper provided a translation from two unidentified Arab professors. The article covers every aspect of the anti-Jewish policy in Germany and its theoretic foundations on the works of writers such as Gobineau and Chamberlain. The study condemns the anti-Jewish policies in Germany and their haphazard ideology. The introduction highlights the author's reliability, citing several years spent in Germany as a correspondent for the London *Times*. Therefore, the introduction explained, the paper had chosen the material to provide "detailed information" about this "subject of utmost importance for the further developments in Europe."[32]

Newspapers like *Filastin* sometimes openly dismissed German anti-Semitism: "The Jews are oppressed only because they are Jews, no more, and there is no justification for that."[33] The same newspaper explained the term *Aryan* in 1933 as the "Indo-European race," making clear that it comprised "Indians, Persians, Armenians, and a group of Europeans," but not Arabs and Jews, who belong to the Semites.[34] The paper dismissed this ideological construct in another article titled "The Truth about the Hitler Movement: Reasons for the Persecution of the Jews": "Hitler followers want to make their race the ruler of all races in the world. One would think, the Nazis are Christians, and is not Christianity a fruit of the Semites and not of the Aryan people? Therefore, the view of Hitler's supporters is very strange."[35]

Palestinian papers repeatedly condemned Italian and German claims to supremacy over other nations as a new type of colonialism. In this context, *Filastin* published excerpts from *Mein Kampf* in order to illustrate Hitler's derogatory opinion of peoples under colonial rule. Hitler had justified British colonial rule by citing their cultural and racial "superiority," and he had ridiculed the "so-called oppressed in India and Egypt" as "chatty snobs" (*schwatzhafte Wichtigtuer*) or "bloated Orientals" (*aufgeblasene Orientalen*). In Egypt, the anger about the publication of these same quotes was so great that the German Embassy in Cairo denied the statements.[36]

On the whole, the Arab press in Palestine provided detailed information on Nazis and Fascism. Although some affirmative voices were heard, many articles rejected the German path. The fierce nationalist stance, which included sharp and violent opposition to the mandate and the Yishuv, was not dependent on those external forces. As *Filastin* pointed out in 1934:

> The Arab Palestinians don't need Fascists or Nazis to be motivated against the Zionists. The hatred against the Zionist plan in Palestine grew long before Nazism and Fascism. . . . But always, when Arabs protest the pro-Zionist policies of England, we heard: Arab Palestinians learned it from the Nazis. And the English believe this? Reality is different. The Arabs don't expel the Jews from the home, but those foreigners want to push the Arabs out of the country.[37]

Arab Perceptions

Several sources indicate a certain amount of sympathy toward Nazism and Fascism in the 1930s throughout the Arab lands. One such document is the report on Adolf Eichmann's trip to the Middle East in 1938, written by his superior Herbert Hagen, who also spoke of an imminent enthusiasm for Hitler. At the same time, Hagen pointed out that this enthusiasm remained necessarily superficial: "For the common Arab, who is overjoyed when he hears the name Hitler, National Socialism and its creator are not political or ideological [*weltanschauliches*] concepts." The "veritable understanding" of the importance of the Nazi doctrine for the Germans would be impossible for the Arabs, according to Hagen, because the "predominant cultural and civilizational influence is English or French and the German mind is not understood." Apart from the racist comments on the Egyptians, to whom he attributed the "oriental law of phlegmatism" and a general inability for spiritual achievements, he stated that a "Jewish question" in the National Socialist understanding did not exist.[38]

Indeed, support or enthusiasm for Hitler in Palestine was in large part emblematic. There was clearly no easier way to provoke the British forces in Palestine in the 1930s than with pictures of or references to Nazi Germany. There are several reports from the 1930s of Arab nationalists using Nazi symbols. Thus, Italian and German flags and pictures of Mussolini and Hitler were displayed on the streets.[39]

Some authors use such sources to paint a picture of omnipresent Arab enthusiasm for the Nazis:

> I would like to point out that the Mufti's so-called "Arab Revolt" took place against the background of the swastika: Arab leaflets and signs on walls were prominently marked with this Nazi symbol; the youth organization of the Mufti's political party paraded as "Nazi-scouts," and Arab children greeted each other with the Nazi salute.[40]

However, such accounts completely disregard existing sources that document different attitudes. On one occasion, the British high commissioner, Arthur Wauchope, mentioned that the Palestinian police exhibited "pictures of Herr Hitler and Signor Mussolini in certain Arab quarters" but dismissed reports on Arab sympathy toward Italy and Germany as "journalistic fiction." Reports in Italian newspapers of pro-Fascist tendencies that the British Embassy in Rome had brought to his attention, he attributed mainly to local correspondent Dr. Mombelli, who was also a Fascist propagandist. Wauchope, in contrast, described the Nabi Musa celebrations in Jaffa: "During the morning and the afternoon processions in Jaffa which were throughout animated by a spirit of holiday-making and of friendliness to the Palestine Police, an Arab band was heard to play 'God save the King' continually."[41]

In the 1930s, Arab Palestinian nationalists led by Husayni tried to gain German support and were open to German propaganda. Some limited financial support was channeled to them through the German Consulate, the Deutsches Nachrichtenbüro (DNB, the press agency linked to Goebbels's Ministry of Propaganda), and the German "Templer" community in Palestine. A "propaganda war" to win public opinion in Palestine had started between the Axis powers — Germany and Italy — on the one hand, and the mandate power on the other. The DNB was represented in Jerusalem since 1934 by two individuals, Dr. Franz Reichert and his deputy Adam Vollhardt, who tried to establish contacts with Arab nationalists. British sources reported that Vollhardt gained some influence in "Arab revolutionary circles" and met with rebel leader Arif Abd al-Razzaq near Tulkarem in mid-1938. Occasionally, Vollhardt had used the Nazi flag while moving into rebel territory. In Jenin he took pictures of British retaliation after the murder of a mandate government official.[42]

The DNB office in Jerusalem temporarily provided propaganda material for nationalist newspapers like *al-Difa'*, which later took a more critical stance. In 1939 Vollhardt declared that he had "never trusted [the editor] Ibrahim Shanti or his companion, both of whom lacked professionalism and could be bought by the highest bidder."[43] That same year, Reichert and Vollhardt had to leave Palestine, which was the end of direct local German propaganda. Now, apart from leaflets dropped from the air, radio broadcasting became the main instrument of propaganda for the Axis.

Throughout the 1930s German propaganda was sometimes met with approval and radical nationalists occasionally hailed the "führer," but the influence on Palestinian society was clearly limited. Attempts to build a Palestinian "Nazi Party" never came to fruition, and the racist anti-Semitism of the Nazis, later embraced by exile leaders such as Husayni, was adopted by neither the mainstream media nor a vast majority of Arabs in Palestine at the time.

Arab Palestinians and the Allied War Struggle, 1939–1945: Changed Conditions of the War Years

During the war years, Arab protest and resistance against Great Britain came to a halt. Aside from being the "enemy," Great Britain was a point of reference and role model for many educated Arabs and was the biggest provider of work in mandate Palestine. Without a doubt, this contributed to the many differing perceptions of Germany held by Arabs in Palestine.

Socialists, intellectuals, journalists, and domestic opponents of the mufti had a different view of Nazi Germany, its racist ideology, and the "world war" that it had started than did the mufti and his collaborators. However, those voices are poorly documented. In a 2007 publication, German historians Klaus-Michael Mallmann and Martin Cüppers present documents on Nazi plans for Palestine and argue that in the case of a German advance to Palestine, "the physical destruction of the local Jews" would have been carried out, "with the far-reaching and active support from the Arab part."[44] They go so far as to speculate about the Holocaust in Palestine as a "German-Arab mass crime."[45] Such conclusions should be met with reservation if they lack sufficient collaboration from Arab sources and rely exclusively on German archival material.

Before the outbreak of the war, George Antonius commented on Arab-British relations in his famous book *Arab Awakening*:

> Nor is the Arab attitude hostile to Great Britain, but just the reverse. The expression anti-British is so freely bandied about in reference to the Arab insurgence that it has given rise to the legend the Arabs are fundamentally hostile to everything English. In actual fact, they are "anti-British" only in the political connotation of that overworked epithet, in the sense that they are determined to resist the present policy in Palestine by every means in their power.[46]

During the unrest of the 1930s, British troop strength was reinforced, and the military used unrestrained brutality against Arab rebels and employed collective punishment to break Arab resistance. Several Arab Palestinian leaders were expelled or deported from Palestine. Most prominently, the mufti had fled to Lebanon in 1937. Members of the Arab Higher Committee such as Jamal al-Husayni, Rashid al-Hajj Ibrahim, and Hilmi Pasha were exiled to the Seychelles and allowed to regain partial access in 1940. Arab Palestinian support for the old political elite disintegrated, and the dissatisfaction with the mufti, which had been growing for quite some time, fed the growing factionalism in Palestinian politics.[47]

The Arab economy in Palestine had collapsed during this time of unrest, and many Arabs—village peasants and urban workers alike—were now desperate for a period of calm instead of continued violent opposition against British mandate policies and the white paper of 1939. Although in 1937 there was collective opposition to the Peel partition plan—an idea unacceptable at the time for a large majority of Arab Palestinians who considered Palestine their homeland and a genuine part of a larger Arab nation—many Arabs were now primarily frustrated with their own poor economic situation. Arab strikes and the organization of a boycott of Jewish goods and businesses had even accelerated economic development in the Yishuv and facilitated the implementation of the Zionist organization's "Jewish Labor" policy for more autarky. Many Arab workers had lost their jobs. Some villages were confronted with violent Arab gangs, whose self-styled rebel leaders kept suppressing and taxing the rural population. These conditions contributed gravely to support for the opposition (to the mufti followers) and more moderation versus the mandate power. The National Defense Party, dominated by the Nashashibi family, and individuals such as Izzat Tannous and George Antonius were more open to negotiations with both British and Zionist officials. In general, the atmosphere in Palestine lost its violent anti-British tone toward the end of the 1930s. A secret Jewish agency report named four reasons for the changed Arab mood at the beginning of the war: the total "exhaustion" of Arab society after years of struggle; "stricter control" by the British; the existence of a "considerable number" of Arabs who clashed with the nationalists' ideology; and the collapse of the mufti's party due to withered lines of finance and communication.[48] In her travel book *The Arab Island: The Middle East, 1939–1943*, Freya Stark recalls an encounter with an Arab Palestinian whom she asked about his view of Great Britain. Regarding the war situation, he answered: "We cannot fight you now, while you are busy. . . . [W]e will fight you later, if we must."[49] "British rule," a British diplomat commented, would without doubt represent a "lesser evil" than a German war victory: "All thinking Arabs will no doubt recognize that nothing would be worse for them than a German or Italian victory, and it is obviously to their advantage to do everything they can to ensure that Great Britain shall win the war, however much they may dislike certain parts of British policy."[50]

Between 1940 and 1942, secret reports to the Jewish agency in Hebron document this as well.[51] In September 1940, about fifty Arabs joined the British forces who enforced recruitment all over the country. In the spring of 1941, the city canceled the annual Nabi Musa celebrations, since there was "nothing to celebrate due to the War situation." The festival was postponed until that time "when England has won the war."[52] The reports show a division within the Arab public in Hebron. Whereas several members of the traditional elite and some young radicals continued their support for the mufti, others favored cooperation with Great Britain. During a public assembly with the mayor, the local mufti, and regional notables, a city council member shouted, "The Satan is in Iraq now," referring to the mufti. The mayor and the other notables agreed that the mufti's insurgence in Iraq would fail soon, as they were increasingly convinced of a German defeat in the war.[53]

Wartime Newspapers against the Axis

With the beginning of the war, Britain continued its restrictive policy on the media. Only three of the traditional daily papers survived: *Filastin*, *al-Sirat al-mustaqim*, and *al-Difaʿ*. A couple of other publications existed during the war, such as the newspaper of the Communist Party, *al-Ittihad*. The Axis war was overwhelmingly condemned by all media in Palestine, who were either generally in favor of the Allies or actively serving as real propaganda tools in the British war effort. The leftist intellectual journal *al-Ghad* commented after the outbreak of the war in 1939:

> The Arab people . . . stand at the side of those who fight Fascism. The differences between England and the Palestinian Arabs . . . do not change this. Those are local struggles, which have to be delayed until the end of the tensions in the world. . . . We are not stupid [enough] to believe the sentence "the enemy of my enemy is my friend."[54]

Al-Ghad warned that Palestine was directly threatened by the prospect of an Axis victory: "If Fascism will prevail, and the Arab lands will be enslaved with iron and fire, our struggle for independence will be set back for years."[55] In *Filastin*, editor Yusuf Hanna predicted the "biggest confrontation in history" and dismissed the idea of a Nazi "preventive war" against communism: "Nazism does not fight communism, but wants to enslave all peoples."[56] In the summer of 1941, *Filastin* predicted that Germany could never win a multifront war: "There is no doubt that we will soon witness the time of punishment for Nazi Germany, according to all the bestialities it has committed."[57] On December 25, 1941, the same paper published a dreadful picture of civilians killed by German forces during the war of extermination on the Balkans with the subtitle "Demonstration of Hitler's New Order in Europe."[58]

Another newspaper covering Nazi Germany with numerous critical reports was *al-Akhbar*, which was issued in Yafa from 1937 through 1942. Its editor was Bandali Hana al-Jarabi, and the editor in chief was Muhammad Najib. Besides critical articles on the German dictatorship, the paper published a series of caricatures by the Egyptian-born cartoonist Kimon Evan Marengo ("Kem"), who drew a large number of anti-Nazi cartoons and served in the British Ministry of Information during the war.[59] The cartoons portray Hitler's Germany as a brutal military regime heading toward defeat in the war. Thus, although Germany had just occupied France at the end of June 1940, *al-Akhbar* printed a cartoon that portrayed Hitler as the driver of a broken limousine that was falling apart.[60] Akhbar commented: "Germany's terrible power was directed against France with all its terror and hatefulness. . . . But the Allies will know how to crush this power."[61]

Another drawing by Kem from March 1941 showed a swastika-festooned carriage equipped with machine guns. Hitler stood next to it, holding a small Mussolini puppet by the neck. In the front, a couple of poor figures were yoked to the carriage, while others who had managed to abandon their yokes flee the scene in panic.[62] In its commentaries, the newspaper often took a similar stance. Hitler was characterized as a "bloodthirsty tyrant" and an "enemy of all students, workers, and religion."[63] In February 1942, Hitler was characterized as "the greatest enemy of humanity."[64]

An editorial in *Filastin* also pointed to the importance of the outcome of the war for the Arab nations: "Every nation is obliged to take this opportunity for resistance against the forces of evil." A victory would mean a "victory for justice" and a victory for "the preparation of unity in Palestine."[65]

In September 1941, *Filastin* published a story about how the Nazi war against the Soviet Union harmed Russian Muslims. More than one thousand mosques, forty-four thousand imams, and several million Muslims were threatened in the East, according to the article. The "great mufti" of the Soviet Union had asked the international community for help to "defend Islam against the enemy that threatens to destroy Islam."[66] Such examples unmasked German and Italian claims of friendship toward Islam. All Palestinian newspapers reported in detail on the progress of the war and the increasing setbacks for the German war efforts.

Radio Broadcasting and Arab Palestinians

The British mandate started its first radio station near Ramallah in 1936. The programs were produced in studios in Jerusalem in English, Hebrew, and Arabic, directed by a British director and one Arab and one Jewish assistant director. The first Arab assistant directors were the prominent pedagogues Khalil al-Sakakini and 'Adil Jabar. The British Information Office was in charge of the coordination.[67] The reception of the program among the Arab population was apparently remarkable; some 8,000

Arabs in Palestine held licenses at the beginning of the war.[68] This number almost doubled to 14,570 registered radios in Palestine in 1943.[69] A radio poll in 1943 estimated that 5.6 persons (half male, half female) would listen to one radio on average.[70] This adds up to an absolute number of 81,500 Arab listeners (still less than 10 percent of the Arab population). In his recent study *Nazi Propaganda for the Arab World*, Jeffrey Herf analyzes transcripts of German propaganda broadcasts recorded by the American Embassy in Cairo. (The originals are lost.) Herf details what the Nazis tried to achieve with their propaganda in the Middle East and how it was produced in Berlin. However, as Herf acknowledges, "information about the size of the listening audience remains scarce."[71] The hypothesis in his and other studies is that German propaganda was credible and popular in Palestine and ultimately had some effect on the recipients.

A scientific wartime radio poll by Stuart C. Dodd, a professor of the American University in Beirut, allows some rare insights regarding the reception of German propaganda.[72] Published in September 1943, it shows that 63 percent of 1,516 listeners interviewed in Palestine listened to the radio at least three times daily; the Berlin station was tuned in by only 13 percent of the radio listeners (8 percent listened only once a month, 4 percent daily, 1 percent listened twice a day, none listened three times). It was among the least popular stations among Arabs in Palestine, who preferred the stations in Cairo (listened to by 98 percent), Jerusalem (98 percent), London (87 percent), Sharq al-Adna (93 percent), Beirut (66 percent), and Ankara (32 percent).[73]

In other sections of the poll, it also becomes clear that German political propaganda was not popular among the interviewed: interviewees said they would tune into the Berlin station only for popular musical programs. Asked about credibility ("truthfulness"), listeners gave Berlin and Bari the worst ratings of all stations.[74] This shows that a majority of those Arab listeners took the German station for what it was: war propaganda.

British sources support these findings and conclude that a majority of Arabs in Palestine preferred the local British station in Palestine or the Cairo station over foreign transmissions, especially the German and Italian stations. According to an assessment of the British Foreign Office, Arabs in Palestine were generally "welcoming the British Service in Palestine" and kept sending "encouraging reports, comments and suggestions."[75]

Similar to the remaining newspapers, the Arab section of the broadcasting service was controlled by the British government and was confronted with censorship or self-censorship. However, there were prominent Arab politicians taking part in these efforts, and there was some genuine room for Arab opinion. While Arab exiles were contributing to the German and Italian broadcasts, Arabs in Palestine shaped the British service. Due to its success, a second, exclusively Arab station named Sharq al-Adna was started in late 1941, and its programs were extended until 1943. Freya Stark, who tried to foster anti-Fascist propaganda in the Middle East, described the station in her traveling book *The Arab Island*. During her visit in 1943, more than one hundred Arabs worked there, providing twelve-and-a-half-hours of daily programming:

> This was an achievement for the war, meant to counteract the Axis, which at that time was giving the Arab world twenty-two daily transmissions in its own language. But what most interested me was the fact that Squadron Leader De Marsac had avoided turning it into a British or Allied station; it was done by the Arabs for the Arabs.[76]

One of the journalists working at the Palestinian radio station was Ajjaj al-Nuwayhid, who wrote about his radio experiences in his memoirs.[77] When he was approached by the broadcasting director and asked to lead the Arab department during the Arab revolt, he presented a number of conditions to the director: he would lead only a free and independent Arab department where he would choose employees, have a secure budget, and experience no British censorship. Although the British authorities initially rejected this proposal, they approached Nuwayhid again after the beginning of the war. This time his conditions were accepted: the Arab news would have to be checked only by an administration official, who was a fellow Palestinian and an old companion of Nuwayhid from the Istiqlal Party.[78] The radio station broadcast lectures by Arab intellectuals and politicians from Palestine and beyond. Nuwayhid repeatedly spoke himself. In 1939, Ibrahim 'Abd al-Qadir al-Mazani spoke on "the Arabs and their position in the current war" and "the Arabs and their position on Nazism and Fascism."[79] Those broadcasts formulated an insistent refusal of German and Italian policies and included reasons for a temporary collaboration with Great Britain. The speeches of 'Azmi al-Nashashibi were also published in various newspapers.[80] In July 1941, Nashashibi dismissed the revolt in Iraq that was led by Rashid 'Ali al-Kaylani and the mufti with German assistance. "The Germans," Nashashibi asserted, "were not motivated by Arab interests . . . , but only the wish to disturb the English in the Middle East. . . . But this German game was obvious to the Arabs."[81] Nashashibi claimed that there were two categories of states: those who submitted to German pressure, resembling "a slave bought on the slave market," and those who tried to save their honor and bravery through resistance. Nashashibi asked a rhetorical question: "To which group [do] the Arabs want to belong?" Then he drew on the German racial theories: "[The Germans] have descended to a low level of stupidity and idiocy. We expect from the Germans that they would treat us well. But while we respect them as a valuable nation, they mistreat the European people. . . . We know that from a German perspective the Arabs belong to the inferior races, who have no right to enjoy life."[82]

Italian Attacks on Haifa

The Arab Palestinian press condemned Italian air raids in Syria and Palestine that took place in 1940 and 1941. On several occasions, Arabs were killed in bombings. *Al-Difa'* reported on "brutal Italian air raids" that destroyed a mosque and a Muslim cemetery, wounding seventy-eight and killing thirty-nine Arabs. That the bombs were deliberately dropped on civilian areas, with most of the victims killed in a coffeehouse, was presented as proof of the bestiality of the Italians.[83] According to another article, there was an overwhelming wave of solidarity with the victims in the Arab community. A solidarity fund was set up and supported by the mandate power and the Red Cross.[84] This was in sharp contrast to German claims that Italian raids on Palestine were welcomed with huge celebrations in "all of Galilee, Palestine, and Syria."[85] In fact, these air raids contributed to the increasingly hostile Arab view of the Axis.

The raids and the Axis's war were also condemned in a brochure that was published as a supplement to *Filastin* and *al-Sirat al-Mustaqim* on July 15, 1940. The booklet comprised twelve pages and three thousand copies were distributed.[86] The author was Muhammad al-Jarkasi, who was engaged in writing anti-Fascist propaganda.[87] He had tried to find support for his activities from the Arab Section of the Jewish Agency and described his motivation as being, "my deep hatred against the Axis powers, because of their anti-Semitism and the damage they have done to the Arabs. I have witnessed this myself, read many articles about it and heard many reports in the Palestinian radio on the Italian actions in Tripoli and Barka."[88] Jarkasi warned that a victory of dictatorships in the war would "end up in an age of slavery unprecedented in history."[89] As an example of Italian brutality, he wrote about the bombing of Palestine that he witnessed himself: "The criminal Italian bombs that were dropped from the air brought destruction to Arabs and Jews likewise, not differentiating men from women and children."[90]

Collaboration and Cooperation with the Mandate Power

Arab collaboration with Nazism had three basic motives: first, partial or full ideological compatibility, reflecting anti-Semitic tendencies or authoritarian elements in Arab and Islamist ideologies; second, the hope for pragmatic or strategic advantages, as described in the adage "The enemy of my enemy is my friend"; and, finally, pure material interests, as the Nazis recruited and paid Arab individuals for their activities.

Much the same is true for Arab cooperation with the British in the 1930s and 1940s: it was either founded in ideological motives, connected to pragmatic interests of parts of the nationalist movement, or fully orchestrated (and financed) by the British. It is remarkable that such historical sources are rarely presented, and if so are dismissed as irrelevant in light of the mufti and his associates. A historical account that reconstructs Arab perspectives using Arab nationalists' diary entries that document sympathy for Nazism—a historical account that also depends upon German internal reports and propaganda—is incomplete and distorted if these Arab voices representing different experiences and attitudes are not taken into account.

Arabs in Service of the Government

Many members of the Arab Palestinian intellectual elite were educated in the West; some went on scholarships to England or attended British-style academic institutions, and they were generally more familiar with British culture, language, and mentality than with those of Germany.[91] Other Arabs serving on behalf of the British forces felt reservation or outright hostility, but still decided to work for the British in times of economic hardship. Although the reliability of Arab servicemen was sometimes questioned, especially during the Arab rebellion, the Palestinian government pointed out in November 1937,

> I strongly deprecate the general and unsupported allegations of unreliability since they tend to discourage a large body of men on whose loyalty we must in any case continue to rely. . . . The morale of the Arab police and other Arab servants of the Government is improving. The

Arab police are working under conditions of great difficulty and danger: some devoted and loyal men among them have as you know paid for those qualities with their lives.[92]

Arabs also served as members of the Royal Army, although their motivation and recruitment were naturally much lower than those of Jewish soldiers, who had served since 1940 in fifteen battalions and in 1944 formed the "Jewish Brigade."[93] In August 1942, a regiment was formed out of three Jewish battalions and one Arab battalion, which was deployed in Egypt and North Africa. One out of six volunteers for the British army was a Palestinian Arab.[94] All over Palestine, the British army set up recruitment offices that tried to attract Arabs, especially among the Christian Arab population, and included the integration of Palestinian Arab women into the "Women's Volunteer Auxiliary Army."[95] Some women served in the regular troops. In total, twelve thousand Arabs from Palestine served in the British army during the war.[96] 'Abdullah's Arab Legion in Transjordan was another army cooperating with the British.[97] However, we know little about the concrete experiences of the Arab Palestinian soldiers fighting on behalf of Britain in the North African or European war theaters.

An increasing percentage of Arabs also worked in factories and companies connected to the British war effort, due to the expanded war industry in Palestine, with quickly growing centers in Haifa and Jaffa. Between 1939 and 1942, the number of Arab industries quadrupled, and the number of Arabs working in the industrial sector doubled by 1945 to some one hundred thousand. This represented approximately one-third of the male Arab population of working age.[98] Their most important employer was the British mandate.[99] In March 1945, British forces directly or indirectly employed sixty thousand Arabs in Palestine and Transjordan. Arab civil employment by the British authorities was estimated at thirty-five to thirty-seven thousand.[100]

Arab-Jewish Cooperation in the Workers' Milieu and News about the Final Solution

At a time when wages were stagnating and prices exploding for Arab and Jewish workers alike, political organization was especially essential for workers to voice their needs and demands. Beginning in 1940, cooperation intensified and became one of the few examples of close Jewish-Arab interaction, albeit one not without problems. However, this wartime con-

tact certainly had an influence on Arab society's attitudes and perceptions. After the Arab workers' movement had been paralyzed during the
1937–1939 revolt, in 1940–1941 the Arab Union of Railway Workers, the
most important organization in that field, resumed its activity. A left-
wing minority, including Hashomer Haza'ir on the Jewish side, tried to
work towards a better Arab-Jewish understanding. The mainstream Jewish labor organization Histadrut had an Arab division that tried to collect
information and make contacts among Arab society and its leaders. Its
power was limited due to its meager financial and personal resources, but
it produced leaflets and material in Arabic that were distributed among
Arab workers. The documents addressed several subjects; some focused
on the fight against Nazism as the common and most important goal.
Thus, a joint appeal from Hashomer Haza'ir and the Histadrut called
upon their "Arab Brethren" on May 1, 1943:

> Two groups fight each other in this war: The assaulting Fascists who
> enslave nations and negate human freedom and happiness, and against
> them the socialist and democratic nations that fight on the path for a
> free world and justice and peace. . . . And our country takes part in the
> war efforts as well. . . . For us all—Jews and Arabs likewise—there is one
> common enemy: Despotic Fascism! And everyone who tries to plant in
> our hearts hatred between you and us is nothing more than a collabora-
> tor with the common enemy.[101]

Following passages in the joint appeal stressed the intention to cooperate
with the Arab population in Palestine. Zionism was explained as a peaceful movement that had done much for the development of the country.
Much of the tension caused by Jewish mass immigration was also linked
to the plight of European Jewry:

> A number of people have been crushed by the boots of Nazism, but there
> are no people as oppressed as our Jewish people. With a cruelty unprece-
> dented in history, the oppressors murdered our people. The blood of
> our brethren and fathers and friends, whose blood is shed in all parts of
> occupied Europe, screams to us and every human being that has a feeling
> heart. Under machinegun fire and toxic gas, day after day thousands of
> human beings are annihilated for one single "crime": for being Jews.[102]

By May 1943, the German extermination policy had reached its peak. It
is difficult to gauge Arab knowledge about the slaughter of the European

Jewish community. In fact, even large parts of the Jewish community in Palestine refused to believe the news for a fairly long period.[103] Since the beginning of 1942, the Hebrew and English press had reported that the inhabitants of the Jewish ghettos in Poland were dying from hunger and/or disease and had covered the killings in Russia, as well.[104]

The literate and generally informed among the Arab public had since 1933 read about the escalation of Nazi persecution against Jews and other victims, so such reports, or the quoted leaflets of the Hashomer Haza'ir and Histadrut that mention the extermination policy, did not seem incredible to them. However, the Cairo declaration of October 7, 1944, from the newly founded Arab League made clear that there was not much space for acknowledging the Jewish drama: "[The committee] regretted the woes which had been inflicted upon the Jews in Europe, but insisted that their question should not be confused with that of Zionism, because it would be unjust to solve the problem of the Jews by inflicting injustice on the Palestinian Arabs."[105]

Arab Anti-Fascist Organizations of the Left

Starting in August 1937, the socialist Arab Students League, active in Bethlehem and other cities, published the journal *al-Ghad*. In February 1940, an English leaflet, "Fascism and Students," came with the paper. The author, identified with the initials T.B., postulated an improvement of Arab education in Palestine and criticized British reluctance to achieve it, making the repulsion of Fascism more difficult:

> Fascism, being a new regime which has been enforced in Italy and Germany without regard to the will of the people, has used a very attractive and inspiring method of propaganda, which deceived the people of the world through the state of chaos in which these countries were left after the Great War. . . . Though this regime was built on iron and on fire, it has found an easy path through [Palestine] for many reasons, which are partly due to the Mandate Government.[106]

For the author, the defense against Fascist influences should have held the highest priority:

> My appeal to the students is to relinquish Fascism and its principles and keep in mind its horrors. Independence and freedom cannot develop under such a regime. My appeal to the students is to seek education in

other directions where they may be taught freedom and fraternity. . . .
My appeal to the government is to help the spreading of schools and education and to facilitate more the means of learning and culture.[107]

The environment for such original critical views of Fascism, independent from British interests, was growing throughout the 1940s. Examples
include the leftist League of Arab Intellectuals. Founded in 1941, its members included 'Abdallah Bandak from Bethlehem, Emile Tuma, Emile
Habibi, and Tawfiq Tubi. Also active were the Nadi al-Sha'b (People's
Club), headed by Emile Tuma, and Shu'a' al-Amal (Ray of Hope), headed
by Emile Tuma and Bulus Farah.[108]

The Communist Party itself was a joint Arab-Jewish organization
until 1943, though nationalist division lines had existed for a long time.
However, until the split in 1943, the party voiced a common rejection of
Fascism, and especially the war against the Soviet Union. Dozens of appeals addressed the terrors of Hitler and Fascism and expressed the hope
for a Communist victory. On June 22, 1942, the party produced an appeal in Arabic marking the beginning of the Nazi war against the Soviet
Union, which was characterized as a "war against all human principles"
and "against all peoples of the world, including the Arab World":

Fascism represents a great danger for our freedom and the future of
our people and has brought destruction and death to all places it entered,
and the fight against it is not just a matter of principle or a matter of love
or hate, but the choice between life and death. . . . And we Arabs close
our ranks in these days, and concentrate our power and unite our efforts
with the common effort of the people of the world in their fight to crush
Fascism and to strive towards justice and freedom and equity among all
peoples![109]

At the end of the year, the party published a leaflet on the occasion of
the German defeat at Stalingrad that expressed the hope for a near end of
the war and a victory over Nazism.[110] However, the party itself fell victim
to internal Arab-Jewish polarity. The disintegration of the party led to
the foundation of two separate parties, including, on the Arab side, the
National Liberation League. This now exclusively Arab organization actively continued its anti-Nazi propaganda. Its constitutional declaration
of February 1, 1944, mentioned nineteen objectives for the war. The old
claims to immediately halt Jewish immigration and Arab land sales to
Jewish owners were among them, together with the need to fight Nazism:

The practical way to overcome aggression and warfare is the liberation of the people and the realization of the right of self-determination, and this is the goal of the people fighting against Nazi aggression, the most terrible and aggressive colonial movement mankind has seen so far.[111]

To mark the German defeats toward the end of the war, celebrations and rallies were organized in several cities in Palestine. For example, in Haifa an assembly was held in a coffeehouse on February 22, 1943, to commemorate the German defeat in Russia, the Allied victory in North Africa, and the twenty-fifth year of the creation of the Red Army.[112]

The Council for the Fight against Fascism and Nazism in Palestine also produced a number of brochures and leaflets, the first one published on October 1, 1942. The leaflet was printed at an Islamic publishing house in Jerusalem, and it emphasized the national interest of Arabs taking an active role in the war. National Socialism in this regard was characterized as an enemy of Arab culture and Islam:

> The Nazis want to make us believe that they are not colonizers who
> occupy foreign land and do not shed the blood of its inhabitants only
> to add to the wealth of the German financiers and barons; they want us
> to believe that our just fight and resolute patriotism are bad things; and
> they try to blemish our honorable history that enlightened the world
> with a grand religion and magnificent culture.[113]

In 1946 the Anglo-American Committee interviewed two young Arabs who were soon to become very well known: Albert Hourani and Ahmad Shuqayri.[114] The latter distanced himself from the mufti and argued, "Let it be known that we are not anti-British, anti-Soviet, anti-American or anti-Semitic. Equally, we are not pro-Nazis, pro-Fascists. We are what we are—Arabs and nothing but Arabs. So help us God."[115]

Epilogue: Mission Atlas

As late as 1944, the German secret service planned an adventurous secret Nazi mission to Palestine. In 1939, the SS and the Sicherheitsdienst had lost their direct representatives in Palestine when they were expelled by the British. During the intervening years, Amt VI (the Auslands-SD, the foreign intelligence service of the SS) of the Reichssicherheitshauptamt, since the autumn of 1941 directed by Walter Schellenberg, had lost touch with reality on the ground and still believed they could foster successful propaganda activities in Palestine. The climax of these German delusions was "Mission Atlas."[116] The mission was prepared by Amt VI in coordination with the mufti and the Arab-German army unit Sonderstab F, which set up a team of two Arab and three German soldiers to embark on a secret parachute mission to Palestine. The unit was supposed to incite against the British and the Yishuv, carry out acts of sabotage, and organize a new Arab rebellion. The Arab participants were long-standing collaborators of the mufti, Thulkifl 'Abd al-Latif and Hassan Salama. In preparation for the mission, it became clear that the mufti was totally out of touch with social and political conditions in Palestine and with the mood of the local Arab community. In a preparatory meeting at the Berlin Wannsee, he declared in the presence of Werner Schellenberg and other German representatives that the German mission would be met with great enthusiasm. Finally, on the brink of German defeat in Europe, the mission was carried out on October 5, 1944. The five agents were flown out of Greece, and at midnight they parachuted into Palestine.

The mission turned into a series of mishaps. One of the few contacts in Palestine the mufti had given the agents, Nafith al-Hussaini, was uncooperative. He told them to leave immediately: "The Mufti made a great mistake in obtaining the co-operation and help of the Germans in trying to accomplish this mission." Within ten days, all five agents were arrested by the Palestinian police or members of the Arab Legion. The failure was complete. The German vision of collaboration with the Arabs in Palestine had fallen apart.

CHAPTER 5

The Spanish Civil War as Reflected in Contemporary Palestinian Press

MUSTAFA KABHA

The Palestinian press included in its reports references to the Spanish Civil War, recognized as an internationally constitutive event, although it vied for space with the Palestinian revolt of 1936–1939. The war in Spain was usually portrayed as part of journalistic coverage of ongoing events, consisting of information on both sides of the conflict: Republican communist forces on the Left and national Fascist forces led by General Francisco Franco on the Right. However, it was not unusual for writers or editorials to express support for one side or the other. The writers' political views were evident from the descriptions and labels attached to each of the opponents and from the emphasis and prominence accorded to atrocities committed by each side. Interestingly, the significant direct involvement of Palestinian volunteers who came to the aid of Republican forces was not manifested in the contemporary Palestinian press.[1]

This chapter seeks to reveal how the war was presented in the Palestinian press of the period, focusing on the two major newspapers published at the time: *Filastin*[2] and *al-Difaʿ*.[3]

During the 1930s, many nations worldwide closely followed global current events, especially the major financial crisis in 1929 and the growing hostility between the democratic bloc and the Axis forces. The Palestinians were no different in this respect. Palestinian public discourse, manifested mainly in the written press, displayed particular interest in events transpiring in places where the involvement of Britain and its allies was evident. The current British mandate in Palestine did not seem to be facilitating independence and self-realization among local inhabitants, and therefore Palestinians tended to support opponents of British policy throughout the world.

To begin with, the Spanish revolt initiated by General Franco in mid-July 1936 was presented among Arab and Muslim countries not as a Fascist revolt but as a revolt against the policies of France and Britain, perceived in these countries as despicable, oppressive colonialist forces. Moreover, Franco and his men were portrayed as sympathizers of Islam and opponents of atheism and heresy. In later stages of the conflict, once the rebels' real ideology was revealed, the enthusiasm and identification with them gradually diminished and were even replaced by sentiments of reservation, if not hostility. This was emblematic of the Arab world in general and of views professed by Palestinian society in particular.

Initial Reports: Endeavoring to Chart and Conceptualize the Situation

The first reports of events in Spain began appearing in the press a week after the war broke out, on July 18, 1936, in the midst of the great Palestinian strike. Naturally, most local press coverage focused on the Palestinian revolt, and scant attention and room were left for other current international affairs. Nonetheless, events in Spain received a surprisingly prominent place in the Palestinian press, featured both on front pages and in editorials and commentaries within the newspapers. At the time, the term *thawra* was being used to indicate the general Palestinian strike and the accompanying circumstances. In Arabic the term means both "national revolt" and "revolution."[4] Thus, it was only natural for other events to be termed *al-thawra* as well, including the Spanish Civil War in its first stages. These developments were presented in a significantly dynamic and diverse manner, with some newspapers changing their views and outlook from time to time.

The bulletin of the Palestinian Communist Party tried to demonstrate the nature of events in Spain by relating the fact that General Franco, backed by the Fascist regime in Italy and Hitler's regime in Germany, headed a Fascist force challenging the rule of the legitimate government of Spain.[5] Later, the newspaper took on a more blunt and blatant tone in its description of the movement:

> General Franco's movement is a fascist war against liberty and democracy; it is an aggressive war not only against the Spanish people but also has the potential to cause heavy damages to the Arab people as well, particularly the Arabs in Morocco who have began to sense the big mistake

they made by supporting fascist Spain. This was made even more clear once he began to harass their leaders and execute some of them.[6]

In a memorandum sent by members of the National Liberation League to the British prime minister in October 1945, they emphasized that they associated the Palestinian national struggle with the international democratic struggle against Fascism and that they would not consent to the Palestinian people's falling victim to this struggle.[7]

Allegedly Neutral Coverage

A conspicuous example is *Filastin*, a newspaper that was initially ambivalent toward the rebels. For example, one of the first reports, headed "Dangerous Uprising in Spain: Rebels Are Trying to Overrun Madrid," said, "Last weekend a serious revolt broke out in Spain. The beginnings of the revolt originated with army units stationed in Morocco, triggered by a local tribal uprising. The revolt is headed by General Franco, who has been joined by several Spanish army units in Spanish Marakesh as well as several navy units. When news of this uprising reached soldiers in Spain they joined the revolt and began fighting the government forces, reinforced daily by residents seeking revenge against the government."[8]

The newspaper attempted to prove its neutrality by reporting that "the situation in Spain remains vague and it is almost impossible to know what is truly happening there; however the French government closed its borders with Spain, and Britain sent a battleship to Malaga to evacuate its citizens."[9] Nevertheless, when describing the rebels' actions, the newspaper left no doubt as to the antipathy they aroused, saying, "Rebel pilots committed terrible, evil deeds, among others, against 6,000 terrified communists fleeing government-held territories."[10] In time, the animosity initially aimed at the rebels was redirected at government forces. The newspaper began stressing that the communists numbered among their ranks many Jews and referred to crimes, theft, looting, and rape committed by government forces and the communists.[11]

The newspaper's growing hostile attitude toward government forces was naturally accompanied by a supportive stance in regard to rebel forces: rebels were now designated *thawra*, the same phrase used to describe members of the Palestinian armed bands or groups of volunteers from Arab countries currently fighting the British under the leadership of Fawzi al-Qawiqji.

By February 1937, the newspaper began labeling government forces "communists" and "atheists."[12] Christian-owned *Filastin* may have had a religious rationale for its views on the belligerent parties, particularly when the news began to feature antireligious acts performed by government forces and their allies, such as the use of church bells as shields for their vehicles and armored cars.[13] This is attested to by its use of the term *Nationalists* to describe rebel forces versus *Reds* for government forces.[14] In contrast, the newspaper reported the ambivalent attitude displayed by the French government, supposedly a major ally of government forces, toward the communists and their allies.[15]

From time to time, the newspaper emphasized its supposedly "neutral" attitude by pointing out the disparities between news originating from government and rebel forces and the problems that these contradictions created for journalists. For example, an article titled "The Spanish Uprising Is a Long-Term Revolt," said,

> There are large discrepancies between the news reported by the Spanish government and reports by the rebels. Each side claims victories and achievements, and no one knows the true facts. An entire week has elapsed and communications have been completely severed, with telegrams being strictly censured. Some believe that the Spanish revolt will be protracted, as both sides are highly committed.[16]

Filastin also emphasized the international character of the revolt and its potential impact on the balance of power in the world:

> The Spanish revolt will transform and interfere with the balance of power in Europe. A victory for the rebels is a victory for Fascism over Communism. It is clear that the Spanish Civil War is being waged between the communists, currently government forces, and the royalist Fascists who are rebelling against them. A victory for one of these will result in the enhancement of its ideology throughout Europe and will probably change the international balance of power.[17]

In contrast, *al-Difaʿ* presented a collection of news items on the views of various countries on each of the Spanish rivals. At first it cited the view of the United States as expressed by Secretary of State Cordell Hull, who instructed U.S. ships to leave Spanish territorial waters for international waters. Hull also directed U.S. diplomatic representatives in Spain to remain in their places and roles until the last possible moment, when they should close their offices and leave the country.[18] Between the lines, we may discern the supposedly neutral U. S. outlook and its patent unwillingness to intervene in local events, perceived as an "internal matter."

In addition, the newspaper presented the view of Portugal, Spain's close neighbor. It depicted the official Portuguese perspective, which conceived of events in Spain as an "international war," albeit not forgetting to mention Portugal's strict disapproval of Communism.[19]

Al-Difa' also presented Germany's and Italy's attitudes toward events in Spain, as follows: "Germany and Italy hold uniform views in regard to their common enemy, communism, and this unity is undoubtedly the safest thing for European peace as it is threatened by the forces of communism."[20]

Describing the two sides of the conflict, *al-Difa'* often used the terms *communists* to describe government forces and *Nationalists* to describe rebel forces.[21] General Franco was described in positive terms as a decisive person with clear goals: "General Franco will not accept any negotiations with government forces and will not accept any option besides surrender."[22] Elsewhere, Franco was designated as the "leader of the Spanish revolt" and cited as saying that he "did not invite the revolt and did not ask for it; rather it was forced on him and his camp. He has no demands aside from removing communism, a foreign offensive concept, from Spain."[23]

Another item stated, "Franco is increasing his pressure on Madrid. The rebel army is being reinforced by new soldiers and preparing for an all-out assault on the capital. Within the capital the situation is becoming grave and there is a shortage of coal and some basic foods."[24] Reading these items, it is possible to sense the atmosphere of chaos and the imminent breakdown of government forces, in contrast to the confident rebels who were proceeding from one achievement to the next and gathering strength daily.

The invasion of Madrid was accompanied by descriptions that implied a sense of sympathy for the victors and ambivalence toward the losers. For example, *al-Difa'* described the rebels' arrival in Madrid as follows: "The Rebels Enter the City of Madrid and the Spanish Government Leaves the Capital for the Town of Valencia — The government left the city early this morning by plane and reestablished itself in the city of Valencia which is now its new center. The government took the opportunity to announce that its departure from Madrid does not indicate that it has abandoned the principle of defense."[25]

During this period, *al-Difa'* found room on its front page for news from Spain, although the major focus was on the still-raging Palestinian revolt. For example, in the issue published on November 8, 1936, the newspaper published two items on the Spanish Civil War in the center of the front page, amidst the news on Palestine. The first item reported that at the end of the third day of the rebel attack on Madrid, government defense forces collapsed and gave way to the rebels, who succeeded in entering the city via several routes. The second item described the state of fear and panic that engulfed residents of Madrid as the rebels bombed them from land and air. The newspaper mentioned in particular the terrible destruction wreaked upon the stretch between the Spanish Ministry of War and the state hospital. The reporter referred to the outcome of these attacks as a *nakba*, a serious disaster.[26]

In another instance, in the issue of *al-Difaʿ* published on July 5, 1937, the entire front page was devoted to Palestinian issues, particularly the recommendations of the Peel Commission, a British Royal Commission of Inquiry, which three days earlier had announced its recommendations regarding the partition of Palestine. Despite the deep import of the recommendations, the newspaper's editorial staff included an item on the Spanish Civil War in the middle of the front page. An item headed "Concern That Europe Would Become Divided into Two Camps," said,

> The French government refused to accept the proposal of the Italian and German governments whereby the rebels [the Fascists] would be recognized as soldiers, as this would mean recognizing the rebel outlook on global affairs, possibly leading to the opening of French borders to Spanish government forces and the transfer of fighters and ammunition through French borders. Fascist countries, on the other hand, would support General Franco and his forces, and thus Europe would become divided into two camps, one aiding the government and the second the rebels, creating the potential for a world war.[27]

Two Issues Missing from Palestinian Coverage of Events

Two issues worthy of mention were conspicuously missing from Palestinian journalistic coverage of the Spanish Civil War: The first is the involvement of Arab Moroccan soldiers and commanders, who fought beside Fascist rebel forces, and the second is the involvement of Palestinian communist activists (side by side with Jewish communist activists) in Spanish government war and propaganda efforts.

The first topic was extensively covered in the international press of the period and in professional literature, and it is currently a source of heated debate among Moroccans and Arabs who seek to reopen the issue and clarify the circumstances in which nearly 250,000 Moroccans were enlisted in support of the Fascist war effort and accusations whereby Moroccan soldiers took part in war crimes against their rivals.[28]

A few short items in the contemporary Palestinian press mentioned the Moroccan identity of some of the rebel companies who conquered Spanish cities, one by one. But they did not refer to the crimes allegedly committed during the occupation. Palestinian journalist Najati Sidqi, asked by the Comintern in Moscow to travel to Spain and take part in the propaganda aimed at Moroccan soldiers among the rebels (and for this purpose was asked to operate under a Moroccan alias, Mustafa Bin Jala), dedicated one chapter of his memoirs to this issue, and described the Moroccan soldiers, their background, and the circumstances in which they were recruited into the rebel corps. In one place, Sidqi describes the attitude of the Spanish public to the Moroccan fighters:

I arrived in beautiful, magnificent Barcelona, with its great cultural tradition, the capital of Catalonia. I suddenly encountered soldiers of the militia [of the government forces]. Their leader approached me, thinking I was Spanish, and addressed me in Spanish: "Why don't you join our ranks?" I smiled, answering in Spanish with the passion of the young: "I am an Arab volunteer. I have come to defend liberty in Madrid, to defend Damascus in Guadalajara, Jerusalem in Córdoba, Baghdad in Toledo, Cairo in Zaragoza, and Tatwan in Burgos." His face displayed astonishment and joy and he answered me in poor French: "Are you indeed Arab? Are you a 'Moro,' [i.e., Moroccan]? It is impossible, Moroccans are standing by the fascist hooligans. They attack our cities, loot our homes, and assault our women." Then I said to him: "These Moroccans who follow the leadership of the fascist generals offend Arabism and Islam with their conduct; they represent only themselves; they have been misled by Spanish military men and a handful of Moroccan leaders who have sold their souls to the devil, such as 'Abd al-Khaliq al-Turaysi."[29]

Sidqi also attests in his book that he was expressing the views of millions in the Arab and Islamic world who shied away from Fascism and Nazism and hoped for the victory of democratic and socialist forces in Spain.[30]

The second topic involved the Palestinian volunteers who teamed up with Spanish government forces. This issue received no coverage or reference in the Palestinian press of the period, perhaps due to lack of knowledge or as a result of the reluctance to speak of Palestinian support for "heretic" or "atheist" forces. The number of volunteers is unknown, but aside from Najati Sidqi, Mahmoud al-Atrash (one of the first Palestinian Arabs to join the Communist Party) is also mentioned, as well as two other Palestinians who died in the war, 'Ali 'Abd al-Khaliq and Fawzi al-Nabulsi.[31]

The involvement of Arab volunteers, among them Palestinians, in the war, side by side with government forces, received little attention in the historical research as well, and only two scholars have treated the subject extensively. The first is Syrian 'Abdallah Hanna[32] and the second is Moroccan 'Abd al-Latif Bin Salam.[33] In both cases, there are no clear grounds for the disregard adopted by the press (excluding communist newspapers and bulletins) toward Arab volunteers who fought beside Spanish government forces as part of international brigades.

Palestinian Support for Franco Rebel Forces

The Palestinian approach to the rise of rebel forces led by Franco in Spain proceeded in phases very similar to those manifested in response to Fascism in Italy and Nazism in Germany. Initial displays of sympathy and admiration changed in time to unenthusiastic sentiments of disappointment, criticism, and later even rejection and antagonism. The actions of General Franco and his men received extensive journalistic coverage. When the civil war broke out, many newspapers published background articles on the opposing sides, with special attention given to the rebel forces. Several newspapers, particularly *Filastin*, devoted their back covers to civil war photos—no small feat at the time. Palestinian sympathy for the rebel forces in the first stages of the war may be explained by three main factors.[34]

The first factor concerns the Palestinian strike and revolt that took place during this time. The largest strike in the history of the Palestinian national movement (April–November 1936) had been successfully launched, and the Palestinians hoped that their support of the Fascists in Spain would facilitate Italian and German support and assistance for their own struggle. The press was convinced that glorifying and stressing the accomplishments of the rebels in Spain would raise the spirits of the striking Palestinian public and prove that it is possible to achieve political and national goals by means of revolt.

The second factor concerns antipathy toward the communist movement. A large portion of the Palestinian national movement and its leadership held extremely hostile views of communism and the Soviet Union and depicted Stalin as a bloodthirsty criminal heretic. Accordingly, Republican forces in Spain were termed *criminal reds, heretic communists, anarchists*, and other derogatory designations. The newspaper *Filastin*, for example, justified its attacks on the communist camp by mentioning the Jews fighting for them. The newspaper frequently reported the many crimes allegedly committed by Republican fighters, whom they described as "looters, murderers, and rapists who rape any woman they encounter."[35] Stories of war crimes were illustrated by photographs taken on the battlefield and published almost daily. In contrast, pamphlets and publications distributed by the Palestine Communist Party reflected the opposite view. They supported government forces and even called upon young Palestinians to volunteer to fight against Fascist right-wing forces in Spain. Reports of Palestinians who had decided to volunteer and even of several Palestinians who had died fighting this war were featured in the pamphlets.[36]

The third reason for Palestinian support of the Fascists in Spain was their antagonism toward Britain and France. The support provided by these two powers, particularly France, to Republican government forces, coupled with their increasing suppression of the local population in their mandate and the occupied countries in the Arab West, strengthened Palestinian identification—particularly among those carrying the banner of Arab nationalism—with their rivals. The newspaper *Filastin* labeled all Republican supporters, i.e., the Soviet Union, France, and Britain, enemies of the Arabs. An editorial published in February 1937 said: "Blum's government in France helped the Reds in Spain by supplying weapons, planes, and tens of thousands of fighters. Thus it would be a crime to claim that Hitler instigated the plague of foreign intervention in Spain. . . . The British press constantly criticizes the involvement of Italy and Germany, but does not mention that of France and Russia, and this is a grave mistake."[37]

That same month, the newspaper quoted a Franco speech in which he said: "Spain is on the verge of becoming liberated from the remnants of Imperialism, abetted by France and the communists." The newspaper even tried to persuade its readers that the purpose of the relationship between the Republicans and their European backers was to torment the Palestinians and that the relationship had a deleterious effect on their sources of livelihood. As proof it cited the flooding of European markets with Spanish citrus fruit, causing a severe drop in the price of Palestinian citrus.

Support in the press for the rebels gradually dwindled, as General Franco's association with the Fascist and Nazi regimes in Italy and Germany became clear. The aversion felt toward these two regimes, on the eve of World War II, was manifested in aversion toward Franco and his affiliation with them. For example, *Filastin* wrote on February 10, 1939, "Naturally, when Mussolini provided assistance to the rebels in Spain it was not their best interests that guided him. By supplying money, weapons, and fighters he sought to gain points for Italy, with the primary goal of advancing his plan to take over the western Mediterranean coastline."[38]

The alliance between Mussolini and Franco was now repeatedly emphasized. For example, one news item on the Spanish Civil War was titled "Mussolini's Fingers in the Spanish War."[39] The article said that Mussolini's fingerprints were evident throughout Spain.[40] Another article stated that the victory of the (Fascist) Falange in Spain meant death for democracy.[41]

At the same time, the attitude toward the Republicans and communists changed and became more positive and sympathetic. A case in point concerns the counterattack launched by these forces in March 1939 in the region of Madrid, which received favorable coverage. This offensive was even designated a "counterrevolution," which succeeded in "releasing from prison thousands of communists subjected to cruel and suppressive treatment by Franco's forces."[42]

During 1938–1940, Franco's allies (Italy and Germany) were vehemently assaulted by writers in the Palestinian press, who targeted Italy first, and then Germany. Akram Zu'ayter began this campaign by publishing an article in *al-Difa'* in which he criticized Mussolini for assuming the title of "defender of Islam," asserting that this was a serious insult to Islam and Muslims.[43]

Al-Jami'a al-Islamiyya further berated Italian propaganda in Arab and Muslim countries and its insistence that "Italians are friends of the Muslims." The newspaper stated that Italy "swallow[ed]" Arab and Muslim countries under the guise of friendly relations.[44] At the same time, the newspaper attacked those Arabs who supported the propaganda, took part in it, and promoted it, and claimed that it was futile and even caused grievous harm to the Arab nation.[45] *Al-Difa'* reproved Germany, specifically renouncing "the disgraceful racial arrogance" of Nazi Germany.[46] *Filastin* continued this trend by maligning Fascism and Nazism and saying that "these two ideologies are reactionary ideologies leading humanity back to an era of indiscriminate racism."[47]

Conclusion

Although in specific instances Palestinians are known to have come to the aid of Spanish government forces, these were mostly the exception rather than the rule. Palestinian society on the whole tended to express more support for the rebels, who were perceived as fighting against communism, and by proxy against Britain and France and their allies.

However, Palestinian support of Fascist forces in Spain diminished over time, and throughout 1938 the newspapers restricted themselves to reporting the civil war as described by international newspapers and news agencies. Toward the end of that year and during 1939, the former support was replaced by outright rejection and, indeed, animosity, a position adopted even by *Filastin*, which had been conspicuous in its support of the Fascists at the beginning of the war. Some articles went so far as to portray Franco as brutal and cruel and alluded to the elimination of rivals within his own camp.[48]

The main factor of this change was the Palestinian discovery of the imperialist nature of Nazi Germany and Fascist Italy. In particular, they realized that the colonial ambitions of Mussolini in the Mediterranean and the Middle East presented a tangible threat to the Palestinians and more generally to the Arab world.

Mussolini on the eve of fascist Italy's invasion of Ethiopia. "Mussolini crushes the dove of peace under his foot." *Al-Musawwar*, September 6, 1935, 1.

Mussolini's propaganda machine attempts to present the imperialist war as a war of defense. He is appealing to the League of Nations: "You are my witness. Ethiopia is attacking me." *Al-Ithnayn wa al-Dunya*, October 14, 1935, 5.

Al-Ithnayn wa al-Dunya reacts to the opening of the Ethiopian (Abyssinian) war. Mussolini is portrayed as devouring Ethiopia, while Haile Selassie sternly warns him against it. November 11, 1935, 1.

(الجيش مسوقة عائد امتقاله بروم الإثنين) ... واشتركت يا أمي فيها إيطاليا)
١٠٢٩
السينيور موسوليني ذاهب للصلاة ومعه شارات السلام ! !

موسولي - ادبي اجعيت في أ كل
الطبة ، لكن يترى ساينبوقى الغرب
البحيرة ؟

A well-armed Mussolini conducting the Ethiopian war while pretending to seek peace. "Senhor Mussolini is walking to pray [for a cease-fire] armed with symbols of peace." *Ruz al-Yusif*, November 18, 1935, 7.

Mussolini ends his military occupation of Ethiopia. "Mussolini: 'I am devouring Ethiopia, will they also let me drink the lake [Tana]?'" *Al-Ithnayn wa al-Dunya*, April 13, 1936, 1.

The Syrian president, Shukri al-Quwatli.

The Iron Shirts (al-Qumsan al-Hadidiyya) salute Dr. Tawfiq al-Shishakli and Najib Agha al-Barazi. From *Mudhakkirat Akram al-Hawrani* (al-Qahira: Maktabat Madbuli, 2000), by Akram al-Hawrani.

Al-Musawwar's reaction to Mussolini's fascist propaganda as the friend of Islam and the Arabs. "Mussolini: 'Oh, Arabs! I am the defender of Islam . . .' The Arab: 'God forbid, oh shaykh, Allah alone is the defender of Islam!!!'" March 26, 1937, 12.

لذ وللحقيقة:

رسالة ارلى الى الشعب العربي

الايطاليون المتوحشون اعداء العرب والمسلمـــين

عريقون فى الاجرام ويسيئون الى العرب بطرق مباشرة وغير مباشره

بقلم محمد الجركس ـ وجموعة قيد من شباب العرب

ويقدران فيضحك القدر وتضحك بريطانيا العظمى ايضا

The title page of a propaganda supplement that came with the newspapers *Filastin* and *al-Sirat al-Mustaqim* on July 15, 1940. The twelve-page anti-Nazi and anti-Fascist propaganda brochure had been drafted by Muhammed al-Jarkasi, and the headline says: "The barbaric Italians are enemies of the Arabs and the Muslims." As explained in the caption of the image, Hitler and Mussolini claim to divide Europe, while in the background Great Britain and "fate" (represented by an angel) are laughing and dismiss their "crazy dreams."

An anti-Nazi propaganda caricature by Egyptian-born Kimon Evan Marengo (signed "Kem" in English and Arabic), showing Hitler's "war machine" falling apart. Although Germany had just occupied France, the cartoon published by *al-Akhbar* in June 1940 implies that eventually the Nazi campaign was going to fail.

Another drawing by "Kem" published in March 1941 by the Palestinian newspaper *al-Akhbar*, suggesting that support for Hitler and his collaborators is decreasing quickly.

على وعلى أعدائي

"المرأة هنا — الجنس المخنون هدم الهيكل على نفسه وعلى أعدائه ... يعني هوه .. أحسن مني!!..."

بين بسائن الغول ..

Hitler after the Munich Agreement: a suicidal Hitler attempts to exterminate all of humanity. "For me and all my enemies. Herr Hitler: 'I heard that Samson destroyed the temple on himself and on his enemies. . . . [I]s he any better than me?'" *Ruz al-Yusif*, October 2, 1938, 10.

Hitler occupies Czechoslovakia. Czechoslovakia is portrayed as a helpless little girl, and Hitler is depicted as a demonic monster with an insatiable appetite for more land. "In the devil's claws . . . Czechoslovakia to Hitler: 'I wonder if I am the first victim . . . or the last one?!' Herr Hitler: 'On the contrary, my dear . . . you are the aperitif of the victims!! . . .'" *Ruz al-Yusif*, March 17, 1939, 9.

A response to the Ribbentrop-Molotov Pact. "The necklace of friendship: Hitler: 'God, what kind of rope did you put around my neck?' Stalin: 'This is a necklace for our alliance and friendship. Could we be friends without it?'" *Al-Ithnayn wa al-Dunya*, October 16, 1939, 1.

On August 26, 1950, Henry Curiel was deported forcefully from Egypt to Italy. The photo was taken on the deck of the boat in the Genoa port, showing Curiel's [*on the left side*] reluctance to disembark (courtesy of Mrs. Joyce Blau, Institut kurde de Paris).

Albert Arie, Hotel Safir, Cairo, February 2007 (photo taken by Rami Ginat).

Marie (Naila) Rosenthal-Kamil and her husband, Sa'd Kamil, both former members of DMNL and Harakat Ansar al-Salam, February 2007, Cairo (photo taken by Rami Ginat).

Tal'at Harb Square, Cairo 2007, the place where Henry Curiel's Maydan bookstore was located in the 1940s (photo taken by Rami Ginat).

A response to Hitler's regular addresses in the Reichstag in which he reaffirmed his commitment to peace. "The address of the week: behind the 'loudspeakers' [of the war]." *Al-Ithnayn wa al-Dunya*, May 1, 1939, 1.

Ruz al-Yusif's response to the outbreak of the Second World War. "History repeats itself: The end of Hitler at the hands of democracy." September 9, 1939, 1.

Al-Ithnayn wa al-Dunya's reaction to Hitler's attempts to present himself as a leader of peace after conquering France and threatening England. "The slogan of Nazism: Peace peppered with blood and extermination." July 29, 1940, 1.

Ruz al-Yusif forecasts what will
happen to Italy if it joins the war
with Nazi Germany against the Allies.
"If she will dare . . . ?! What will be
Italy's destiny if she joins the war
against the Allies?" This cartoon
demonstrates how Mussolini was
squeezed between the vise of
England and Egypt. May 11, 1940, 1.

Two witnesses—Gestapo leaders—tell of the Nazi atrocities. Hitler and Himmler are
responsible for the annihilation plan of the Jewish race. *Al-Ahram*, January 4, 1946.

بولندا

Al-Ithnayn wa al-Dunya mistakenly believed that Hitler would not be able to swallow the bread of Poland and would be stuck there. "He cannot swallow it." September 18, 1939, 1.

استئناف محاكمة زعماء النازي في نورمبرج

اعدام اليهود بالجملة ـ هتلر يأمر بقتل جنود الكوماندو

The beginning of the Nazi leaders' trial at Nuremberg. Mass execution of Jews— Hitler commanded the killing of commando soldiers. *Al-Ahram*, January 3, 1946.

PART III

IRAQ

CHAPTER 6

Iraqi Shadows, Iraqi Lights: Anti-Fascist and Anti-Nazi Voices in Monarchic Iraq, 1932–1941

ORIT BASHKIN

The grandmother of the protagonist in Khalid Kishtainy's autobiographical novel, *Tales from Old Baghdad: Grandma and I*, suffers from insomnia. Having been married to a Turkish officer and longing for the return of the glorious days of the Ottoman Empire, the grandmother relies on the advice of a "German" doctor. In her mind, Germany is connected with the much-missed Ottoman past:

> My father had to step in and call Dr. Max Macowiskey, the Polish family doctor whom grandma insisted in identifying as German, for all good Europeans, to her, were German, just as all wicked Europeans were English. The worse of it is that not only was he not German, but he was actually Jewish. Dr. Macowiskey prescribed that every night before going to bed she should take a tablespoonful of *arak mustaki*, the national drink of the country.[1]

When a good Muslim doctor suggests sleeping pills as an alternative medication, the grandmother dismisses his advice, saying, "He knows nothing. . . . [W]hen you need a doctor, call in a German one." The grandmother's medication, however, necessitates frequent visits to Michael Atisha, the Christian owner of a liquor store. In addition to the *arak* he sells, Michael's political analysis of current events offers her some hope. According to Michael:

> Hitler is not attacking Turkey . . . because he has a secret agreement with the Turks. . . . As soon as he finishes with that atheist, Stalin, and his gang of anti-Christian communists, Turkey will join him in marching on Iran. . . . Turkey is run by a bunch of drunkards. Hitler knows that. And

he will soon put things right. He will bring back the sons and heirs of the Sultan. . . . I tell you, he'll put an end to this idiotic state we have, to all these lackeys the British imperialists brought with them.[2]

The grandmother and Michael, however, do not like Mussolini, "the fat fellow . . . who pretends love and devotion to God, calling himself 'Protector of Muslims'": "He sold guns to the Jews in Palestine. But . . . Hitler will know what to do with them once and for all. There will be no Palestine for the Jews."[3]

The novel, very tellingly, exposes some of the conflicts Iraq experienced during the 1930s. The confusion in the grandmother's mind between the Germans "she knew," namely, the allies of the Ottomans, and Hitler; the ignorance of the lower middle classes concerning Hitler and Mussolini's true intentions; and the muddling of anti-Zionism and anti-Semitism were all typical of this period. Yet in addition to the grandmother's ignorance, and love of all things German, we hear other voices. The grandmother's son and grandson mock, albeit lovingly, her misinformed opinions, knowing full well that her opinions are a matter of the past, and, more important, they rely on a Jewish doctor, whom they consider a friend and a member of their community.

The novel raises important questions regarding the degree to which Nazi and Fascist ideologies were received in Iraq. It encourages us to think about what the Iraqi people knew about Hitler at the time, the support Germany gained, and the extent to which the pro-Palestinian sentiment of the Iraqi people was translated into anti-Semitic notions. These questions, beyond their historical importance, also have extremely important contemporary implications. In recent years, a new market has emerged for books detailing the connections between radical Islamists, Middle Eastern elites, and Fascist and Nazi groups. The activities of Nazi sympathizers, such as the Palestinian religious leader Hajj Amin al-Husayni, in the war years and the appropriation of anti-Semitic motifs by Islamist movements have caused some scholars and media pundits to draw a connection between Islam and Fascism more generally.[4] These historical analyses, in their popularized forms, have found a receptive audience in conservative circles in the United States that have connected the need to fight "the global danger" of radical Islam at present with the need to combat Nazism and Fascism in the past.[5]

Furthermore, the Ba'athi state itself has been compared, on several occasions, to Nazi Germany. No book was as influential in this regard as

Kanan Makiya's *Republic of Fear*. Makiya provides horrifying, yet accurate, depictions of Saddam Hussein's violence and the ways in which Ba'athi authoritarianism penetrated every aspect of Iraqi society. The book's premise is that Iraqi civil society, completely crushed by Ba'athi murderous brutality, could not rescue itself, and hence was in need of outside assistance. In describing Ba'athi terror, Makiya argues that Ba'athist ideology was consistent with broader twentieth-century ideological trends, originating in Europe at the turn of the century: "In light of the precedents that culminated in the interwar years in Fascism, Nazism, and Stalinism, Saddam Husain was an imitator, not an innovator." Makiya also emphasizes Ba'athi anti-Semitism, evidenced by public executions of Iraqi Jews following the Ba'ath's rise to power and a state-sponsored study about Jewish and Shi'i education in Iraq, into which anti-Semitic motifs were integrated.[6] His analysis also reflects on Iraq prior to the Ba'athi regime, as he seeks to find the roots of the Iraqi Nazi-like regime in the years when Iraq was a constitutional monarchy (1921–1958). Examples cited include the 1933 massacre of the Assyrian community, the coup in 1936 (the first instance of a military takeover in the Arab world), and the military coup of 1941.[7] The book became a best seller in the period before, and immediately after, the Gulf War of 1991. Makiya himself was also one of the architects of American plans for post-Ba'athi Iraq. Not surprisingly, the outlook of the book colored much of the American postoccupation effort; the failed efforts at de-Ba'athization, for example, were modeled after the attempts at de-Nazification in Germany.[8] Although I have no doubt that Makiyya was committed to issues of human rights and uncovered crimes committed against Iraqi civilian populations, the endeavors to find the origins of the Ba'ath in the monarchic past have led to many misrepresentations of interwar realities.

In this chapter, I offer an alternative reading of the Iraqi past. I do not wish to ignore the fact that Nazism and Fascism had important supporters in the Iraqi public sphere. Furthermore, there is no doubt that the activity of pro-German sympathizers did much to shatter the belief of Iraqi Jews in the ability of the Iraqi nation-state to protect their rights as citizens. I do, however, wish to underline the alternative voices present in the public sphere and to emphasize the connections among various anti-Nazi groups. I am not alone in this endeavor; scholars such as Peter Wien, Sami Zubaida, and Eric Davis have advanced similar evaluations.[9] Given that depictions of Iraq as hopelessly undemocratic have colored the war discourses in America, historians, I feel, have an ethical responsibility to chart out the makeup of the anti-Nazi and anti-Fascist Iraqi camp. We must explain its origins and its importance, as well as present the richness of the intellectual sphere and its democratic and humanistic voices.

Fascist, Anti-Fascist, and Anti-Nazi Voices, 1932–1941

During the 1930s, Iraqi militarist and nationalist groups affiliated with the state considered cooperation with Nazi Germany. Prominent Iraqi intellectuals, officials, and policy makers admired Germany's program of modernization, which had led to its military and economic triumphs. Fascist aesthetics and vocabulary began to take root in Iraq. Youth movements, in particular the paramilitary organization al-Futuwwa, were seen in nationalist circles as key to the cultivation of healthy notions of masculinity and manhood. Speakers at the Pan-Arab club al-Muthanna, home to many of the nation's intellectuals, hailed the efforts of Germany to modernize and reform. Yunis al-Sab'awi, a Mousuli writer, translated sections of *Mein Kampf* into Arabic and worked for the German Embassy as a translator of pro-German material.[10] British diplomats were concerned by the efforts of the German Legation and the German minister to Iraq, Fritz Grobba, to sway Iraqi public opinion in favor of Germany: Grobba and the legation cast Germany as a power opposed to Great Britain and hence a possible strategic ally of Iraq. A British report from 1939 noted that "German cultural propaganda is in reality the preparation of the minds and the souls or part of the people to be receptive of political propaganda." On October 24, 1940, the Iraqi press reported on Germany's declaration of sympathy with the Arabs, which was met with approval by journalists and considered a great honor in certain nationalist circles. An important figure in the dissemination of pro-German propaganda was Hajj Amin al-Husayni, who had arrived in Iraq in October 1939.[11]

Iraq had experienced a period of continual political instability following the military coup orchestrated by Bakir Sidqi (October 1936–August 1937). After the coup's failure, a group of four nationalist colonels wielded tremendous political power so that they could ensure the installation of prime ministers sympathetic to their concerns. In September 1939, the pro-British Nuri al-Sa'id was appointed prime minister and declared that Iraq would not enter World War II unless attacked. He confirmed that Iraq would help Britain in the war, though only to the degree specified in the Anglo-Iraqi Treaty of 1930. Disagreements regarding Iraq's relationship with Germany led to the appointment of Rashid 'Ali al-Kaylani as prime minister in March 1940. He resigned, rather than cut off relations with Italy, at the end of January 1941, but returned to his post as a result of pressure from the military. Upon his return to power, Kaylani announced the establishment of a military regime, at which point Sa'id and the pro-British Iraqi political elite fled Iraq. This turn of events did not please the British, who were aware of the nationalist inclinations of the new government. Kaylani was unable to navigate between British pressure, on the one hand, and the nationalist and pro-German demands of some of his supporters, on the other. He promised British officials that he would honor the 1930 treaty, but they did not consider him trustworthy. British forces entered Iraq in April and after a short military campaign, lasting through April and May, reoccupied that country.[12]

The revolt affected the lives of Iraqi Jews. On May 7 and 8, Jewish stores were looted in Basra following the departure of the pro-Kaylani forces. On June 1 and 2, as Kaylani and forces loyal to him left Baghdad but before the British entered the city, Jews were attacked by groups composed of policemen, soldiers, civilians, Bedouins, members of youth groups, and young people. The rioters, in a series of assaults that came to be known as the *Farhud*, attacked the poor sections of the Jewish quarter and some of the city's mixed neighborhoods. When the *Farhud* ended, somewhere between 135 and 189 Jews had been killed, between 700 and 1,000 had been wounded, there were at least 10 cases of rape, and around 550 stores and 900 apartments had been looted.[13]

Admiration of Nazi Germany and Fascist Italy certainly influenced a group of nationalist, Pan-Arab intellectuals and policy makers centered in Baghdad, whose voices became hegemonic in the 1930s and who played a key role in the 1941 coup. The pro-Fascist camp hoped that the implementation of Fascist models in Iraq would allow the state to mold the souls and bodies of the nation's subjects, attain military successes, and improve Iraq's regional position by siding with England's geopolitical rivals. British and Iraqi politicians of the time (as have later historians) were quick to point out that Pan-Arabists were more inclined to absorb Nazi ideas. The Pan-Arabists' animosity toward Britain made Germany an alluring ally, and their ideas about a Pan-Arab nation that united all speakers of Arabic paralleled, in some ways, the German ideal of *lebensraum*. Indeed, most supporters of Fascism and Nazism in Iraq came from the Pan-Arab camp. Historians have claimed that Syrian, Egyptian, and Palestinian teachers in Iraq likewise advanced this chauvinistic Pan-Arab model.[14] Reeva Simon subsequently notes that, "borrowed from the German 'volk' historians, the theory of a primeval ancestor nation transmitting civilization to the rest of the world during its meanderings from an original homeland to its present abode had been 'Turkified' by the Ottomans. . . . Similarly, the pan-Arabs extolled both the historic role of the pre-Islamic Arabs and the geographic unity of the territory which was to be the modern Arab nation."[15]

One of the Pan-Arab intellectuals whose writings are often cited in the academic discourses about pro-Fascist tendencies in Iraq is Sami Shawkat. Born in Baghdad in 1893, Shawkat graduated from the Military College of Medicine in Istanbul in 1916 and served as an officer in the Ottoman army during World War I. He joined the Arab army in Syria in 1919. In Iraq Shawkat served in various posts at the Ministry of Health and later became director general of education (1931–1933, 1940–1942) and a minister of education (1940). He also served as a minister for social affairs (1939).[16] Historian Sylvia Haim identifies Shawkat as a key figure in the conceptualization of Arab anti-Semitism. Haim pays close attention to his book *Hadhihi Ahdafuna* (These are our aims), "a collection of Fascist addresses to schoolteachers" that "praises Hitler and Mussolini for their wisdom in making the annihilation of internal enemies—the Jews—the first condition of national revival." To Haim, Shawkat

> obliquely establishes the necessity for their [the Jewish] annihilation with the help of the Hegelian idea of the state. . . . The Jews are internal enemies in Arab countries, since they have betrayed their Semitic race and deserve the treatment meted out to traitors.[17]

Shawkat's writings are, indeed, profoundly undemocratic. He constantly cautions against certain "criminals" within the Iraqi society who spread their poisonous propaganda against the national principle. Lest "we fight such enemies," he admonishes, "we would not free ourselves from our ailment, and accordingly, would not undergo an effective and sincere revival."[18] Shawkat, however, is often unclear as to the identity of these perilous elements, although he refers to individuals, especially foreigners, disseminating unfound misinformation, which resulted in hostility among the Arab nations and sectarian tensions in Iraq.

Hadhihi Ahadafuna clearly evokes nationalist and romantic notions, with all their kitsch and sentimentality. Shawkat hails the premodern world as a universe typified by mercy and devoid of materialist inventions that gave humanity hellish innovations and turned the world into a perpetual battlefield.[19] Though appreciative of modern technologies, he employs an imagery that rests upon instincts and intuitions and not on things one acquires in schools or reads about in books and newspapers. His perception of the national leader, King Faysal I, is shaped by this romanticism. Shawkat's depictions of Faysal accentuate absolute and irrational subordination to the perfect leader of Iraq, thanks to his lineage as a descendant of the Prophet. Shaking the king's hand, he felt it transmitted "determination, spirit and holiness":

> When talking, an aura of light seemed to surround him. A man thus felt his sacred power. . . . My heart jolted with unyielding excitement every time I was in his presence. . . . I wholeheartedly wished I could grant him everything I had to offer, including my life and my youth. . . . For this reason, I was often reminded of the words "May I sacrifice my mother and father for your sake" and "May I sacrifice my soul for your sake," words which the Arabs addressed to the Prophet Muhammad and to the Caliphs. I was persuaded by and committed to the idea that the rationale behind the sensation that occupied me at His Majesty's presence was not simply the result of fawning and obsequiousness but came from pure, truthful sentiments! The ancient Arabs felt towards their caliphs and their leaders as I have felt when standing in front of Faysal.[20]

Faysal, then, was important to Shawkat not merely because of his good statesmanship, but also—and more significantly—because of the sanctity surrounding his persona. Faysal's body was encircled with light and provoked an emotional turmoil in Shawkat whenever he spoke to him. As leader of the nation, Faysal was almost an equal to the Prophet himself and was referred to in the same words with which the Arabs addressed their caliphs during the seventh century.

Shawkat, a staunch supporter of Kemalism, suggests similar models in order to contemplate questions of leadership and sovereignty in Iraq. An important figure was the second righteous caliph, 'Umar ibn al-Khattab (586-644). He argues that the caliph "knew the people simply by gazing and conversing," and "identified the character of a person by a swift look." As one of the greatest Arab leaders, it was his role "to give our men and leaders a firm political outlook, which would enable them to know people."[21] Shawkat does not narrow the potential of such leadership to the ancient past and points out that such leadership is acceptable and even desirable at the present time, and that even leaders like Disraeli knew their own subjects in a similar fashion. Shawkat, nevertheless, never specifies who the true successor to Faysal I or 'Umar was. Although he invests much effort in highlighting the legitimacy of the Hashemite monarchy, neither Ghazi nor Faysal II fitted these images of heroic leadership. Thus, although his writings about leadership very much resemble the personality cult that emerged in Nazi Germany, it is obvious that he saw no parallel to such great leaders in the contemporary Arab world.

Shawkat's vision of the state is similarly undemocratic. The state is paralleled to the institution of the family, an establishment typified by love, loyalty, and obedience.[22] Shawkat addressed his writings mainly to Iraqis, feeling that Iraq was superior to Egypt and the coastal parts of Syria, Lebanon, and Palestine in its Arab character, because, unlike the former, Iraq was relatively isolated from Western influence, an isolation that enabled it to preserve a cultural distinctiveness lost in more Westernized Arab cities. Nonetheless, he thought his views were suitable for the entire Arab nation and wrote frequently on the history of the region and about Pan-Arab geopolitical units.[23] To Shawkat, the history of the region was the history of ancient Semitic empires. He portrays the Arab empires of the past as units whose parts functioned in perfect harmony. These empires thrived by granting full rights to whoever adopted the Arabic language, thus succeeding in Arabizing the newly conquered lands and avoiding internal fragmentation and violence.[24] For example, Musaylima (d. 633), a false prophet who challenged the leadership of the Prophet Muhammad, was of Arab origins, yet being a traitor he was killed by other righteous Arab tribesmen, whereas the convert Salman al-Farisi (seventh century), who was not an Arab, adopted the Arabic language and thus served the Arab nation.[25] Another example suggested by Shawkat was the Arabization of the Copts and their integration in the Arab empire, which proved that "every individual who lives among us, speaks our language and does not possess in his heart hostility to us, is one of us and deserves our love as we love ourselves."[26] The subjects of Arab empires had unique moral characteristics. Shawkat alleges that in the same way that the Englishman was typified by fine character and personal dignity, the Jew by an obsessive interest in gold, and the Japanese by adoration of nationalism and self-sacrifice, the Arab was characterized by his pride in tribal ancestry, honor, dignity, and diligence. These qualities had made the Arabs very similar to the Englishmen. The way to achieve a national revival was thus to strengthen these qualities and to direct them toward military, economic, and educational venues.[27] Islam, in this domain, was significant as a sort of intellectualized civilizing mission. The Arab colonization process entailed a colonization of the soul: whereas the Roman Empire disintegrated both from within and from without through foreign attacks, Islam and the Arabic language survived for many years despite foreign occupation; even at times of decline, the number of Arabs increased without hardly any cases of conversion from Islam.[28]

Shawkat's construction of the medieval Arab empire is vital to his conceptualizations regarding the contemporary Iraqi nation and its models of leadership. His concept of empire is influenced by European examples; he refers to the unification of Italy and Germany as a successful way of unifying other small countries that shared the same language and religion.[29] Nevertheless, British ideas regarding the nature of their empire are essential to Shawkat's writings no less than either Bismarck and Mazzini or Hitler and Mussolini. Evocation of Disraeli as a great imperial administrator, drawing parallels between the character of the Englishman and the Arab, making references to the fact that the Arabs conquered India, and ending *Hadhihi Ahdafuna* with a translation of Rudyard Kipling's (1865–1936) "If"[30] epitomize the impact of British imperial ideals on Shawkat's thinking. His imagined Arab empire, moreover, was far better than the British Empire because Arab empires allowed the assimilation of various subjects into the state. Akin to the Arab leaders of the past who fused a political unity out of diverse populations, current Iraqi leaders ought to mold a new nation, Iraq, out of various tribal and religious elements.

Shawkat's antidemocratic ideas can be summarized in one word: *unoriginal*. His positions were extremely popular in interwar Europe as well as in the Middle East. As Mark Mazower points out, the 1920s and 1930s were an era in which "biological metaphors were widely applied to international relations, when the fears of population decline were widespread," and subsequently nations were perceived as bodies, facing extinction, unless they survive within safe and defendable borders.[31] Shawkat's understanding of the national battle for survival and his interest in hygiene, education, and demography should thus be contextualized in the interwar era and in nineteenth-century Middle Eastern politics of reform. Such views could not be categorized as German, Fascist, or imperial because they were always a mixture of several elements. His views, nonetheless, assumed popularity in Iraq; articles advocating opinions similar to Shawkat's were published by the press as editorials, columns, and news items. Shawkat implemented some of his ideas in the ministry of education and contributed to its militarization. His theories, however, did not simply represent an actual proto-Fascist reality, but rather represented a *desire* to change contemporary Iraqi actualities, in which the state's attempts to assume hegemony were frequently met with resistance. In other words,

Shawkat's theories imply not that Iraq was like the German and Italian states, but that it was quite different from the Fascist states that emerged in Europe.

Antidemocratic voices such as Shawkat's encountered substantial opposition in interwar Iraq. Prior to the outbreak of World War II, the espousal of totalitarian political philosophies was limited to Shawkat's relatively small fraction of the Baghdadi nationalist elite, yet the state faced far more formidable *internal* challenges. Tribal revolts, namely, the Shi'i and Kurdish protests against the state's discriminatory policies, occupied the state's politicians. Kurdish uprisings broke out in 1930, 1931, and 1935. In 1935 the Yazidi tribes and especially the mid-Euphrates Shi'i tribesmen challenged the authority of the state in a revolt whose crushing necessitated a great deal of military force. Furthermore, Shi'i writers and intellectuals objected to universal conscription, one of the main aims of the nationalist camp (which was finally achieved in 1935), and, importantly, protested the abuse of democratic rights, especially the underrepresentation of Shi'is in the democratic institutions of the Iraqi state. The Shi'i intellectual and *mujtahid* Muhammad Husayn Al Kashif al-Ghita called for a new electoral system in Iraq and for legal equality among the nation's various religious communities. Thus, for the southern and the Shi'i parts of the nation, concerns about fair representation and distribution of national resources far outweighed the debate about Fascism and Nazism.[32]

The military coup led by the Kemalist Bakir Sidqi was quite different from that of Kaylani. The leaders of the coup were initially open to cooperation with the social democrats and other reformist elements. Some were also proponents of Iraqi territorial nationalism. They viewed the Pan-Arab tendencies of the previous governments with great suspicion, and hence marginalized many of the Pan-Arab supporters of Germany. Moreover, during the years of the military regime, Jewish rights were protected and respected.[33] Matters changed after the war broke out, yet even then a prominent group of Iraqi politicians, mainly the country's pro-British elite whose political hegemony relied on its connections to Great Britain, did not want to pursue a relationship with Germany that might erode their power. First and foremost among them was Nuri al-Sa'id, Iraq's most powerful politician and the nation's premier for multiple terms. Sa'id repeatedly stated his commitment to fighting German propaganda in Iraq and reported to the British about German activities. He protested the activities of Grobba and the German Legation to the German minister of foreign affairs and even threatened to dismiss all German teachers in Iraq and expel Grobba himself. Some cultural and political activities promoted by Grobba were blocked by Iraqi officials, including Sa'id.[34]

During the years 1933–1940, the British themselves took steps to counter pro-German propaganda efforts. The British maintained an espionage network aimed at gathering information on the activities of prominent Iraqis. Who hired a German governess for his children, who studied in Germany, who wrote pro-German articles in the press, and who visited Grobba or got a bottle of whiskey from him—all were recorded and documented. The British were also quick to identify pro-Fascist and pro-Nazi items in Iraqi newspapers and knew whom to pay in order to have stories favorable to Great Britain published. They also encouraged pro-British propaganda efforts via the BBC, youth organizations like the British Boy Scouts, and the pro-British 'Alawaiya Club. Grobba, for his part, complained about anti-Nazi and anti-German publications in Baghdad that blunted his propaganda efforts.[35]

The Sherifians (Sunni Iraqi officers who had participated in the Arab Revolt and became the backbone of Iraq's political leadership) and the Pan-Arab elites regarded Mussolini less favorably than Hitler because of the former's imperialist campaigns in North Africa. Mussolini's self-representation as a man fighting on behalf of Islam fell on deaf ears. Ambassador Archibald Clark-Kerr reported:

> I have asked several Iraqi friends what impression has been made by Signor Mussolini's recent declaration on Italian policy towards Islam and the Arabs, and I have found that they all treat these declarations as ridiculous bombast.[36]

Furthermore, not all Sherifians and Iraqi nationalists, even the most anti-British, were eager to accept German and Italian backing. Peter Wien shows convincingly that Iraqi nationalists—intellectuals, politicians, and generals alike—did not wholeheartedly adopt Fascist and Nazi theories. Iran and Turkey, and their leaders and reforms, were far more significant than overseas enemies or allies. Moreover, Wien demonstrates that not all allusions to Germany should be understood as evidence of sympathy for Nazism; many of these narratives celebrated Prussian, rather than Nazi, models and reflected a nostalgic view of the Ottoman past.[37] To corroborate Wien's argument, I turn to an important publication of the time, the satirical journal *Habazbuz*. As Wien has shown, despite the journal's enthusiastic support of militaristic tendencies in Iraqi society, the paper's editor, Nuri Thabit (b. 1897, Baghdad), never favored the adoption of a Fascist or Nazi model in Iraq.

Habazbuz is interesting for a few reasons. First, Thabit had much in common with Iraq's national elites. He was educated in an Ottoman military academy, fought on the Ottoman side during World War I, and became part of Iraq's intellectual elite during the interwar period. Furthermore, he, like many of his peers, believed in the positive power of the military to shape society and hailed the militaristic character of Turkey and Iran. Second, the journal enjoyed some currency; its issues reference the responses of Iraqi journalists and intellectuals to its articles. Because of its satirical nature, articles were often written in the colloquial, and cartoons were featured prominently—mostly on the front page. Therefore, we may assume that many more people saw the paper or that articles from the paper were read aloud to them. Third, *Habazbuz* was merciless in its skewering of various elements in Iraqi society, including the pro-German and pro-Fascist camp, and we can therefore gain insights from its contents into the nature of the anti-Fascist and anti-Nazi critique within national Iraqi circles.

Thabit's objections to Nazism and Fascism focused on two lines of reasoning. First, he took issue with the colonialist actions of Germany and Italy, which he saw as the attacks of strong nations on weaker ones. The concern about weak nations facing monstrous imperial powers dated back to the early days of the mandate, when Iraqis protested the disrespecting of their rights—and those of other Arab states—to sovereignty and self-governance by strong nations. Second, Thabit implicitly argued that Arab-Iraqi nationalism, modeled on the Nazi ideology, in which ethnicity and racism were prominent, did not fit the multilingual and multiethnic nature of Iraqi society. The journal, in fact, celebrated Iraq's multiplicity of dialects and cultures, even while parodying them. Hilarious, vulgar, nationalist, and heterogeneous, Iraq, as represented in *Habazbuz*, could not have endured a purely racial and authoritarian rule.

Habazbuz attacked Mussolini on a number of occasions. When Mussolini proclaimed that he was the protector of Islam, *Habazbuz* reminded its readers that the British imperialists had also pretended to "protect" certain peoples: "When was the defense on religions or peoples [*aqwam*] established out of good intention[s]? Wasn't this wretched word [*protection*] the starting point for colonialism in any of the stages of history?"[38] Similarly, when the newspaper *al-Sabah* ran an editorial defending Il Duce, *Habazbuz* mocked the daily, hinting that its editor might have received financial encouragement to print such an item. Ridiculing the language of the editorial, *Habazbuz* rephrased *al-Sabah*'s flattering depictions of the Italian dictator thus:

> God [*Allahuma*] protect the protector of religion . . . and support our Sultan, the ruler of land and sea [*sultan al-barayn wa khaqan al-bahrayn*], the Sultan, son of the Sultan, the Khaqan, son of Khaqan, Il Duce![39]

The titles evoked here had previously been bestowed on the Ottoman sultan. By using this terminology, Thabit reminded readers who the true protector of Islam is (or, rather, was) and, more important, insinuated that Mussolini harbored imperialist ambitions concerning all the former lands of the Ottoman Empire. On other occasions, the paper cheered the Ethiopians fighting against the Italians, expressing the hope that they would soon be victorious.[40]

Thabit explained that Hitler and Mussolini could not be compared to Mustafa Kemal (Atatürk) in terms of leadership, and in fact the former would not even be privates under the latter's command. When Hitler came to Germany, wrote Thabit, he destroyed its existing culture and did not create anything new, but rather exiled the productive economic elements of German society, namely, the Jews, in the name of fighting communism. Mussolini fought his old party, the Socialist Party, replaced communism with Fascism, and wished to return Italy to the glory of ancient Rome by colonizing weak nations.[41] Such nations were thus unworthy of either admiration or emulation. Thabit found the violence of the Fascist regimes disgusting. In an article recognizing the good services of Dr. Max Macowiskey (the same doctor mentioned at the beginning of this chapter), the following question was posed: which profession served humanity's best interests? Thabit acknowledged that a military commander who defended his noble country was worthy of humanity's respect, yet one should wonder, "What happiness has General Franco brought to Spain?" Inventors were praiseworthy, but one should also take into account the fact that they invented deadly military weapons and other destructive materials. The answer, then, was the doctor, the man who assists his fellow men without question or hesitation.[42]

Thabit supported the spread of militarism among the Iraqi youth and even viewed the shirt organizations in a favorable light. Yet as a teacher, he was alarmed by the introduction of Fascist aesthetics into Iraqi schools and the militarization of Iraqi education. The article "The Time of Exams" opened with Thabit's shocking depictions of the ignorance of Iraqi youth, which had become apparent to him as he corrected the exams of graduating high school students. One student had written that Egypt was born in the time of Adam and was ruled by Abraham for a thousand years. The latter had left Egypt to Khediv Isma'il Pasha, who in turn left it to his son, King Fu'ad, whom Umm Kalthum praises in her songs. Another student wrote that Harun al-Rashid was one of the four rightly guided caliphs (*al-Rashidun*). This ignorance, Thabit observed sadly, was typical of students at all levels of education. The reason was that students simply had no time to study, because of all the military exercises they were required to perform in schools: "Every day a sports competition! Every day a sporting exercise! Every day a parade!" Thabit decried the propensity for having students perform in parades in honor of visiting dignitaries, arguing that the result was that "when you ask a student on Khalid ibn al-Walid he tells you he is Napoleon's cousin!"[43] Thabit contended that education ought to come first and that parades and military performances should never come at the expense of true education—the knowledge of one's history and cultural values.

A Pan-Arabist, Thabit was extremely proud of Arab and Islamic history and ridiculed those who did not know the Arabic language well. At the same time, however, he appreciated his Turkish education and was much enamored of Turkish literature.[44] Highly sensitive to the variety of dialects and languages in Iraq, he wished to record and preserve this diversity. *Habazbuz* in fact included a great deal of information about Turkish literature and quoted complete sentences in Turkish. The paper's vocabulary, a very Iraqi combination of Turkish, Persian, and Kurdish words, as well as the transliterations of various Iraqi colloquialisms, made some items almost incomprehensible to non-Iraqi readers, even if they were Arabs. *Habazbuz*, moreover, parodied al-Muthanna Club as well as the Iraqi Broadcasting Station for their promotion of pure Arabic (*Qahtaniyya khalisa*). Thabit's insistence on the colloquial thus stirred conflicts between himself and those who called for the adoption of classical Arabic (*fusha*) in order to unite the Arab world.[45]

More crucially, Thabit insinuated that Iraqi elites privileged Egyptians, Syrians, and Palestinians over other Iraqis. The paper made fun of the Egyptian propensity for declaring the champions of Arab poetry, arguing that they invented more and more titles for the leading poets in the Arab world, such as *amir al-shu'ara, sheikh al-shi'r, sha'ir al-nil*, and so on.[46] Thabit also wondered why al-Muthanna Club frequently invited Egyptians and Syrians to talk about al-Muthanna ibn Haritha: "We are Iraqis, we know more about al-Muthanna than any Syrian journalist. Why haven't they had an Iraqi?"[47] Thabit, moreover, did not hesitate to joke about any leading personality in Iraq, including Hajj Amin. When the editor of *al-Zaman*, Tawfiq al-Sam'ani, printed a photo of a famous individual with the wrong caption underneath, Thabit suggested further mistakes might be made by *al-Zaman* such as running a photo of the Jewish intellectual Anwar Sha'ul with the caption, "His Highness the great Mufti of Palestine, Hajj Amin al-Husayni," and a photo of the nationalist journalist Salim Hasun with the caption, "The Respected Sasson Khaduri, the Head of the Jewish Community in Baghdad, May God Prolong his Life [Hebrew: *ha-shem ya'arikh et hayav*]."[48] Although such satirical commentaries were tolerated in the Iraqi context, as we shall see they were not received with much joy by the Palestinians living in Iraq.

Moreover, Thabit took issue with the conflation by Iraqis of Judaism and Zionism. The paper did make fun of Jews, but also made fun of Christians, Arabs, Shi'is, Sunnis, Turkmen, Kurds, Persians—in short, everyone in Iraqi society. I found only one article that could be seen as anti-Jewish.[49] Most articles represented Jews as full-fledged Iraqi citizens. Furthermore, Thabit either employed Jews or knew quite a lot about Jewish Iraqi culture, since the paper used Hebrew expressions to typify the speech of Iraqi Jews. This practice was not entirely new; Shmuel Moreh has drawn attention to the Hebrew and Aramaic words in the poetry of the popular Shi'i poet 'Abbud al-Karkhi.[50] Karkhi, however, was a southerner, whereas Thabit was a Baghdadi. In December 1936, *Habazbuz* ran a story, "Excommunication" (Hebrew: *al-herem*), that used colloquial language to depict a conversation between a few friends reading to their Jewish brethren:

—Adon [Mister] Schwartz . . .
—Who is he?
—A Zionist!
—Published an article in the newspaper *Ha-Boker*. . . regarding the declaration of Iraqi Jews that they disassociate themselves from Zionism, and said that the declaration caused much pain to the hearts of the Zionists. May a thousand pains befall on their heads!

The friends later discover that Adon Schwartz wanted to prevent Iraqi Jews from leaving for Palestine as a punishment for their pro-Palestinian sympathies. The Jewish state had no place for such pro-Palestinian Jews. They needed to be excommunicated. The friends therefore concur that Iraqi Jews know that Palestine is Arab and will stay Arab forever. They also realize that Iraqi Jews are Iraqis "who [have] lived with us for thousands of years" and have no relation to Zionism. One of the friends lists names of Iraqi Jews who contributed to Iraqi society by building hospitals and schools. He concludes, "The Jews of Iraq are Iraqis before anything else, and prefer their country to the rest of God's lands!"[51]

The story was written less than a year after the general strike in Palestine began in April 1936, an event that marked the beginning of the national Palestinian revolt against Britain. Jews in Iraq were criticized sharply and at times physically attacked in this period by some radicals affiliated with the pro-Fascist camp because of the presumed connections between Judaism and Zionism. The Jewish Iraqi intelligentsia, however, were themselves highly critical of Zionism. In October 1936, a letter by the community's rabbi, Sasson Khaduri, appeared in the nationalist daily *al-Istiqlal*: in it the rabbi claimed that his community had no connection to Zionism, since the Jews of Iraq were Iraqis and shared the concerns of their countrymen.[52] Several other pro-Palestinian statements by Iraqi Jews during the revolt were made in the press.[53] It was consequently important for Thabit to show his support for such opinions and to establish that Zionism and Judaism should be distinguished from one another. Iraqi Jews, in his opinion, were loyal citizens and for this reason had received the scorn of their Zionist brethren and deserved the support of their fellow Iraqis.

I have given much space to Thabit's ideas because of his background, which, as I noted, had much in common with the Sunni elite of Iraq, and because his *Habazbuz* was very popular. Significantly, Thabit's views were shared by other members of the Iraqi national elite. The educator Sati' al-Husri, a passionate nationalist, shared Thabit's positions on education and objected to the transformation of education into a military endeavor that would prepare students to die for the motherland (as suggested by Shawkat), while the influential politician Jamal Baban felt that al-Futuwwa disrespected the meaning of true militarism.[54] Shi'is, Turkmen, and Kurds were alarmed by the exclusionist model of Arab ethnicity and employed a discourse sensitive to conditions in Iraq. Thabit's admiration of all things Turkish was certainly not unique. Many Sherifians, as well as members of the Iraqi officers corps who had served in the Ottoman army until the end of World War I, believed in Atatürkism (*ataturkiyya*), a term with many, often conflicting, significations. For Nuri al-Sa'id, it signified one-party rule and a commitment to modernization. Iraq had formerly been linked to Turkey by the bonds of Ottomanism, Sa'id argued, but now it could relate to Kemalist Turkey based on the shared commitment to modernization and reform. Kaylani and Sidqi both referred to Atatürk in their writings. Admiration of Atatürk did not necessarily mean turning one's back on Arabism, however. On the contrary, some Iraqi Pan-Arabists felt that Arab culture should play the same role that Turkish culture played in the Kemalist model. Many of the laws either codified or proposed in the 1930s (the obligation to wear a *sidara*, the limitations on celebrating '*ashura*', the attempts to settle tribes) were modeled after Kemalist reforms. As Peter Wien has observed, Iraq's Sunni neighbor was far more important to the Arab elites in these years than any developments in Europe.[55] *Habazbuz* thus provided a forum for concerns current in the Iraqi public sphere.

Secular Kemalism, however, offered very little to the state's religious populations. Yet the objections to Nazism and Fascism came also from religious circles, as religious scholars feared the secular character and imperialist intentions of these closely related ideologies. Such views were reflected in a letter written by the mufti of Mosul, Habib al-'Ubaydi. Following Mussolini's declaration that he was the protector of Islam, 'Ubaydi published a letter in *al-Bilad* addressed to Signor Mussolini, in which he stated:

> By venturing to assume for yourself the title of Protector of Islam, you did nothing new. . . . The Moslem, while welcoming friendship of whatever kind, abhors protection of no matter what character. The butcher must not be deceived by the submission of some female sheep.
>
> Tripolitania is an Arab and Moslem country. For a quarter of a century Rome has been in control of the destinies of the Arabs and Moslem population of that unfortunate territory. What factors of modern civilization, other than fire and steel, has Rome introduced into that country? What kind of science, culture or economic development other than despotism and subjugation, has Rome conferred upon that land? Is this the sort of friendship that Rome means to have with the Arabs and Islam?[56]

The message of the letter was clear: a colonial power could not claim to be a friend, let alone a protector, of Islam, when oppressing another Arab and Muslim country. Like Thabit, the mufti reminded Mussolini that promises of protection and friendship, so central to the rhetoric of colonialism, were all too familiar to Muslims.

The influential Shi'i *mujtahid*, Hibbat al-Din al-Shaharastani (1883–1967), was a key figure in the rejection of Nazi ideology in Iraq. Shaharastani had established himself as a critic of ethnic nationalism before World War I. In 1910 he proposed that the answer to colonialism was Islamic unity, one encompassing Turks, Arabs, Iranians, and Indians, and issued a condemnation of ethnic exclusivity (*'asabiyya*).[57] A democrat, Shaharas-tani enthusiastically supported the constitutional revolutions in Iran and in the Ottoman Empire.[58] These positions were most important in the 1930s. Shaharastani stated in 1937 that Islam was a religion based on the brotherhood of all men, regardless of their race, and that it celebrated the dignity and importance of the individual. Theories of racial supremacy and a political system that deified the state at the expense of the individual thus contradicted key elements of the Islamic and Arab spirit. Nazism, moreover, was alien to the Islamic conviction that religion provided a foundation for complete democracy, on the one hand, and for strong indi-vidualism, on the other.[59]

Islamic legal theory that specified that the religious rights and the reli-gious autonomy of *Ahl al-Kitab* (Jews and Christians) were protected was used to challenge anti-Semitism. Adherence to this tenet was very strong in both the North and the South, where religious and tribal values con-cerning the protection of Jews as a minority were deeply ingrained. In the South, tribal leaders and *mujtahids* assisted the Jewish population; for ex-ample, tribal militias protected Basran Jews during the looting of Jewish property in the month of May.[60] Northern Sunni religious leaders like-wise supported Jewish Iraqis and objected to the activities of Hajj Amin al-Husayni in Mosul.[61] After the war, the propaganda efforts of both the British and the pro-British Iraqi elites portrayed Islam as a Semitic reli-gion that rejected ethnic nationalism.

A vital voice in the anti-Fascist and anti-Nazi camp was that of Jew-ish Iraqi intellectuals. With the 1908 Ottoman constitutional revolu-tion, the Jews of Iraq had taken their place among the nation's intellec-tual elite. They were prominent writers and journalists, and they used their clout to combat Nazi propaganda efforts. Jewish intellectuals such as Anwar Sha'ul, Ezra Haddad, and Shalom Darwish addressed their anti-German critiques to the Arab-Iraqi community via the Arabic-language press and participated in the BBC anti-German Arabic broadcasts. Sha'ul was the editor of Iraq's most important cultural magazine, *al-Hasid*, to which many Sunni and Shi'i intellectuals contributed. His harsh criti-cisms of Germany and Italy in *al-Hasid* caused him to be mentioned in complaints filed by representatives of those nations with the Ministry of the Interior. Haddad, in a series of articles in *al-Hasid*, condemned totali-tarian regimes for denying their citizens basic human rights, deifying the leader of the state, and suffocating the spirit of freedom. The overarching point of many of these articles was that Iraqis should reject Fascism as a threat not only to Jews, but to all men seeking democracy, freedom, and independence.[62] Iraqi Jews also used their economic power to influence reporting on Jewish affairs and the war and made various contributions to the British war efforts.[63] It was also difficult for the Germans to screen pro-Nazi films in Baghdad. As Ambassador Clark-Kerr reported in 1936:

> [German] political propaganda is conducted mainly by means of cinema-tography films, depicting the emergence of Germany as an equal of other powers, with all that this entails; the triumphs, oratorical and others, of the Fuhrer and his followers. Only one hall is available to this kind of display, since five of the six theaters in Baghdad are owned by Jews, who refuse to lend themselves to the spreading of German political ideas.[64]

The most resolute opponent of Nazism and Fascism in Iraq was the Left, both the legal and illegal. The former was a group called al-Ahali (the People). Led by students and middle-class youth, al-Ahali promoted a Fabian and social-democratic agenda. The group was established in 1932 under the leadership of intellectuals such as Muhammad Hadid (b. 1905) and Kamil al-Chadirchi (b. 1897). In the early 1930s, Mussolini had appeared to be a reformer whose reorganization of the Italian economy had been quite successful. By 1933, however, Ahali journalists were criticizing all forms of Fascism, although they did not support war against Germany at this stage.[65] Their newspaper, *al-Ahali*, published a translation of an article by American historian Sidney Fay, which argued that the United States should not interfere in German politics. Fay acknowledged Nazi anti-Semitism and discussed it in detail in tracing the roots of the phenomenon back to medieval times.[66] Nazi anti-Semitism was reported, and condemned, in other instances, such as in the article, "The Psyche of the Hitlerists and the Reasons for Their Animosity towards the Jews."[67] In addition to stories about Germany and Italy, there was also much concern about the outcome of the civil war in Spain.[68] *Al-Ahali* also made mention of general abuses of civil rights in Nazi Germany, such as the power accorded to the secret police or the restrictions on the press.[69]

Al-Ahali's most interesting intellectual was 'Abd al-Fattah Ibrahim (b. 1906). Ibrahim received his bachelor's degree in history and political science from the American University in Beirut (1926) and continued his graduate studies at Columbia University, working on his master's thesis under the supervision of Thomas Parker Moon. In Iraq he worked as a teacher, writer, and journalist. Ibrahim edited the newspaper *al-Ahali* and was a leading force behind major ventures of the group in the mid-1930s. He left *al-Ahali* because of his objections to its role in the 1936 coup.[70] In 1939 Ibrahim published *Muqadimma fi'l Ijtima'* (Introduction to sociology). The work offered something new to the Iraqi, and indeed the Arab, public sphere. Whereas other Iraqi intellectuals at the time referenced French and German theoreticians from the eighteenth and nineteenth centuries in their reflections on nationalism, Ibrahim evoked a new range of thinkers. In addition to Mill, Hume, Kant, Smith, and Paine, his work also referenced Benedetto Croce (on culture), Carlton Hayes (on nationalism), and Malinowski (on sexuality). *Introduction to Sociology* saw two subsequent editions. Ibrahim's writings continued to be read extensively through the 1950s; his works were quoted by prominent nationalist 'Abd al-Rahman al-Bazzaz and historian 'Abd al-Razzak al-Hasani and are mentioned in memoirs of Iraqi intellectuals. In other words, although Ibrahim was never able to shape state policies, despite his political activity, the readers and students he gathered around him were influenced by his writings and incorporated his ideas into their thinking.[71]

To Ibrahim, Nazism represented a new type of regime at the core of which was a leadership positioned above the law. Ibrahim was particularly troubled by Nazi racism and its emphasis on "racial homogeneity" (*wahdat al-jins*). This theory, he wrote, assumes that races battle one another in order to survive, that each race possesses a unique culture, and that each race must preserve the purity of its blood in order to ensure its progress. Most of the people who believed in such theories also believed in the superiority of their own race and in its right to dominate other "inferior" races and cultures. Ibrahim noted that the Nazis based their theories of race on previous writings, most notably those of Arthur de Gobineau and Houston Stewart Chamberlain. To illustrate how the Nazis developed these theories into a full-fledged science, he quoted arguments in favor of racial purity and against racial integration put forth by Nazi leaders and theorists. In particular, he cited *Why the Aryan?*, a 1934 pamphlet by Dr. E. H. Schulz and Dr. R. Frercks that argued for the need to protect the cleanliness and wholesomeness of the Aryan race. Ibrahim then went to great lengths to debunk such theories, attempting to prove that they were illogical, unscientific, and harmful to society.[72]

Ibrahim contended that the concept of "purity," which served as the basis for ethnic nationalism in general and for Nazism in particular, impeded the description of cultures, nations, and peoples. There was no such thing as the purity of a single language, as all languages included remnants and influences from other languages. The idea of a culture unique to a nation or a race was likewise unsupportable, as culture was the product of all of humanity and tended to arise from the fruitful interactions of various peoples and traditions. Ibrahim treated the "natural features" of nations as mere stereotypes. The Germans themselves, he said, were once considered barbaric and impetuous, whereas now they were thought of as a hardworking and highly orderly people. The features of a nation, therefore, related to who represented the qualities of that nation and at what period; the Romans, for instance, had termed the Germans barbarians, whereas contemporary Germans used this word to describe other peoples.[73]

Based on his readings of Carlton Hayes, Ibrahim did not view nationalism as the manifestation of the dormant desires that had shaped the mentality of the national community from antiquity and sprung to life in the modern age, but rather saw it as a modern phenomenon and a form of societal consciousness, which was the product of capitalism, industrialization, literacy, and education. Instead of organizing a society on the basis of racial or ethnic features, a truly modern community ought to be based on democratic citizenship (*muwatana*).[74] Nationalism, however, could assume a very destructive form if not grounded in democracy and if "it is established for the service of one class, and takes colonialism as a basis for its foreign policy and oppression as a basis for its internal policies, based on the myth of national glory or the lies of foreign threats."[75] Ibrahim concluded by saying that culture, the product of humanity, changed according to time and place and that it gave humans in the modern age industries, sciences, arts, and new social formulations. How horrible it is, he concluded, that some societies seemed to cling to the cultures of bygone eras.[76]

A second leftist group that challenged Nazism and Fascism was the nascent Iraqi Communist Party. The ICP emerged as several local groups coalesced in March 1935 into the Committee against Colonialism (Lajnah did al-isti'mar). The ICP initially supported Sidqi, yet he attacked the Communists and restricted their activities. They also supported Kaylani in his coup, viewing him favorably as an anticolonialist, but urged him not to pursue collaboration with Germany. Initially, the Communists regarded World War II as a battle over imperial spheres of influence, in relation to which the Arab world should remain neutral.[77] Nonetheless, *Sawt al-Sha'b*, the journal of the ICP, reprinted the very negative opinions of Nazism voiced by Egyptian literary critics such as Ahmad Hasan al-Zayyat and Tawfiq al-Hakim.[78] During the 1941 coup, the ICP warned against attacks on Iraqi Jews.[79] Following the *Farhud*, the Communists denounced the acts of violence against "their Jewish brothers" and characterized the looting, killing, and abuse of fellow Iraqis as illegal, unjust, and incompatible with Iraq's national spirit. The Communist reaction proved effective; from that point on, the number of Jews who joined the party increased substantially.[80] The pro-Jewish stance of the ICP was rooted in its appeal to minorities, such as the Armenians and the Kurds and the ICP's vision of the Iraqi state, which included the nation's various ethnic and religious minorities.[81]

A prominent Communist writer of the period was the novelist and short-story writer Dhu Nun Ayyub (b. 1908). His collections of short stories mocked the Fascist and Nazi regimes of Europe and their Iraqi supporters. Nadi al-Muthanna and its pro-Fascist supporters were a favorite target of Ayyub. In the introduction to his collection of short stories *Al-Kadihun* (The workers), Ayyub ridicules the paramilitary education in Iraq inspired by Fascist models:

> In the near future, we should find amongst the Arabs a man who believes that the mere wearing of military uniforms is enough to give birth to national feelings, and another, who gathers around him a large number of children in order to lead them, armed with nothing but simple clubs, to conquer the world. I do not wish to waste too many words on this subject, which is more the area of a psychiatrist.[82]

Those who introduced Fascist aesthetics and military practices into Iraqi schools, as did the paramilitary organization al-Futuwwa, should thus be considered insane. In Ayyub's opinion, a Nazi model of nationalism had found a footing in Iraq, because Germany, in the words of one of the characters in his novel *Doctor Ibrahim*, "easily understood the language that this people comprehended, that is, the language of meaningless words, shining dinars, hatred of the British and of the Jews."[83] Ayyub reminds his readers that Fascism destroyed the independent spirit, corrupted culture, and obliterated any sign of humanism. In Germany and Italy, Ayyub writes, "this type of dictatorship obscured the national literature, colored with [a] humanistic palette. . . . One cannot find these days the equal of Goethe in German literature; of Dante and Boccaccio in Italian literature[;] . . . this living literature had been replaced by cacophony and nonsense."[84] The narrator in his short story "The Prophet" believes that Germany and Italy were "greedy imperialist nations" and cautions Iraqis against the promises of the Germans to grant freedom to the Arabs. He points out that the exact same promises were made by the British and the French during World War I, when those colonial powers sought the help of the Arabs against the Turks. He compares Mussolini to an aggressive gorilla and Hitler to a rapacious tiger to indicate the peril in replacing one colonial power with another, potentially a more dangerous one.[85]

(Images of Mussolini as a gorilla were quite common and appeared also in the Egyptian press.) Ayyub believed that in a nation as ethnically and linguistically diverse as Iraq, the combination of ideas of ethnic purity with nationalist ideology was hazardous to the heterogeneity of the nation.[86]

Finally, anti-Semitic propaganda could not undermine the relationships among friends, neighbors, business partners, and colleagues. During the *Farhud*, many Jews who resided in mixed neighborhoods were saved because their Muslim neighbors and friends came to their aid. While Jews reported that their non-Jewish neighbors joined in the riots and looting, they also testified that Muslims sought to help them. A Zionist account written by Eliyahu Epstein shortly afterward acknowledged numerous instances of Muslims assisting Jews.[87] Some accounts mention people who sheltered up to seventy people during the days of the riots. One Arab woman, seventy years old, was reported to have had many neighbors in her home for more than twenty-four hours.[88] At times, ideology had very little to do with the assistance provided to the Jews. A man who worked for the rail company, whom a Zionist document identified as "a Nazi," refused to fire his Jewish workers and kept a close eye on them during the riots.[89] Sa'ib Shawkat, the brother of Sami and Naji Shawkat, opened his doors to Jews and gave them refuge.[90] Similarly, in Basra Muslims aided their Jewish neighbors during the riots in early May on the basis of religious and tribal values.[91] A British account mentioned that many notables in Basra "gave asylum in their own homes to Jews and other members of minorities who were in fear for their lives."[92] The protection of Jews in Baghdad and Basra sprang from a sense of intimacy in the mixed areas, which could not be dislodged by pro-Fascist, pro-German, or anti-Semitic propaganda.[93]

Beyond Iraq's borders, Egyptian newspapers expressed anti-Fascist and anti-Nazi opinions. Egyptian intellectuals, some of whom resided in Iraq and were admired by its Pan-Arab elite, led a campaign against Nazism. Ahmad Hasan al-Zayyat, the influential publisher of the Egyptian literary magazine *al-Risala* (which was widely read in Iraq), resided in Iraq during the 1930s. He viewed Italy as an imperialistic force and objected to its militarist character. 'Abd al-Razzaq al-Sanhuri, an Egyptian legal theorist who taught law in Baghdad, contended that Nazi anti-Semitism was not only anti-Jewish but also anti-Arab, and that for the Nazis the Arabs were an inferior race as well. These intellectuals were highly influential in the Baghdadi cultural and literary arena. In addition, the Baghdadi public sphere was flooded with Egyptian cultural products, and novels by Egyptian luminaries like Tawfiq al-Hakim and Taha Husayn were esteemed in Iraq. The latter two were also known for their critiques of Fascism and Nazism.[94]

It has been argued that the truly influential non-Iraqi Arabs were the Syrian and Palestinians residing in Iraq.[95] In the aftermath of the *Farhud*, an Iraqi government investigation report determined that much of the pro-German and anti-Jewish sentiment had been fomented by Syrians, Egyptians, and especially Palestinians living in Iraq (most of whom were teachers).[96] Hajj Amin al-Husayni was marked as a key agent in the deterioration of the relationship between Jews and Muslims. Nonetheless, whereas Hajj Amin and his Palestinian supporters were welcomed by the Pan-Arab Sunni elites in Baghdad, the Palestinians were viewed as outsiders (*dukhala'*) by the Iraqi press. The diaries of Akram Zu'aytar evidence the difficulties encountered by the Palestinian elite residing in Iraq. Zu'aytar was a Palestinian teacher and writer who worked in Baghdad in the 1930s, whom the British identified as being pro-Nazi.[97] Zu'aytar's diaries (published posthumously) make no mention of his Nazi connections. They do, however, provide many details concerning his activities at al-Muthanna club, the various pro-Palestinian organizations that emerged in the Iraqi public sphere, and pro-Palestinian events in Iraq. Although the Palestinians were valued as teachers and professionals, many were also refugees and hence relied on the protection of the Pan-Arab elite in Iraq. Though welcomed, Palestinians (and Syrians as well) were also resented because they were given jobs Iraqis believed they themselves should have had.[98]

Zu'aytar's diaries depict a series of confrontations with local Iraqis based on their critique of the Palestinian camp. For example, in 1934 the satirical journal *Abu Hamd* lampooned the Pan-Arab Syrians, calling them *dukhala'*.[99] In response, Zu'aytar threatened to resign from the Ministry of Education, arguing that as a man deeply committed to Pan-Arabism, he would not stand by while the Syrians and the Palestinians were insulted. His resignation was addressed to the prime minister, Minister of Education Sami Shawkat, and others, but was not accepted.[100] Zu'aytar's friends in turn applied political pressure, and *Abu Hamd* was forced to apologize; even *Habazbuz* defended Zu'aytar's opinions.[101] Zu'aytar despised al-Ahali for similar reasons. Its members criticized the Syrians and the Palestinians for turning a blind eye to the wrongs of the Iraqi state, and consequently Zu'aytar labeled them communists and proponents of perilous regionalism (*iqlimiyya*). One incident that was particularly alarming to Zu'aytar involved an attack on Palestinian teachers, including Zu'aytar himself, printed in the leftist press. The Shi'i politician Ja'far Abu Timman, who was connected to the al-Ahali group, printed in his journal, *al-Mabda'*, a complaint by Kurdish students that the teachers from Palestine harbored anti-Kurdish opinions and hurt the feelings of their Kurdish students.[102] Again, Zu'aytar threatened to resign, but his colleagues in al-Muthanna Club and politicians close to him pushed for an investigation of the Kurdish students' complaints. The investigation eventually ruled in favor of the Palestinian teachers.[103] These accounts demonstrate the power of the Palestinian contingent: it was able to pressure Iraqi politicians to silence its opponents in the Iraqi public sphere in order to promote its agenda. Yet Zu'aytar's diaries testify that he was extremely troubled by the activity of al-Ahali and that the Palestinians, together with the Syrians, were criticized in the local press. They were tolerated guests, but not, as was later indicated, the primary shapers of public opinion.

Similarly, the diaries illustrate that Zu'aytar failed to understand the Iraqi milieu. On the one hand, the Palestinian intellectuals found in Baghdad a home. The Iraqi public sphere was genuinely pro-Palestinian. Conservatives, nationalists, social democrats, and communists, all agreed that Palestine was being colonized by the Zionists and the British. The Pan-Arab camp welcomed the Palestinians upon their arrival, and they, in return, were quick to contribute to Iraq's educational system and its vibrant cultural scene. They enjoyed more freedom in Baghdad than they had in mandatory Palestine (especially after 1936).[104] On the other hand, Iraq was far more multicultural and multilingual than its Pan-Arab elites were willing to admit. Kurdish culture was very dominant in the North. As we have seen, Turkish language and literature were greatly appreciated by many Iraqi intellectuals, and Reza Shah and Atatürk's secularizing reforms were also much admired, even by the Iraqi Pan-Arab elites. In addition, many Iraqis, especially in the South, knew Persian well. Non-Arab Shi'is made pilgrimages to the shrine cities Najaf and Karbala in southern Iraq, and Jews had contributed to the development of Arab Iraqi culture. This did not sit well with Zu'aytar, who characterized Iraqis who called for collaboration with either Iran or Turkey the enemies of Pan-Arabism.[105] In many ways, Iraq failed him because it was not the beacon of Pan-Arabism he hoped it would be. It should be noted that Zu'aytar reproduced in his diaries the anxieties of his Sunni nationalist patrons regarding the Shi'is and the Kurds. Although he befriended many Shi'i intellectuals, most notably the educator Fadhil al-Jamali, his sectarian position put him at ideological odds with many Shi'is. Consider, for example, his depictions of Karbala:

> I visited Karbala together with a group of my brethren. We learned that there are 21,000 Iranians in the city. It was the time of Ramadan, and

we went, while fasting, to the Shrine of al-Husayn, Peace be upon him. We found the preacher [*wa'iz*] there giving a sermon [*khutba*] . . . commemorating the killing of our lord [*sayyiduna*] 'Ali, Peace be upon him, saying: "When 'Ali was killed, the people of Syria cried with joy, and Mu'awiya ordered that all the Syrian lands be decorated, out of hate for 'Ali the martyr [*shahid*]." . . . This is how enmity between Syria (*Sha'm*) and Iraq is inherited . . . and no one is there to fight it!![106]

He later added that he knew that enlightened Shi'is decried these sentiments, but lacked the courage to challenge them.

Although Zu'aytar respected the Shi'i imams 'Ali and Husayn, by adding the titles "peace be upon him" to each of their names, he also identified the elements in Shi'i society he found lamentable: their Persian and hence non-Arab character and their abhorrence of the first Umayyad caliph, Mu'awiya ibn Abi Sufyan, with whom he associated the glory of Syria (and whom Shi'is identify as the enemy of Imam 'Ali). Although these positions might have been received favorably among Sunni Pan-Arabists, they would clearly be objectionable to many Shi'is in Iraq, including those whom Zu'aytar had befriended. These opinions also testify to the great rift between himself and the Iraqi Shi'is. Indeed, some of the attacks on the *dukhala'* came from Shi'i writers who saw the arrival of the Sunni Palestinians as an attempt to minimize their role in Iraqi culture.

Zu'aytar, of course, did not expresses the views of all Palestinians residing in Iraq. Not all shared his antidemocratic agenda. Many simply hoped to find allies in Iraq. Yet I have chosen to describe his diaries in some length because in both the historiography of modern Iraq and in Iraqi and British documents after June 1941, the Palestinian intellectuals are represented as exercising a great deal of power in shaping Iraqi politics and contributing to its anti-Jewish and pro-German actions. However, during the 1930s, they were actually quite vulnerable; the British spied on them, and any Iraqi government could have ended their stay in Iraq. Their integration in Iraq and their ability to promote an agenda that concerned Iraq, rather than Palestine, was rather limited.

Conclusion

I have proposed in this chapter that despite the apparent hegemony of militaristic, antidemocratic, and sometimes pro-Fascist and pro-Nazi voices in the Iraqi public sphere, Iraqis were not of one mind regarding

Fascism and Nazism. It was possible to express critical opinions in the Iraqi print media because of the activities of leftist and liberal groups that, albeit nonhegemonic, still impacted the political debate in Iraq.

The analysis that I have offered, moreover, concerns several historiographical narratives. One popular narrative, which was developed by Makiyya and appears in other sources on Iraqi history, delineates an uninterrupted continuum of authoritarian activity beginning with the pro-Fascist voices of the 1930s and leading up to the Ba'athi violence in the 1970s. Certainly, we can identify a flow of ideas from the nationalist groups of the 1930s to the Istiqlal Party of the 1940s and 1950s to the Ba'athi organizations of the 1960s. These groups loom large in Iraqi history, but they were definitely not the only players in Iraqi politics and culture. In fact, when we consider the cultural and intellectual scenes, it seems that the groups that emerged from the marginal anti-Fascist groups in the 1930s were those who shaped Iraq's culture in the decades after 1941. After the British reoccupation of Iraq, the British exiled a great number of Kaylani supporters and turned a blind eye to the activities of the Left, which consequently grew in strength. The war against Nazism and Fascism in the Communist public sphere became a key issue. Contesting Nazism pointed up not only the ICP's commitment to the anticolonial struggle, but also its opposition to the supporters of Nazism in Iraq. Communist organizations, such as the important 1943 feminist group the Women's League against Fascism, held up their anti-Fascist agenda as underscoring their commitment to socialist ideology, while the Communist press glorified the heroic Soviet war against Fascism. The social democrats emerged as yet another important power in Iraq, and the National Democratic Party played a key role in Iraqi politics in the 1940s and 1950s. Moreover, during the years 1941–1952, most of the influential Iraqi intellectuals were identified with Socialist and Communist goals. Under the leadership of 'Abd al-Karim Qasim (1958–1963), they rose to power and did much to shape Iraq's cultural agenda. Pro-Communist and left leaning, these elites marked their enemies as Fascists and Nazis. The intellectuals who cherished the Kaylani movement did not assume center stage until 1963.

A second popular narrative (or, rather, a mishmash of several historical narratives) links Pan-Arabism and pro-German ideologies. Although it is true the proponents of the pro-Fascist camp were mostly Pan-Arabists, other Pan-Arabists did not hold such views. The conservative elites affiliated with the state, such as the pro-British Nuri al-Sa'id, emphasized Pan-Arab notions identified with the Arab Revolt, yet were very much at odds with the Kaylani faction. The anti-Fascist Egyptians, such as Zayyat, were Pan-Arabists and enjoyed wide support among Iraq's Pan-Arab elites. Similarly, the pro-Fascist and anti-Fascist camps in Iraq cannot be divided according to sectarian lines. The former were mostly Sunni, but included some Shi'i intellectuals as well, and the latter included many Sunnis. Al-Ahali members mostly belonged to the Sunni middle class, and Dhu Nun Ayyub, a Communist, and Nuri Thabit, a humanistic nationalist, were also Sunnis. The debate about Nazism and Fascism, in other words, like many other debates relating to Iraqi history, should be liberated from the simplistic binaries of good Shi'i/bad Shi'i or good Sunni/ bad Sunni, as this was a debate about ideas, visions of society, and perceptions of modernity.

Within this Pan-Arab context, it is also vital to comment on the ever-popular equation between the critique of Zionism and anti-Semitism. Hajj Amin al-Husayni was a Nazi sympathizer, as were some of his supporters. Yet even in Palestine itself, Husayni did not reflect the entirety of the Palestinian national movement that was composed of women's organizations and labor movements, as well as other organizations.[107] As shown in Rana Barakat's work, for example, Husayni's undemocratic leadership was heavily criticized by various political actors in the Palestinian public sphere.[108] Supporting Germany because that country had taken the side of the Palestinians was reasonable to some Iraqis, but was also rejected by other intellectuals, in particular the Social Democrats, the Communists, and the Jewish intelligentsia. Yet all three of these groups were themselves anti-Zionist and pro-Palestinian. Bluntly put: if we are to connect any anti-Zionist statement in the 1930s to a pro-Nazi stance, we need to include the pro-German group and the chief rabbi of Iraq, as well as the prominent Jewish intellectuals who were at the forefront of the anti-Nazi camp.

Finally, as Iraqis—especially Nuri Thabit—recognized, Iraq was probably the least fitting place to promote a racist ideology of a pure Arab ethnicity, modeled on the role accorded to Aryan culture in Nazi Germany. Iraq had contributed much to Arab culture: its neoclassical poetry, for instance, reflected the profound knowledge of its leading poets concerning their Arabo-Islamic heritage. But the Iraq of the 1930s was also typified by bilingualism, multiculturalism, and a richness that emanated from the country's interaction with Iran and especially the Ottoman Empire. Not all Iraqis, even the most vocal opponents of British colonialism, were willing to give up this diversity. In fact, many Iraqis still cherish this diversity today.

PART IV

EGYPT

CHAPTER 7

The View from the Embassy: British Assessments of Egyptian Attitudes during World War II

JAMES JANKOWSKI

Some appreciation of Egyptian attitudes regarding World War II and its protagonists can be obtained from the assessments of Egyptian public opinion found in the reports of British officials posted in Egypt. British evaluations of the mood of the Egyptian public during the war provide a partial, although indirect and tangential, indicator of wartime Egyptian sentiment. Maintaining control of Egypt was vital to the British war effort, especially in the early years of the war when North Africa was an active theater of combat. Accordingly, British officials in Egypt paid close attention to the state of Egyptian public opinion and how shifts in Egyptian sentiment could potentially influence the British position in Egypt and the fortunes of war.

This chapter examines a selected body of British Embassy reports, primarily those of British ambassador Sir Miles Lampson (from January 1943, Lord Killearn), regarding Egyptian attitudes toward the war. It concentrates on the years 1940–1942, when the threat and eventually the reality of Axis attack made the war a subject of vital importance to Egyptians. It pays less attention to the period from 1943 until 1945, when the threat of invasion had lifted and Egyptian attention turned to the postwar settlement.

There were certainly gaps in the information about Egyptian attitudes available to British officials, as well as questions as to the accuracy and reliability of the information that did make its way into British reports. Estimates of Egyptian public opinion found in British Embassy reports passed through several filters. First, it was a picture derived primarily from their contacts with the Egyptian establishment and officialdom. British officials maintained close personal connections with members of the Egyptian political and commercial elites, connections through which they assessed the views regarding the war that existed within Egypt's upper classes. The quality of information available to the British concerning popular attitudes was unquestionably less than that available for the country's elites. Nonetheless, through tapping the sources of information available to the British officials who still staffed positions in the Egyptian police and security services, and through periodic tours of the provinces undertaken by embassy officials for the purpose of sampling the mood outside Cairo, British officials accumulated and transmitted a steady flow of information concerning the state of Egyptian public opinion regarding the war.

The information concerning Egyptian developments provided to the British by pro-British Egyptians and officeholders (the main source of British information about domestic trends) was of course in part tailored to serve the interests of those informants. Accordingly, caution is necessary in weighing its reliability. But British diplomats were not unsophisticated babes in the woods who uncritically accepted the information passed on to them as gospel. Well aware of the partisan inclinations of their informants, they made a diligent effort to assess the validity and utility of information received. Although they may not always have been successful in their efforts to separate the wheat from the chaff, British reports were critical assessments that attempted to take into account misinformation generated by partisan concerns.

At the same time, the information that British officials received and reported home was inevitably refracted through the prism of British assumptions and prejudices about Egyptians. The extent to which the latter could color British assessments is indicated by the condescending if not racist tone of a 1941 commentary by Charles Bateman, an official with extensive service in Egypt, lamenting that mounting pro-Allied propaganda in Egypt was "an impossible job because Egyptians do not share our passionate will for victory and because there is no such thing as Egyptian courage. . . . At heart all Egyptians are defeatists in as much as they are ruled by fear."[1] Although not as blatantly prejudiced as Bateman, Sir Miles Lampson was a committed imperial proconsul who occasionally expressed a similarly supercilious attitude toward Egyptians and what he once termed "the timorous Egyptian mind."[2] The following account must be read with an awareness of British assumptions about and stereotyping of Egyptians and how these influenced their evaluations of wartime Egyptian opinion.

British Embassy reports concerning wartime Egyptian public opinion were selective in their content. Their primary focus was on dangerous trends and potential threats that might adversely affect the British position in Egypt and the successful pursuit of the war against the Axis. More favorable currents, such as Egyptian statements of support for the Allies or routine Egyptian cooperation with the Allied war effort, received passing notice but less extensive commentary and analysis.

The overwhelming concern with security issues and the relationship between Egyptian domestic conditions and the British war effort lent British Embassy reportage an alarmist quality. Obsessed with imperial security during wartime, and colored by their own prejudices about Egyptians, British reports may be biased toward the negative. Viewing everything through the prism of wartime security, Ambassador Lampson's commentaries in particular are drawn in black-and-white, with few shades of gray. Mirroring the fluctuating fortunes of war in the North African theater from 1940 to 1942, Lampson's reports swing from a mood of self-satisfied optimism about Egyptian conditions at moments of Allied military success to a mood of bleak pessimism when the fortunes of war favored the Axis. It is difficult to know the degree to which these frequent pessimistic British evaluations of Egyptian public opinion accurately reflect Egyptian conditions on the ground or are in part the consequence of British anxieties at a time of unparalleled national crisis. The views expressed by the British about the effect of adverse wartime developments on the state of Egyptian opinion in the crucial years of 1940–1942 may in part have been a product of their own preoccupation with British national survival.

Initial Egyptian Responses to the War, 1939–1940

In later 1939 and early 1940, the relatively calm period of the "phony war" following Nazi Germany's rapid conquest of Poland in September 1939 and prior to its Blitzkrieg in France and the Low Countries in May and June 1940, British evaluations assessed the Egyptian mood as basically pro-Allied. British frustration regarding the decision of the newly installed independent ministry headed by 'Ali Mahir not to declare war on Germany in September 1939 notwithstanding,[3] Lampson's reports at the beginning of the war emphasized that in other respects initial Egyptian cooperation with Great Britain's war-related demands had been "entirely correct and most helpful."[4] The ambassador was sanguine about public opinion: after meeting with a number of editors and proprietors of the Arabic press of Egypt in mid-September, Lampson's comforting conclusion was that "they are all solidly with us: and their papers could not be more satisfactory. One and all they take the line that this is not due solely to the Alliance but also largely because they realize that the rights are entirely on the Allied side."[5] In his November 1939 overview of the Egyptian scene during the first two months of the war, the ambassador's overall assessment was that "the feeling of the great majority of the Egyptian people was whole-heartedly in favour of the democratic Powers and anti-Nazi."[6] Without providing specifics, Lampson's review did assert that members of what he termed "the Turko-Egyptian 'aristocracy,'" as well as other "anti-British and pro-German elements" centered around the Egyptian Palace, were engaged in promoting "either pro-German propaganda or in equally undesirable defeatism." He went on to note, however, that up to late 1939, "the anti-British and pro-German intrigues of the Palace and its hangers-on still remain largely in the domain of talk and intention."[7]

A fuller appreciation of popular sentiment in the early months of the war comes from two reports based on tours of Upper and Lower Egypt by John Hamilton, assistant Oriental secretary. After visiting Upper Egypt in December 1939, Hamilton reported on "considerable nervousness displayed amongst all classes regarding the possibilities of the situation" upon the outbreak of the war. An initial fear of an Italian attack upon Egypt, rumors that the British would conscript an Egyptian labor corps for compulsory service as they had done in World War I, and low cotton prices all contributed to this initial mood of apprehension. When Italy remained neutral, any intention to raise a labor corps was officially denied, and cotton prices rose, public opinion "reverted to normal." Evaluating the impact of the new medium of radio, Hamilton reported that Egyptian State Radio was by far the most popular source, foreign stations being listened to only by "selective listeners." Of foreign stations, his sources cited still-neutral Italy's broadcasting as the most popular; in contrast, according to his informants, "German broadcasts are immediately switched off as being offensive rubbish." Overall, Hamilton found "a general confidence in eventual Allied victory" in Upper Egypt, but also "a feeling of respect for Germany's might" in educated circles. His conclusion combined a positive assessment of the current situation in Upper Egypt with caution that opinion could shift if the military situation took a different turn: "The situation in Upper Egypt would seem for the moment generally satisfactory, and, pending any serious developments in the Near East and Mediterranean, it is likely to remain so."[8]

Hamilton found a similar set of circumstances when he toured Lower Egypt in February–March 1940. As in Upper Egypt, he reported the prevailing attitude toward the war in Lower Egypt to be "satisfactory." In his view, Egyptians had "a genuine feeling of sympathy with the Allied cause and a realization of what happens to small countries who come under German sway. The treatment meted out to the Czechs and Poles has impressed the public with what might happen to themselves in like case." Hamilton's report cited conflicting estimates concerning the effectiveness of Axis propaganda in Lower Egypt by early 1940. "According to official informants, i.e., mudirs and consular agents, there is no very active German or Italian propaganda in the provinces at the present time, and independent inquiries failed to find any concrete evidence of such." Yet Hamilton's report also noted the existence of contradictory assessments: "This information is, I know, contrary to certain reports recently received at the Ministry of Interior." Hamilton went on to express concern that economic issues, specifically the rise in the cost of living already under way by early 1940 and worry over the disposal of Egypt's cotton crop in wartime, could produce internal instability and offer "a fertile field for enemy propaganda" in the future.[9]

Ambassador Lampson took a more alarmist view of the impact of Axis propaganda in the early months of the war than did his subordinate Hamilton. In April 1940, he stated that "reports, both secret and otherwise, indicate [the] spread of anti-British feeling and propaganda in Egypt and the Near East."[10] Lampson credited this anti-British trend both to economic grievances and to ongoing Arab concern over Palestine.[11] (In retrospect, Lampson's concern about the effectiveness of Axis propaganda in Egypt may have been exaggerated; a 1943 assessment of the Research Department of the Foreign Office concluded that wartime Axis propaganda efforts in Egypt had had, "on the whole, surprisingly little effect.")[12]

Lampson's reports on conditions in Egypt during the war paid considerable attention to economic matters and their impact upon public opinion. The potential economic impact of the war was a subject of major concern to Egyptians. Primary was apprehension concerning how the export of Egypt's vital cotton crop might be reduced by the war and its accompanying constraints upon international commerce. This concern prompted the British government in late 1939 to commit to pledge to purchase any shortfall in the export of Egypt's cotton crop.[13] This commitment notwithstanding, economic concerns perturbed the domestic political scene. In early 1940, the ambassador noted the beginning of both an ominous rise in the Egyptian cost of living and shortages in the availability of vital consumer goods due to the war.[14] In April the Wafdist opposition raised the issue of wartime constraints over cotton exports in parliament,[15] and in May Lampson was reporting that "supposed griev-ances [regarding wartime controls on cotton exports] are one of the main causes of the latest anti-British feeling in Egypt today."[16]

In May 1940, as the phony war approached its end, Ambassador Lamp-son's general view was that "the majority of the Egyptian people is still well-disposed towards us." Echoing Hamilton's reports, Lampson main-tained that "the provinces are politically apathetic, absorbed in purely material problems and at present irresponsive to attempts to stir up anti-British feeling." But the ambassador counseled his government that the current favorable situation could change: "It would be risky to count on an indefinite continuance of Egyptian goodwill. Behind the present ami-cable feelings there lurks always the fundamental anti-foreign bias in any country subjected to foreign occupation." As Lampson saw it, "The de-velopment of anti-British feeling in the Egypto-Arab world will depend in the main on the fortunes of the war. The success hitherto of Germany has contributed more than any German propaganda to the belief that the German military machine is too strong for us."[17] The prospect that war-induced economic strains and further demonstrations of German mili-tary prowess could combine to erode the initial pro-Allied attitude of the Egyptian public was a frequent theme in British assessments thereafter, as the war entered its more expansive and (for Egypt) dangerous phases.

Italy Enters the War, 1940

Egypt's relationship to the war took a dramatic turn in June 1940. Italy's formal entry into the war as an ally of Germany raised the prospect of an Italian invasion of Egypt, as well as the possibility of Italian air and naval attacks upon Egypt's population centers. Both conditions soon materi-alized; beginning in September 1940, Italian forces crossed the Libyan-Egyptian border and advanced into Egyptian territory as far as Sidi Bar-rani, while the second half of 1940 witnessed Italian air raids directed particularly at Alexandria and cities along the Suez Canal.

Italy's entry into the war had almost immediate political repercussions in Egypt. Ambassador Lampson was still resentful of the 'Ali Mahir gov-ernment's September 1939 decision not to enter the war as a formal bel-ligerent, suspecting Mahir of being engaged in seeking a secret arrange-ment with Italy,[18] and finding Mahir "systematically obstructive" in regard to meeting British demands regarding the internment of Italian nationals and the restriction of the publication of pro-Italian material in the press subsequent to Italy's entry into the war.[19] In late June 1940, he pressured King Faruq to dismiss the Mahir ministry. Mahir resigned on June 23; he was replaced by a pro-British ministry headed by Hasan Sabri.[20] Sabri remained prime minister for most of 1940; upon Sabri's sudden death on November 14, 1940, he was replaced by Husayn Sirri, who remained prime minister until February 1942.

A contributing factor to the British insistence on the dismissal of the 'Ali Mahir ministry from office in June 1940 was the fact that, upon Italy's entry into the war in that same month, Mahir took the position that Egypt, while continuing to honor its obligations of support to Great Britain as specified in the Anglo-Egyptian Treaty of Alliance of 1936, would become a formal belligerent only in case of direct Italian attack upon Egypt.[21] Italy's subsequent invasion of Egypt notwithstanding, the Sabri ministry maintained this stance of nonbelligerence that had been adopted by its predecessor. Nonetheless, when in office, it proved itself a compliant wartime ally of the British, removing officials suspected of pro-Italian inclinations and satisfying British demands regarding the surveillance or internment of Italian citizens resident in Egypt.[22] Upon his death in November 1940, Lampson privately referred to Sabri as "a very staunch friend of Great Britain."[23] Although maintaining this policy of formal nonbelligerence, a similarly cooperative stance marked the ministry of Husayn Sirri, a politician whom Lampson characterized as "consistently friendly and pro-British."[24]

The issue of cotton remained a central Egyptian concern for much of the war. To assuage domestic fears over the export of Egypt's main crop, in August 1940 the British government reached an agreement with the Egyptian government to purchase all of Egypt's 1940 cotton crop.[25] Ambassador Lampson's assessment was that the terms of the deal had been generally accepted in Egypt and had "afforded wide relief from anxiety and engendered [a] feeling of economic security for [the] immediate future, as well as [a] measure of real gratitude towards Great Britain."[26]

The later months of 1940 were when military hostilities for the first time seriously affected Egypt. The Italian invasion across the Libyan-Egyptian border in the fall, as well as the air attacks that accompanied it, are reported to have significantly and adversely affected Egyptian attitudes toward the war. The generally optimistic and pro-Allied mood identified in British assessments of late 1939 and early 1940 rapidly gave way to commentaries in which the dominant theme was Egyptian apprehension concerning the likely adverse consequences of the war for Egypt. In September, as Italian forces entered Egyptian territory, Lampson observed that the "Italian advance in Western Desert is now causing some alarm amongst Egyptian public."[27] Lampson's view in the fall of 1940 was that, despite recent calls for Egypt formally to enter the war on the side of the Allies by Sa'dist Party leaders Ahmad Mahir and Mahmud Fahmi al-Nuqrashi,[28] the Egyptian public "remains anxious to keep out of hostilities."[29] He attributed this to two factors. One was the disastrous military events of the spring and summer of 1940 (the fall of France and the Low Countries, along with the prospect of a German invasion of Great Britain), which he credited with having produced "the general belief that we [the British] would not be able to go on with the war." The other was a theme that was to reappear in British reports during the fraught years of 1940–1942, as Axis air attacks repeatedly struck Egyptian cities. This was the Egyptian public's "genuine fear of the destructive results for Egypt of Italian enmity." According to the ambassador, "This fear was shared by the majority of the Egyptian public." Commenting on "the disinclination of the great majority of the Egyptian public to commit themselves to hostilities with Italy as long as they remain doubtful of our ability to hold back the invading army," Lampson's view was that "the consequent demoralization of public opinion and of the army has become a serious factor in the internal situation at a moment when the military threat of Italy has become imminent."[30]

The Italian offensive into Egypt is reported to have fostered anti-British agitation. In early November, Lampson noted a recent "increase in [the] distribution of anti-British pamphlets."[31] More ominous to the British was the state of morale in the Egyptian army. Both the efficiency and the loyalty of the Egyptian army became a concern of the British authorities in Egypt in 1940. Already in June 1940, Lampson was citing reports regarding what he termed the "rot which was rapidly spreading through [the] Egyptian army as a result of [the Mahir ministry's] equivocal attitude towards Italy."[32] By October the ambassador perceived a "possibility that the Egyptian army, under Palace directive, will not fight if the Italians attack positions, such as Siwa, entrusted to Egyptian forces for defence, and may even be hostile to us in the event of a successful Italian advance."[33] Apprehension as to the morale and loyalty of the Egyptian military units stationed along the Libyan border led the British, from July 1940 onward, to force the withdrawal of Egyptian units from border areas and their replacement by Allied military units.[34] In early 1941, Lampson observed that "in Egyptian military circles there was some feeling of shame that the Egyptian army had taken no part in the victories [of late 1940] which had freed Egyptian soil from the invaders."[35] This cavalier British treatment of the Egyptian military turned out to be a self-fulfilling prophecy: resentment over the marginalization and humiliation of the Egyptian army in 1940 reinforced the anti-imperialist sentiments of younger officers and led some to attempt to organize plans for an anti-British military uprising.[36]

The cloud of British anxiety concerning Egyptian support for the Allied war effort lifted, if only partially, toward the close of 1940. In December the tide of battle in the Western Desert turned, as the British army defeated Italian forces and advanced to the Libyan-Egyptian border; by February they moved into Libya, destroying the Italian Tenth Army and occupying all of Cyrenaica. This shattering of Italy's offensive capability was seen by the British as having transformed the mood in Egypt, producing "jubilation among [the] Egyptian public" by relieving Egyptians of their "fears of invasion" and of the prospect of further Italian air bombardment.[37]

In his review of the Egyptian scene in the year 1940, Ambassador Lampson credited the combination of British military successes against the Italians in the Western Desert and the successful resistance of the Greeks to Italian invasion in late 1940 with having "shattered any illusions regarding Italian power and changed the whole atmosphere of fear which had so long prevailed in Egypt."[38] Yet the military situation in North Africa was not totally favorable to the Allies at the close of 1940: in another report of the same date, Lampson cautioned that the recent appearance of the German air force in the Mediterranean theater "has given of late the anti-British and defeatist elements the opportunity to exploit the fears of an easily frightened people that our victories with the Italians were relatively unimportant, and that we should soon find how different it was to deal with a forthcoming German offensive."[39] The British ambassador was largely satisfied with the situation in Egypt as 1940 ended: "The repulse of the German attacks on Great Britain and the resounding British victories in the Western Desert had restored belief in the power of British arms, and had for the time being done much to remove the acute apprehension which had been evident amongst all classes regarding an enemy invasion of Egypt."[40]

A counterpoint to these British assessments of 1940 comes from the occasional comments on the Egyptian public mood made by members of the American Legation. During the crisis of June 1940, American chargé Raymond Hare emphasized particularly the popular desire to avoid being dragged into the war: "There is no doubt that public opinion here is still strongly against the entry of Egypt into the war."[41] American minister to Egypt Hamilton Fish said much the same in August: "The predominant feeling in Egypt is still against involvement in hostilities."[42] Like his British counterparts, Fish also commented on a general Egyptian disposition toward the Allied rather than the Axis cause. As he put it in September, "Generally speaking public opinion is opposed to becoming involved in the war but at the same time there is no doubt that the vast majority of the population dislike the Italians intensely and hope for a British victory."[43]

Axis Offensives and Internal Disruptions, 1941

British success against the Italians in late 1940, and the mood of relief that it is credited with having produced in Egypt, proved short-lived. Early 1941 witnessed major reverses for the Allies in the Mediterranean theater. In North Africa, the arrival of German forces under General Erwin Rommel first stabilized the collapsing Italian war effort and by the spring resulted in the second advance of Axis forces into western Egypt. North of the Middle Sea, the Balkans was a disaster area for the Allies. German forces conquered Yugoslavia and Greece in the spring of 1941, in the process expelling a British expeditionary force sent to assist the Greeks. This was followed by the German conquest of Crete as a base for further offensive operations in the eastern Mediterranean. In the Middle East proper, in April anti-British Iraqi nationalists seized control in Baghdad, sought German assistance, and by May were engaged in active if ultimately unsuccessful hostilities with British military forces.

German advances in the Mediterranean and the Middle East were reported to have had immediate repercussions in Egypt. Pessimism was the buzzword in British reports about the popular mood in Egypt in the spring of 1941. By early April 1941, the British credited Rommel's counterattack in the Western Desert with having "thoroughly frightened the Egyptian public which has been quick to repeat the old refrain that the British can deal with Italians but not with Germans."[44] A week later, another report cited "more pessimism than ever before" in Egypt as a result of the successful Axis advance.[45] Ambassador Lampson's evaluation of the Egyptian mood at the end of April 1941 was a bleak one: "The effect of our reverses in Libya and the Balkans has been profound. . . . The Egyptian public is now fundamentally pessimistic regarding the outcome of the war. The general feeling is that, while we are able to repel the Italians from the soil of Egypt, we shall be unable to deal with the Germans in a similar way."[46] The loss of Crete as a result of German airborne assault was credited with generating "a profound defeatist impression amongst Egyptian public which is inclined to regard this German overseas success as [a] serious blow to the hitherto unquestioned legend of British sea power."[47] Air raids on Alexandria that disrupted economic activity and produced a refugee flight from the city further eroded Egyptian faith in the British ability to defend Egypt from Axis attack.[48]

The Axis successes of early 1941 encouraged domestic opposition to the British position in Egypt. In mid-March, one dispatch cautioned that the prospect of a new Axis offensive in the Western Desert was likely to be "used by mischief makers to influence the public in a defeatist and anti-British sense."[49] This soon materialized: by late April, the embassy was reporting that "fifth column activities are on the increase," as a wave of anti-British pamphlets began to appear in Egyptian cities.[50] The military clash between Iraqi nationalists and British forces in May 1941 added fuel to the anti-British mood: a report of late May stated that "the Iraqi rebellion is being increasingly exploited by anti-British agitators."[51] According to Lampson, a "rain of anti-British pamphlets continued undiminished" through May 1941; it included pamphlets attributed to Ahmad Husayn of Young Egypt that called on Egyptians to obstruct British defense measures,[52] while others also credited to Husayn "calling for revolution" were found posted at Egyptian tramway stops.[53] Some pamphlets seized by the Egyptian security services reportedly advocated the assassination of British officials and pro-British Egyptian politicians.[54]

This surge in anti-British agitation in early 1941 produced a British-encouraged crackdown on suspected anti-British elements by the ministry of Husayn Sirri. As a preventive measure, early in the year Hasan al-Banna of the Muslim Brotherhood, an employee of the Ministry of Education, was posted from Cairo to the more remote locale of Qina in Upper Egypt.[55] In April 'Ali Mahir, the presumed hub of anti-British agitation, was confined to his country estate, with "all political contacts cut off."[56] The famous attempt of former chief of staff of the Egyptian Army General 'Aziz 'Ali al-Misri to flee Egypt by air, either to go to Iraq to participate in the nationalist uprising there or to join Rommel's forces (accounts differ), failed when his aircraft malfunctioned and crashed; Misri was apprehended in early June.[57] Drastic action was taken against Young Egypt, the organization believed to be behind much of the anti-British pamphleteering. In May the organization was banned and its newspaper suspended. Although Ahmad Husayn himself fled and succeeded in evading arrest until July, by mid-June 1941 the bulk of the membership of

Young Egypt was reported to be either arrested or under "strict supervision" by the authorities.[58] Overall, Ambassador Lampson found the Sirri ministry's efforts to prevent anti-British activity effective: "Recent repressive measures of the Government against agitators have had good effect and some of the most prominent fifth columnists are at present keeping their mouths shut."[59] This repression of dissent by a pro-British Egyptian government worked: although there may have been an attempt by some anti-British politicians, notably 'Aziz 'Ali al-Misri in tandem with vehemently nationalist civilian movements such as Young Egypt, to organize an anti-British uprising in Egypt similar to that under way in Iraq in the spring of 1941, anti-British activism in Egypt in 1941 never moved from the stage of clandestine preparation to positive action.[60]

Evaluations of the Egyptian scene by the American Legation in early 1941 ran parallel to those of the British Embassy. Stating that "fifth column and general subversive activities . . . have increased noticeably of late," America's minister Alexander Kirk also noted the growth in anti-British agitation that accompanied Axis advances in the spring of 1941. Kirk attributed part of the cause to "the considerable effect of radio broadcasts in Arabic from Bari and Berlin, particularly the latter." But the American diplomat also emphasized the limits of anti-British agitation in the first half of 1941: "There is little evidence of the organization of such activity on an important scale. . . . [T]he situation here is not regarded as critical for the moment."[61]

By mid-1941 the fortunes of war began to improve for the Allies. Iraq's anti-British rebellion was crushed in May, and the successful British and Free French invasion of Syria and Lebanon in June was credited with producing "satisfaction and relief" in Egypt and with having been greeted with "almost universal approval" by the Egyptian public.[62] Paradoxically, the German invasion of the Soviet Union in late June was also seen as having a positive effect in Egypt. Viewing wartime events through an Egyptian prism, the Egyptian response to the news of the opening of a new and massive theater of war in Eastern Europe focused primarily on its probable implications for Egypt: "The entry of Russia into the war has been welcomed by the Egyptians, who think that it will at any rate postpone a German attack on Egypt."[63] Regardless of the sweeping German victories in the early weeks of their Russian campaign, in Egypt "public opinion continues to be buoyed up by the hope that Russia will distract Germany from an immediate offensive against Egypt. Egyptian sentiment is anti-Russian but the hope is freely expressed that Russians and Germans may devour one another on a large scale."[64] Nonetheless,

Germany's massive military conquests of 1940–1941, culminating in its occupation of much of Eastern Europe, served to buttress the Egyptian perception of German military superiority: although Germany's new preoccupation with the conquest of the Soviet Union assuaged Egyptian fear of an immediate Axis invasion of Egypt, nonetheless "the majority of Egyptians still remain convinced of German invincibility." [65]

The clash of arms on the war's numerous battlefronts was not the only concern of the Egyptian public in the tense year of 1941. In the summer of 1941, Axis air raids on Alexandria and the canal cities resulted in loss of life, in a refugee flow, and in producing significant economic disruption.[66] The political result was public agitation, including calls in parliament, for the evacuation of British military forces from Cairo and for the Egyptian government to declare Cairo an open city in order to avert similar attacks upon the Egyptian capital.[67] According to an American report, when Prime Minister Sirri raised the subject with Ambassador Lampson in September 1941, Lampson vetoed any effort on the part of the Egyptian government to declare Cairo an open city.[68] The American minister also noted the censorship's efforts to discourage the press from sensationalist reporting of destruction due to Axis air attacks.[69]

The Mediterranean theater stabilized in mid-1941, by which time the Axis advance in the Western Desert had been checked by the British, British forces had defeated the Iraqi nationalists and reasserted British control of Iraq, and the British and Free French invasion had brought Syria and Lebanon under Allied control. The opening of a successful British offensive against Rommel's forces in November 1941 was credited with being "acclaimed with considerable relief" by the Egyptian public. According to Lampson, "The fear of invasion had not yet been entirely removed by the end of the year, but our success in Cyrenaica produced a much more favourable attitude towards us." At the end of 1941, Pearl Harbor, the entry of the United States into the war, and the expansion of the war to global dimensions reportedly had only a marginal impact in Egypt: according to Lampson, "Few Egyptians take account of events outside the Middle East, and public reactions were limited to fears that the Far Eastern development would prolong the war and affect Egypt's essential supplies." [70]

By late 1941, the hostilities that had raged across the Mediterranean and North Africa since mid-1940 were having severe economic repercussions in Egypt. In contrast to the previous year, the terms of the British government's agreement to buy the 1941 Egyptian cotton crop were reported to have been negatively received, becoming a subject of Wafdist criticism in the Egyptian Parliament.[71] More fundamental issues were the continuing rise in the cost of living and shortages in the availability of vital necessities due to the wartime constriction of imports from abroad. In September 1941, the British prodded the Egyptian government for legislation reducing the acreage allotted to the cultivation of cotton in order to free agricultural land for the production of food crops. A measure to this effect was eventually enacted by the Egyptian Parliament, but nonetheless generated resentment against Great Britain among cotton cultivators.[72] The shortage in food supplies, a problem that was reinforced by hoarding on the part of speculators, was only partially resolved by official limitations on cotton acreage and an increase in that allotted to cereals. The rising cost of living, a burden that had not been accompanied by a concomitant increase in wages and had been left unaddressed by successive Egyptian governments, in turn produced labor agitation and a wave of strikes; in response wage increases that only partially alleviated the problem were mandated by the Egyptian government. Ambassador Lampson emphasized that many of these economic problems were popularly attributed to Great Britain's predominant position and wartime demands. In specific terms, "the shortage of foodstuffs is wrongfully attributed to purchases by British troops"; more generally, "the cotton issue, the high cost of living, the food shortage provide excellent grievances to exploit against us." These economic problems, along with Axis air raids on Alexandria, the Canal Zone, and eventually the environs of Cairo added to the popular perception that Egyptian support for the British war effort was resulting in a host of calamities for Egypt. Together, all served as fertile soil for anti-British agitation: "As the hardships of the people increase through growing economic difficulties and more intensive air raids, so will the opportunities increase for enemy exploitation of popular feeling against us."[73] In Lampson's opinion, Egypt's economic problems in 1941 "undoubtedly contributed very largely to the unsatisfactory attitude of the country towards Great Britain during the last quarter of the year."[74]

The Year 1942: February 4, the Wafd, and al-'Alamayn

Two events of 1942 — one political, the other military — were crucial for the evolution of Egyptian internal politics and the military course of the war in North Africa. The political event occurred on February 4, 1942, when British authorities in Egypt used the threat of force and imminent abdication to compel a reluctant King Faruq to install a Wafdist ministry headed by his nemesis, Mustafa al-Nahhas.[75] Nahhas and the Wafd, sub-stantially anti-Fascist in outlook and by the early 1940s willing to align with Great Britain in order to regain office, governed Egypt for most of the remainder of the war (February 1942–October 1944). Beyond its in-tended purpose of installing a stronger government that would cooperate effectively with the Allied war effort, the incident of February 4, 1942, left an indelible mark on Egyptian politics. Neither the Wafd, thereafter viewed by many Egyptians as having lost its essential nationalist character because of its willingness to collaborate with the British occupier in order to attain high office, nor the monarchy, stained by its inability to stand up against the same occupier, recovered from the loss of legitimacy suffered by both as a result of the incident of February 4.

The military event was the culmination of the clash of arms between the Axis and Allied forces in Egypt's Western Desert at the battle of al-'Alamayn. The year 1942 witnessed dramatic swings of fortune in the desert war. In the first half of 1942, Rommel's forces broke the British de-fensive line in Libya and by June had stormed across the Egyptian border to within sixty miles of Alexandria. A successful Axis invasion of the Nile Valley was a distinct possibility by mid-1942. The front line stabilized in the summer, as the arrival of reinforcements and new commanders (Alex-ander and Montgomery) reinvigorated the Allied cause. The military situation was transformed in September–October 1942 when the British Eighth Army, now superior in both manpower and matériel to Rommel's overstretched forces, first checked the last Axis offensive at 'Alam al-Halfa and subsequently defeated Rommel's now depleted forces at al-'Alamayn. By January 1943, Allied forces had advanced to Tripoli; by May the Axis had been totally expelled from North Africa. The Axis threat of an in-vasion of Egypt was definitively repulsed in late 1942.

The first half of 1942 was a particularly ominous time for the Allied cause in North Africa. According to Lampson's review of early 1942, Axis advances in Libya in January "came as a great shock to the Egyptian pub-lic, which, in the first panic, already saw the Germans successfully invading Egypt." The British setback in Libya "has greatly discouraged even our friends, who are beginning to accept the claim of our enemies that, while we can deal with the Italians, we cannot stand up to the German military machine."[76] Egyptian apprehension concerning Axis invasion accelerated when German forces mounted their major offensive into Egypt in the spring of the year. By July Lampson reported that the Axis advance into Egyptian territory had "naturally given the country a thorough fright."[77]

German advances at the beginning of 1942 combined with accumu-

lating economic tensions to produce manifestations of anti-British sentiment and activism. "Our military setbacks during the month of January
gave great encouragement to the anti-British elements in their campaign
against a pro-British Prime Minister," Lampson later observed. Noting
that "as on previous occasions, enemy military advances synchronized
with internal agitation," Lampson cited increased domestic opposition to
the ministry of Husayn Sirri in parliament, unrest and protests by Azhar-
ites and other students, and eventually street demonstrations in which
cries of "Long live Rommel!" were heard.[78] It was the combined popular weakness of the Sirri ministry vis-à-vis these public manifestations of
anti-British sentiment that in early February 1942 prompted the British
to compel King Faruq to install a more popularly based and pro-British
Wafdist ministry in office.

Anti-British or pro-Axis activity (or both) within Egypt thereafter
does not seem to have been as extensive in 1942 as it had been during German advances in early 1941. This was in large part due to the new Wafdist
government remaining a loyal ally of their British sponsors and its ability
to take vigorous action to counter anti-Allied activism. In March 1942,
Lampson reported that "the attitude of the new Government has been
excellent. It has put a stop to practically all open anti-British agitation.
Manifestations have ceased, and even anti-British pamphlets have become
rarer."[79] In a statement before the newly elected Chamber of Deputies in
April 1942, Nahhas coupled a firm resolution to "spare Egypt the horrors of war" with a pledge to remain faithful to Egypt's existing alliance
with Great Britain and a promise not to tolerate "any action by any Egyptian or foreigner of a nature to endanger in any way the military security
of our Ally or to give cause for any anxiety to those now fighting for the
very existence of democracy and freedom."[80] The same pro-Allied commitment was made in the Speech from the Throne delivered before parliament in April.[81]

The Wafdist ministry maintained a pro-British stance throughout the
crisis months of mid-1942. The major Axis advance into Egyptian territory in the spring generated an increase in the clandestine distribution
of anti-British propaganda within Egypt. "There have been a considerable number of anti-British pamphlets distributed, some of obvious enemy
authorship and others composed by 'Young Egyptians,'" Lampson reported in July 1942.[82] Nonetheless, the ambassador also emphasized that
the new Wafdist ministry had been "most co-operative" in maintaining
internal stability in the face of the menacing Axis advance.[83] Nahhas him-

self told Lampson that the government had made some three hundred arrests of suspected anti-British individuals and closed the Royal Automobile Club, a center of pro-German sentiment; eighty-four additional actions included dissolving the palace-linked special police, interning "high-placed fifth columnists" including 'Ali Mahir, and the "wholesale arrests of lesser undesirables." [84] The maintenance of internal stability was assisted by a partial rapprochement between the new Wafdist ministry and the Society of the Muslim Brothers in 1942; "by a mixture of bribery and threats," Nahhas was able to obtain "the professed adherence of this society, and has persuaded it to disown any anti-British intent." [85] Lampson's assessments of mid-1942 continued to report an overall situation of "calm," thanks in good part to the Wafdist administration, which in his view had remained "as staunch as ever." [86] In the fall, the ambassador credited Egypt's stability in the face of the Axis threat in mid-1942 primarily to the pro-Allied policy of the Wafdist government: "Largely as the result of [Nahhas's] actions and attitude during that critical period the country remained completely quiet and no complications were created for us while our army was stemming the enemy army almost on the threshold of cultivated Egypt." [87]

Reminiscent of Benjamin Franklin's maxim to the effect that the threat of hanging in the morning tends to concentrate the mind, the British ambassador speculated that the "appearance of the enemy at the doors of Egypt has caused a very general realization of the unpleasantness of an Axis occupation, even amongst elements hitherto notoriously anti-British. Result has been a considerable turn of feeling in our favour." In addition to Nahhas's pro-Allied public declarations, similar statements came from non-Wafdist politicians. The Sad'ist Ahmad Mahir, faithful to his pro-Allied track record throughout the war, publicly supported the measures of internal security taken by his rival, Nahhas; other leading opponents of the Wafd such as Muhammad Husayn Haykal of the Liberals and Isma'il Sidqi, the latter previously a leading advocate of Egyptian neutrality, also made statements supporting the Wafdist ministry's pro-Allied stance in early 1942. Lampson's judgment was that Nahhas "could hardly have carried out this [pro-Allied] policy had not the general feeling of the country at the time been favourable." In Lampson's view, both ideology and self-interest lay behind Nahhas's vigorous support of the Allied cause in 1942: "It is obvious that his attitude was not dictated purely by love of us. The fact is that he and the Wafdist leaders realized that their fate was more or less bound up with us. As champions of the democratic idea in Egypt they could not hope for any future with the Germans in Egypt and King Farouk no longer restrained by us. The Wafd was therefore forced to gamble on our victory." [88]

A recurrent concern of the British in the wake of the incident of February 4, 1942, was uncertainty regarding the reliability of the Egyptian military. The national humiliation of February 4 had immediate effects in military circles. In the wake of the episode, unnamed junior officers reportedly attempted to hold a public demonstration of loyalty to the king and a protest at the British Embassy, but were dissuaded from such actions by their seniors. [89] As the British ambassador summarized the effects of February 4 in his annual report on 1942, Egypt's army officers were "very sore" over the king's humiliation by the British; "indiscipline and disloyalty" had surfaced in the wake of the incident. [90] In August 1942, Lampson reported a meeting with Prime Minister Nahhas in which the latter cited "various signs of danger of disloyalty in [the] Egyptian army"; Nahhas referred specifically to the recent arrest of two German agents who had penetrated Egypt to establish contact with the Egyptian military (Operation Condor), [91] to the attempted flight of two air force officers to the German lines, [92] and to "reports of a secret society amongst the army officers, which he believed to be true." [93] Late in 1942, Lampson commented on "a feeling of instability in the army owing to the struggle between the King and the Wafd"; [94] other reports cited a dispute between the palace and the ministry over the disciplining of officers who had penned "insubordinate and libellous letters dealing with political matters, copies of which they broadcast." [95] The postrevolutionary narrative that traces the roots of military discontent and clandestine protorevolutionary organization to the war years finds partial confirmation in the contemporary British record.

The turning point in the military situation in the Western Desert came in the second half of 1942. In the British view, by July 1942 the stabilization of the front line had "caused some return of public confidence." [96] The repulse of the final Axis offensive at 'Alam al-Halfa in September "greatly encouraged the Egyptian public, although the fact that we have not yet driven them back to their original line somewhat moderated the optimism. Public still remain dominated by [the] natural feeling that the enemy at Alamein are too close for safety." [97] The Allied victory at al-'Alamayn and the beginning of the rapid Axis retreat from Egyptian territory by November 1942 in turn led to "immense general relief and joy in practically all sections of the population and all parties," [98] and the victorious entry of the Eighth Army into Tripoli in January 1943 was evaluated as having "caused general delight as definitely relieving Egypt of [the] invasion bugbear" that had loomed over Egypt from 1940 through 1942.[99]

As the military tide turned in late 1942, Lampson continued to credit the Wafdist ministry of Mustafa al-Nahhas with a significant role in maintaining Egyptian stability: "The attitude of the Government towards ourselves has been on the whole very satisfactory. Nahas Pasha has not hesitated repeatedly to make public declarations in favour of the Allied cause, even before our victories made it safe to take up such an attitude. He has hitherto, in spite of some weaknesses, done more or less what we desired regarding internees and censorship. Fifth columnism has now become a negligible quantity in view of our victories, but great credit must be given to Nahas Pasha for his resolute action against manifestations of this nature."[100] In his retrospective annual report on the Egyptian scene in 1942, Lampson (now Lord Killearn) reiterated the Wafdist ministry's "unequivocal attitude of cooperation with Great Britain" throughout 1942. The Wafd's "openly declared sympathy with our cause put a stop to nearly all overt anti-British agitation; demonstrations ceased and even anti-British pamphlets became rare."[101]

Whereas British evaluations regarding the pro-British and anti-Axis stance adopted by the Wafd once it assumed power were positive, the same was not the case with the Wafd's economic performance. The British found the Wafdist ministry ineffective in addressing or resolving Egypt's war-induced economic stresses. Efforts of the new ministry to alleviate the problem of food supplies by lifting restrictions notwithstanding, the hoarding of wheat by speculators and resultant price rises continued under the Wafd.[102] The ambassador's report at the end of 1942 was critical of the economic record of the Wafdist ministry: "Previous governments showed themselves incapable of handling supplies, and the Wafd Government has proved no better in this respect at a time when the problem has become one of greater urgency and importance to the life of the people. . . . The continuous rise in the cost of living is another problem with which the Wafd Government has so far failed to cope." Government-set prices for cotton and rice "were fixed too high in order to please the agricultural proprietors and without regard for the consumer," and the government had "failed to take effective measures by way of increased taxation, subsidizing essential commodities, &c., to check inflation."[103]

The cost of living continued to climb throughout the tenure of the Wafdist ministry. In November 1943, the ambassador lamented that "it is a pity that the Wafdist Government has not been able to deal more effectively with the questions of supplies and the rise in the cost of living.

This is one of the weakest points in its armour. The phenomenal increase in the cost of living is weighing heavily on the consuming masses, and causing great discontent against the Government, which is accused of inefficiency and corruption in dealing with this problem."[104] His review of Egypt in the year 1943 noted the popular repercussions of the Wafd's economic shortcomings: "In respect of supplies and the cost of living, however, the Government's record is distinctly weak; its failure to check the continued rise of everyday commodity prices or to ensure equitable distribution of locally produced goods inspired accusations of corruption and inefficiency in dealing with these problems."[105]

Postwar Aspirations, 1943–1944

The critical years of the war for Egypt were 1940–1942. In 1943–1944, as the battlefield receded from Egypt, British reports on the attitude of the Egyptian public concerning the war become much thinner. Intermittent British assessments of the Egyptian public mood concerning the course of the European war in 1943–1944 indicate the war becoming a diminishing concern for Egyptians once it no longer posed a direct danger for Egypt. Whereas the fall of Tunisia and the complete expulsion of the Axis from North Africa in May 1943 were reported to have been "hailed with universal enthusiasm" in Egypt,[106] the ambassador's almost offhand comment to the effect that the Allied invasion of Sicily in July 1943 had "reawakened the flagging interest of the public in the general war situation" indicates diminishing Egyptian interest in the course of the global struggle after the Axis ouster from North Africa.[107] By late 1944, British assessments of the Egyptian press noted only passing attention being given to events in the now distant European and Pacific theaters of war.[108]

What embassy assessments after 1942 emphasize is a corresponding growth in Egyptian attention to the postwar settlement and how it might affect Egypt. At the same time as reporting Egyptian relief over the Axis defeat in North Africa, Lampson was noting that "Egyptian attention is now turning from war to post-war settlements, particularly as regards Egypt herself and the Arab countries."[109] He expanded on this theme in an overview of the Egyptian scene in early 1943: "As the tide of war recedes from Egypt and runs against the Axis Powers, politically minded Egypt is turning its attention from the war itself to the problems of postwar conditions and settlements."[110] Such attention increased over time; press interviews of leading politicians concerning their views on Egypt's postwar goals were a feature of Egyptian journalism as the war moved toward its close.[111] By mid-1944 the ambassador was reporting that "recently the press had been full of articles detailing Egypt's national requirements of us in unambiguous terms. . . . In the press the Government has frequently been urged not to let the opportunity slip and to make clear its nationalist program before the end of the war."[112]

Embassy reports in 1943–1944 gave considerable attention to how Egyptian commentators now stressed Egypt's role in facilitating the Allied victory in order to buttress Egypt's postwar claims. In September 1943, *al-Ahram* published a special issue to commemorate the fourth anniversary of the start of the war. To demonstrate Egypt's contribution to the Allied war effort consequently to establish its claims to the consideration of its national aspirations after the war, the newspaper cited a recent speech by Winston Churchill praising Egypt's wartime assistance to the Allied war effort, noted the efforts of the various ministries that had maintained internal security and provided logistical assistance to the British, and extolled King Faruq, who was described (with no apparent sense of irony) as "the first and principal factor in keeping Egypt free from the horrors of war."[113] In the same month, *al-Ithnayn wa al-Dunya* similarly cited statements by Churchill, Roosevelt, and Allied generals as evidence that "Egypt had been doing her duty as an honourable ally and a faithful friend. So far from stabbing her allies in the back she had stayed by them in their darkest hours."[114]

The same points featured prominently in statements by Egyptian political leaders in 1943–1944. Prime Minister Nahhas's address to the major Wafdist conference held in November 1943 made a point of expounding on "the services which Egypt had rendered to Great Britain in loyal execution of the [Anglo-Egyptian] alliance, a loyalty which had been frequently appreciated by the British Ally."[115] The Speech from the Throne in the same month emphasized "the fidelity of Egypt to its treaty obligations, particularly those towards Great Britain, and on the profound devotion of Egypt to the principles of democracy and liberty."[116] Prime Minister Nahhas stated the case again upon the eighth anniversary of the conclusion of the Anglo-Egyptian Treaty of Alliance in August 1944, shortly before his abrupt dismissal from office: "Democratic Egypt had taken her place beside her great ally and had scrupulously kept her engagements and fulfilled all the obligations imposed by the treaty. . . . It was his duty as leader of the Egyptian people and Prime Minister to record the signal services rendered by Egypt which had remained faithful and loyal to the cause of liberty and democracy."[117] The trope that Egypt had made a significant contribution to the Allied war effort and as a consequence deserved a sympathetic hearing for its national aspirations became a staple of Egyptian commentary as the war wound toward its end.

Conclusion

Several conclusions emerge from these British wartime assessments of Egyptian opinion. It is perhaps banal to note that, as presented in British reports, Egyptian opinion about the war was shaped primarily by how Egyptians perceived the course of events possibly influencing Egypt. Central in this respect were considerations of whether the ravages of war would extend to Egypt, as they intermittently did in 1940-1941, when Axis armies crossed into Egyptian territory and when the country's population centers came under Axis air bombardment, and more intensely in 1942 when Rommel's forces threatened to conquer the Nile Valley. In the later years of the war, by which time the Allies had been victorious in the Mediterranean, the focus of elite opinion became how Egypt might benefit from the new world order that it was assumed would emerge after the war. As presented in British assessments, Egyptian attitudes toward the war were primarily shaped by considerations of the war's consequences for Egypt.

A second conclusion from the British record concerns the volatility of Egyptian views regarding the war. Although British evaluations periodically note an underlying affinity for the democratic cause rather than for the Fascist powers, they also emphasize that the victory of the democracies was not taken for granted by Egyptians. Especially from 1940 through 1942, the British found the Egyptian mood swinging as wildly as did the fluctuating fortunes of war in the Mediterranean theater. Axis advances from Libya into Egypt were credited by the British with producing a mood of "defeatism" that was often accompanied by surges in anti-British propaganda and activism by Egyptian opponents of the British occupation; correspondingly, Allied counterattacks and advances elsewhere were seen as leading to relief that Egypt had been saved from the ravages of war and a decline in anti-British propaganda and activism. As noted previously, here it is difficult to disentangle the true state of Egyptian public opinion from the obsessions of British observers of the Egyptian scene; the vacillation in Egyptian public opinion from a mood of optimism to one of pessimism reported by British observers may in part have been due to their own wartime anxieties. Nonetheless, at least as seen by the British, no teleological Egyptian assumption of faith in the eventual victory of the Allies existed throughout the conflict. At critical points in the war, Egyptian opinion as seen by the British was dominated by fear of Allied defeat and what that might portend for Egypt.

A corollary to the above was the hearty respect for the power of German arms reportedly possessed by the Egyptian public in the early years of the war. Germany's sweeping European victories in 1940–1941 appear to have produced a widespread belief of the superiority of the German military to the forces of the Western democracies. (Save for a short period in mid-1940, until the British defeat of the first Italian advance from Libya into Egypt, the same view was not held in respect to the Italian military.) It was not until late 1942 and early 1943, with the British victory at al-ʿAlamayn and the subsequent advance of Allied armies across North Africa, that Egyptian belief in German military superiority faded. The assumption of German military prowess colored Egyptian views of the course of military events from 1940 through 1942, reportedly feeding the swing toward anxiety that set in with every apparently inexorable German advance.

What do contemporary British reports add to our knowledge of Egypt during World War II? The frequent references to surges in anti-British, pro-Axis sentiment and activism at moments when Axis forces were advancing confirm the presence of anti-imperialist sentiment in the country and of the willingness of nationalist Egyptians to attempt to use the circumstances of war in the attempt to liberate Egypt from British occupation. At the same time, the fact that pro-British administrations in Egypt, once installed in office from mid-1940 onward, were able to control anti-Allied propaganda and activism and to prevent any substantial subversion of the Allied war effort would seem to indicate that the breadth of anti-British sentiment was more restricted than is sometimes assumed. Moreover, the references to an underlying sympathy with the Allied as opposed to the Axis cause, to Egyptian relief at Axis setbacks, and to fears of what Axis invasion and occupation might portend for Egypt undercut any essentialist image of Egyptians being fundamentally sympathetic toward the Axis powers. Although security and subversion rather than the ideological inclinations of Egyptians were the primary concerns of British reporting on the Egyptian mood, their assessments give no reason to presume sweeping Egyptian ideological sympathy with the Axis during World War II.

The material presented also refines our knowledge in several respects. Although the references to the subject are intermittent, British reports do not bear out the assumption that Axis radio propaganda had a major effect on Egyptian public opinion in the crucial years of the war. The material examined confirms the presence of clandestine wartime discontent and anti-British organization within the Egyptian military. In regard to 1942, it shows the degree to which the previously anti-imperialist Wafd had made common cause with the British and acted vigorously to support the Allied war effort by maintaining internal order in the face of impending Axis invasion.

British reports also suggest that the crucial period in terms of Egypt's domestic stability may have been the spring of 1941 rather than the summer of 1942. It was in the early months of 1941, when Axis advances in North Africa, the Balkans, and Mediterranean plus the presence of regimes partially inclined to the Axis in Iraq and Syria-Lebanon posed the threat of hostile envelopment of Egypt, that domestic opposition to the British position in Egypt may have been strongest. It was then that both military and civilian elements, still at liberty, attempted to organize an anti-British uprising similar to that being mounted in Iraq and were repressed by the security services. By mid-1942, when Rommel's forces stood at the edge of the Nile Valley, some of the anti-British elements that had been apprehended in 1941 were no longer in circulation, a stronger Wafdist government stood firmly in support of the British, and the potentially dangerous movement of the Muslim Brothers had reached agreement with the Wafd and remained politically quiescent. Thus, Egypt's moment of potential internal crisis may have been in 1941 rather than 1942. At the same time, the assessments offered in British reports, as well as those found in the more fragmentary American diplomatic material, indicate that the threat of internal subversion never reached critical proportions. Even in 1940–1942, the most fraught years of the war, Egypt does not appear to have been a seething cauldron of discontent whose populace would have welcomed Axis invasion with open arms.

The Rise of Homemade Egyptian Communism: A Response to the Challenge Posed by Fascism and Nazism?

RAMI GINAT

From the late 1930s, links between international communism and the last remnants of the Egyptian communist movement had hardly existed. This state of affairs would affect the course of the latter's development. At the same time, the existing labyrinth of Anglo-Egyptian relations and the growing national and social discontent led to the appearance of new radical platforms—both leftist and rightist in their content.

Whereas right-wing orientations were formulated and led by educated Egyptians, notably Muslims, left-wing trends were a combination of both veteran communists (members of the communist movement of the 1920s and 1930s) and, more noticeably, new ideological frameworks founded by foreigners, *mutamassirun* (foreign nationals, who were permanent residents) and Egyptians, many of them of Jewish origin.

Since the early 1930s, Egypt had witnessed a growing social and political discontent, deriving from disappointment of the immersed parliamentary system, the economic crisis, and the political repression of the Ismai'l Sidqi's dictatorial regime (1930–1933). This development manifested itself in the rise of street politics and the appearance of young, educated middle-class groups, known as the *effendiyya*. The latter perceived itself as a vanguard force acting in order to rescue Egypt from social and economic distress with the aim to lead the country toward political independence. Parts of the *effendiyya* integrated within the old political establishment, mainly within the Wafd, whereas other groups were active within new extraparliamentary radical political frameworks, such as "Young Egypt" (Misr al-Fatat) and the Muslim Brothers.[1] The gradual structural change within the Wafd's socioeconomic composition in the 1930s manifested itself in pressure from within to introduce social reforms. The Wafd's left-wing faction became more conspicuous, yet the party was still dominated by the old-guard right wing.

In the international arena, the tightening alliance between Italy and Germany, two rising European powers, was a source of concern worldwide. Moreover, the occupation of Ethiopia by Fascist Italy (1935–1936) and Britain's hollow and inept reaction to this development were to affect considerably Egyptian public opinion and the internal political discourse on Fascism and Nazism. Following the occupation of Ethiopia, many Egyptians realized that the Fascist menace to Egypt was closer than ever before.

Large segments among the Egyptian liberal educated classes and a considerable number within the foreign and *mutamassirun* communities were frustrated with the sociopolitical situation at the time. They were disappointed with the Wafd's failure to introduce social reforms and, in particular, with its failure to reach a satisfactory treaty with Britain in 1936. At the same time, they perceived the alternative to the Wafd—the solutions suggested by the two strong extraparliamentary movements, the Muslim Brothers and Misr al-Fatat, namely, radical Islam or radical nationalism, respectively—with growing concern, especially under the prevailing international circumstances, i.e., the rise of Fascism and Nazism.

For Muslim and non-Muslim Egyptians, communism could offer a revolutionary solution to the contemporary social problems that both Islam in the past and the current liberal democracy failed to provide. Communism could also offer secular and modern alternatives.[2] It became particularly attractive for young Jews for several reasons: it was an international movement; it was Western, modern, and progressive without being imperialist; and by de-emphasizing religion it was socially inclusive for Jews. They were looking for an alternative, and the communist formula of worldwide anti-Fascist popular fronts, as presented by the Seventh Congress of the Comintern, appeared attractive to young, educated Jews.

This chapter examines the factors behind the emergence of the home-made Egyptian Left, focusing on the impact of two contextual occurrences, the first internal and the second external. On the domestic front, it aims at discerning the possible influence that the appearance of radical right-wing groups may have had on the decision made by non-Muslims to embrace leftist ideas. In the international arena, it intends to probe the impact that the rise of European Fascism and Nazism had on the tilt leftward of young, educated Egyptians, particularly Jews—a development that led gradually to the appearance of a homemade brand of Marxism.

The chapter will scrutinize the development of the Egyptian Left, in particular with regard to its attitude toward Fascism and Nazism. The time frame covers the period from the mid-1930s until the mid-1940s.

Communism, Fascism and Nazism, and Jews:
Historiographic Overview

There are several explanations in the literature as to why Egyptian Jews boarded the leftist boat. Beinin and Lockman have examined the relationship between Egyptian Jews and communism and conclude that for Jews, "communism was the only political alternative to the declining Wafd, that promised to protect their status in Egypt." In their view, this may explain the involvement of a large number of Jews in the reorganization of the Egyptian communist movement. "These Jews, especially those fluent in Arabic in addition to European languages," they argue convincingly, "provided a bridge between the foreign communists and the indigenous Egyptian intelligentsia and helped forge the link between communist intellectuals and the workers' movement."[3] Indeed, as we shall see, Jews played a central role in the formation of nearly every leftist organization.

Some studies regard the emergence of new extraparliamentary radical political frameworks, such as Young Egypt and the Muslim Brothers, as manifestations of the influence of Fascism and Nazism on the educated Egyptian youth.[4] Rif'at al-Sa'id, the most prominent scholar of the Egyptian communist movement and a former member of the Democratic Movement for National Liberation (Hadetu)[5], maintains that the Egyptian "reaction" embraced Fascism as a means to confront the Left. He argues that the reactionary forces published books and articles glorifying Mussolini and that the press was looking for "an Egyptian Mussolini, who could free the country of the peril of Bolshevik and communist revolution."[6] The "reaction" also allowed Italian Fascists to form organizations within the Italian community in Egypt. Mussolini, notes Sa'id, founded Italian schools in Egypt to provide Italians and Egyptians with a Fascist education. These schools intended to replace the socialist schools of the Popular League (al-Jami'a al-Sha'biyya), which left-wing Italians founded in Alexandria in the early 1920s. Hitler too, stresses Sa'id, was given prominence by the newspaper *al-Fallah al-Iqtisadi*, especially in its column "Germany Today . . . Adolph Hitler." His decisive role in defeating Bolshevism was praised. Parties such as Misr al-Fatat, the Nationalist Party, and even the Wafd were attracted to Fascism and formed youth organizations such as the Wafdist "Blue Shirts." This development led to a counteraction, democratic in its essence, with the formation of anti-Fascist unions and clubs. Abundant articles written and published by various important forums raised the alert against the Fascist menace and urged fighting it. Leftist organizations sprouted out of these frameworks. The British authorities deliberately overlooked their emergence and, with the outbreak of World War II, even sought cooperation with the newly established Egyptian Left.[7]

Sa'id also addresses the Jewish role in the movement's development. Whereas Sa'id equates Jewish communist activity in Egypt in the 1920s with that of other foreign groups—seeing them as constituting a unit—he begins to view the Jews as a separate group by the end of the 1930s. Unlike most other scholars, Sa'id asserts that communist activities continued throughout the 1920s and 1930s. Indeed, the Comintern dominated Egyptian communist activities from behind the scenes until the mid-1930s, as my recent study clearly shows.[8] In the mid-1930s, however, an additional type of activity emerged among foreign groups in general and Jews in particular as a reaction to Fascism. Around that time, the first attempts were made to form a left-wing movement other than the veteran Egyptian Communist Party. The people involved in these attempts had different ideologies and aspirations, which would ultimately lead to further divisions within the Egyptian Left. At the same time, the role of "foreigners" in Egyptian politics grew stronger; anti-Fascist activities increasingly gave way to outright communism. This, claims Sa'id, afforded "foreigners" a more central role than strictly necessary; they now took the lead in the movement.[9]

Indeed, the stormy 1930s led "foreigners," particularly Jews, to increase their political activity in Egypt. Jews, Sa'id asserts, faced a rising dual threat: externally, European Fascism and Nazism, the Italian occupation of Ethiopia, the back gate to Egypt, and the rise of Hitler and his anti-Semitic policy; internally, the antiforeign activities (xenophobia) directed by the Muslim Brothers against Jews, foreigners, and the British. The Muslim Brothers, he reasons, forged an alliance with the palace and the Axis powers in the early stages of World War II.[10] For Hasan al-Banna, the movement's omnipotent leader, the regeneration of Islam "must begin in Egypt, for the rebirth of 'international Islam' in both its ideal and historical sense, requires first a strong 'Muslim state' (*Dawla Muslima*)."[11] Misr al-Fatat and its leader, Ahmad Husayn, were also cause for worry for the foreign community. For "foreigners," stresses Sa'id, the fear was even more substantial because the king's inner circle sympathized with both radical movements. Moreover, Mussolini's Fascist ideas reached Egypt and were embraced by members of the Italian community that was divided into anti- and pro-Fascist factions.[12]

The proposed solutions to Egypt's severe economic and political crisis of the 1930s, reasons Sa'id, were not essentially revolutionary, but rather were based on delusive semi-Fascist and religious ideas and practices, which attracted bourgeois circles.[13] Organizations such as the Muslim Brothers and Misr al-Fatat, he argues, were a tool in the hands of the palace in its struggle for power against the Wafd. In the 1930s, he notes, the popularity of Nahhas Pasha and the Wafd was the main obstacle hindering the spread of religious extremism and Fascist tendencies.[14] The events of February 4, 1942, Sa'id goes on, created an opportunity to form new political margins—nationalist and revolutionary. These two trends were represented by the "Free Officers' movement" and the "leftist movement," and they both situated the Wafd in its appropriate place—as a force that understood well the national problem, but endeavored to solve it peacefully without much reliance on the public. Part of the Wafd's method of advancing the nationalist goal was to maneuver between the palace and the British. At the time, the British, for their part, took pains to cooperate with the Egyptian communists against the Fascist forces. The communists who raised the banner of a broad anti-Fascist front, however, condemned the British occupation. They formulated the slogan "Against fascism . . . but not with the English" (*Didda al-Fashiyya . . . wa-lakinna laisa ma'a al-Ingiliz*). The communists opposed negotiations with the British and called to launch an armed struggle (*al-kifah al-musallah*) against them, thus introducing a new political school to the awakening public nationalist discourse. Following the Soviet victory over Germany in Stalingrad, the image of the USSR in Egypt improved, and the communists benefited from that development.[15]

A different explanation of the complex relations between right-wing radical groups and the Jews of Egypt is provided by Ahmad Sadiq Sa'd, a prominent figure in the group al-Fajr al-Jadid (also known and referred to as Tali'at al-'Ummal), who was attracted to Marxism for its interpretation of historical materialism. Sa'd joined Ittihad Ansar al-Salam (IAS, the Union of Peace Supporters) in 1937, where he established close links with Paul Jacot Descombes, the leader, as well as Yusuf Darwish and Raymond Duwayk, with whom he continued his political and intellectual activities for many years to come.[16] Drawing on his own experience with members of Misr al-Fatat as a young Jewish student, Sa'd explained that their anti-Semitic approach derived from ignorance—they believed that all Jews were also Zionists. Indeed, articles published in the movement's mouthpiece journal, *Jaridat Misr al-Fatat*, in the late 1930s followed such a line, blaming all Jews for robbing Palestine from its Arab inhabitants.[17] Sa'd recalled his experience as a student at the college of engineering, where he witnessed anti-Jewish activities conducted by students who were members of Misr al-Fatat. At some point, he took the initiative to explain to them that although he was Jewish, he was at the same time anti-Zionist. Zionism, he reasoned, was an imperialist movement, and he asked his audience to boo Zionism. Later he founded a student committee to support the Palestinian anti-Zionist struggle. IAS, noted Sadiq Sa'd, condemned Zionism. He, Yusuf Darwish, and other members were propagating in the streets against Zionism and, instead, supported the rights of the Arab Palestinians to Palestine.[18]

The Emergence of the New Left

It was in the late 1920s that Leon Castro, a leftist Jewish lawyer who was closely associated with the Wafd, founded les Essayistes, a scientific-cultural society. Castro was against the idea of compromising with the British on the issue of independence. His activities for the Wafd paralleled his Zionist activity in Cairo. He was among the founders and leaders of the Egyptian Zionist Union (al-Ittihad al-Sahyuni al-Misri) in 1917.[19] Les Essayistes represented a variety of ideological trends—liberals, democrats, and leftists—that attracted many Jews, Italians, Greeks, and other foreigners as well as a small group of Egyptian intellectuals. Castro and his followers campaigned against Nazism and anti-Semitism. They called for the boycott of German goods and literature.[20] As part of his anti-Fascist campaign, Castro also founded the League for the Combat of Anti-Semitism (Jam'iyyat Mukafahat al-'Ada'a li-l-Samiyya), which had many Jewish members and was very active in the school network of the Lycées.

A leftist trend was consolidated within that group that maintained contacts with the French Communist Party.[21] Many of them joined Paul Jacot Descombes's new leftist organization, IAS, which was founded in 1934. Descombes's group was linked to the international organization Rassemblement Universel pour la Paix, and its main goal was to attract as many Egyptians as possible to its ranks.[22] IAS operated as a legal platform, which—for outward appearances—focused on issues related to democracy, anti-Fascism, and antimilitarism, but was actually a leftist organization. Its members were mainly Greeks, Britons, and Jews, and there was also a small group of Egyptians—most of whom were educated young-sters. The group laid the foundation for the future cooperation between "the foreign Egyptian left and local Egyptians," as Edward Levi, a Jewish member of IAS, who was also the president of the League for the Combat of Anti-Semitism in Alexandria, pointed out. Veteran communists such as Sheikh Safwan attended the meetings of IAS, recalled Levi.[23]

Descombes strongly believed that communism in Egypt could be suc-cessful only if it was solely based on Egyptians. Foreigners, he maintained, could merely assist temporarily in providing Egyptians with Marxist guid-ance and education. Descombes was very cautious in his activities within Egyptian society, which until World War II remained mainly within the framework of theoretical discussions. His group, however, was mostly known for its anti-Fascist campaign. It attacked the Italian occupation of Ethiopia in the mid-1930s and supported the Republicans (who were also supported by the USSR and the socialist camp) in their war against the nationalists (promonarchists, who were supported by Fascist Italy and Nazi Germany) during the Spanish Civil War (1936–1939). IAS expressed a willingness to send volunteers to fight along with the Republicans—a popular front comprising a variety of political groups: democrats, social-ists, communists, and anarchists.[24]

Eli Mizan, the chief of the Cairo branch of IAS, noted that their group called for the formation of a broad popular front to the fight against Fas-cism. The slogan of a popular front, which was endorsed by the USSR, became the essence of the group. To quote him: "We started as Jews fight-ing against anti-Semitism, and we ended up as communists." The founders of the group, he added, were leftists—a matter that affected its course of development.[25] It is noteworthy that many young Jews, including Marcel Israel, Henri Curiel, and the teenage boy Hillel Schwartz (the three were to form three different communist frameworks in the early 1940s), wanted to volunteer to fight on the side of the Spanish Republicans or at least to provide them with material support. The case of Israel is particu-larly interesting. He established contacts with the Spanish Embassy in 1937, asking to volunteer in the international brigade that fought against Franco. His plan did not materialize—the ambassador persuaded him that it would be better for him to support the Spanish democratic forces by conducting anti-Fascist and anti-Franco propaganda activities within Egypt. Israel followed the ambassador's advice and joined forces with a variety of anti-Fascist frameworks, publishing and distributing books and articles on Republican Spain and the danger of Franco and his Fascist movement. His dedication and contribution to the anti-Fascist campaign were highly appreciated by the international brigade, which awarded him a silver medal.[26]

Yusuf Darwish received his higher education in France, where he studied law and commerce from 1930 to 1934. Upon his return to Egypt, he worked as a lawyer in the Mixed Courts, and in 1944, after studying Egyptian law, he received from the University of Alexandria a license to appear before Egyptian courts. In France he was introduced to Marxist literature, which attracted him. He became active in the French Students' Committee against Fascism and War, which was founded in 1933 and sponsored by the French Communist Party. Along with his work as a lawyer, he joined IAS in 1934. In his autobiography, Darwish argues that IAS focused its activities on anti-Fascism, antiracism, antimilitarism, and the promotion of peace among the nations, and that therefore IAS fought against the Zionist movement, which they regarded as racist.[27]

With the outbreak of World War II, IAS ceased to exist. By that time, there were a few schools that took different routes. A small group of Jews continued to work together with Descombes in the Groupe Études until the early 1940s. Among them were Yusuf Darwish, Raymond Duwayk, and Sadiq Sa'd; the three were to play a central role in the communist movement in the 1940s and 1950s.

The Democratic Union (al-Ittihad al-Dimuqrati) was founded in 1938–1939, and its founding nucleus was based on Marxist dissenters from IAS.[28] The Democratic Union was significant for the future development of Egyptian communism. Among its leading figures were Henri Curiel, Hillel Schwartz, and Marcel Israel. The Democratic Union maintained contacts with Arts and Freedom (al-Fann wa-al-Huriyyaa), a group of Egyptian artists and intellectuals led by Georges Henein, who held Trotskyite views. Members of that group published a Marxist newspaper in French called *Don Quichotte*. The threat of European Fascism and the urgent need to oppose it were the paper's main themes along with social and class issues.[29]

The Democratic Union was ephemeral because it could not sustain the conceptual differences of opinion and personal rivalries among its main leaders. Curiel, for his part, placed greater emphasis on the role played by the Egyptian authorities in interrupting the activities of the Democratic Union. The latter, he condemned, were sympathetic to Fascism and dissatisfied with the anti-Fascist nature of the Democratic Union. With the outbreak of World War II, he narrated, the Democratic Union debated fruitlessly the possibility of cooperating with the British against Fascism.

Curiel was against any cooperation with the British whatsoever, stressing the need to, simultaneously, fight both Fascism and imperialism.[30]

Shortly before the outbreak of World War II, Curiel, like many other communists worldwide, was displeased with the conclusion of the Ribbentrop-Molotov Pact (August 1939). He took the side of the Western democracies and wanted to enlist in the French army—a move that was politely declined by the French Consulate. His close ally George Pointée[31] took pains to persuade him of the realpolitik behind Stalin's diplomatic move: "The die was cast at Munich, when the Western democracies demonstrated their refusal to join a broad European alliance against Nazism. Stalin confined himself to playing them at their own game by deflecting the Hitlerian wrath which London and Paris hoped to see fall on him. The time gained would be useful for preparing the Red Army for the inevitable onslaught, for no one was in any doubt that the pact would bring about only a very short breathing space."[32]

Curiel was an autodidact as far as his Marxist education was concerned. He searched in this literature for solutions to Egypt's manifold problems. The German invasion of the Soviet Union in 1941 motivated him to intensify his anti-Fascist campaign. According to Curiel, in the first half of 1942, when the situation on the battlefield was not in Britain's favor and Rommel was heading toward Egypt, many political circles in Egypt that wanted to see Britain defeated welcomed that development. Curiel, unlike many communists who left for Palestine, courageously stayed "to organize the anti-German resistance."[33] With the assistance of a handful of followers, including Pointée, Curiel distributed leaflets addressed to the Egyptian people, saying, "Don't think that the Germans are better than the English." In June 1942, the Egyptian political police arrested Curiel. In his opinion, he was arrested because the Egyptian political police considered him a collaborator with the British and believed that the arrest of "a communist Jew could be used to prove their true feelings, when the Germans would take control of Egypt."[34] He was jailed for several months in al-Zaitun prison, where most of the prisoners favored the Axis and—according to him—were anti-Semitic. The period in prison was a formative experience for Curiel. He got protection from an unexpected source—Husni al-'Urabi, the former leader of the Egyptian Communist Party, who converted to Fascism. 'Urabi took pains to persuade Curiel to convert to Islam. The latter refused, reasoning that such a move "would reflect weakness and a selfish attempt to save my skin. I thought that there was a need to fight for Egypt and religious conversion was not a real war."[35]

Soon after his release, encouraged by the Soviet victory at Stalingrad, Curiel decided to form a new communist organization, al-Haraka al-Misriyya lil-Taharrur al-Watani (the Egyptian Movement for National Liberation, or EMNL), which was composed of a small group of educated Egyptians, workers, Nubians, Sudanese, a few former members of the Egyptian Communist Party, and a small number of Egyptian Jews.[36]

The New Egyptian Left: Self-Evidence of Communist Members

The early 1940s witnessed the emergence of new communist organizations detached from the old communist guard of the 1920s and early 1930s. The reasons for their emergence are well explained by Henri Curiel. According to him, the period starting in June 1941 (the German attack on the USSR), continuing with the national humiliation of February 1942 (the British ultimatum to King Farouk), and reaching its peak in February 1943 (the great Soviet victory at Stalingrad) may be regarded as the formative phase of the new wave of organized communism. The first years of the 1940s witnessed the formation of various communist organizations, most of which were founded by Jews: Iskra (Hillel Schwartz), the Egyptian Movement for National Liberation (EMNL, Henri Curiel), the People's Liberation (Marcel Israel), and the group al-Fajr al-Jadid (Ahmad Sadiq Sa'd, Yusuf Darwish, Raymond Duwayk, and Rushdi Salih, the first three of whom were of Jewish origin). These organizations differed over a variety of issues that not always justified splits.

The following section examines whether Fascism and Nazism played any concrete role in the decision made by Jews to join communism in the period under discussion. To start with, note that for some of the founders of the new communist organizations, the decision to join communism had nothing to do with the appearance of sporadic manifestations of anti-Semitism among right-wing trends. Yusuf Darwish, for instance, acknowledged that he did not experience anti-Semitism or feelings of ethnic and religious alienation in his youth. The only time he experienced such a thing in Egypt was when he was beaten up not by members of indigenous Egyptian right-wing circles, but rather by gangs of Italian Fascists that started to roam the streets of Cairo in their notorious brown shirts in the early 1930s.[37]

Albert Arie, a former member of both Iskra and the Democratic Movement for National Liberation (DMNL), argued that in the 1930s most Egyptian Jews had little interest in politics and were happy to lead their own lives in peace. Arie and Darwish did agree that there was no discrimination against Jews in Egypt prior to 1948. When the Arab-Zionist conflict intensified, it led radical voices in the Muslim Brothers and others in society to denounce the socialist movement that had attracted so many Jews to its banner as "just another face of the Zionist coin." Arie, like Sadiq Sa'd before him, categorically rejected out of hand those attempts to draw a link between Zionism and communism. True, Jews joined communism as a natural alternative at the time, because the communist movement had always stressed that Jews were part of society and belonged to Egypt. Arie admitted that he was attracted to communism following the developments during World War II that he witnessed: the French collapse in 1940, the German Blitz on British cities, Rommel's military achievements in the Western Desert of North Africa, and, the turning point, the Soviet victory at Stalingrad. Consequently, his admiration for the Soviet Union and his appreciation of communism increased considerably. Arie ruled out the possibility that he joined communism in order to save his skin from Fascism. Why communism, he asked, and not Zionism? "Palestine could be a better refuge for me to protect myself of fascism. Why would I join communism and take the risk that one day I may be arrested? By choosing communism, I made it clear that Egypt was my homeland, and only from here I could fight fascism. My roots were in Egypt, and I had never considered the possibility of uprooting myself from there."[38]

Like Sadiq Sa'd before, Arie blamed right-wing circles for employing anti-Semitic terminology in order to defile Zionism, which they ignorantly deemed as the equivalent of Judaism and communism. To quote him:

> I remember reading books warning that the Jewish octopus was spreading its tentacles everywhere into the nation's social, economic and political life . . . that the Zionists had planted their eyes and ears in Communist cells and were seeking control. . . . [T]he [Muslim] Brotherhood's activities against the Jews and its equation of Judaism with Zionism worsened the situation. The Jewish Community Council was loyal to the regime. Cattaui and Cicurel [leaders of the Jewish community] tried to hold the pieces together until the last minute.[39]

Zionism and communism represented the margins of the Egyptian Jewish community, whereas the vast majority regarded themselves as Egyptians, concluded Arie.[40]

Sharif Hatata got his start in Schwartz's Iskra just before joining forces with Curiel, and it was only recently that he had the courage to divulge his secret—his Jewish roots. To quote him: "It is not useful to sacrifice the fact that my grandmother [on my mother's side] is Jewish, especially, as one of the weapons used to attack socialism in Egypt is the argument that socialist thought is closely linked to Zionism. Therefore, the disclosure of this fact could become a disgrace."[41] Hatata did not ignore the key role played by Jews in the communist movement's formative years. He openly acknowledged the role of "foreigners and Jews" in introducing modern socialism to Egypt and in connecting the wave of socialist sentiment, which enveloped much of the world, to the growing national and social movement in Egypt. Hatata, nevertheless, placed greater emphasis on the external Nazism-Fascism factor as a generator of political consciousness among Jews. In his view, "Jews had a bitter experience with fascism under whose cruelty they so greatly suffered, and it was therefore just natural that many of them were western-democratic in orientation and joined the Allied armed forces, or provided them with material assistance in their war against the [Nazi-Fascist] aggressors."[42]

Some Egyptian communists viewed critically the motives behind the decision of Jews to join communism. Tariq al-Bishri, a veteran Egyptian leftist,[43] had no doubts as to the existing links between Jewish communist leaders and the Zionists: the top brass among the Jewish communists had acted on behalf of Zionism.[44] For Bishri, Jews opted for organized communism as a tool by which they advanced Zionist interests. Bishri even went so far as to assert that the Jewish presence in the Egyptian communist movement, particularly in the 1940s, was such that the movement's tactics in Egypt were not altogether different from those of Zionists in the Levantine countries bordering on Palestine. Their presence meant that the movement's activities in Egypt aimed at forming a popular front to counteract the Islamic and Pan-Arab nationalist movements, which both the communist movement and the Zionists considered to be offshoots of Fascism, or even Nazism.

Bishri opined that the Jewish sympathy for the communist movement in the mid-1930s was a result of the abolition of the benefits for foreign residents by the 1936 British-Egyptian treaty. This made foreigners in Egypt more likely to take up politics; they attempted to intervene in government decision making in order to prevent a crackdown on local foreign strongholds. They began to take up positions in Egyptian party politics, while attempting to enlist public figures and groups (including the communist movement) to form a front that could withstand the forces of Islamism and Pan-Arabism and fight the growing wave of xenophobia and discrimination in Egypt.[45]

Later, Bishri discussed Curiel's view of the political climate in Egypt as he understood it in the late 1930s. According to Curiel, this was the same worldview that drove young *mutamassirun* to take up political activism. The nationalist movement in Egypt, he claimed, experienced a significant renaissance, having been joined by a large number of "fascists and Nazi sympathizers." The impact of the nationalist and intra-Egyptian issues on Egypt's Jews was negligible; most of their attention was focused on attempting to neutralize the threat of Fascism, to which so many Egyptian nationalists seemed to be drawn. Curiel explained that communism was the only ideology that viewed Egypt's Jews as Egyptians. At this point, Bishri asked why Curiel did not see the Jewish involvement in Egyptian politics as anything out of the ordinary. On the contrary, wrote Bishri, what puzzled Curiel was the inability of some communists to accept the presence of a sizable Jewish minority in Egyptian political life. Furthermore, claimed Bishri, Curiel saw nothing strange in the fact that these foreigners, who enjoyed certain legal privileges and whose motives for taking part in Egyptian politics were a function of the interests of the communities they represented, were among the leaders of Egyptian political organizations that competed with more "grassroots" movements—Islamic and nationalist, labeling them "fascist."[46]

Curiel, wrote Bishri, maintained that the first priority for the communists—both foreign and Egyptian—was a campaign to promote their ideology and to attract people to join their ranks. The first step was to advance communism as an idea; implementation was still a distant prospect. In other words, concluded Bishri, the activity was more theoretical-ideological than practical, the goal being to foster an "ideological base" within the wider spectrum of Egyptian politics, which could in turn draw in young Egyptian supporters and legitimize the foreign contingent in Egyptian politics. The priorities set by the foreigners were not Egyptian nationalist per se, but rather international: a rejection of Italy's policy of aggression in Ethiopia, opposition to Japan's policy of aggression in China, and opposition to Franco's regime in Spain. It can thus be said that the movement was more anti-Fascist than anticolonialist and, therefore, essentially European in orientation.

Moreover, the factors contributing to the establishment of Curiel's movement pertained to external developments rather than internal social currents, which lay at the heart of Marxist thinking. For example, Curiel pointed to the Nazi aggression against the Soviet Union in June 1941 as well as the victory at Stalingrad in February 1943. Bishri also noted the events of February 4, 1942, as an internal Egyptian event that contributed to the movement's founding.[47]

For his analysis of the history of the communist movement, and particularly the role of Jews in the movement, Bishri relied on Muhammad Sid Ahmad's book *Mustaqbal al-Nizam al-Hizbi fi Misr* (The future of the parliamentary regime in Egypt), published in 1984.[48] Sid Ahmad, wrote Bishri, admitted in his book that Jews were the most prominent figures among the founders of the Egyptian communist movement in the early days of World War II. Sid Ahmad did not at all question the Jews' loyalty to Egypt and maintained that many of them had been his friends. Still, he claimed that one could not but question their motives, particularly during that period. He believed that this could not merely be a coincidence. It seemed unlikely that the goal was to create an independent workers' movement, as Jews often claimed—in reality, they had little to no affiliation with this social class. More plausible was the notion of an ulterior motive, of which the Jews themselves were not consciously aware: the need to prepare public opinion, including that of nationalist intellectuals and highly motivated young people, to extend them their protection as a heterogeneous minority in the face of the rising popularity of Nazism. Sid Ahmad went on to note that Jews sought to maintain their standing in the movement's leadership—a fact that later had a negative impact on the communist movement, particularly following the establishment of the state of Israel.[49]

In his attempt to argue that Jews had exploited Marxism for their own ends, Bishri relied also on Sa'd Zaharan's book *Fi-Usul al-Siyasa al-Misriyya* (The roots of Egyptian politics).[50] Zaharan asserted that in the late 1930s, Britain encouraged several forms of "popular" anti-Fascist activity among the expatriate communities in Egypt. Among the groups that joined these efforts was a group of foreigners and *mutamassirun*, chiefly Jewish Marxists, who feared Hitler and therefore seized upon Marxism as a way of attaining their goal—defending themselves from Fascism and Nazism. The communist movement was fraught with schisms, particularly during the period when most of its leaders and high-ranking cadre were foreigners, mainly of Jewish origin. According to Zaharan, this situation persisted even after many of them had left Egypt in 1948, due to their lasting influence on the new local leadership.[51]

In an article entitled "The Jews in the Egyptian Communist Movement and the Arab-Israeli Conflict," Sid Ahmad openly questioned the extent to which the identification with communism on the part of the Jews, who reestablished the Egyptian communist movement in the 1940s, stemmed from the "Jewish" component of their identities, i.e., an attempt to preserve the latter in the face of adversity. This included Rommel's early military victories in the region, together with the general threat of an Axis-led invasion of the Nile Valley. This would have subjected the Jews to the same sort of existential danger that had ravaged the Jews of Europe.[52] Jews who turned to communism did so with the full knowledge that their only goal was to preserve their Jewish identity — in other words, to find an ideological, internationally minded isle of refuge that was naturally geared toward fighting racism and, ultimately, anti-Semitism.

Yet Sid Ahmad reminded his readers to take note of Curiel's statements regarding his own Jewish identity and the way in which it led him to turn specifically to communism. Curiel claimed that at the end of the 1930s, the Egyptian political arena was essentially closed to Jews. Political parties, even the two largest ones, the Wafd and the Liberal Constitutionalist Party, did not accept Jewish members. The communist movement was the only outlet for Jews who wished to be politically involved in Egypt. Sid Ahmad wrote that Curiel gave several reasons for the enthusiasm of Jews for communism: a positive impression of the communist movement worldwide, a deep distaste for Fascism, a feeling of alienation from Egyptian political life, and, finally, the lack of allegiance to any other political movement.[53]

Sid Ahmad claimed that the destruction of the communist party in Egypt in the mid-1920s had eliminated all traces of communism or internationalism in Egyptian political life. The signing of the 1936 British-Egyptian treaty enraged the Egyptian Right that then began to view Germany as a possible ally. This led the Right to support Germany's war against Britain, in keeping with the adage that "the enemy of my enemy is my friend." Sid Ahmad noted that in those days, Egypt was too narrow-minded to realize that Nazi Germany was simply imperialism at its worst.[54] In the years 1940–1941, stated Sid Ahmad, a number of upper-class Jews created Marxist organizations, separated from each other. In his view their motives were as follows:

I think, at that time, the reasoning was the following: Rommel was at the doors of Alexandria; if he had occupied Egypt, he would have gone to Palestine. I am not talking of a plot at all, but this was a sort of normal reaction. What happened then probably is that they knew about the persecution of Jews; it was known to some extent or other, not like afterwards. They were looking for an ideology that could be a protection, that could identify them with Egyptians standing up to fascism; so it was communism at the time. The ideology of communism was an anti-racist ideology which could give them protection.[55]

As Rommel drew nearer, demonstrations broke out, with many chanting such slogans as "Press on, Rommel!" This led to much unrest among the British authorities and foreign expatriates, particularly Jews, who had a particularly acute sense of the dangers of any Nazi victory. The ramifications for Jews would have been much more immediate than the ramifications for Egypt as a whole. According to Sid Ahmad, it was here that the confusion regarding the reestablishment of the communist movement in the 1940s arose: had the movement been founded—even unwittingly—solely in order to protect its Jewish founders or to provide an outlet for the ideology it espoused, to represent Egypt's workers, irrespective of the identity of the movement's founders? According to Sid Ahmad, the confusion over this point greatly influenced the development of the movement in the years that followed. Even if one accepted the first alternative, namely, that the communist movement was founded in order to protect its Jewish founders, this should not have affected the manner in which the communist movement developed and pushed for the "advancement" of Egyptian society. The idea of protecting Jews from Nazi persecution in no way excluded the notion of liberating the Egyptian people—nationally and socially. The contradiction between the two emerged only after the concept of defending one's Jewish identity came to be identified with the state of Israel, which negated the basic principles of Egyptian national liberation.[56]

Some veteran communists analyzed acceptably the motives behind the formation of communist organizations and the participation of many Jews in them. Yusuf al-Jindi, a prominent figure in the DMNL and the Egyptian communist movement, spoke favorably of the Jewish communists of the 1940s. Jews, he asserted, played a major role in the reemergence of the communist movement in the early 1940s. That was their reaction to the rise of Fascism in Europe and its anti-Jewish policy. Although Fascism was still far away from Egypt, Jews concluded that they should be prepared to fight the danger in advance. Some Jews joined the existing anti-Fascist organizations, and some chose to revive the Egyptian Left by forming new organizations that offered a radical sociopolitical platform perceiving Fascism as the main enemy. The Soviet Union's entry into World War II and its military achievements contributed significantly to the rise of the new Egyptian Left and enhanced its positive image among the people. This development facilitated the spread of Marxist and socialist thought. Curiel's bookstore,[57] Jindi pointed out, played a decisive role in this process.[58]

Didar Fawzi-Rossano, who joined EMNL in 1943, was born in Cairo in 1921 and socioeconomically came from a well-to-do background. Her father instilled in her his hatred of Fascism and Nazism: "We belonged to a generation that experienced the anti-fascist struggle and the awakening of the Egyptian national movement. As Jews we had to make our choice."[59] Reasoning that Jews were among the pioneers of organized communism in the 1930s, she stated unequivocally that the rise of Fascism and Nazism had an enormous impact on the Egyptian national movement, leading many educated youngsters, many of whom were Jews, foreigners, and occasionally of Muslim families, to join al-Ittihad al-Dimuqrati—an anti-Fascist and anti-Nazi organization.[60] Jews like herself, explained Fawzi-Rossano, were excited about the victory of the Soviets over the Germans. Because they had come from a cosmopolitan milieu, they were not attracted by Zionism. French was their culture and language, and Marxist literature was accessible for those who were interested.

Fawzi-Rossano's recollections of the late 1930s and early 1940s resemble those of Yusuf Darwish. Jews, she noted, were mainly attacked by Italian Fascists. For instance, she referred to the violent clashes between the Italian sport club and the Jewish "Maccabi" club. The Greek community was also divided between anti- and pro-Fascist trends.[61]

Mustafa Tiba, a veteran Egyptian communist who started his activity as Curiel's ally and ended up as Curiel's political adversary, had no doubts: Jews had played "an important role" in the reestablishment of the communist movement in the early 1940s. Whereas Curiel had denounced the Muslim Brothers and Misr al-Fatat as "Fascist," Tiba opined that the two groups were, in fact, anti-Semitic. Tiba referred to the demonstrations on November 2, 1945, the anniversary of the Balfour Declaration, that had been organized by the Muslim Brothers, with Misr al-Fatat as a junior partner. Tiba claimed that the demonstrations were not intended to express solidarity with the Palestinian people, but rather meant to attack Jewish institutions and businesses. This added a sinister anti-Semitic dimension to the national struggle. According to Tiba, these demonstrations served the Zionists, driving Jews to leave Egypt and obscuring the fact that Zionism, and not Judaism, was the true enemy of Egypt and the Arabs.[62]

Post–World War II Years: Misusing the Term
Fascism in the Internal Political Discourse

Abu Sayf Yusuf of Tali'at al-'Ummal gives an accurate picture of the division of the Egyptian national movement, as seen through the lenses of the Egyptian Left, pointing at two nationalist trends: chauvinist and Fascist parties versus liberal and progressive parties.[63] It is noteworthy that in the post–World War II years, the terms *Fascism* and *Nazism* were often misused by leftist organization to attack right-wing organizations, such as the Muslim Brothers and Misr al-Fatat, and those politicians associated with the palace. For instance, al-Tali'a al-Wafdiyya (the Wafdist left wing) published a political manifesto in 1947 calling for the protection of democracy, the people's rights, and the immunization of religion against delusive elements and for launching a war against Fascist elements such as the Muslim Brothers and like-minded groups.[64] In December of that year, Tali'at al-'Ummal (formerly referred to as al-Fajr al-Jadid), a group that cooperated at the time with al-Tali'a al-Wafdiyya, issued a leaflet explaining their motives and incentives for that cooperation. At that crucial junction in Egypt's history, it was stressed, supporting the Wafd was an essential measure to combat the spread of Fascism represented by 'Ali Mahir, Hasan al-Banna, Ahmad Husayn, Salah Harb, and 'Abd al-Rahman 'Azzam. The Wafd's opposition to these Fascists prevented them from founding Fascist armed groups. The Wafd protected democracy and the parliamentary system and advanced a reformist and democratic agenda: the law of trade unions, a campaign to eradicate illiteracy, the promotion of popular culture, compulsory and free education, and the use of Arabic language in foreign institutions.[65] Despite the Wafdist declaration of war on internal Fascism and the defeat of international Fascism, the Egyptian Fascist group remained intact and was likely to betray the homeland for the sake of foreign imperialism. Despite these words of courtesy, the Wafd was criticized for prohibiting appropriate representation of the working classes in its ranks, despite the fact that the latter proved to be its main supporters and the supporters of democracy. Certain adverse elements existed within the Wafd that tried to divert the party in antidemocratic directions.[66]

Several years later, when the Wafd was in power (1950–1952), the leftists continued to perceive the Muslim Brothers as Fascists: "They are fascists, enemies of the workers, communists and the Soviet Union. A tool, serving reaction and imperialism."[67] The image of Misr al-Fatat, which by then was called the Socialist Party, did not improve, and it was still

seen as a Fascist organization. The group supported the Second International, along with well-known imperialists such as British foreign secretary Ernest Bevin and his government. For that reason, Misr al-Fatat
supported the reactionary idea of the unification of the Nile Valley under
the Egyptian crown and the colonization of the Sudan by Egyptians. It
supported Ibn al-Sa'ud, the reactionary king of Saudi Arabia. The organization still regarded the Misr Bank as a national financial institution, even
though the bank had been taken over by Americans and Britons. Ahmad
Husayn, the Misr al-Fatat leader, had always deemed the Muslim Brothers
as the most nationalistic elements in terms of their loyalty and willingness to sacrifice themselves for the sake of the nation. He also instigated
domestic clannish conflicts, calling vehemently to fight against Egyptian
Jews. His organization employed terrorist means to achieve its goals. In
conclusion, this group was a mixture of anarchism, terrorism, and socialism of the house of learning of the Second International.[68]

Fu'ad Mursi, a founder of the Egyptian Communist Party, popularly known as al-Raya, in 1949–1950, condemned the alliance created in
the post–World War II years between the national bourgeoisie and the
"feudalists, the allies of fascism," in order to defeat the Wafd Party. Consequently, a terrorist despotic regime was established, and its chief goal
was to eradicate the progressive movements by encouraging Fascist and
terrorist elements, such as the Muslim Brothers, to act freely. In the meantime, the reactionary regime occupied the public's attention with issues
such as the unity of the Nile Valley and the war over Palestine. It did so in
order to distract the people from its revolutionary urge: the liberation of
Egypt from British imperialism, the large landholders, and monopolists.
The communists favored the Wafd Party, and particularly its left wing,
and were pleased with the formation of the Wafdist government in 1942
following the "February events"—a development that marked the victory
of the progressive forces over the Fascists. In this regard, the communists
followed the line dictated by the Seventh Congress of the Comintern in
1935, which called for the formation of an anti-Fascist national front based
on the communists, socialists, and the progressive national bourgeoisie.[69]

The armed struggle against the British forces along the Canal Zone
in late 1951 to early 1952, in which members of the Muslim Brothers and
Ahmad Husayn's Socialist Party featured prominently, was a cause for
worry for Tal'iat al-'Ummal (unlike its rival, Hadetu, that supported
it). In December 1951, al-Muqawama al-Sha'biyya criticized the Wafd
government (1950–1952) for allowing the formation of militias by these
organizations—a dangerous development that might lead these forces

to undertake a coup d'état that would overthrow the Wafd government. Former prime minister 'Ali Mahir, who was referred to as "the former German agent," along with Ahmad Husayn and members of the Fascist parties, implemented the policies of American imperialism. They pretended that they were fighting against British imperialism, but their real goal was to establish "a terrorist barbaric and exploitative regime."[70]

Tali'at al-'Ummal and other communist groups (with the exception of Hadetu) continued with their antiestablishment declarations even after the revolution of July 23, 1952. The derogatory terminology employed by Tali'at al-'Ummal to describe the Free Officers' regime rehashed familiar terrain. Muhammad Naguib's inner circle was perceived as a "military dictatorship," which was fighting against the free men. The people should topple "Naguib's fascist and treacherous government." Naguib's government was taking harsh measures to prevent the reemergence of an armed anti-imperialist popular movement to bring an end to British occupation. This Fascist regime, it was declared, was conducting an antidemocratic war to destroy the Wafd Party and the communist movement.[71]

Conclusion

People of Jewish origin were prominent among the founders and leaders of the newly emerged communist and left-wing organizations in the 1930s and early 1940s. As we have seen, some joined the movement on ideological grounds, and some viewed leftist ideas, generally, and communism, particularly, as a means to contain the spread of European Nazism and Fascism to Egypt. Indeed, the Fascist and Nazi hazard had gradually come in close proximity to Egypt—by the mid-1930s, Italian Fascism was stationed at the back door of Egypt, whereas the early 1940s witnessed the galloping of Nazi troops through the Western Desert toward Egypt. That was not the only reason, however, that educated young Jews founded or joined left-wing frameworks. The political frameworks that existed in Egypt at the time closed their gates for Jews, and the only way for the latter to express their political and social consciousness in deeds was to establish or join new leftist frameworks. As I have shown in a broader study,[72] many young Jews joined the communist organizations only in the mid-1940s— after both Fascism and Nazism were defeated. An atmosphere of admiration for the Soviet Union and communism prevailed among young, educated Egyptians, including Jews. Young Jews perceived communism as a secular and modern doctrine that would allow their integration in society regardless of religion, ethnic, and socioeconomic origins. Communism could sort out their question of identity—the ideal solution to the question of "who we are." In this regard, it is noteworthy that the prominence of Jews in the communist movement was not an exclusively Egyptian phenomenon, as Jews played a central role in the international socialist movement during the period of the First, Second, and Third Internationals.

Indeed, in the first part of the twentieth century, many Egyptian Jewish communists operated most of the time in illegal dissident organizations that demanded radical sociopolitical changes within both Egypt and the Sudan. They were altruistic human beings with farsighted visions—the bearers of universal and humanist revolutionary ideas that challenged the existing order. They belonged to a tiny minority group, and as such they realized that their leading role was temporary—to lay the foundation for dissent frameworks and to act as mentors for their compatriots, who would soon take over the leadership.

The rise of a domestic Egyptian right wing that was inclined toward xenophobia and showed sympathy for the anti-British Fascist-Nazi alliance was still far from being a branch of the latter. True, anti-Jewish manifestations were uttered in words and in deeds by both Muslim Brothers and Misr al-Fatat, before and during World War II. However, their bearers did so mainly because they confused Judaism with Zionism. Moreover, those Jews who boarded the leftist boat did not do so because they were anxious over the rise of Egyptian right-wing radicalism. In fact, the latter played a negligible role in their decision.

CHAPTER 9

"The Crime of Nazism against Humanity": Ahmad Hasan al-Zayyat and the Outbreak of World War II

ISRAEL GERSHONI

Historical and Historiographical Setting

A commonly held theme in the narration of Egyptian intellectual history in the interwar era is that the 1930s ushered in "the shift of Egyptian intellectuals to Islamic subjects."[1] This trend coalesced and expanded in the latter part of the 1930s and the beginning of the 1940s, as it was expressed through the production of a vast corpus of texts and publications about seventh-century Islamic history, particularly biographies of the Prophet, the rightly guided caliphs (*al-khulafa' al-rashidun*), and other Islamic heroes. The very shift to Islam was a topic that was widely debated and contested in scholarly literature. An early narrative produced in the 1960s defined this shift as a "crisis of orientation": a dramatic and chaotic intellectual retreat from a Western-oriented system of values, humanism, liberalism, secularism, science, and rationalism (dominant in the intellectual community of discourse in the 1920s) to a romantic Islamic religiosity, imbued with "confused" irrational, emotional, and strong anti-Western motifs. The intellectuals' Islamic publications were by their very nature reactionary and regressive, often a reproduction of Islamic orthodox or reformist ideas, and sometimes *mahdist*/fundamentalist Islamic themes. In "destroying" their own intellectual liberal and progressive project, this narrative charged, the intellectuals "betrayed" their task to modernize, secularize, and advance their society into a modern era.[2] According to this approach, the shift to Islam also involved the intellectuals' general denunciation of democratic parliamentary values and practices, while at the same time they deliberately adopted authoritarian concepts and values, heavily influenced by contemporary Nazism and Fascism.[3]

A later revisionist narrative, developed in the 1970s and 1980s, challenged the early narrative of crisis. According to the new narrative, the shift did not reflect a crisis of orientation and did not involve a total retreat from Western-oriented liberalism, humanism, and the belief in the power of science and rationalism. Rather, the intellectuals were attentively responding to profound sociopolitical transformations that were occurring in the 1930s, particularly the rise of urban mass society, mass culture, and mass politics. Pressures from below prompted them to adjust the public discourse and to adopt new strategies of Islamic writings as a tactical maneuver and instrumental means by which to create new discursive forms of communication with "the masses" in order to maintain "social order."[4]

The revisionist approach was generally more cautious about linking the "shift to Islam" to the abandonment of the values and principles of liberal democracy and the adoption of a Fascist-inspired authoritarian orientation.[5] However, some scholars who shaped this narrative did emphasize the connection between these two trends. For them, the shift to Islam was part of a general evolving intellectual mood that reflected disappointment with liberal democracy and the "failure of the liberal experiment," and as a result intellectuals expressed growing admiration for Mussolini and Fascism, and eventually, during the war, Hitler and Nazism.[6]

A third narrative was developed in the 1980s and onward by social historians who studied social thought and social movements. This narrative did not specifically treat the intellectuals' shift to Islamic topics, but it argued that the intellectuals and other social forces in the 1930s—through the radicalization of the anticolonial struggle to end British rule in the Nile Valley—developed sympathy for Fascist Italy and Nazi Germany as liberating powers. The intellectuals and other social nationalist forces held that "the enemy of my enemy is my ally." As such, this narrative assumed that the anti-British struggle ipso facto necessitated Egyptian sympathy or collaboration (or both) with Fascism and Nazism. Support for these latter powers in their war against Britain would secure Egyptian independence. Additionally, according to this narrative, oppositional left-wing socialist forces heavily criticized Egyptian democracy, which was based on a constitutionalist parliamentary system and was supported by the Wafd, the mainstream nationalist force. They viewed it as an institution totally controlled by the landed and commercial elites that promoted their own class interests and neglected the plight of broader sectors of Egyptian society.

Thus, in their impressive work on Egyptian social history and the labor movement, which became a classic in the field, Joel Beinin and Zachary Lockman adapt a similar argument. They assert in a generalized manner:

In the 1930s important sections of the intelligentsia in the colonial and semi colonial countries viewed fascism primarily as a militant form of nationalism. In Egypt, some of the *effendiyya* abandoned the secularism and liberalism of the Wafd as a result of their dissatisfaction with the 1936 treaty and the continuing economic and social crisis of the country, and began to embrace more radical nationalist ideologies. Fascism also had a certain appeal, and because it was imported from Italy and Germany, the rivals of Egypt's British overlords, it seemed to those who despaired of the Wafd's failed liberal parliamentarianism an appropriate ideology to guide a resolute struggle against the British occupation . . . more diffuse pro-German sentiment was widespread at the outbreak of the war.[7]

This chapter is an attempt to demonstrate that these narratives are misleading. It is part of a larger project that problematizes and deconstructs this master narrative of the ostensible sympathetic attitudes of the "important sections of the intellegentsia" to Fascism and Nazism. It is evident that the principal mistake of these narratives derives from a lack of serious and systematic research on the intellectual discourse regarding the following major topic: the status of liberal democracy versus forms of authoritarian and Fascist political culture and political regimes. The Egyptian public debate on this crucial topic earnestly preoccupied many intellectuals and journalists within the broader landscape of print culture in the interwar era. In the specific context of the 1930s, against the backdrop of a dramatic ascendance of Fascism and Nazism (and communism), and due to the Egyptian democracy's chronic setbacks and malfunctions, this intellectual discourse became a hegemonic force in the field of print and visual media. Given the overconcentration on discourse analysis of the shift to Islam or the study of social thought—or, for this matter, the study of national identity and imagination—intellectual historians did not identify and investigate this discourse. Hence, it appears that intellectual historians neglected the very discourse that should interest us, as it is our indicator of the intelligentsia's concrete attitudes toward Fascism and Nazism. Moreover, a systematic study of this particular discourse clearly shows that even for those newcomers to Islam-oriented intellectualism or for established Islamist intellectuals, the "shift to Islam" did not necessarily lead them to support Fascism and Nazism. Similarly, oppositional nationalist and left-wing socialist forces that challenged the parliamentary government also were not necessarily sympathizers. Even the syndrome of "the enemy of my enemy" was less salient than it has been represented.[8]

I seek to embody my claim by analyzing the thought and position of Ahmad Hasan al-Zayyat (1885–1968) on this subject. I did not arbitrarily select Zayyat. As a founder, owner, and editor of *al-Risala* (the Message), Zayyat became a prominent and authentic intellectual voice in the 1930s and 1940s. Symbolically, the first issue of *al-Risala* appeared in mid-January 1933, a few days before Hitler assumed power. Due to Zayyat's efforts, *al-Risala* became the most successful and widely circulated intellectual weekly in Egypt in the 1930s. Because a third of its issues were circulated throughout the capitals of the Arab world, his influence on the Arab intelligentsia at large was discernible. Along with the most influential Egyptian intellectuals, other prominent Arab writers and intellectuals contributed to this periodical. Perhaps more than any other intellectual weekly in Egypt and in the Arab Middle East, *al-Risala* aptly represents the distinctive intellectual dilemmas and predicaments of the decade and the ideological and cultural trends that emanated from the intellectual community. Zayyat's role in the editorship and decision-making processes of *al-Risala* lent him great public notoriety and cultural capital. By the end of the decade, he was one of the most influential public intellectuals of the era.

Aside from his prominence and archetypal attribute, I selected Zayyat due to an additional important reason. Zayyat and *al-Risala* were mouthpieces of the "intellectual shift to Islamic subjects in the 1930s." In contrast to individual intellectuals who advanced this process through their distinctive publications, such as Haykal, Taha Husayn, or 'Abbas Mahmud al-'Aqqad, Zayyat reinforced the trend through the entirety of essays and reviews published in his magazine. The dissemination of *al-Risala* was much wider in scope than the aforementioned intellectuals' publications. Whereas between two and four thousand books on Islamic subjects (*Islamiyyat*) were circulated and in an extraordinary case even reached ten thousand copies per edition, each weekly issue of *al-Risala* was circulated to thirty or forty thousand (average for the years 1933–1945) throughout Egypt and the Arab world. Beyond its Islamic and Islamist orientations, *al-Risala* also promoted a strong Arab national cultural orientation. Zayyat was a main agent in shaping the Arab national image of Egypt. He strove to forge an Egyptian Arab national identity that would be integrated into the broader Pan-Arab nationalist framework.[9]

Ostensibly, these pronounced Islamist and Arabist orientations led Zayyat to display his disappointment with liberal democratic values and institutions, to underline liberal democracy's "failure," and to be captivated by the authoritarian charm of Fascism and Nazism. Nevertheless,

Zayyat became one of the most assertive voices against any form of auto-cratic government or authoritarian political culture. With the same en-thusiasm that he denounced Fascism and Nazism, he strove to reassert liberal democracy and its values and principles in Egypt, Europe, and other parts of the world.

The Search for a Redeeming Leader and the Preference for Democracy, 1937–1939

Zayyat's anti-Fascist and anti-Nazi view had already evolved into a solid position during the years 1933–1937. In writing about this subject on the eve of the war and during its early years, he articulated and entrenched his stance. In front-page editorials in *al-Risala*, Zayyat and other contributors made a clear distinction between Fascism and Nazism, between Italy and Germany, and between Mussolini and Hitler. His criticism of Italian Fas-cism and of the Duce was far more acerbic and systematic. At times it bor-dered on venomous, biting attacks. Zayyat exposed the imperialistic drive of Fascist Italy and its Mediterranean, Middle Eastern, and African am-bitions. The fact that Mussolini was a direct threat to Egypt and the Suez Canal and regarded them as part of the Mediterranean *lebensraum* (*mare nostrum*) of the Italian empire further intensified his hostility. However, the war in Ethiopia in 1935–1936 was a major milestone in the development of this position. The murder of hundreds of thousands of Ethiopians with a modern war machine and poison-gas bombs dropped indiscriminately from the air, the conquest of the country, and its annexation to the Fascist empire all shocked Zayyat. The atrocities of the Fascist army, the murder of innocent citizens, and the arbitrary elimination of Ethiopian indepen-dence, a member of the League of Nations, provided him with incontro-vertible proof that Fascist imperialism was worse and more destructive than traditional British or French imperialism. Zayyat, who viewed him-self and his periodical as a front in the national struggle against British colonial rule, understood that Fascist imperialism was far more cruel, racist, and demonic. In fact, the war in Ethiopia led *al-Risala* to mobilize in a systematic, crushing attack on Mussolini. In addition to denouncing the "oppressive imperialism" of the conquest, the weekly exposed the ugly "white" Fascist racism against the "black Ethiopians," which provided a horrifying justification for violent mass murder. Moreover, Zayyat noted the essential link between the totalitarianism of the Fascist state, the op-pression of the civil society, the destruction of freedom of expression and freedom of the press, and internal terror against political rivals, on the one hand, and its external militarism and expansionism, on the other. On the eve of World War II, when Zayyat learned that Mussolini's rule over Libya and East Africa would place a noose around Egypt's (and Sudan's) neck and pose a direct threat to its independence and sovereignty, he and other contributors escalated and intensified the denunciation and rejection of Mussolini and Italy.[10]

During the same period, Zayyat and *al-Risala* also leveled criticism at Hitler and the Nazi regime in Germany. In particular, Muhammad 'Abdalla 'Inan, a prominent intellectual of the weekly, was the writer who led an aggressive anti-Nazi line. In a series of articles, he exposed Nazi totalitarianism, rejected and refuted the theory of Aryan racial superiority, and expressed his disgust with its application in an official set of racist laws by the Nazi state's agencies and policies. He repeatedly renounced the Nazi regime and pointed to the danger it posed to Europe and the world. 'Inan and *al-Risala* condemned the persecution of the Jews, denounced anti-Semitism, and identified with the persecuted Jews and their suffering.[11]

But, at the same time, Zayyat and other writers on the weekly—somewhat in contrast to 'Inan—did not overlook what they viewed as the Nazi regime's domestic achievements, in particular in the area of economic and social reforms. Zayyat expressed sympathy for Hitler's ability to rehabilitate the German economy, to ensure the welfare of millions of Germans, to raise the national morale, to rebuild the country's military strength, to defy the Versailles agreements that had suppressed German independence, and to turn Germany into a European and international power. Above all, he was impressed by Hitler's display of resolute leadership that brought the Germans self-confidence, pride, and prestige.

Zayyat discussed Hitler's achievements in rehabilitating Germany in the context of a broad public discourse in Egypt about the proper relations between the Fascist and Nazi dictatorship and the liberal democracy: can and should democratic Egypt, based on a constitutional parliamentary government, learn anything from the accomplishments of the Nazi dictatorship? Although Zayyat had serious reservations about key components of Nazism, in particular dictatorship and racism, he did find some positive points in the overall change that had taken place in Germany. He regarded Hitler as an inspiring leader. Moreover, until 1938 the processes of the Nazification of Germany seemed to be focused on the domestic rehabilitation of German society and economy. It appeared to Zayyat that Germany was not intent upon territorial expansion and imperialist conquests. Hence, he concentrated on learning about the internal "constructive" changes and Hitler's central role in bringing them about.[12]

In the spring of 1937, in a series of articles titled "On Democracy," Zayyat tried to reformulate his attitude toward democracy. His articles were constructed as a dialogue between a young, "perplexed" man (representing Egyptian Arab youth) seeking his political path and an older man possessed of a solid worldview (Zayyat) attempting to guide him on the basis of democratic principles. The implication was that the young man embodied a new generation that found itself in a state of crisis and disorientation. This generation displayed skepticism about the parliamentary democratic form of government and its ability to put forth reforms and mobilize national forces to liberate Egypt from colonial rule. A dangerous potential developed in this generation that might lead its members to despair of democracy and become enthralled by Fascism or Nazism. Zayyat strove to strengthen support for democracy in the "confused and tormented" minds of these young people and to explain to them that despite its flaws and shortcomings, it is still the only form of government appropriate for modern man and society, including Egypt and the Arab countries. In this dialogue, Zayyat begins by surveying the history of democracy for his young readers. He states that "it is the most worthy form of government which protects human dignity and ensures world peace. This form of government was established by the free thinking man in Athens." This classical enlightened system collapsed in the dark Middle Ages when it encountered "the spread of ignorance, emotional stupidity and egotistical instincts" in human societies and was supplanted by the form of "absolute rule." In this dark, benighted age, democracy remained only a dream and vision.

However, beginning with the early modern era, a vast human struggle took place to reinstate democracy, "a struggle for the sake of which many precious lives were sacrificed" until "the modern European man, in an ongoing heroic struggle and making even greater sacrifices, engendered its renewed victory." The new democracy arose in the eighteenth century on a new basis of reason and science and on the modern principles of freedoms, rights, and justice promised to all human beings. Then, Zayyat stresses to his young readers, democracy took on a new garb, more humane and universal than ever before: "Through it, every individual has the right in his homeland, to voice his view in a trial and to elect the government." This was democracy of the people, by them, and for them. Moreover, in Zayyat's view, only this democracy could ensure equality alongside freedom. Hence, "the poor worker, the hired apprentice, or the impoverished *fellah* can [in a democratic system] oust officeholders who are not effective and can even overthrow a government that is guilty of injustice." This is the essence of democracy: "it is equality in rights and duties, the sharing of riches and of shortages." It is a free public space, open to full equality of opportunities in which each individual can fully realize his talents and capabilities to reach the highest status regardless of his origin, wealth, or title.[13]

The young man listens attentively to Zayyat's arguments in praise of democracy. But he is still seeking an answer to a specific question that is bothering him. "What do you say about Mussolini and Hitler?" he asks provocatively. Zayyat, as if prepared for the question, replies placidly, while expanding his liberal views to include Fascism and Nazism as well, "I claim that they are a clear manifestation of democracy. After all, they are two men who are acting in the name of the people for the sake of the people; they represent the power of the nation and are fulfilling the will of that nation." Zayyat has the impression that the young man is "persuaded" by his words. He is planting in the youth's mind his own fear that Egyptian youth is liable to be seduced by the false charms of Fascism and Nazism.[14]

This position reflected an internal tension, typical of Zayyat and other writers for *al-Risala*: a tension between support for democracy and a par-liamentary constitutional system and an effective leadership that would realize this democracy ideologically and practically. Zayyat believed that Egyptian democracy was in need of a resolute, strong leader who knew how to lead the nation. He was unquestionably expressing his longing for Sa'ad Zaghlul and the heroic national leadership that had inspired the Egyptian people to carry out the national revolution of 1919. Later, Zaghlul was the first elected prime minister under the new constitution-alist parliamentary system. Atatürk and the Kemalist revolution also pro-vided Zayyat with an ideal model of effective national leadership: "We are yearning for a leader who will serve his nation and not himself, for his people, not for his party, a leader for tomorrow, not for today; a leader who will provide these hard-working people with the pleasure of brotherhood under the shelter of the homeland, pride in national freedom realized under the wings of the constitution, and the beauty of equality achieved under a worthy [democratic] form of government." Only such strong visionary leadership can cure Egyptian democracy of its ills and put it back on the right course.[15]

This was the intellectual and psychological context that induced Zay-yat to look at Hitler's leadership in his search for distinctive qualities for that ideal leadership he aspired to find. In early May 1939, in an article entitled "This Is the Man," Zayyat tried to appropriate some of Hitler's leadership qualities for Egypt's parliamentary experience. True, Hitler had always been for him a "dictator" unrestrainedly controlling Germany, which was blindly obeying his every desire and whim: he was a despot imposing totalitarian tyranny on his people, a tyranny unparalleled in human history. Nonetheless, Zayyat argued that it was impossible to overlook Hitler's impressive oratory skills as manifested in his electrifying and mesmerizing rhetoric so that his voice "filled the entire world" and "his speech, or a translation of it, was heard in every country on the globe, in every city in every country, in every house in every city, and in every ear in every house." For Zayyat, behind the führer's remarkable oratory there was a genuine charismatic form of leadership backed by his impressive achievements as the leader of Nazi Germany. "This surprising man," Zayyat said, "has succeeded in six and a half years to build with fire and iron, out of a sense of anger and revenge, resolve and national zeal, a state that after the Versailles Treaty was stricken by disgrace, and almost annihilated by hunger. . . . When it tried to touch its body, it found only broken limbs scattered all about. But Hitler arose and imbued the nation with the spirit of struggle, gave it the power of weaponry, and thus Germany became the master of the states in matters of life and death, decreeing peace or war upon the nations. And Hitler managed to do all of this without a revolution and without a war." Through these extraordinary achievements, Hitler became a leader "who embodies the [German] state; and through whom the new generation is stirring and rising up and in whom history is being fulfilled." Indeed, with his unique ability to redeem Germany from the grave crisis in the aftermath of the Great War, Hitler restored its greatness and power and provided a constructive model of leadership for Egypt.[16]

Of course, Egypt was not lacking in skilled people and abundant resources. Zayyat stressed that the country had many material treasures and talented people and was endowed with "unique qualities" stemming from its distinctive geographical location and rich history as a glorious, ancient civilization. Egypt had people who excelled in a variety of fields, in politics, law, culture, the press, literature, and art. Egypt thus did not lag behind in assimilating modern science and technology and "is no less unenlightened than Turkey just as Germany is no more learned than France." But Egypt's fundamental problem was that its "forces are split and shattered," and they acted to further contradictory aims guided by opposing interests and desires. Hence, many of its qualities were "latent, or cut off from one another, or dispersed in every direction." Egypt lacked a centralized, cohesive leadership that was capable of realizing the vast skills and talents the country possessed. Therefore, its "leaders have not succeeded in working together in the last twenty years to do what Hitler alone has done in six and a half years." Egypt lacked that charismatic leader who could utilize the country's latent virtues and resources and harness the power that characterized a determined and unified nation striving to achieve a superior goal. It was such a leader that Zayyat longed for and was convinced that Egypt merited.[17]

Nevertheless, Zayyat definitely did not want to create the impression that it was possible to emulate Hitler, "the Nazi dictator," for Egypt and the Middle East. In the leadership that he demonstrated, Hitler was a general inspiration but not a concrete model for emulation. Zayyat concluded his article with explicit words of reservation: "Heaven forbid that you, my dear reader, should think that I advocate a sole rule [dictatorship] because I want to see a [worthy] man at the head of our leadership. The leader we desire, the leader we want, should lead, not control, should be an advisor not a prince, should take us on the path of struggle and sacrifice, not to enslavement and hubris." Zayyat drew a clear distinction between Hitler's dictatorial leadership of the "West" and the desirable leader for the "East." "The leader whom we desire for ourselves and for every beloved nation in the East cannot be a tyrant because he is a believer, and faith by its nature limits rule and kills the passion [for power]. Such a leader cannot enslave because he is a Muslim, and in Islam in its laws is the freedom of man and consultation in government." Thus, from an essentialist approach, which does not allow for a possibility that the "Hitlerian dictatorship" can be adopted in the local political culture, Zayyat rejected Hitler as a role model. Egypt and the eastern Arab nations deserved a leader who would be a genuine leader of their own, a strong democratic leader who acted within the limitations of a parliamentary representative system.[18]

Hitler Endangers World Peace, 1938–1939

Hitler and Nazi Germany have far uglier and more demonic faces that are directly linked to German foreign policy. During this same period, Zayyat and *al-Risala* became more aware of the aggressive, expansionist, and imperialist nature of Nazi Germany and its aspirations to dominate *lebensraum* in Europe. Zayyat's qualified admiration for Hitler's leadership did not preclude his understanding of the danger posed by Hitler's ambition to establish a "greater Germany." The developments on the ground only intensified and sharpened these fears. The Anschluss and the conquest and annexation of Austria, Hitler's claims and annexation of Sudetenland, the threat to and invasion of Czechoslovakia, and, at the eve of the war, the claim to Danzig and the escalation of the conflict with Poland that led to the outbreak of the war—all rendered Hitler and Nazism a new type of Western, dictatorial, and racist imperialism. Zayyat and many other writers in *al-Risala* argued that Hitler was stirring up a new European war whose first victims were "the small, weak nations."[19]

The crisis of the summer of 1938, which peaked with the Munich conference and agreements, elicited a harsh reaction from Zayyat. Prior to concluding the agreement, while Chamberlain shuttled back and forth between London and cities in Germany in an attempt to achieve a compromise with Hitler, Zayyat reacted in a front-page article entitled "Democracy vs. Dictatorship: A Frantic Week." It was a pessimistic and depressing article that predicted how humankind was sliding downhill in the wake of the conciliatory concessions being made to Hitler's aggressive and menacing whims. Zayyat, who had been following Hitler's path since 1933, understood all too well the meaning of the "Munich week." "The bleak week" proved to him that Nazi Germany was bringing a catastrophe upon enlightened men and modern society and that if the democratic powers placated him, they would sentence mankind to a terrible fate. In his eyes, Germany was dictating a new, appalling, and dangerous international agenda that would drag mankind down to "bestiality and barbarism." Zayyat chose an arsenal of extremely acerbic, harsh words to describe the situation. "In these very days," he wrote, "human beings have forgotten that they are committed to religion, civilization, and philosophy." Power, passion, hubris, and evil had taken over all of their deeds. "They only speak in the language of force, argue with one another with the logic of wolves, and attack one another with the fanaticism of *Jahiliyya* [*bi-'asabiyyat al-jahiliyya*]." "Extreme tyranny has taken over. They have cast off their independent will and have become a herd of sheep led by one stick to the field or the slaughterhouse!!"[20]

Who was the shepherd leading his herd to a "field or a slaughterhouse"? That same Hitler and that same Germany were the cause of a regressive shift in the evolution of the human species. Under the violent and hypnotic influence of Nazism, the human species in the twentieth century had turned aside from all its achievements in science, reason, culture, morals, and aesthetic refinement that it gained through so much hard work and so many heroic struggles. "Man has abandoned all that and now stands again in the primordial wilderness to which his forefathers were expelled from the Garden of Eden. His naked body is free of the spark of culture, his soul is empty of the nobility of religion, and his emotions lack the beauty of literature and art. He stands ready to devour his bleeding prey, his mouth foaming with saliva, his spear dripping blood." Hitler had violated all the laws of civilization and mocked all the principles and norms of the Enlightenment and humanism. He was taking humanity back to the primal form, the primitive and bestial species of precivilization. "In Hitler's soul passion constantly burns and power rages in his mind. He bellows the roar of the mad lion and opens wide his hellish mouth." As he lowered humanity to this bestial and despicable level, Hitler was adept at dictating to it new game rules that furthered his satanic aims: "Humankind suffers, democracy is fearful and alarmed, civilization bows its head and hides from the Satan, and the League of Nation has fallen silent." "The entire world is delirious with the mad fever of fear for the fate of its peace and its civilization." In this frightening situation that Hitler had imposed upon the enlightened world, it was clear that "Chamberlain's arguments against Hitler's drives are like efforts made by a tiny sprinkler to extinguish a huge fire." "Peace is dying" because Hitler was not interested in it and Chamberlain was hesitating, trying to appease and in doing so only abandoning "world peace" to the cunning, crude game rules of the führer. And thus, the path to a world war was under way: "The whole world, for the first time in its history, sees in all four directions one illusion that arises from one delirium: a declaration of war, the catastrophes of war, and the results of the war!" Indeed, Hitler had brought about a situation in which "human beings are beyond repair." Zayyat likened this to a man with a terminal disease that leads to the end of human civilization.[21]

Despite this desperate situation, Zayyat still expressed his confidence in democracy as the only form of government fit for human beings. He reminded his readers that "humans were the ones who established democracy on the foundations of freedom and equality; they based it on philosophy and laws; they disseminated it through literature and art, and they enveloped it in peace and security." But the takeover by "the absolute tyranny" (*al-tughyan al-mutliq*) of several nations, in particular Germany, had destroyed democracy in those nations, "undermined its effectiveness and deprived it of its prestige, so that the ruled citizens have been denied the special qualities of its [democracy] power and utility. Therefore, dictatorship is the disaster [*naksa*] of the bestial disease that has beset enlightened and civilized man. It is dragging him back to instinctual madness and barbaric rabies [*al-kalab al-wahshiyya*] so that he no longer understands any language but that of the beast of prey, nor can he get out of the bloody cycle of conflict other than through another conflict."[22]

Zayyat strongly opposed the irrationality and barbarism that fueled and incited this intolerable human situation. He was appalled by the ability of the "absolute dictatorship" to control the minds of men, to cause them to deny the values of democracy and enlightenment, and to succumb to primitive bestial drives. Had the "controversy between Berlin and Prague," he asked rhetorically, exceeded the control of logic? Indeed, it had. Hitler had turned this diplomatic controversy into a pretext for inciting all men to wage war against one another: "From the very moment that the wolf has determined to devour the innocent lamb every proof is void and all evidence is groundless"; as soon as the "volcano" had erupted and boiling lava was spilling out, burning everything in its path, "it no longer recognizes logic, criteria or boundaries." Hence, there was no point in trying to persuade the führer to change his mind or to present him with rational or practical arguments in order to placate his fury and prevent a war. Hitler was determined to liquidate Czechoslovakia on his campaign "to devour" additional weak nations, and the attempt to stop him with the logic of negotiation was futile. World peace now did not have a leg to stand on and was collapsing in the face of Hitler's resolute decision to destroy it. The democratic world was fighting against Hitler with means that were ineffective and hence defective and useless. The policy of appeasing Hitler would not "stop the epidemic," nor would it ensure peace. "Peace which is a hostage of the force of weaponry is a peace that can only be relative and temporary." What, then, was the solution? Zayyat was convinced that Hitler's savage power could be blocked only by force. Nazi power must be confronted by an equivalent power. "Only if the strong force is challenged by an equivalent force will it fall." Hitler was dictating to democracy militant rules of the game: it must desist from all efforts of appeasement and turn to armed means. Perhaps with these, there was a chance to save the "moribund peace."[23]

Who were the victims of "the new barbaric situation"? Zayyat did not doubt that those were the "weak nations" and the "small states." They had paid and would continue to pay the price of the takeover of world order by the "barbaric forces." Zayyat's identification with Ethiopia, Austria, Czechoslovakia, Albania, and later with Poland stemmed from the fact that he regarded them as sharing a common fate with Egypt and the Arab countries, all (or most) of whom were born as a result of international arrangements made after the Great War. In the spring of 1939, as *al-Risala* closely watched the breakdown of "world peace" in the wake of Hitler's continued campaign of military and political expansion, Zayyat analyzed the dangerous developments. In an article entitled "Kill Poverty, Kill the War," he added an economic, materialistic dimension to his explanation of the rising tension and the imminence of the war. The explanation is somewhat simplistic, but it gives us an additional vantage point from which to observe Zayyat's anti-Fascist and anti-Nazi position. He argued that the struggle between "dictatorship and democracy" was also based on the desperate economic crisis in which large parts of human society found themselves early in the decade. Peace, he said, depended on the wealth of human society, on stability, on economic and social security, and on the elimination of poverty and ignorance. A satisfied, stable society that enjoys economic, social, and cultural well-being will not tend toward war. Referring back to the Great Depression, he asserted that France, Britain, or Switzerland successfully coped with the economic and social crisis. The United States through the New Deal and under the leadership of President Roosevelt, whom Zayyat admonished, managed to extricate itself from the difficult social and economic crisis through the democratic means of government intervention in the economy and the construction of an infrastructure for a welfare state. In contrast, the grave economic and social crisis in Germany and Italy gave rise to "dictatorship," to the "two dictators." The severe distress and despair that struck millions in these two countries paved the way for the rise of Hitler and Mussolini. Zayyat was convinced that if "the inhabitants of Berlin and Rome" had not been "struck by poverty" as a result of the serious economic crisis and had enjoyed genuine economic well-being, social security, and a high standard of living, "like the inhabitants of London and Paris," "we would not have seen how they turn their backs on humanity, become alienated from civilization and adopt the patterns of brute force . . . a force that impels them to kill." Nazi Germany with Hitler at its helm was the complete, terrible embodiment of the attempt to "kill poverty" by means of a racist dictatorship: "The Germans are expelling the Jews from their homes in order to take over their property and money. They are conquering nations by military force in order to take over their territory. They are threatening the strong states with the fever of madness by stoking anxiety, fear, and bewilderment; and as for the weak states, they are placing their greedy hands upon their resources and the sources of their livelihood." The force driving German expansionism was also material greed. Hitler warned, frightened, and deceived the superpowers; for the small, weak nations, he "prepared" invasions and annexations for the purpose of exploiting their material resources and economically enslaving them.[24]

"The Crime of Nazism against Humanity," September 1939

About a month after the outbreak of World War II, Zayyat published a seminal essay, "The Crime of Nazism against Humanity." The title of the article speaks for itself. Zayyat was devastated, as he clearly understood the monstrous nature of what the war involved and that it would bring unprecedented death and destruction to mankind. In his neoclassical style, Zayyat employed the sharpest language, at times apocalyptic, to exclusively blame Hitlerian Nazism (*al-naziyya al-hitlariyya*) for the outbreak of the war and its horrific results. His opening words reflect his shock and profound distress. "Oh, what a distortion of reason! Oh, what a perplexity of logic! Human history is today confronted with an unprecedented horrific and overwhelming earthquake that man has never encountered since God's creation of earth."[25] Zayyat admitted that human reason remained powerless and incompetent in comprehending how mankind was led into such a horrendous war. The Nazis had conquered the great German nation, which brought humanity the finest intellectual works in science, philosophy, literature, and art. "The Nazis," Zayyat wrote, "silenced the thoughts of German people, eradicated the people's will, recreated it as a huge herd of elephants of hell [*afyal jahannam*], who aspire to conquer the whole world—the military forces as well as civil populations—either by totally destroying them or by planting terror and hunger!" In a more empathetic tone, Zayyat pontificated that if "Hitlerian Nazism would establish its authoritative dictatorship on one good principle or one constructive school of thought, then we would attempt to excuse the total enslavement of the German people to Nazism, and its fomenting of disarray to the humane world." However, Zayyat found that reality was starkly different. "Nazism is a gross deviation of chauvinism and racism [*al-'asabiyya wa-al-'unsuriyya*], of ethnocentrism and hubris." He was amazed by the follies of history. How could the enlightened German nation be relegated to a barbaric crowd of warriors, and, even more troubling, how could Europe and the enlightened world let such a demonic phenomenon flourish and be dragged into such an all-encompassing war?[26]

For Zayyat, Nazism was a demonic power that was viciously waging total war against two major cultural traditions of enlightened mankind: war against the monotheistic religious traditions—Judaism, Christianity, and Islam—and war against secular human civilization, as it was reshaped in the Renaissance and the scientific revolution of the sixteenth and seventeenth centuries and particularly during the Enlightenment of the eighteenth century (Zayyat and contributors to *al-Risala* included the Arabic *nahda* in these modern secular trends).[27]

Zayyat vehemently rejected Hitler's theory of race as it was conceptually framed in *Mein Kampf*, and as it was implemented in Germany through racist laws and regulations in the 1930s. Appealing to broad communities of readers, including Muslims, Christians, and Jews, Zayyat employed macabre parody as a literary device to convey his message. He attacked Hitler and *Mein Kampf* by presenting Hitler as a self-proclaimed prophet and *Mein Kampf* as a holy book. In Zayyat's sarcastic analogy, Hitler assumed that his book descended to him or mankind from the heavens, and "thus, it is *Shari'a* that invalidated all other holy books except for *Mein Kampf*; it erased all ruling authorities except Nazi rule, and obliterated all races other than the German [Aryan] race." In this macabre construction, Hitler is an apostle (*rasul*) and *Mein Kampf* a message (*risala*), a new sharia brought from heaven to the "new chosen people," the German Aryan race. In Hitler's racist doctrine, the Semites, the Semitic race, "is the scum of the human race [*huthalat al-nas*]." The religious messages of the Semites are inferior and indeed invalid compared to the sealed message of superiority that the Aryans brought to the world, according to this construction. "How can the Semites not be inferior to the Aryans? For they [the Aryans] are the epitome of the races; their revelation and apostle are superior to any other mission [revealed or human] in the world?"

Zayyat used this literary strategy to reject all the racist theories and concepts in *Mein Kampf*, as well as the racist policies of the Nazi regime. Hitler was a false prophet, and his book was not the sharia, but a demonic message of brutal inhumane racism. In contrast, Zayyat reasserted the distinctiveness of the universal messages, which the "so-called Semites" brought to the world through "Moses and Judaism, Jesus and Christianity, and Muhammad and Islam." He reminded the führer that the three Semitic monotheistic religions introduced the world to new laws and norms for human behavior. They brought messages of humanism, compassion, and love, and thereby eased human adversity and predicaments. In particular, Zayyat emphasized that "no race is superior to another, no race may oppress another, and no nation shall commit injustice towards another." In other words, for Zayyat, the Semitic universal messages prove the complete falsity and hollow deception of *Mein Kampf*. Zayyat added, "Who is the German deity who selected Hitler, Göring, Hess, and

Ribbentrop from the Aryans to exterminate the world nations, crushing human civilization, and annihilating all the brilliant achievements of mankind?" They undermined both God's law and secular enlightened human conscience and sought to replace them with a totalitarian political order "that does not honor agreements, disregards treaties, and has neither laws nor principles." In his poetics of evil, Zayyat defined Nazi racism and anti-Semitism as "the Nazi doctrine which humiliates human races, denies the natural rights of peoples, disregards laws and norms," and aimed only to rule by power, deception, manipulation, corruption, and trickery while totally rejecting all other worldviews. Zayyat rhetorically asked if this was Hitler's superior pure Aryan, scorning this presumption.[28]

Reasserting his prewar arguments, Zayyat presented Hitler as an international provocateur and manipulator, obsessed with undermining the contours of the international order that emerged after the Great War. Zayyat challenged Hitler by asking what Luther, Kant, Goethe, and Beethoven, and "their enlightened German descendants," would say about the führer's conduct. How would they respond to the tyrant, "the same frustrated artist [Hitler was an amateur painter], who lies in the name of the German state, signs agreements on behalf of its nation's honor and then disregards them, and turns his nation of hardworking people into a demonic enemy of peace, who instills terror in every heart, and sows misery in every home." How would the great forefathers of the German nation regard Hitler, who, after ardently opposing communism as the most loathsome doctrine and notorious regime, "lets the swastika slowly but surely be squashed between the hammer of communism and its sickle." (Zayyat vehemently attacked the nonaggression pact between Soviet Russia and Nazi Germany in late August 1939, known as the Ribbentrop-Molotov Pact.) *Al-Risala*'s contributors, similar to many other Egyptian papers and magazines, were convinced that Hitler's aim in provoking the war was to establish a "new world order" (*al-nizam al-'alami al-jadid*), the Nazi order.[29]

Zayyat firmly rejected Nazi dictatorship (*al-tughyan al-nazi*). He reiterated that the Nazi regime repressed all civil rights and liberties, silenced all opposition, barred the press, and turned Germany into a police state. Reminding the reader of his positive assessment of Hitler's domestic performance, just a few months before, he conceded his grave mistake. Zayyat toiled to quote the paragraphs in which he erred in his praise for Hitler's leadership abilities in an early-May edition of *al-Risala*. He recounted that at that time, "I did not expect that God would strike Hitler with the lowest human defect—with a most devastating form of rapid extermination. His head is taken by hubris, his soul is full of obstinacy to the point that his passions are limitless and his whims are unstoppable." By the same token, Zayyat emphasized that Hitler, who was initially admired by the youth of many nations of the world, was now viewed by them as a "warmonger" whose aim was to drag the world into the "blaze of war."[30]

Zayyat returned to one of his central themes: the real victims of the war that Hitler imposed on the world were "the small peoples [al-shu'ub al-saghira]," including Egypt and the Arab peoples. The Nazi dictatorship aimed at "controlling the world based on enslaving the weak, exploiting all natural and human resources for a single-race rule and the will of one dictator." He emphasized that the only guarantee for the continued existence of these nations was a stable international order, a strong League of Nations, "honor, justice, and peace among nations."[31]

Having ardently rejected Nazism, Zayyat reasserted human freedom, liberal democracy, religious, racial, ethnic tolerance, and a multiparty, pluralistic parliamentary government. For him, the traditional-religious and modern-secular legacies that brought culture, morality, and social and political orders to mankind can "only be safeguarded and sustained by the free democratic powers." Therefore, "the small nations cannot live in liberty only through active participation in the unyielding and committed defense of democracy." Accepting reality, Zayyat adopted a pragmatic approach according to which the "only guarantee for the survival of the minority within the majority, of the weak under the wings of the strong, is anchored in the social virtues which first emerged in the monotheistic religions and were then developed and refined in the shelter of democracy." Nevertheless, Zayyat apocalyptically warned, "if heaven forbid" the totalitarian dictatorship should prevail, "human rights will be trampled and human brotherhood will be replaced by one-race ethnocentrism. Rather than equality among nations, a single nation will control the world, and a single dictator will suppress human liberty, we will witness a new world conquered by evil, and we do not want to live in such a world!"[32]

Zayyat's conclusion was clear-cut: death was preferable to living in a world where Nazism had triumphed. Hence, in a world confronting a fateful zero-sum game of war, democracy must win and Nazism must be defeated. For democracy to triumph, Egypt and the Arab world must support the democratic camp and the Allies.[33] More generally, it appeared that for Zayyat, the historical anticolonial, anti-British struggle for independence must be postponed until the war against Nazism was won.

The Horrors of the War: "The Politics of Sharks and Minnows," 1939–1940

From the fall of 1939 until the summer of 1940, Zayyat continued to closely follow how "the crime of Nazism vis-à-vis humankind" was expanding and deepening. The events of the war and the use of scientific knowledge to create deadly weapons and sophisticated military technology that killed hundreds of thousands of soldiers and civilians seemed to fulfill his apocalyptic forecasts of the inferno and horrors that the new war would bring upon the human species. Zayyat understood that this war would rapidly turn into a killing industry that would lead to the deaths of millions and that it would be far more brutal and possess greater killing power than any previous war. In his gloomy mood, Zayyat pondered the desperate predicament of man and society who were by their own actions bringing about the end of *Homo sapiens* as a civilized creature. He lamented the alarming dialectic between science and the sophisticated scientific culture, on the one hand, and the destruction and killing that this same science and scientific culture made possible, on the other. Zayyat believed that in the present war, "science was destroying everything it had built" from the scientific revolution of the seventeenth century until the present day: "Everything that modern civilization gave rise to is being destroyed by science [through modern weaponry]."[34] He feared that the inferno of the new war would annihilate "rational human thought" because men of reason and literature were incapable of preventing the extermination of thought, as reason was itself enslaved to the war machine. He derided Germany as the complete and terrifying embodiment of the loathsome use of science and technology for mass murder. That same Germany that produced "high culture" was the one that had created "atrocious science and the exploding civilization." It was Germany that "gave rise to the barbaric, bestial, fanatically tribal Hitlerism, which is causing so much damage, tribulation, and destruction." Zayyat frightfully observed how science and culture were becoming one of the anticultural, inhumane, demonic means. "Science, through which human reason discovered the fundamentals of existence in order to better understand the secret of life and harnessed the forces of nature for the betterment of human beings — that same science has emptied out the human conscience, making it conscienceless, and enabled wickedness to take it over and extract evil from everything good it produced and from all the creations of civilization. It has attacked them with weapons of destruction such as aircraft that blindly drop bombs from the air, or the tanks that shoot poison bombs or armored vehicles that spew out fire!" Thus, in the bosom of enlightened, humanistic science, "devastation and extinction," the most satanic and wicked that exist in mankind, had emerged. "Are not thought, literature, science and culture, which scientists, intellectuals and writers have sought to defend, the very ones who have made Hitlerian Germany into a hell blazing with the fire of an inferno, gases and killing?"[35]

In June 1940, when Nazi troops conquered northern France and Paris fell, Zayyat's apocalyptic mood peaked. Zayyat, who studied in Paris, suffered from traumatic shock due to his affinity with the city. It was his alma mater and the origin of his worldview, his approach to culture and art, his ethical and aesthetic sensitivities, and his criterion for observing and comprehending human experience. For him, "ill-fated France [*fransa al-mankuba*] was a new victim of the menacing forces of corrupted, distorted science." France, the mother of reason and the producer of cultural and scientific achievements, the country that had imparted modern thought and culture to Germany, was now the victim of science and culture. "God have mercy on Jean Jacques Rousseau who fought all his life to prove that science was corrupting man. If he had continued to live until the Nazi era, he would have seen and been convinced that it was man that was corrupting science!" The fall of France to the Nazi invader was incontrovertible proof of the detestable use that man was making of science to destroy enlightened civilization.[36]

In other articles from that period, Zayyat focused on the battlefields and analyzed them in detail. His concrete analysis only further illuminated the "horror" and "catastrophe." A major focus in this discussion was Nazi Germany's campaign of conquests and military expansion into North and West Europe and the terrible sacrifice being made by the "weak nations" it was invading. To Hitler's crimes, Zayyat added the crimes committed by Stalin and Soviet Russia ("two barbaric powers"). Italy remained neutral and did not join in the war; it had become less relevant, and Zayyat temporarily spared it the rod of his criticism. It is clear that Zayyat's emphasis on the fate of the "small nations" stemmed from his constant fear that the war would reach Egypt and other Arab countries and would inflict damage on the "small nations" in the Middle East.[37] He described for his readers the special character of new Nazi imperialism, the ways in which it was conquering, destroying, and brutally enslaving the occupied populations. He did this to prove to them that Egypt and the Arab world actually did not have the option of joining Nazi Germany. Zayyat used a metaphor taken from the subterranean jungle, in which the new imperialistic powers, the "sharks," are devouring the "weak states," the minnows. He defined it as "the politics of the fish" (*siyasat al-samak*). In a key article on the subject, he opened with the motto of Hitler's declaration that "the present war will overthrow the existence of the small states." Zayyat once again portrayed the "terrible injustice" that underpinned this frantic forecast made by Hitler. "The small nations," he explained, are the outcome of the Great War. "The guarantee of their existence and independence is that same political arrangement that the great powers established [after the war] and described as the 'international balance.'" This arrangement was anchored in regulations, agreements, and international treaties agreed upon between the powers and the establishment and operation of the League of Nations. They were intended to ensure the existence of this world order and the existence of the small states within "separate, agreed boundaries." These boundaries defined their political and national entities and defended their independence and sovereignty against any arbitrary acts by "those who would trespass and use force." "But then Hitler, the emissary of satan [*rasul al-shaytan*] and prophet of the Germans . . . came and proclaimed a death sentence on the small states. He decided that the world would be solely ruled by only two superpowers: a ruling state (the king's state in chess), which is Germany, and a pawn state (the queen in chess), which is England as he thought yesterday, and Russia [instead of England] as he believes today!" In Hitler's vision, which was "rapidly being fulfilled" in the war, the small states would be erased from the world map.[38]

A central dimension of the article was an analysis of Russia's brutal military attack on Finland in November and December 1939. Zayyat stated that "the Russian bear is now swallowing up Finland just as the German tiger has swallowed up Poland." These "two barbaric powers" had no restraints and would go on taking over the small states and expanding the territories of their empires. The "small states" remained helpless: they had no choice but to "observe these greedy eyes and gluttonous mouths" that longed to "swallow them" and were confronting them with "the danger of an assault and a menacing end, the outcome of which is unknown." Zayyat's description of the new imperialism was clear: "Nazism and communism have denied the laws of God and human norms and are grasping the world with the 'politics of the fish,' the rules of which say that the weak is always the food of the strong." The outcome was the dominance of the politics of belligerent conquest in which there was no room for the weak and the small, just as Hitler made clear in his frightening forecast. "In this way, order has been disrupted and peace has been rejected, the balance has been upset and life has been abandoned to upheaval and chaos. Justice has been debased, logic has been refuted, and the community of small, tender fish has been struck by confusion, bewilderment and fear, prey to two beasts: the dictatorships [the sharks] that annihilate them down to the last minnow and the alligators of democracy that try to liquidate the sharks down to the last one." Thus, at the end of 1939, Zayyat did not see how the democratic Allies preparing for an immense war against Nazi Germany and Soviet Russia could find the time or means to save the small states that had been abandoned to their fate.[39]

A few months later, it turned out that Finland had fallen into the hands of the Russian invader. Zayyat, out of complete identification with the victim, lauded the heroism of the Finns who fought bravely despite their clear military inferiority and resisted determinedly for "three and a half months." Although numerically, "every Finnish soldier fought against sixty Russian soldiers," the small Finnish army caused many casualties to the great Russian army ("about two hundred thousand Russian soldiers were killed") and destroyed some of its finest military equipment—thousands of weapons, tanks, armored cars, and aircraft. "Finland fought a heroic war in the cause of justice, peace, and civilization." This was "heroism based on great devotion, the honor of the race, readiness for self-sacrifice and the sanctity of the homeland." In contrast, Russia had fought a barbaric and loathsome war of conquest whose only purpose was to demonstrate its power, to expand its territory, and to sow destruction and killing. But even when universal justice was on Finland's side, no one came to its aid, and it was defeated and lost its independence. This conquest of "a small, helpless state" seemed to completely corroborate Zayyat's forecast about the desperate fate of the small states. He described this as the "Finnish tragedy" (*al-ma'sa al-finlandiyya*). Undoubtedly, the fall of Finland was "a failure of human conscience and human intelligence, with whose failure right and justice died." "Wretched, miserable Finland" had been abandoned to its fate, and the democratic powers were also responsible for that: they did not "break down" the wall of neutrality of Sweden and Norway in order to defend "their little heroic neighbor." Zayyat had expected them to come to the aid of Finland, but they failed to do so, just as Sweden and Norway failed in a simple humane act, help to a neighbor. Zayyat asked his readers whether in this emergency of life and death, the objective should not have sanctified the means. "Can you be accused of trespassing across the border with your neighbor if you did so in order to put out a fire in his home?" Zayyat was convinced that if Finland's neighbors, with the backing of France and England, had mobilized to help it, "the Satan Stalin would have withdrawn as a wretched coward and Bol-shevism would have been beaten and been overwhelmingly humiliated forever!" In reality, Finland was abandoned, left to its fate, destroyed, and occupied. Zayyat traumatically expressed his fear that the small states in the Middle East would suffer a similar fate. The tragedies of Poland and Finland, Zayyat said, were "two warning lights for the small nations which show they cannot rely on anyone, and points to the danger of being help-less and abandoned to isolation and aloneness."[40]

But even when he expressed his profound disappointment with the be-havior of the democratic powers, Zayyat remained convinced that only they are capable, after they realized the severity of the situation, of pro-viding protection for the "small states." As a matter of fact, "the small states have no other option but to stick with the Allies and to hope they will triumph." "The painful, horrible fall of Poland and Finland is a divine warning for all the small states in the West and the East that the victory of Nazism and communism would mean the victory of barbarism [*fawz al-wahshiyya*] which does not recognize the individual's right to live nor the nation's right to independence." Moreover, the victory of Nazism would be "the victory of naked force so that life would not be possible at any mo-ment or in any situation."[41] Hence, the clear-cut conclusion: even if the small states in the Middle East were conducting an anticolonial struggle for national liberation against Britain and France, they could not seek to gain that independence with the help of Nazi Germany. The enemy of one's enemy could not serve as an ally because the imperialist methods that this enemy used were far crueler and demonic.

This conclusion led Zayyat, in those articles of the winter and spring of 1939–1940, not to despair of the possibility of finding a solution. He suggested a twofold resolution. The first was the creation of a bloc (*al-tajamu‘* or *al-takatul*) of the small states into one front that would defend them against "the politics of the fish." The second was a renewed reliance on the democratic powers as the only life preservers that could ensure the independent existence of the "small nations." On the first level, Zayyat proposed a union and mutual aid between the regions of "neighboring states like the Baltic states, the Balkan nations and the Islamic peoples." This union should adopt the model of the United States of America: "a unified foreign policy, overall defense [a joint army], one constitution and government." In this way, no one small nation-state would remain alone exposed to the imperialist ambitions without being able to defend itself by means of a regional defense belt: "This unification policy is the only one that can provide security against the policy of the fish." In the region close to Egypt, Zayyat proposed the creation of a unified front of four-teen Arab Islamic states: Morocco, Algeria, Tunis, Libya, Egypt, Sudan, Palestine, Syria, Hijaz, Yemen, Iraq, Turkey, Iran, and Afghanistan. If these states united according to the American model, Zayyat believed ("they have no choice but to follow in the path of the United States of America"), they would not only effectively protect themselves, but "they will bring constant betterment to the world and a permanent guarantee of peace!" The small-states union must rely on the support of the democratic powers. Here Zayyat came to his second solution. Unions and federations of the small states must be part of the effort of the democratic states to win the war. "The small states must join the democratic nations fighting for peace, freedom, and civilization, as part of their own struggle. Only if the Allies defeat this militaristic, heretic, chauvinistic dictatorship will the small states, today and tomorrow, be able to overcome their weakness and [defend themselves] just as nature provides protection for the weakness of the ants, the bees and the monkeys." Thus, by means of their regional union, they would be able to build, jointly with the democracies, a new world order, one that was safe, stable, and peace loving. Moreover, only the support of the Allies could ensure their ability to achieve national liberation and independence.[42]

Conclusion

Zayyat's anti-Nazism was decisive and vehement. He identified Hitler and Nazi Germany as the perpetrators who created the international crisis on the eve of the war. He squarely blamed Hitler for provoking the war and held him responsible for its horrific results. True, his neoclassical and emotional rhetoric, rife with neotraditionalist metaphors and symbols, was sometimes archaic and overdramatic. Through this language, Zayyat carved out a special niche for himself within the broader anti-Nazi discursive sphere. However, it is imperative to consider that Zayyat's positions were not extraordinary. On the contrary, he was the rule, not the exception. He authentically represented the mainstream public opinion and accurately reflected the widespread moods that dominated the intellectual community of discourse and broader sectors of literate Egyptians.

Zayyat also represented an important intellectual current that simultaneously engendered the "shift to Islamic subjects," yet was starkly anti-Nazi. Public intellectual luminaries such as 'Abbas Mahmud al-'Aqqad, Taha Husayn, Tawfiq al-Hakim, Salama Musa, 'Abd al-Razzaq al-Sanhuri, or second-tier writers such as Muhammad 'Abdalla 'Inan, Ibrahim al-Misri, 'Ali Adham, Niqula al-Haddad, Muhammad Lutfi Jum'a, and Huda Hanum Sha'rawi, each in their own language and mode, expressed an anti-Nazi stance no less pronounced or clear-cut in this period.

When the war broke out, this intellectual community was united in its rejection of Nazi Germany, Nazi doctrine, and above all Hitler, or what they referred to as "Hitlerism" (*al-hitlariyya*). This rejection derived from four enduring elements that were loathed by all of these publicists and intellectuals: Nazi totalitarian dictatorship, Nazi racism, Nazi imperialism, and the Nazi-initiated war's dangerous threat to eliminate the "small nation-states."[43]

All of these intellectuals were also an integral part of the Egyptian national movement and its struggle for independence from British rule. They perceived themselves and their writings as a front in this anticolonial project. Nevertheless, confronting the Nazi challenge, they always preferred British semicolonialism (resultant from the Anglo-Egyptian Treaty of Alliance of 1936) that secured for Egypt substantive independence under a constitutionalist parliamentary government. In the context of the coming war and its unfolding, intellectuals supported liberal democracy, Britain, and the Allies for a plethora of reasons. These reasons ranged from the view of Britain as the lesser of the evils, the defense of democracy and rejection of dictatorship, and their perception of the Allies as the only defense against Nazi annihilation. As Zayyat clearly stated, a triumph for Nazism would usher in the fall into a dark and barbaric world in which simply "there will be no human existence" and "we will not desire to live in it." Hence, only total defeat of Nazism and the unequivocal triumph of Britain and the Allies were the guarantees for the creation of a new world in which Egyptian and universal human existence would be possible. Furthermore, it would renew hope for Egyptian and Arab national liberation, dignity, and sovereignty.

CHAPTER 10

The War and the Holocaust in the Egyptian Public Discourse, 1945–1947

ESTHER WEBMAN

Post–World War II Egypt was a country of great expectations for the ful-fillment of its national aspirations in accordance with the promise epito-mized in the advent of a new era of world order. Although its parliament resolved to join the war on the Allies' side in February 1945 with a very small margin and Prime Minister Ahmad Mahir paid with his life for it, official spokesmen and the newspapers went out of their way to express their joy over the victory of democracy, and of humanitarian, liberal, and universal values. Moreover, they emphasized Egypt's role in the war and contribution to the Allies' victory, reflecting a prevailing trend since early 1943 with the turn of the tide in favor of the Allies.[1] Yet the feeling of ela-tion that grasped major groups of the Egyptian public was short-lived, giving way to frustration and disappointment from the postwar global peace resolutions and the failure of the Great Powers to meet their pledges during the war. This fluctuation in mood soon led to the reevaluation of the war and Egypt's role in it.

The references to the Holocaust also witnessed a change, fluctuating from empathy to the Jewish suffering and a humanitarian approach to the victims to their representation as the major cause of the injustice that be-fell the Arabs. The themes in reference to the Holocaust stemmed from the growing political controversy over the fate of Palestine that had been linked with the problem of the Jewish displaced persons. The responses to the Holocaust were hence rooted in the unfolding reality, as was the rep-resentation of the war. The developments in the regional arena were per-ceived as an integral part of the broader international scene, and the disap-pointment from the Great Powers' attitude, and particularly the Western ones, toward the Palestine problem was intertwined with the disappoint-ment from their attitude toward Egypt's national aspirations. Moreover,

Egyptian dealings with them was also part of a broader preoccupation with the past and collective memory and was heavily affected by the degree of acceptance of Western cultural and ideological influences.

This kind of elation and disillusionment after the war were typical of not only the Egyptian political and intellectual scenes. Other countries under colonial rule striving to gain independence underwent a similar process. Algeria is one case in point, despite the differences in its colonial experience and situation during the war. The French Third Republic was overthrown with France's defeat in June 1940 by Nazi Germany, and its replacement, the collaborationist Vichy regime, imposed racial policies that favored the *pieds-noirs*, the European settlers in Algeria, and abrogated the Jews' French citizenship, alienating Algeria's Muslim population. The Anglo-American landing in Algiers on November 8, 1942, put an end to the Vichy administration in Algeria and gave rise to great hope for liberation among the nationalists, especially after General de Gaulle's arrival in June 1943 and the establishment of a new administration.

But disillusionment was quick to come. The Manifesto of the Algerian People, signed by fifty-six Algerian nationalist and international leaders, was submitted to the French authorities and the Allies in March 1943. It demanded an Algerian constitution that would guarantee immediate and effective political participation and legal equality for Muslims, but General Catroux, who had been appointed *gouverneur général* of Algeria by de Gaulle in June 1943, refused to even consider it. Instead, the French administration in 1944 instituted a reform package ("ordonnance" of March 7) that granted full French citizenship only to certain categories of "meritorious" Algerian Muslims. The first explosion of discontent occurred on V-E Day, May 8, 1945, when a display of Algerian nationalist flags in a Muslim march at Sétif was met with violence that ended in the massacre of about one hundred European settlers and led to countermeasures resulting in the deaths of about fifteen hundred Muslims, according to a French committee of inquiry. Other estimates vary from six thousand to as many as forty-five thousand killed.[2]

The events of the Second World War and the Sétif event, which later became a founding myth in Algerian collective memory, put an end to any hopes of a substantial change in France's colonial policy. The loyal soldiers (the *tirailleurs*) who returned home after the war became disillusioned at the realization that their sacrifices for the sake of the empire were not going to be rewarded by any real improvement in their situation.[3] Disappointment convinced moderate Muslim nationalist Ferhat Abbas, who believed in assimilation with France, that colonialism was "a racist enterprise of domination and exploitation," in which even the most enlightened strands of French republican opinion were fully implicated.[4] Nationalist activist Ahmad Tawfiq al-Madani clearly expressed these prevalent feelings on the second anniversary of victory day:

> May 8 was a day of victory of the Allies against the Germans. It was a day of the collapse of the tyrannical German forces. . . . From a military point of view it was a significant victory, but . . . this was not the victory of freedom as they [the Allies] claimed and still claim. There are still nations under foreign rule around the world. . . . Those believed the promises and agreements and made sacrifices in order to gain their freedoms, self-rule and independence. . . . What was May 8 for these nations? It was a day of bitter disappointment, and collapse of hopes.[5]

This chapter focuses on the changing image of the war and Nazi Germany in Egypt, in an attempt to examine a possible correlation between these changes and the volatile representation of the Holocaust and zooms in on the early period of two to three years, between the last months of the war and 1947.[6] Historian 'Abd al-Rahman al-Rafi'i spoke of a shorter period, describing the year 1946 as "the golden era" of the San Francisco Convention that unfortunately changed already in 1947 due to a serious diversion from the convention's decisions, and a return to the old principles in international relations. Similarly, Tariq al-Bishri referred to the period between the end of the war to mid-1946 as one of the "most pleasant" (*muwata*) periods. Egypt presented its problem at the Security Council, he said, and expected support for a resolution on British evacuation.[7] This period was not only crucial, as it laid down the foundations for the future perception of the war and for the Holocaust discourse, but unique in its diverse representation of both events. The chapter's basic assumption is that there is a correlation between them, although not a direct causal relation, that is reflected in the changes in the perceptions of the war and the emerging attitudes toward the Holocaust. It does not seek to dwell on the representations of the Holocaust and the war,[8] but attempts to explore the relationship between the references to World War II as well as Nazism and the responses to the Holocaust in the Egyptian mainstream discourse, as it was reflected in the press, particularly *al-Ahram* and three major periodicals—*al-Hilal*, *al-Risala*, and *al-Thaqafa*.

This chapter contends that the period under review was indeed a formative period that laid the foundations for the discourses on both the war and the Holocaust and that Egyptians eventually perceived themselves as being reluctantly involved in both cases. Egypt was not an integral part of the scene in both events, but followed them closely. The intellectual interest in the war and negative standing toward Fascist Italy and Nazi Germany[9] had no immediate bearing on actual Egyptian politics. Egypt was keen on keeping out of the war and officially avoided identifying with either side, yet since it was still under British domination, it had to sever its relations with the Axis, turned into a supply base for the Allied forces, and had to subordinate its resources to the war effort, according to the 1936 agreement. Bitter debates raged over the question of the entrance to the war among politicians and intellectuals, partly reflecting ideological differences and dividing them into camps. The palace and a few politicians and army officers identified with the Axis and even created some contacts with Germany,[10] exacerbating Britain's fears and suspicions, which culminated in the February 4, 1942, British ultimatum to the king and intervention for the establishment of a pro-British Wafdist government, headed by Mustafa al-Nahhas. Hence, the issues of the Egyptian public's tendencies during the war, Egypt's entrance to the war, and the February 4 incident that became a founding myth in the narrative of national liberation continued to preoccupy the public discourse and historiography and were integral to the discussions on Egypt's identity and place in the international arena. Debates erupted again by the end of the war when the Great Powers conditioned the participation in the postwar international bodies in declaring war on the Axis.

If on the eve of the war and during the first couple of years the attitude toward it stemmed from a position that it was a European war that did not concern Egypt, the German military defeats and the Allies' foreseen victory created a shift in its perception. It became a war in defense of sublime values against evil forces in which Egypt consciously took part. The mainstream Egyptian political-historical discourse in the immediate aftermath of the war presented the country decidedly on the side of the Allies in the fight against Nazi tyranny, proud of its sacrifices and of its belief in the future new world order that was to secure its national aspirations. However, as it became clearer that Egypt's road to full independence and the complete evacuation of British troops from its soil were far away, this attitude changed again. The first shift hence occurred in the middle of the war, whereas the second gradually occurred during the period under review, in a way like a pendulum, gliding back to its initial position. The war came to be seen as a war of two imperialist camps that Egypt was not responsible for and had nothing to do with, but it had been reluctantly entangled in it and had to pay some of its price, casting doubts on the war's essence and goals. Whereas Nazi Germany was still perceived as deserving all condemnation for its transgressions and crimes, these were now belittled compared with Britain's and the Allies' misdeeds. The moral equation between Nazi Germany and the Allies was made possible by disregarding or belittling the racist and genocidal component of Nazi ideology and practice, particularly the Holocaust.

Similarly, Egyptians observed the Jewish tragedy from afar, they were aware of what had been happening, and they reluctantly became involved in the efforts to resolve the problems created by it. The Holocaust became a matter of growing concern to Arab leaders due to political developments even before the war had ended. The Zionists' calls to abolish the restrictions imposed by the 1939 British White Paper on Jewish immigration to Palestine, invigorated by the emerging problem of Jewish survivors and refugees in Europe, in addition to Zionist demands to establish a Jewish state in Palestine, obliged them to address the Holocaust, directly or indirectly. "We, the Arabs, found ourselves, despite our will, a party to anything that is related to the Jews, including the story of antisemitism," explained leftist writer Ahmad Baha' al-Din two decades later.[11] The evolving discourse clearly shows that there was a flow of information and knowledge about the scope of the horrors. As the solution of the Jewish problem increasingly led to the establishment of a Jewish state in Palestine, Egyptian preoccupation with the Holocaust focused on its political ramifications, on its perceived political exploitation by the Zionists, and on minimizing its scope.

Elation and Identification with the Universal Values of the New World Order

The assassination of Ahmad Mahir, the head of the Sa'dist party, on February 24, 1945, was a manifestation of the political and social tensions that troubled Egypt during and immediately after the war. Mahir, who had been a consistent propagator of Egypt's entrance to the war with the Allies since its beginning, mainly out of pragmatic national considerations, was appointed as prime minister with the removal of Mustafa al-Nahhas by King Faruq on October 8, 1944, one day after the Alexandria Declaration on the establishment of the Arab League. Mahir's proposal to declare war on the Axis to afford Egypt to join the peace negotiations and to take part in the establishment of the new United Nations (UN) organization reignited the controversy that had typified the Egyptian political scene since its eruption. Particularly vociferous was the Wafd opposition to the declaration, which considered it an aggressive act that could entail further Egyptian sacrifices beyond its capacity.[12]

Three major issues engaged Egypt: its political future, its socioeconomic situation, and the redefinition of its national identity. The stage was ripe for the demand to revise the 1936 agreement and for British evacuation. The values for which the war was fought and on which the UN was founded cherished hopes of independence in nations that were under the Great Powers' control. For Egypt, it was an opportunity to integrate into international bodies and gain at the same time an advantage in the negotiations with Britain. Hence, the year 1945 did not only mark the end of a tragic epoch in world history, and Jewish history in particular, but also stood for new hopes for a better world order. It marked growing expectations for a new dawn of independence and sovereignty. Although concerned first and foremost with its domestic affairs and primarily the attainment of complete liberation from British domination, Egypt was deeply involved in all issues pertaining to the Arab lands, including the Palestine question, especially in view of its leading role in the newly established Arab League.[13]

Perhaps a most glaring example of the shift in the attitude toward the war at this stage one can find in two contradicting fatwas, issued by Mufti 'Abd al-Hamid Badawi, defined as *faqih Misr*,[14] in Muhammad Hasayn Haykal's memoirs. The first fatwa was issued on the eve of the war (no exact date given), asserting that according to the 1936 agreement Egypt was not required to declare war that took place in Europe. Similarly, Shaykh al-Azhar Mustafa al-Maraghi, who reportedly had a great influence on the king, stated that this war in Europe "does not concern Egypt" (*la naqa laha fiha wa-la jamal*).[15] However, on February 18, 1945, Badawi issued another fatwa with an opposite message, according to which Egypt should be an active partner in the establishment of the new world order even if this meant declaring war on Germany. In any case, the fatwa added, Egypt took part in the fighting and in defeating Germany since it put all its resources and facilities at the Allies' disposal.[16]

The Egyptian mainstream public in the immediate aftermath of the war, except the Islamists and the ultranationalists, was carried away by the new expectations and emphasized total identification with the Allies in the fight against Nazi tyranny.

Ahmad Mahir declared in February 1945 that he expected Britain to recognize Egypt's independence after the war. "In its approach to the war

Egypt proved that she is a reliable ally, fulfilled its commitments not only according to the agreement's requirements but mobilized all its possible capabilities in the service of democracy that the Allies set out to defend."[17] Tawfiq al-Hakim, who spoke via the mouth of his donkey, described the foundations on which the new world order should be established, reflecting the prevailing belief that emerged from the barrage of articles in the daily press and periodicals: "There are no small nations and big nations," declared the Egyptian delegate to the peace conference. "We are one nation, one world . . . and four liberties. . . . We all undoubtedly agree on the principles presented by the democracies before the end of the war . . . the freedom of thought and speech, the freedom of religion, the liberation from poverty and destitution, and the liberty from oppression and slavery."[18]

After the declaration of war, Mamduh Riyad asserted in *al-Ahram* on March 2, 1945, that the war was a defensive war carried out by the Allies and Egypt with them against the Axis aggression. Egypt, he explained, was part of the Allies' alignment and in a state of war with the Axis since its outset, and even its citizens were considered enemies in occupied Europe. Moreover, its share was bigger than that of other nations who declared war on the Axis before it. An editorial in the same paper on March 9, marking the fiftieth anniversary of the death of Khedive Isma'il, boasted of Egypt's traditional linkage to Europe and its place in the international arena since Isma'il's days. "Western civilization is mankind's legacy" that all should integrate in. By going to San Francisco, Egypt was getting out of its isolation, which meant backwardness and stagnation, in order to integrate into the international scene, fulfill its national demands, and play a role.[19] Similar views were expressed by King Faruq and Prime Minister Isma'il Sidqi, who stressed that Egypt welcomed the Allies' victory out of a belief in the principles of liberty and justice for which they fought. "Democracy suits our spirit," they declared. From the plethora of articles in the same vein, it was made clear that Egypt not only fulfilled its commitments but was a conscientious partner in the war effort, and even if its losses were not as big as the losses of the European nations, it paid a high social and material price in subordinating its economy to the war conditions, and it expected to be compensated for it. Egypt did not require anything except being treated according to the values of the winning camp,[20] "and now it is time for action!" declared an *al-Ahram* editorial, enumerating Egypt's national demands.[21] Muhammad Husayn Haykal even asserted that Egypt's performance in the war was among the reasons for the victory of the Allies in the African fronts.[22] Striving to be part of the League of Nations did not mean, however, neglecting the idea of Arabism (*'uruba*) and belonging to the Arab and the Muslim worlds.[23]

Mustafa Amin, who bemoaned the human victims of the war, for being mostly innocent civilians, also stressed that Egypt fulfilled its commitments and was a friend in times of sorrow and of victory. "Our allies won the war and now they have to win peace and compensate Egypt."[24] The war was perceived as a clash between good and evil, as Hasan al-Zayyat and others implied.[25] He wondered how a man like Hitler, "with no faith like Luther, no statesmanship like Bismarck, no literature like Goethe and no philosophy like Nietzsche could rule 60 million people, who belong to the European distinguished race [*jins mumtaz*], and hypnotize them for ten years." He and Mussolini drowned Berlin and Rome with "a misleading darkness and a suffocating gas which blinded eyes that used to see," he wrote. Nazism impaired the beliefs of the people with its propaganda, bought the conscience of politicians, damaged the spirit of nationalism, sowed death everywhere, and imposed its tyranny. Nazism was destroyed, and in fact it collapsed like a mountain into itself.[26] Responding to Zayyat's article and specifically his astonishment that such a progressive and educated nation yielded to such a tyrant, 'Abbas Mahmud al-'Aqqad pointed to the characteristics of the German political culture, which does not allow freedom of thought, a possibility to judge its leadership, or participation in government. German obedience, he explained, stemmed from historical and geographical circumstances. Germans lived in the middle of the continent and they needed absolute military obedience because they were often in a state of war with their neighbors. Hitler succeeded in deceiving his people not only due to the lack of political culture but also due to his initial victories, which led them to believe that he had both the wisdom and the might to subdue Europe and the world. Drawing a lesson from Hitler's experience, 'Aqqad suggested to the "peoples of the East who waver between schools and views" that they should not sacrifice freedom for merits offered by tyranny in substitute for freedom and independence.[27] During the 1940s, 'Aqqad wrote a few books and many articles and gave weekly talks on the Egyptian radio on Hitler, Nazism, and World War II, which were later compiled into books, reiterating his belief in democracy; attacking the Nazi regime, its methods, and its leader; and consistently perceiving them as a threat to Egypt itself.[28]

Nazi ideology and precepts, the German people's responsibility for the Nazi regime's deeds, and the lessons to be drawn preoccupied the Egyptian public debate during the period under review, especially due to the

Axis defeat, the conditions imposed upon Germany, and the trials of Nazi leaders. The victory was not only the victory of the Allies or the defeat of Nazi Germany; it was the victory of "sublime principles that humanity strived for — a victory of justice, freedom and equality over the principles of tyranny, oppression and brute force," elaborated Muhammad 'Abdallah 'Inan.[29] Germany discussed for years the philosophy of materialistic power, developed by Nietzsche into a national political theory, maintaining that the world was composed of the strong and the weak, the master and the slave. Then came Hitler who declared the superiority of the Aryan race and Germany's right to rule and dominate and to create its required living space. Grieving the sight of "beautiful Europe" bleeding in its ruins, like Zayyat, 'Inan described Germany's "barbaric methods" and "unscrupulous aggression," with which it crushed European civilization and abused the civilized world, not realizing that physical power was not enough for establishing hegemony. Touching upon the question of the German people's culpability, he concluded that since the German people supported "the Hitlerite gang" (*al-'usba al-hitleriyya*) to the end, there was no room to differentiate between the German people and the German state. "The tendency to aggression is rooted in the soils" of the Germans, and Hitlerism was its manifestation. The dissolution of the Nazi Party was not enough. Time was required for uprooting the remnants of Nazism and the German aggressive spirit. 'Inan repeated his belief in democracy in another article published on September 4, boasting of the expansion of democracies to additional states.[30]

Two people were responsible for "the dreadful war," claimed another editorial in *al-Thaqafa*, hoping that with their disappearance "the hated dictatorial system" vanished as well. The two regimes were established, the editorial explained, due to certain circumstances, and the people in both cases believed that it was a temporary phase. But the two tyrants amassed power and consolidated their ideological and cultural grip to fight and destabilize democracy, doubting its ability to resist them. The initial swift victories of Germany seemed to prove that, but the dictatorship's claim has been undermined, and reality proved to support democracy. In conclusion, the editorial asserted that every regime that did not respect the individual's freedom was doomed to failure, and although democracy had its flaws it was able to correct itself.[31]

Muhammad Farid Abu Hadid also spoke of "a cruel philosophy based on egoism, struggle and violence," which should be replaced by a new mentality and a process of reeducation in the spirit of the new principles of the time, whereas Sami 'Azir Jubran indicated that "another Germany, democratic and submissive," should be established.[32] Muhammad 'Awad Muhammad as well shared these views about the war and the Nazi regime's passion for aggression and domination, but found a positive aspect in its conduct. Beyond its organizational qualifications, precision, and capacity to mobilize the whole nation, it clearly declared its intentions. The Nazi leader wrote a book in prison, he said, with no literary value, yet it was sincere (*sarih*), with an accurate description of his plans.[33] Assuming that the German people were submissive and obedient, he wondered nevertheless how there were no more attempts to revolt and assassinate Hitler.[34]

Al-Hilal published an imaginary sentence translated from an English source, in which four judges, "great leaders" of the past—Alexander the Great, Friedrich the Great, Genghis Khan, and Napoleon—unanimously denounced Hitler. He was presented as shedding the blood of humanity, exploiting his country for his needs, and launching a war with no noble goals that only caused destruction everywhere. Although the short play is a translation, its publication meant acceptance and identification with its contents.[35] 'Aqqad added an epilogue to *Mein Kampf*, mocking Hitler and comparing his ambitions to his achievements. "I lied, and lied. . . . I went to a world war without having adequate weapons, except iron and fire and treason and words. . . . My weapon broke and I stood without weapon. My struggle is gone with no remains except these pages."[36]

In his story "My Donkey and Hitler," Tawfiq al-Hakim refers to Hitler's bloodshed. The donkey falls asleep and dreams about "the new shehriyar" the "blood spiller" (*safil al-dama'*), who is not a king but a führer that was not satisfied by slaughtering a virgin every morning and needed a more horrific "blood bath" (*hamam al-dam*). In his dream, Shehrezad went to see Hitler to prevent him from the massacres. Wondering how she got there, he warns that she is really brave if she belongs to the democracies, but she replies that she has no connection either to democracy or Fascism, since she belongs to an era that was not familiar with those terms. Hakim invents an exchange of views between them, in which she asks for freedom of speech for a limited time, states that she abhors violence, and introduces her beliefs in the freedoms of man, thought, persuasion, and faith. After commenting that his military victories are not unique, she suggests that those who rely on the power of God (the prophet and the messenger) and those who rely on the power of thought (the scholar and the artist) persist more than those who rely on the power of the military. His biggest mistake, she contends, was his love of one race and hatred of all the other races, as well as his aspiration to subordinate the nations to the Aryan race by compulsory and aggressive means.[37] Through his imaginative Shehrezad, Hakim expresses his utmost repulsion of Nazism for its racism and militarism and defends his basic belief in democratic principles, albeit avoiding the term.

'Ali Adham wrote about the "crazy ideas" of the Nazis, who exploited the myth of the white man's superiority, invented lies, and adhered to them as an excuse for their deeds, dragging the whole world to "a stormy unrestricted war."[38] Historian Muhammad Fu'ad Shukri also did not mince words in expressing his repulsion of Nazism and Hitler, defining the Nazi ideology as "a limping perverted ideology," based on falsehood, causing only sorrow and pain.[39]

Tyranny is doomed to failure, asserted Sami al-Jaridini, who published a few articles in *al-Hilal*, discussing Nazism and the lessons of the war. Intrigued whether Nazism emanated from German culture or was an aberrant phenomenon, Jaridini reached the conclusion that Nazism as well as Fascism were manifestations of the fanatic nationalist spirit, which seeks to keep other nationalisms inferior and remain superior. In his article on "the struggle of peace," he described the war as a social revolution that started in the aftermath of World War I. Hitler and Nazism were not responsible for causing the war, but the German people were because of their upbringing and philosophical perceptions as well as their military, industrial, political, and spiritual leaders. They assumed that the West was inferior and that Germanic domination over Europe was inevitable, and hence they carried out a revolution against the European order (*nizam*) to impose the German economic, industrial, and cultural mentality. In his postwar article "The Nazi Beast," Jaridini dealt with the question of whether it was feasible to uproot Nazism after its military defeat, reiterating that Nazism was not alien to the Germanic spirit and Hitler only gave vent to its aspirations. "It is a militant people saturated with traditions," he wrote. Defining race theory as "a myth" (*kharafa*), he explained that the Germanic race claimed to preserve its Aryan pure blood. Then Alfred Rosenberg, the ideologue of Nazism, added another element, according to which the Germanic purity made the people infallible and inclined to great achievements. In translating these theories into practice, Nazism subordinated everything to the military authorities and substituted law with power. He portrayed the regime as a military regime and the führer as "pharaoh," as he was perceived as God, both being arrogant and deserving their end. Nazism was an enslavement tool, and Britain faced the German tyranny and fought it out of its love of freedom and independence, he concluded. In his article "The War after Five Years," in the issue of July–August 1944, he identified three results to the war: the emergence of human respect, the effort of reconstruction, and the transformation of economic and social policies from the national to the international sphere.[40] Ahmad Amin as well assumed that the new mentality after the war would strive to unify the world on a universal rather than national basis.[41]

Amir Buqtor believed that history would pass a harsh (*ashadd sarama*) judgment on Hitler and Mussolini, which would be even less sympathetic (*'utfan*) than toward Napoleon. Describing Hitler and Ribbentrop as two "venomous snakes," Buqtor, like Jaridini, considered Hitler as a result of the old Prussian philosophy, whose most important propagators were Nietzsche and Bismarck, "the enemies of democracy, Christianity and justice." The hatred of the Jews as well was not invented by Hitler, he said, describing the rise of anti-Semitism in nineteenth-century Germany. Hitler despised law and justice and had a tendency for revenge and destruction. He hated the Jews and designated women to slavery roles, he added. Buqtor labeled Ribbentrop as "the first criminal," who "was full of arrogance, stupidity and cruelty"; Himmler as "the butcher"; and Goebbels as "a criminal dwarf." The human mind, he concluded, is incapable of grasping the barbaric horrors in the concentration camps and the suffering of their inmates.[42] Buqtor, Jaridini, and others did not ignore Hitler's and Nazism's animosity toward the Jews, yet most of the articles did not raise the issue of the Jews' persistent persecution and their systematic annihilation as a cause for their denunciation.

Addressing the Holocaust

With these perceptions in mind, the flow of information on the Holocaust and the terminology used are of no surprise. The Egyptian press covered the developments in Europe, including the fate of the Jews, quite extensively. The interest and reference to the Jews under Nazi rule did not stem only from the narrow prism of the evolving Middle Eastern conflict. What Israel Gershoni has shown in his study on Egyptian attitudes toward Fascism and Nazism during the 1930s[43] was true for the postwar period as well. Egyptian interest evolved, at least among those agents of culture who led the public debate, from a sense of affiliation with the victorious camp and its cultural values. In this atmosphere, reports on Allied advances and the horrors that they encountered in the Nazi camps or the coverage of the Nuremberg trials were not unusual, and the same could be said about the reference to the Jews.

Most of the descriptions brought here came from the Egyptian dailies, mainly *al-Ahram* and *al-Misri*, which published regular news items on the war. The coverage was factual, mostly neutral, usually quoting news agencies or foreign sources. In some cases, the dailies dispatched their own correspondents to the scenes of events. The number of editorials that reflected a clear political or ideological stance was relatively small. Still, the mere transmission of data was of great importance. The dailies, as Gershoni says, "sought to express the voice of the safe center and the lowest common [political] denominator" in order to reach out for the large literate, not necessarily intellectual, public.[44]

As early as January 1945, we can find reference to the massacre of the Jews (*madhabih al-yahud*)[45] and German atrocities (*faza'i' al-alman*), with a precise, detailed description of the death factory (*ma'mal al-mawt*), which included gas chambers (*ghuraf al-ghaz*) and crematoria to get rid of bodies (*ghuraf al-muhraka lil-takhallus min al-juthath*).[46] Other reports spoke of the "selections" (*'amaliyat al-farz*), crematoria (*ifran*) in the Nazi death factories (*masani' al-mawt*), as well as the German death camps (*mu'askarat al-i'dam al-almaniyya*), the camps of horrors (*mu'askarat al-ahwal*), and torture camps (*mu'askarat al-ta'dhib*).[47] References to human carnage (*majzara bashariyya*), extermination (*ibada*) in crematoria (*maha-riq*), or Nazi brutality (*quswat al-nazi*) were also frequent.[48] Nor did the paper ignore the Jewish identity of the victims, speaking of Jewish martyrs (*shuhada' al-yahud*) or of the catastrophe of the Jews (*nakbat al-yahud*). Reporting on memorial ceremonies held by the Jews in Palestine in March 1945, *al-Ahram* pointed to the "Jewish casualties of the Axis which led to the extermination of a third of the Jewish people." Later it quoted U.S. president Harry Truman, saying that 5.7 million Jews perished by the Nazis.[49]

All of these phrases were faithful to the English and Hebrew terminology. The idioms *faza'i'* and *idtihad* became entrenched in Arab terminology at the time, just as their respective English equivalents, *atrocities* and *persecutions*, were most common in official documents and journalistic writings, referring not only to the Jews but to all victims of Nazism. Although the terms *Holocaust* and *Shoah* appeared during the war, they acquired their meaning as denoting specifically the Jewish suffering and genocide under the Nazis only years later.[50]

Concurrently, a parallel terminology emerged in reference to the Jewish refugees, which reflected the evolution of Arab attitudes toward the Holocaust and its survivors. In the early reports appearing toward the end of the war, the word *refugees* (*laji'un*) was most frequently used to denote Jewish and other displaced persons in Europe. But once the issue of Jewish immigration to Palestine entered center stage, the term *immigrants* (*muhajirun*) most often replaced it.[51] Occasionally, the survivors were described as "the Jewish remnants in Europe" (*ma baqiya fi Urubba min al-yahud*), as "victims of Nazi madness" (*dahaya al-junun al-nazi*), as "survivors of Nazi horrors" (*al-najun min ahwal al-nazi*), and as "the dispersed refugees" (*al-laji'un al-musharradun*).[52] Writing in *al-Katib al-Misri* in mid-1946, on his sailing from Alexandria to Beirut through the port of Haifa, Taha Husayn described his impressions of Jewish displaced persons on their way to Palestine. On the ship, there were "about 1000 weak Jewish refugees," he said, children, young girls, and women who lost their husbands and all they had, "even the ability to smile a sad smile at the slightest hope." Some of them had lost all, but new life was flourishing inside them, "enlightening their wounded hearts with hope and despair, satisfaction and loath, comfort and pain." Husayn added that these immigrants were imposed on Palestine and there were many other places that could absorb them better than Palestine, but when the ship anchored in Haifa he was filled with a mixture of "rage, anger, compassion and pity."[53] This essay apparently angered many Egyptian intellectuals, who thought that he was repeating Zionist propaganda, as Siham Nassar commented in her book on Egyptian Jewry and its press, published thirty-five years later. Yet, she added, it was also a proof that Egyptian intellectuals differentiated between Zionism as a political movement and Judaism as a religion and between their antagonism toward Zionism and their sympathy toward the persecuted Jews.[54]

It was clear at this stage that the issue of the "persecution of the Jews by the Nazi regime" posed a burden on the outright rejection of Jewish immigration. Therefore, writers made attempts to separate it from the discussion of the Palestine problem and present it as a humanitarian universal problem, the solution to which they were willing to take part in. In this way, one could identify with the Jewish pain and at the same time oppose Jewish immigration to Palestine and Zionist political ambitions. This approach befitted the prevailing perception of the new world order and Egypt's role in it. "Undoubtedly, a solution has to be found for the Jewish problem, but colonizing Palestine is not a solution to the universal Jewish problem, and it would be unjust to demand solely from the Arabs to solve it at their expense," *al-Hilal* wrote, adding that opposition to Zionism did not contradict Arab compassion to past Jewish plight.[55] The dailies' reports indeed reflected the changes in the attitudes toward the Jews as the conflict escalated, although they lagged behind the periodicals that were unequivocally identified with specific political and ideological orientations.

The coverage of the Nuremberg trials held against the leaders of the Nazi regime between October 1945 and November 1946 sheds additional light on the representation of the Holocaust as well as the perceptions of Nazism and the war. Although the murder of Jews was not discussed as a distinct subject, it was included in the more comprehensive category of war crimes and crimes against humanity.[56] In general, the coverage in *al-Ahram* was comprehensive, in its discussion on the meaning of the trials, in reviewing the charges, and in producing the testimonies against and by the defendants. Moreover, it seems that *al-Ahram* adopted a moral position vis-à-vis the defendants, both in style and in content. It used phrases such as *Nazi war criminals* and emphasized the charges against the Nazi leaders, accusing Karl Dönitz, for instance, of waging "an inhumane war."[57] Likewise, the coverage of the Jewish issue was extensive, giving details of the "mass killing of Jews," charges, and testimonies.[58]

Most revealing was the publication of an eight-article series by an unnamed Egyptian correspondent in Germany during February 1946, based on interviews in addition to his impressions from the Nuremberg trials and from visits to German cities and Nazi camps. Clearly, in these reports the writer allowed himself to express his personal views much more explicitly than in the regular news items. His second story focused on the Nazi leaders. He labeled Göring an "arch-criminal, a criminal of the brutal kind" (*shaykh al-mujrimin, mujrim min al-naw' al-qasi*). Rudolf Hess appeared to him as being at a "total loss of consciousness as far as human heart and conscience are concerned," whereas Alfred Rosenberg was presented not only as "the philosopher of Nazism" but as hating Muslims, and Julius Streicher was depicted as the "implacable enemy of the Jews and Judaism."[59]

In his account of his visit to Dachau, the "grave of the living" (*maqbarat al-ahya'*), he refuted allegations already spreading that the atrocities against the Jews were considered "figments of [the] imagination" (*shubuhat*). "The matter is neither Jewish lies [*akadhib*] nor Anglo-Saxon propaganda," as some people said, but rather "the most horrifying crimes that human beings had ever or will ever commit."[60] However, the correspondent described the trials as "a dangerous precedent and a revolution in the history of law." If the idea was to try the Nazis for what they committed after August 1939, that is, "invasion of foreign lands without warning, the destruction of cities and their civilian population, the destruction of countries, the extermination of populations, torturing people, killing of hostages, the theft of treasures and the expertise in methods of killings, then it is the duty of anyone who wishes well for future generations." But it would be a "crippled ['arja'] justice" if the goal was to punish them for annexing Austria and eliminating Czechoslovakia without putting on the bench with them those who enabled them to do so, "sang the praises of their good intentions," and promised to look the other way so long as they left the West and turned their forces eastward.[61] The writer's criticism of the trials, in his otherwise balanced and comprehensive reporting, was increasingly reinforced in the Egyptian discourse and reflected dilemmas that were not overlooked in Western debates on the trials.

Disillusionment and Disappointment

The first expressions of feelings of missed opportunity appeared already by the end of 1945, especially in view of the British ambiguous messages as to Egypt's demands for independence.[62] Jacques Berque described the period between the end of the war to 1950 as "a dark period, during which Egypt experienced disappointments as great as her hopes, the anger of the under-privileged flared up in violence, and the contrast between the maturity of men's demands and the indefinite postponement of solutions reached its highest pitch."[63] Egypt was given the chance to participate in the newly established international bodies, but it soon realized that those did not provide it with any advantage in its negotiations with Britain over the issues of British evacuation and full independence and did not change its domestic situation. Unemployment due to the end of the war, the rising inflation rates, and the continuing urbanization process created growing discontent, which had been aggravated by similar problems in other Arab countries and by the Palestine problem.

Egypt participated in military operations and mobilized all its economic resources, asserted the government's memorandum to the peace conference in 1946 and Prime Minister Nuqrashi's speech to the Security Council on August 11, 1947, and therefore, it was surprised that its demands were completely disregarded.[64] The hope to end the Fascist aggression was mixed with other hopes, which were not being fulfilled, wrote Muhammad 'Awad Muhammad. The foreign ministers' conference in London (in the beginning of October) failed, and the inability to decide on a new one made it difficult to look to the upcoming year with hope. 'Awad Muhammad emphasized that Egypt and the Arab and Muslim worlds supported the Allies, although they were aware that they made mistakes in their relations with them and that the crimes committed by the Nazis had parallels in the conduct of the non-Fascist countries. The Nazis were not the first rulers to violate agreements and hurt the weak. The peoples of the East were firmly aware that the defeat of the Axis was indeed a victory of the whole world, and the disillusionment did not prove that they regretted the destruction of the Axis aggression, but they believed that this would put an end to all kinds of aggression. The U.S. policy in relation to the Italian colonies and the Palestinian problem—"two of the most horrific crimes" (*min afza' al-atham*)—was disappointing, he concluded.[65]

'Abdallah 'Inan also spoke of the prevailing pessimistic mood and concern just a few weeks after the end of the war due to those unresolved problems. He pointed to the UN as violating its own promises and agreements. "As the war became more comprehensive and dangerous [*arwa' wa-ashadd khataran*], the promises became more shining and benevolent [*alma' wa-a'zam*]," and so the awakening from the pleasant dreams was swift and painful, he wrote. Egypt was not invited to participate in the peace conference, and the Anglo-American Committee passed a death sentence on Palestine. It made many sacrifices for the Allies and for the democratic front and assumed that "by making those heavy sacrifices she serves her national cause," but a year had passed since the end of the war and Egypt was still grappling with economic problems and social concerns.[66]

The disappointment was manifested in a poll that the monthly *al-Hilal* conducted among 6,417 students in June 1947. To the question, if they would address international organizations for resolving disputes, most of them answered that they had no confidence in them because they would not stand by the small states. Lack of confidence in international organizations was also the result of the question of the best way to achieve full independence; more than two-thirds of the respondents indicated "struggle and self-reliance" were better. Most students also preferred Egypt to maintain neutrality in international affairs rather than commit itself to either bloc.[67]

As Egypt faced more difficulties in achieving its full independence and the evacuation of British forces, the damages incurred to it during the war, the sacrifices it made, and its feeling of deception were highlighted, while casting retrospective doubts on the war and its goals.[68] Nazi Germany was still perceived as deserving denunciation for its misdeeds and ideology, but those started to shrink in comparison to Britain's behavior.

These two motifs—magnification of the Egyptian effort during the war and the comparison between the two fighting camps—were the core of the shift in the representation of the war.

An *al-Ahram* editorial marking the anniversary of the Balfour Declaration considered the war as a conflict between two sets of beliefs that emerged from Christianity and the French Revolution, between a model of a new state and a new regime embodied in the Axis states and an old model of state and regime.[69] The British deceived Egypt, claimed 'Abd al-Majid Nafi'. They introduced the Second World War as "a revolution against the Nazi tyranny," but it seems that Britain went to war not to defend democracy and the liberties of nations but to defend its empire.[70] World War II was an imperialist war, as was the previous world war. "The most horrific tragedy [*arwa' ma'asa*] in human history deeply shook the essence of civilization [*hadara*]," but man did not learn anything.[71] The agreements after the war were also seen in a different light. Nafi' contended that they resembled the agreements made after World War I, and attacked the international court for wavering with the wind and proving that "justice is for power." The Nuremberg trials showed, he argued, that the civilized [*mutamaddin*] man mocks justice for the sake of his killing instincts. Among those Nazi leaders who were executed, there were innocent men whose only crime was their "allegiance to the service of their state." They would become legends in the future, and their memories would be cherished.[72]

'Ali Adham also pursued this logic, claiming that all the leaders during the war deceived their people. They spoke of ideals and moral values, but in fact they believed only in their interests and aspirations. There was no room for moral ideals in the political world and international relations, he concluded. The situation quickly deteriorated, said an editorial in *al-Thaqafa*. The Great Powers forgot their promises and returned to their old ways and disagreements.[73] Similarly, Sami 'Azir Jubran, who published the book *Al-Mushkila al-almaniyya* (The German problem) in 1946, attributed the responsibility for the war to both sides. The view that a people had an aggressive character was false, he claimed. Nazism and Fascism were not German or Italian phenomena but international phenomena that existed in different parts of the world. The German people were a peaceful people and should not be punished for the crimes of Nazism. The themes of the book, reviewed by historian 'Abd al-Rahman al-Rafi'i, appeared in an article dealing with "the responsibilities of peoples and their attributes" in view of the Nuremberg trials. The Germans were accused of being complacent with the Nazi regime, he posed, but the British and the French also did not respond to their governments' acquiescence to Hitler's demands, although they lived in democratic countries and had the means to express themselves. Rejecting the notion of collective responsibility, Jubran concluded that the vanquished were measured by a double standard, sowing the seeds of the next world war.[74]

Ahmad Hasan al-Zayyat, who expressed harsh criticism of Hitler in the 1930s,[75] was longing for him in 1947. Outraged by the French and British continued colonization of North Africa and the Middle East, he described Hitler as having "good intentions and sincere views," who understood that the biggest trouble was capitalism, "which means the Jews and their pimps, who strive on the blood of society like fleas and lice," and that their annihilation would uproot corruption and thefts. For this, "the deceased" was sentenced to death by Weitzman and Churchill. "Had God wanted peace on earth," Zayyat went on to say, he would have rendered this sentence to Roosevelt and Stalin and set the criminal free. "Had God enabled Hitler to be a judge [in Nuremberg], there would have been no problem in Palestine, in the Sudan, in North Africa or Indo-China."[76]

During the period under review, the debate over Egypt's role in the war did not deal with the attitudes and sentiments of the Egyptian public and leadership toward the Axis and Nazi ideology. This seems to have started later in the late 1950s and early 1960s with the new historiography on the war initiated by the regime. This topic, as Salah al-'Aqqad and 'Abbas Mahmud al-'Aqqad indicated, touched upon a sensitive nerve in the collective memory and aroused heated discussions on the nature and development of the national struggle and the role of each political group in it.[77] The only references to the Egyptian public tendencies during the war were reports on articles published abroad or on the British accusations in the UN General Assembly, and they were vehemently rebuffed. *Al-Misri* published a report on an article in a Swiss paper that maintained that Egyptians still felt sympathy toward Germany. The journalist described meetings with lawyers and doctors who showed him German anti-Semitic pamphlets, found in the German Legation in Cairo before the war, and he was impressed by their conviction of their accuracy. He claimed that German propaganda found a tentative ear in the Middle East, since the Arab world shared the German animosity toward the Jews, and this had increased since the events in Palestine. *Al-Misri*'s reporter, however, was surprised by this information, finding the article "full of strange imagination" and therefore worth reporting.[78] A year later, *al-Ahram* published a letter that appeared in the *Guardian*, claiming that many Egyptians would have welcomed Rommel if he had occupied Egypt. The letter quoted an unidentified Egyptian, who emphasized that Britain did not save Egypt during the war; on the contrary, Britain exposed Egypt to danger and hence should compensate it. This reporter was also surprised by the dissemination of this "old story," but attributed it to Britain's depreciation of Egypt's efforts during the war.[79]

A major issue in this mood of disillusionment was the Palestinian problem, which had become, since the end of the war, an urgent issue on the public agenda, intertwined in domestic politics and in the struggle for national liberation, reaching its peak on May 15, 1948, with the launching of war against the nascent Jewish state in parts of Palestine. It provided a further impetus to attack Western powers by comparing them to Nazi Germany or accusing them of scheming with Zionism against the Arabs. Egyptian intellectuals were mobilized by a deep conviction when writing about the Palestinian problem, the intentions to turn part of Palestine into a Jewish state, and the dangers posed by Jewish immigration to the Arab states.[80] Muhammad 'Awad Muhammad considered the Palestinian problem the "test case" of the new world order. "Imposing a Jewish state on Palestine exceeds in its tyranny and aggression the greatest crimes [atham] carried out by the Axis states," he contended. The Axis states indeed committed awful crimes in the occupied areas, but they did not claim to establish a regime based on justice, and they did not enforce a foreign people in a country under their control.[81] "Where are you, the Atlantic convention!?" posed Muhammad Tawfiq Diyab. Arabs fantasized in their dreams of a new America after the war, but they realized that both the United States and Britain were "our enemies," conducted a crooked policy, and complied with Zionist and Jewish machinations.[82] Calling Arabs to wake up and beware the Western deceit, Sayyid Qutb, then a literary critique and later an Islamist thinker, attacked the Jewish immigration to Palestine and criticized both politicians and intellectuals for believing in Western civilization and the bankrupt Western conscience. Qutb bluntly reiterated his views in October 1946, following the publication of the Anglo-American Committee's findings, stating that all Westerners had "a rotten conscience, a false civilization, and a huge deception called 'democracy.'"[83]

"We thought that the fall of the dictatorship in Europe and Asia would enable the great democracies to provide a just treatment to the problem emanating from the persecution [idtihad] of the Jews," said 'Abd al-Rahman al-'Azzam, secretary-general of the Arab League in his response on August 19, 1945, to President Truman's proposal to enable the immigration of Jews to Palestine. Such immigration would harm Arab interests and lives and would be a "pointless factor" in resolving the universal Jewish problem, he said, adding that "the persecution and oppression of the Arabs in order to help persecuted Jews is not a moral or practical solution."[84]

Following the publication of the Anglo-American Committee's recommendations, the Egyptian press, while stressing the need to distinguish between the Palestinian and the Jewish problems, agreed that the recommendations meant a "death sentence for Arab Palestine." Tying the two issues was perceived as a crude political mistake, which proved the indecent intentions of the international community to unjustly impose upon Arab Palestine the burden of the Jewish problem. Sayyid Qutb, who advocated terrorist activity against the British at the time, concluded that the Jews had achieved their goals in the war.[85] His point gradually took center stage in the Arab discourse, which presented the Jews as the real victors of World War II.

The Egyptian Parliament discussed the government's response to the Anglo-American Committee's report on May 14, 1946, and parliament member Fikri Abaza was quoted by *al-Ahram* the following day as supporting the government's criticism of the report. The committee chose to nullify the white paper and transfer one hundred thousand European Jews to Palestine, "even though there is no linkage between the problem of the Jews in Europe and the Palestine question," he said. "It needed courage to tell Britain to relocate the Jews to Australia or another place in its vast empire, but it did not find a solution except of bringing a catastrophe [*nakba*] on Palestine." If the problem of European Jews was a universal one, the whole world should have decided on the means to solve it. "The evil acts perpetrated in Palestine by the Zionists are threatening all Arab countries," he added. Abaza expressed his disappointment with the disappearance of the "noble principles that we have heard during the war from the Allies," and concluded, "Hitler died, but in his place 100 Hitlers have emerged."[86]

The struggle against Zionism became a major component in the public discourse of all ideological trends and an integral part of national identity and commitment for national liberation. Egyptian intellectuals perceived the need to confront Zionism as an existential challenge, as they perceived Nazism in the 1930s.[87] The debate over the Zionist movement, its ideology, its political ambitions, and its nature focused on the allegedly racist aspects of the Zionist ideology, which reflected Nazism and Fascism. In his writings, 'Aqqad exemplified this shift from Nazism to Zionism. The Egyptian public debate on Nazism diminished at the end of the period under review. Instead, debating the attributes of Zionism exposed the prevailing perceptions of Nazism as a benchmark of evil. Ibrahim 'Abd al-Qadir al-Mazini also identified a potential danger in a "Zionist state" to all the Arab countries neighboring Palestine, equating Zionist ambitions in the Middle East with Hitler's "living space" and racism.[88] A similar portrayal of Zionism was published in an editorial of *al-Thaqafa*, accusing Zionism of exploiting the Jewish tragedy in Germany to encourage immigration to the "promised land, cherished by their myths." They dreamed not only about Palestine, it said, but about all the Near East as their "living space." Moreover, they perceived themselves as "the Chosen people" who had the virtues and schemes to control the whole world.[89]

Zionism was also perceived as impairing the course of history. The belief that reality was changing and the world was moving toward the dissolution of nationalism and sectarian interests turned Zionism into the epitome of the old values and ugly nationalism.

This duality was manifested in the representation of the Holocaust as well and allowed writers, such as 'Aqqad and others, to create texts that complied with the basic paradigms of the war and the Holocaust and included accurate historical details and events, but at the same time expressed different views. 'Aqqad continued to preach for democracy, yet the introduction to his book on the war, published in 1970, urged the readers to remember "the black history" of the old Nazis for learning a lesson on the Zionists, who "resemble them, imitate them and follow their criminal course."[90] Anwar Kamil published a book as early as 1944, comparing Nazism and Zionism while recognizing the horrors of the Holocaust.[91]

The Holocaust became a matter of growing concern to Arab leaders due to political developments even before the war had ended. The Zionists' calls to abolish the restrictions imposed by the 1939 British White Paper on Jewish immigration to Palestine, invigorated by the emerging problem of Jewish survivors and refugees in Europe, in addition to Zionist demands to establish a Jewish state in Palestine, obliged them to address the Holocaust, directly or indirectly. As the solution of the Jewish problem seemed to lead to the establishment of a Jewish state in Palestine, Egyptian preoccupation with the Holocaust focused on its political ramifications and on its perceived political exploitation by the Zionists. Unlike the earlier matter-of-fact reports during 1944–1946 about the horrors that were revealed during the liberation of the Nazi camps and by the Nuremberg trials, the ensuing references to the Holocaust became highly charged, and their point of departure was that of conflict and confrontation. The Holocaust was no longer viewed as a neutral fact but seen

as a catalyst to an adverse course of events and a major justification for
the enemy. The Holocaust and "pangs of conscience" in Western countries for the failure to help the Jews during the war came to be seen as a
major means for rallying international support for the Zionist solution to
the plight of the Jews. Three basic approaches could be discerned in the
references to the Holocaust: One still recognized the Jewish tragedy but
sought to separate the survivors' issue from the question of Palestine and
present it as an international humanitarian problem, in whose solution
the Arabs could take part. Thus, it was possible to express compassion for
Jewish pain together with unequivocal rejection of Jewish immigration
to Palestine and of Zionist political goals. Such an attitude was congru-
ent with the aspirations of Arab elites to be integrated into the postwar
world order and with their awareness of Arab dependency on Britain and
the United States. The second approach, stemming from the belief that
because of the Holocaust, Zionism succeeded in realizing its national,
political aspirations, sought to understate or minimize the meaning of
the Holocaust by using ambiguous terms or depicting it as a problem of
civil discrimination, going as far as partial or complete denial. The third,
seeking to delegitimize Zionism, blamed the Zionist movement or the
Jews for what befell them.

The reactions to UNSCOP's recommendations published on August
31, 1947,[92] calling for the partition of Palestine into two states, a Jewish and an Arab, were unequivocal in their rejection. They were seen as
"a further violation of the principles of justice and [legitimate] right"
and "a mark of disgrace on the forehead of human justice." How could
the world, which fought the Nazi tyranny and founded the United Nations, agree "to the results of that awful partition," wondered Egyptian
writer Ahmad Hamza.[93] Christian writer Niqula al-Haddad, who portrayed the Jews in negative terms, accused them of taking advantage of
the humanism and compassion of the Christian Europeans following the
recent persecutions, which he defined as expulsion and expropriation of
their property.[94] Beside these first signs of denial and relativization, two
points assumed ever-growing importance: first, the accusation of inflat-
ing the scope of the persecution of the Jews in Europe by Zionism to justify the claim over Palestine and extort universal conscience, and, second,
the argument that a Jewish state would not provide security to the Jews in
general and to Middle Eastern Jewry in particular.[95] Mahmud Muhammad Shakir warned that the Arabs who opened their doors for Jews fleeing
persecution would no longer have any compassion toward the Jews. "We
pitied them when they were persecuted. We provided them with shelter

when they were expelled, and opened our lands to them when they were driven out like leper dogs by the ancient Christian peoples. But they denied and forgot it all, and they had bitten the hand that healed their pain and wounds throughout history." Shakir described the Jewish immigrants as "the scum [*hathala*] of the Jews," as "the lowest [*ardhal*] creatures," and as "human carcasses," and charged the Great Powers with committing an unprecedented crime by imposing them on another people.[96]

Conclusion

By the end of 1947, compassion toward the Jews had faded in both the official and the public discourses, giving rise to a growing alienation toward the Holocaust and to an approach emphasizing that the Arabs were not responsible for it and that if they would bear its brunt, it would be a tragedy no less serious than the Holocaust. In the coming years, all the themes that were identified during this formative period were developed and came to typify the discourse on the Holocaust. Although they did not constitute a systematic coherent narrative, one can discern a trend moving from recognition of the event as a human disaster whose burden the Egyptians and Arabs in general were ready to share to alienation, relativization, denial, and justification. The diversity of voices and the willingness to deal evenhandedly with the Holocaust were substituted by a more monolithic discourse that increasingly utilized it in the rhetoric of the Arab-Israeli conflict and referred mainly to its political ramifications.

A similar process occurred in relation to the war, and it came to be seen as a war of two imperialist camps that Egypt was not responsible for and had nothing to do with, but it had been reluctantly entangled in it and had to pay some of its price. However, if in relation to the discourse on the war, one could discern a pendulum movement in relation to the Holocaust, it was a linear development, and only since the mid-1990s can one identify a change in the mainstream discourse and a return to acknowledging the Holocaust as a historical fact. The discourse on the war during its last phases and immediately after its termination conformed with the Western perceptions and had an impact on the references to Nazi Germany and on the attitudes toward the persecution of the Jews by the Nazis. This explains the empathy toward the Jewish victims by some writers, the embarrassment that the international and regional political developments created, and the crisis of faith when the hopes for a better reality were shattered in view of the Great Powers' reluctance to acknowledge the

Egyptian right for independence. Nevertheless, *Nazism* remained a pejorative term to delegitimize the West and particularly Zionism. This transformation was clearly seen in the writings of major intellectuals, such as 'Abdallah 'Inan, Hasan al-Zayyat, 'Abd al-Qadir al-Mazini, and Muhammad 'Awad Muhammad, and in the approach of the major mainstream periodicals. This leaves one wondering how the shift could be so swift and whether it indicates a fragile belief in democracy, dependent on pragmatic considerations and concrete gains.

The moral equation between Nazi Germany and the Allies was made possible by disregarding or belittling the racist and genocidal component of Nazi ideology and practice, particularly the Holocaust. Ahmad Baha' al-Din asserted that Germany should not be blamed for the imperialist war, in which two capitalist regimes fought for world dominance. Just as the Germans had destroyed and killed in the countries which they occupied, so did the Allies cause great destruction in Germany, "and that should suffice to settle the account," he concluded.[97] The 1962 National Charter, the major ideological program of Nasserist Egypt, stated that the "people expressed itself by its adamant refusal to take part in a war that was nothing but a conflict over colonies and markets between Nazi racism and Franco-British imperialism, which brought upon humanity as a whole unlimited disasters of mass killing and destruction." The Egyptian people rejected the slogans that both sides voiced "in order to deceive world nations."[98]

Writing in the late 1960s, Egyptian historian Muhammad Kamal Dissuqi of the nationalist camp denounced both Allied and German historians for not taking an objective position and for presenting their side as fighting for high moral values. He described Nazism as a racist expansionist movement and referred to the Nazi system of oppression: the concentration camps, the plans to Germanize large areas of Europe by exterminating the local population and settling Germans, and the murder of invalids and mental patients in Germany.[99] Yet, for Dissuqi, the evil inherent in Nazism did not justify the Allies, as the war was a struggle between two imperialist forces whose economic interests clashed. The difference between them was mainly in the terminology they used, not in their deeds. Churchill, the French, and the Japanese used the term *colonies* (*musta'marat*) unabashedly, Hitler spoke of a "living space," Stalin demanded territorial gains, whereas Roosevelt spoke of "financial profits." The true meaning of all of these terms was one: the enslavement and plundering of the small nations. Worst of all was world Zionism, which played a leading role in pushing the world toward war and incited the other states against Hitler. Dissuqi expressed his solidarity with the German people, explaining that he fully shared their "pains and hopes." Had historians objectively described the atrocities that the Allied forces committed in Germany, he says, "we would have seen more severe crimes beyond anything that the human mind could describe."[100]

The question of Egypt's entrance into the war or its position toward the fighting camps, which aroused bitter controversies among politicians and intellectuals, and even in later years seemed to elicit passionate debates whenever it was raised,[101] was not a major issue during the period under review. The number of historical studies on Nazi Germany and the war published in the Arab world is strikingly low, especially when compared with the "explosion" of such publications in the West, claimed Salah al-ʿAqqad. In an attempt to explain this paucity, he pointed to the common misperception of Arab passivity during the war compared with their more important role during World War I, the cultural-ideological shift that they had experienced then from Ottoman-Islamic identity to nationalism, and an alleged lack of historical perspective. He found the latter reason particularly unsatisfactory, considering the sources available to Arab historians. In subsequent decades, this lacuna has been filled by several works.[102] However, there is a remarkable void in historical studies on the Holocaust despite the frequent reference to it in the public discourse, in contrast to the vast volume of literature on Zionism, Israel, and Judaism.

PART V

OTHER ARAB VOICES

CHAPTER 11

The Tiger and the Lion:
Fascism and Ethiopia in Arab Eyes

HAGGAI ERLICH

Double Conceptual Dichotomy

The "Ethiopian Crisis" of 1935 had a tremendous impact on global history. It destroyed the "collective security" concept of the League of Nations and opened a chain of developments that eventually led to the outbreak of World War II. In Arab societies of the Middle East, the international crisis inspired the emergence of a new "political generation." The students' riots in Egypt of November–December, the youth demonstrations in Damascus in December, the Palestinian revolt that began in April 1936, and the military takeover in Iraq of October 1936 marked new beginnings in the region's political culture. Some of the new energy stemmed from tensions created by Mussolini's multidimensional challenge to the strategic order in the Middle East. His threat to destroy the neighboring Christian empire of Ethiopia while directly defying British and French international hegemony, and his propaganda in which he portrayed himself as a champion of Islam and a supporter of Arab nationalism, combined to galvanize Arab publics and present them with serious dilemmas. On the one hand, there was the option of sympathizing with the Italians as "the enemy of our enemies." As a new power, positioned on the periphery of Libya, Eritrea, Somalia, and Ethiopia, the Italians could humiliate the occupiers of the core Arab countries, the old and now seemingly weary British and French. The Italian Fascists offered a dynamic ideology of integrative, idealist nationalism, a unifying force bursting from the young soul of the nation. For many Arabs, the hymn of Italian Fascism, "La Giovinezza" (the youth), was compatible with the rising Arab concepts of *futuwwa* or *shabiba*, as signifying the renewed leadership of a rejuvenated spirit. The hope that Italy, from the periphery and through the rising Arab youth, would help to achieve freedom and unity inspired a political wing, already alive and kicking, in core Arab publics and countries.

On the other hand, there were forces no less powerful that conceived Mussolini and Fascism as the worst manifestation of Western aggression. Many already understood that Fascism, by its very nature, cannot be an ideology of international solidarity, but only one of aggression and dominance. Mussolini made it clear in 1926, his "year of Napoleon" and of "Mare Nostrum," that he intended to revive Roman rule in the East. He demonstrated this in Libya where he showed his brutal hand, especially by hanging, in September 1931, the local freedom fighter 'Umar al-Mukhtar. Moreover, as of early 1935 and the beginning of the Ethiopian Crisis, Fascism was also showing its racist dimension. Italian propaganda, especially as of 1932, tried to radiate friendliness toward Islam and Arabs, but once preparations began to conquer Ethiopia, the Fascists made no effort to conceal their sense of white superiority. The entire imperialist enterprise of conquering Ethiopia was presented by Rome as a "civilizing mission," depicting Ethiopians as clearly inferior and resorting to racist terminology, which was often harsher than that of nineteenth-century imperialists. For many members of Arab publics, Fascism and Mussolini's Italy were dreadful, compared to which the British and the French seemed a lesser evil. The Ethiopian Crisis, they thought, should be exploited to convince London and Paris to more strongly support parliamentarian nationalists in the Middle East and to expand the local spheres of political autonomy.[1]

Needless to say, the dichotomous conceptualization of the Italian Fascist "other" reflected trends that competed for the nature of the nationalist "self" in Egypt and the Fertile Crescent. The aim of this chapter is to revisit that conceptual dilemma from another angle, integrally connected.

The discourse in the Middle East about Fascism and Italy was inescapably also discourse about Ethiopia as a neighboring Christian, African, and Eastern state. Like elsewhere in the world, people had to take sides, and the discussion of Ethiopia among Muslims gave the arguments an even deeper historical significance. Whereas Italian ambitions and Fascist ideology presented very modern challenges, Ethiopia presented the essential dichotomies that had been recycled from the early days of Islam. It is necessary to briefly mention this historical background, for the crisis makes it relevant to the process of redefinition of the political culture in Arab and Islamic societies.

Ethiopia was the first foreign relations case in Islam. The Prophet's earliest followers, the *sahaba*, who were persecuted in Mecca by the local

Arab pagans, were instructed by Muhammad in 615–616 to seek asylum with the Christian king, *al-Najashi* (*negus* means "king") Ashama of al-Habasha (Ethiopia). Thus, the first hegira was to Christian Ethiopia, and Najashi Ashama, recognizing the refugees as believers in one God, gave them shelter and enabled them to prosper in his country. This episode, a story of early Islam's survival, redemption, and success, left a double message for Muslims.

The Ethiopian Christian *Najashi*'s generosity, his refusal to betray the first small community of Muslims to their Meccan persecutors, his befriending of and corresponding with the Prophet, and his contribution in other ways to Muhammad's victory have continued to resonate among Muslims across the centuries. The Prophet was said to have dictated that his followers should "leave the Ethiopians alone as long as they leave you alone," which, for many ever since, has been a message of flexibility and tolerance. For moderates, the Ethiopian benevolence and the Prophet's attitude and teachings meant that Islam accepts Ethiopians as legitimate neighbors and that in spite of their Christianity, they deserve eternal gratitude.

However, later in the story, according to Islamic sources, in the year 628, after Muhammad had emerged victorious, the *Najashi* answered the Prophet's call and himself adopted Islam. But he was soon betrayed by his Christian subjects and died an isolated Muslim. This second part of the episode left a different, contradictory, message that has been recycled ever since by less tolerant Muslims—namely, that once the Ethiopian king accepted the Prophet's mission, Ethiopia had become a part of the "land of Islam." According to this interpretation, the *Najashi*'s demise was the first defeat and humiliation of Islam, and Ethiopia's betrayal was the ultimate sin of *irtad*, that is, of being a Muslim and returning to heresy. Moreover, Christian Ethiopia went on to conquer and suppress Muslims, never really "leaving them alone." Ethiopia, it followed, must be redeemed under a Muslim king. "*Islam al-Najashi*" was, and still is, the goal and the slogan of the less compromising wing of Islam, ever in dispute with those preaching tolerance and acceptance.

Throughout the ages, whenever Ethiopia was on the agenda of Muslims, their arguments over policies and strategic options always revolved around this initial dichotomy. Those who stood for promoting good neighborliness could derive legitimacy from the Prophet's history and sayings; those who advocated militancy could do the same, and from the very same reservoir of traditions. In time, this multinuanced Islamic heritage concerning Ethiopia was also transmitted to modern nationalism,

Egyptian and Arab. It was couched in new vocabulary but ever returned to the initial formative Islamic dilemma. In 1935, when Mussolini put Ethiopia squarely on the agenda of the Middle East, the vibrant discussions in Arab and Islamic publics over Fascism or parliamentarianism, Italy or Britain and France, nearly always turned to a discussion of Ethiopia and its role in Islamic history. The "Ethiopian question" attracted attention and ignited arguments of historical depth until the final occupation of the country by the Fascists in May 1936, and somewhat after.

Arab responses to the crisis had some practical aspects. On the one hand, in February 1935, the al-Azhar mosque-university sent two Azhari shaykhs from Cairo to Addis Ababa to open a madrasa in the Ethiopian capital and help rally support for the emperor. In late 1935, soon after the beginning of the Italian invasion, Egypt actually sent volunteers (mostly Ethiopians residing in Egypt), led by two retired Ottoman generals, and three Egyptian Red Crescent medical teams, all of whom saw action on the Harar front. On the other hand, King Ibn Sa'ud of Saudi Arabia sold camels to Mussolini's army in spite of the sanctions imposed by the League of Nations. But these concrete actions were negligible. Of much greater significance were the public debates during these two years.[2]

Pro-Ethiopian Voices: Mussolini and Fascism Will Be Defeated

In hundreds of newspaper articles, pamphlets, and books published in 1935 and 1936, Ethiopia was discussed in historical terms. Those who denounced the Fascists now wrote of Ethiopia as an Eastern sister, Semitic by virtue of its ethnicity and language, Eastern by virtue of its ancient connection to the Coptic Church, even Islamic by virtue of the religion of half of its population. It was a close neighbor, who from antiquity shared the waters of the Nile and the history of the Red Sea. They admired the country's ability to retain its independence for many centuries and mobilize military power to face Europeans and even defeat them during the "Scramble for Africa." Among Palestinian Arabs, the pro-Ethiopian side was adopted mainly by the so-called *al-mu'arada*, the opposition to the *majlisiyyun* of the al-Husayni camp. Their attitude was expressed, for example, by the Jaffa-based *Filastin*: "The Muslims always remember Abyssinian favor with early Islam, the same as they remember the Fascists' recent atrocities against their fellow Muslims in Libya. The Arabs support Ethiopia because of Eastern solidarity and historical love."[3] A "Friends of Ethiopia Association" was active in Jerusalem. According to *Filastin* of

October 31, 1935, it held a symposium on Ethiopian history, with the main lecture being on the Ethiopian victory over the Italians at Adwa in 1896. This victory symbolized Ethiopia's successful stand against European imperialism in the late nineteenth century and ensured its proud entrance into the international family of independent nations. (By the time the Jerusalem event was held, the Fascists had redeemed their pride by capturing Adwa, on October 6, 1935.)

A number of politicians in Syria and their newspapers expressed sympathy for Ethiopia. The most persistent pro-Ethiopian among the Syrians was the exiled nationalist hero 'Abd al-Rahman Shahbandar, who wrote in Cairo:

> I shall not hesitate to sacrifice my life for Ethiopia just as I was not hesitant to do so for Syria in 1925. I do not hesitate to stand by Ethiopia and identify with her, for indeed the highest obligation to freedom and liberation commands us to do so. . . . We are proud to see that we stand for freedom and that our brothers in the Arab world pursue a noble line with regard to Ethiopia.[4]

In Iraq, the Christian Razuq Shammas, one of the country's leading journalists, wrote that "all the Eastern people regard Ethiopia as their sister who is brutalized and with whom they identify," and the Jewish poet Anwar Shawul published a poem in the Baghdad literary weekly *al-Hasid*, in which he compared Ethiopia to Joan of Arc, who "fights for justice when evil-doers try to extinguish freedom."[5] In Egypt the *al-Ahram* newspaper advocated a clearer pro-Ethiopian line. It sent a correspondent to Addis Ababa who stayed in the Ethiopian capital until the Italian captured it in early May 1936 and sent daily reports, including interviews with the emperor.[6]

Egypt, with its long historical ties with Ethiopia, was naturally the center of Arab public opinion. At least four books on Ethiopia appeared in Cairo in 1935. They were devoted substantially to Ethiopian and Ethio-Islamic history and inescapably returned to Muhammad and *al-Najashi* as the starting point of any discussion on Ethiopia. Two of these were written by supporters of the Italians and will be mentioned below.

In his introduction to *The Ethiopian Question from Ancient History to the Year 1935*,[7] Egyptian lawyer, judge, and journalist 'Abdallah al-Husayn wrote that Ethiopian society, with a few exceptions, was Semitic in culture and origin, similar in ethnicity to the Arabs of the Arab peninsula, and that much of Ethiopian culture came from the ancient Egyptians. His interpretation of history was full of respect for Ethiopia. His recounting of the "Muhammad and the *Najashi*" story was clear. He quoted the Prophet's saying, "Leave the Ethiopians alone as long as they leave you alone," and added:

> And because of this order, none of the rulers of Islam ever even contemplated occupying Ethiopia or exerting their influence over it. On the contrary, the states and principalities of Islam always lived in peace and friendship with the Ethiopian Empire, until after the Middle Ages. Even now, some of the *ulama* and the *mufti*s of Somalia published a decree forbidding the Muslims to fight Ethiopia.[8]

In narrating modern Ethiopian-Egyptian relations, as well as Islamic-Christian relations within Ethiopia, Husayn painted a rosy picture. Throughout, he emphasized Ethiopia's affiliation to the Eastern world as well as its successful facing up to Western imperialism. A long chapter devoted to the prospect of Italian use of poisonous gas in Ethiopia implied that it was the Fascists who were barbarians while depicting Ethiopia as a respectful neighbor deserving of full support.[9]

The more famous pro-Ethiopian and anti-Fascist book was *Between the African Lion and the Italian Tiger*,[10] by Muhammad Lutfi Jum'a,[11] which appeared in the last weeks of 1935. Jum'a had already blamed Mussolini for the Italians' atrocities in Libya and in his 1932 book, *The Life of the East*, had exposed Fascism as a dictatorship and the embodiment of Western imperialism and aggression.[12] A lawyer and well-known intellectual, he was one of the promoters of the cultural-national identity of Easternism (*al-sharqiyya*), an idea developed at the time by secular-minded Egyptians. The people of the Orient, they maintained, irrespective of their religious or ethnic differences, share a common culture and must unite to stem Western imperialism.[13] For Jum'a, Emperor Haile Selassie was thus a lion symbolizing the hopes of the East, and Ethiopia was the symbol of its dignity, its leader in the areas of bravery and survival. Eastern Ethiopia deserved sympathy and support in facing Fascism and would reciprocate by helping fellow Easterners, Arabs, Egyptians, and others, in their common secular, progressive struggle for the redemption of the entire Eastern world:

> Egypt and the rest of the East both Near and Far, and Arabism ['*uruba*], embracing its many peoples and states, are all concerned with Ethiopia, with its centrality in the world and its present crisis. If Europe is inter-

ested in the Ethiopian Crisis because of fear for the world order, or resistance to Italian aggression, with us, it is different. We are interested in Ethiopia because it represents both the East and Africa at their very best and most lofty—in terms of beauty, form, quality and dignity. What is more honorable than maintaining freedom, generation after generation and era after era, and resisting foreign enemies whatever their might? And indeed the Ethiopians (like us) conceive freedom to be the most precious value in life.[14]

Jum'a's book, subtitled *A Social and Psychological Analytical Study on the Italo-Ethiopian Question*, was a historical survey. The first chapter was devoted to Ethiopia's early relations with Islam, particularly the Muhammad-*Najashi* story.[15] The emphasis was on Ethiopia's saving of the *sahaba* and on the "beautiful special relations" between the *Najashi* and the Prophet. There was no mention in the book of the possibility that the *Najashi* converted to Islam; by Jum'a he simply answered Muhammad "in a kind and polite manner."[16] The reader was left with the impression that the Ethiopian king remained a good Christian, together with his priests:

The Ethiopians headed by *al-Najashi* and by the priests proved that they were a noble people, lofty in spirit and humanity, having mercy on anyone oppressed, be he of their religion or of other persuasion. They, *al-Najashi* and his people, proved that they were men of principles and justice, and that the Prophet was right in sending the *sahaba* to their country, the land of righteousness.[17]

In later chapters, the author chose to gloss over cases of Christian-Islamic conflicts in Ethiopian history, like the wars of Ahmad Gragn, the Islamic holy warrior from the town of Harar who, with Ottoman aid, temporarily destroyed Christian Ethiopia in the sixteenth century (1529–1543). Jum'a focused instead on the relations between Egypt and Ethiopia's modern emperors and presented them in positive terms. At one major point, he even accused the Egyptian Khedive Isma'il of helping European imperialists against Ethiopia.[18] The great Ethiopian emperor Menelik II (1889–1913) was Jum'a's hero. His benevolence was such that "all his subjects, Christians and Muslims alike, loved him and admired his beauty."[19] The Egyptians, wrote Jum'a, have never forgotten that the Ethiopians never intervened in the flow of the Nile.[20] For the Muslims in Ethiopia, Egypt was the spiritual center, as was Alexandria for the Christians. Ethiopia was portrayed as a neighbor, an important part of the East.

Its enemy was and remained the West. The Italian conquest of Eritrea and reducing it to a colony, argued Jum'a, was "stabbing Ethiopia in the heart with a dagger." [21]

In contrast with Ethiopia as a sister land of benevolence, Jum'a analyzed Fascism as a dictatorial system bound to be oppressive and ever ready to inflict misery on all. [22] "Fascism is a strange system," he wrote, "which simplifies and reduces the significance of the nation. It identifies the nation with one individual and subordinates it solely to his will, betraying all the nation's hopes." [23] Although in the short run Fascism may prove successful, it must fail in the long run:

> Some observers wrote about fascism contending it was an efficient and good system. However, because this system depends inherently on one leader and his views, it would [inevitably] deteriorate with his age, or when his health worsens. In such a case, the whole system will be paralyzed in anticipation of a new savior of the nation who would replace the old one. The right system is the one based on laws, the general ones and the particular ones. . . . It is possible that a good leader may make good use of a bad law, but it is also possible that a good law would turn into an instrument of evil in the hands of a dictator. [24]

Jum'a had a rather pessimistic view of human nature under any system:

> Time has changed and the world has developed but the human killing instinct, the urge to go to war, the blinding greed and the drive for enmity remain, and it makes no difference if the ruler is a dictator, a president of a republic or a fascist leader. [25]

But Fascism, he maintained, is a sure prescription for endless and racist wars among nations:

> It seems that the fascists think that all those who are not under their control, and those who do not obey their orders, are not civilized people. That they are reckless barbarians, unworthy of being a recognized nation and members of the League of Nations. [26]

The Duce, he wrote, himself refused to cooperate with the League of Nations and sought war, blood, and death in Ethiopia. [27] In a chapter on the essence of leadership that praised statesmen like American president Woodrow Wilson, British prime minister David Lloyd-George, and French prime minister Georges Clemenceau, Jumʿa stated that "the lowest of them all in quality and by any standard, are Mister Mussolini and his likes."[28] Mussolini's way, Jumʿa argued, could not but lead to chaos:

> The Italian leader succeeded in reforming his country in ten years. He instilled a new spirit in the people and engraved on their consciousness that they are sons of a glorious nation and a vast empire. . . . However, when he thought there was an opportunity to attack Ethiopia, when the eyes of the world were elsewhere and nobody seemed to bother about east Africa, then began the real problem.[29]

The title of Jumʿa's book was significant. The author called Haile Selassie the "African lion" but went on to mention that the Ethiopian emperor was rather "the lion of Judah."[30] Indeed, in 1930 the Ethiopian had been crowned and proclaimed "Haile Selassie I, Conquering Lion of the Tribe of Judah, King of Kings of Ethiopia and Elect of God." Behind those words was the medieval Christian Ethiopian ethos that the kings of Ethiopia were descendants of King Solomon of Israel and that all Ethiopians, whose Christianity contained vivid Judaic and Hebraic aspects, were "the true children of Israel." Jumʿa discussed this deep spiritual and genealogical Ethiopian connection to the concept of Israel and mentioned that it had lasted three thousand years, since the days of King Solomon.[31] In later years, during the era of Nasserite Pan-Arabism in the 1960s, this traditional "Israeli connection" would be condemned by Arab public opinion makers, and Haile Selassie would be attacked as a "Zionist lion of Judah," but not by Jumʿa.[32] For the liberal Egyptian of the 1930s, this was a traditional dimension of Ethiopia's identity, an integral aspect of a respected "Eastern" culture. Jumʿa even implied that this biblical connection was indirectly confirmed by the Koran.[33] Choosing the lion metaphor to depict the Ethiopian emperor in the very title of his book seems to attest to his conceptualization of Ethiopia as a part of a pluralist, suprareligious East. Mussolini, to distinguish, was for him a tiger, a crude killer, a beast of primitive social skills, a predator to be feared, not respected.

In the first page of the book, there appears a picture of Haile Selassie, majestic in his dress as a Christian king, wearing a crown with a big cross at its top. Mussolini's picture appears only on page 107, dressed as an ordinary person and described as "the leader of Italy and the initiator of the war." On page 95, Jumʿa explained:

An observer can distinguish between two great leaders. The one began as a prince who made it to the imperial throne with cunning and bravery. He is said to be from the tribe of Judah, of the dynasty of Solomon and Queen Sheba. He represents one of the noblest nations in terms of loving freedom and defending it. The other is a man who came from the ranks of the people, endured and persisted until he came to full power in his country, and built his name among his like. He represents a nation which was among the noblest, in terms of military and political might, which had gloriously ruled the entire world during the periods of pagan cultures [namely, in Roman times].

When Jum'a concluded his writings, just as Mussolini invaded Ethiopia, he was sure that "mankind is facing a tragedy of an unprecedented scale, worse than the World War [I]," but was hopeful that justice would prevail in the conflict between the majestic Eastern lion and the dictatorial tiger from the West.[34] The Fascist Italians, he concluded, sought revenge for their defeat at Adwa, but Ethiopia, the Eastern, Christian-Muslim country, would triumph:

> The Italians could invest fortunes and sacrifice thousands of young souls along many years of fighting, and still be far from fulfilling their goal. They would face problems, challenges, and difficulties that could turn children's hair gray. They should remember the legacy of Adwa, for their coming defeats will be many times worse.[35]

Not only liberals like Muhammad Lutfi Jum'a raised their voices in support of Ethiopia and against Fascist aggression. One of the prominent activists for Ethiopia in Egypt was the distinguished leader of the *salafiyya* movement for Islamic revival, Shaykh Muhammad Rashid Rida. Rida's political platform was strongly anticolonial and flexible enough to conceive of Christian Ethiopia in Islamic terms of pluralism and coexistence. Back in 1896–1897, he admired Menelik II for defeating the Italians and for building an independent, strong Eastern empire.[36] Rida was also behind the publication, in 1908 in Cairo, of a book by Sadiq al-'Azm, a Syrian Ottoman general and an envoy of Sultan 'Abd al-Hamid II to the court of Menelik, which was a detailed tribute to the land of the Christian *Najashi* as a safe haven for Muslims. When the 1935 crisis began, Rida stated that all the peoples of the East should identify with Ethiopia's struggle against Mussolini, whom he regarded as the worst manifestation of Western aggression and not a champion of Islam. Rida established his own contacts with Ethiopian Muslims, sent them messages and books—he wanted to modernize their Islam—and urged them to remain loyal to Haile Selassie. He also corresponded about Ethiopia with the Saudi king Ibn Sa'ud and tried to persuade him to help the Ethiopians and not the Fascists.[37]

Pro-Italian Voices: Fascism and the Demonization of Ethiopia

Shaykh Muhammad Rashid Rida, in our context—one of the more important advocates of the Ethiopian cause—was also a lifetime friend of Amir Shakib Arslan, a Syrian Druze and Mussolini's most ardent supporter in the Arab-Islamic world. Both were members of a group of inter-Arab politicians called the Syrian-Palestinian Congress, which had been established in the immediate aftermath of World War I and supported the more active anticolonial leaderships in the region. In the 1920s, they flirted with the idea that Mussolini could help the Arab cause, but like many others they were disillusioned with the Fascists when they crushed the Sanusis in Libya. Whereas Rida remained in strong opposition to Mussolini until his death, Arslan and other members regained their faith in Italy in 1933–1934. In fact, he had already developed quite a negative attitude toward the Christian empire of Ethiopia. Back in 1928, Arslan had written to Ras Tafari, the future (as of 1930) emperor Haile Selassie, demanding the restoration of basic rights for Muslims in Ethiopia. He received no reply, and it was perhaps because of that insult that he continued to refer to Haile Selassie as Tafari throughout the 1930s. When Mussolini quelled the Sanusiyya, for a while Arslan lost his anti-Christian Ethiopian sting. In 1933 he published a long article, "The Muslims of Ethiopia," that included extensive passages from an Arabic manuscript on the Ahmad Gragn conquest. The article implied that Islam in the Horn of Africa had had its share of victories and dignity. But he soon returned to admiring Mussolini and spreading the Italian's word about saving Islam from Ethiopian oppression. In October 1934, Arslan returned from a tour in the Italian colony of Eritrea and published an article in his journal, *La Nation Arabe*, full of praise for Mussolini's treatment of Islam. In January 1935, he published another article in *La Nation Arabe*, warning Ethiopia that it should enact autonomy for its Muslims or face destruction. In February 1935, Arslan was twice summoned by the Italian leader and emerged from the meetings convinced that the Arabs would have no better deal than Mussolini's victory in the East. If such a victory were at the expense of Ethiopia's existence, Arslan would not mourn. Immediately afterward, he began an active campaign in support of the Italian cause in Africa and the Middle East.[38] Of the dozens of articles he published in Arab media from that time until after the final collapse of Ethiopia, it is worth quoting an article in the Palestinian newspaper *al-Jami'a al-'Arabiyya*, on March 4, 1935:

> All those who would like to defend Ethiopia have first to read about its history, and particularly regarding the Muslims living there and what they received from the Ethiopians. They will see that apart from the Muslims of Spain, no other Muslim people has suffered over the centuries such atrocities as the Muslims of Ethiopia.

He then claimed that six million Muslims were living in Ethiopia, deprived of their rights, barred from access to government posts, and living in conditions worse than under European imperialism. Italy, he wrote, was the true friend of the Arabs and of Islam. He then asked:

> Are we so strong and secure as to forget our own needs and give our attention and aid to the land of the Najashi? We should not alienate a power like Italy just for the beautiful eyes of a certain people who for years did nothing but oppress Muslims who lived on the same land.[39]

In September 1935, Arslan organized a congress in Geneva, attended by some seventy scholars and politicians, at which Italy was praised as the true ally of Islam and Arabism.[40] After the beginning of the Italian invasion of Ethiopia, he published an article in *al-Ayyam* of Damascus, which barely concealed his racist attitude:

> And now Palestine is about to fall to the Jews and I see no Muslims in the entire world do anything comparable to their interest and sympathy to Ethiopia. . . . Now Britain is about to declare war on Italy while she herself is in control of Egypt, Palestine, Iraq and Transjordan, countries which are far superior in culture to Ethiopia.[41]

In January 1936, Arslan published in *al-Ayyam* his last letter to his friend Muhammad Rashid Rida (Rida had died in August 1935):

> What do we remember about Ethiopia? That she ruined seven flourishing Islamic emirates, . . . the mass Christianization of 1880 by emperor Yohannes. The destruction of mosques. When did we ever see Ethiopia

doing anything for Egypt, Syria, Palestine? For ten years, she has been a member of the League of Nations; has she done anything for us?[42]

While disputing Rida's anti-Italian ideas, Arslan was fully supportive of the ideas of Egyptian Yusuf Ahmad, as expressed in his book *Islam in Ethiopia*, published in Cairo in November 1935. *Islam in Ethiopia* deserves more attention than can be given here.[43] It was an intensive effort to completely destroy the image of Ethiopia and Ethiopians in the eyes of Muslims. It narrated the history of the country as a chain of anti-Islamic atrocities and went back to the initial story of the Prophet, the *sahaba* and the *Najashi*, to depict it as one of Christian hatred for Islam. "Some writers talk of the *sahaba* as a reason to support Ethiopia. . . . As to the honor given to the *sahaba*, it was by one man only, Najashi Ashama. Indeed, he converted to Islam. But he had to conceal it from his people until he died. . . . As to the priests and the people, they gave the *sahaba* only trouble. They rebelled against the Najashi because he was good to the Muslims."[44] Yusuf Ahmad's book became quite popular and is still often quoted today. Yusuf Ahmad often drew on Arslan's articles, and Arslan did his best to promote his book. In a review he published in the Egyptian newspaper *Kawkab al-Sharq* on February 23, 1936, Arslan praised Yusuf Ahmad for expressing the state of mind of the true courageous Muslim.

Chapters from Yusuf Ahmad's anti-Ethiopian book were published in various newspapers in the region, notably the Syrian *al-Jazira*, which reprinted parts of the book on January 9, 1936. The newspaper's editor, Syrian journalist Tayasir Zabiyan al-Kaylani,[45] deserves our attention, as he represented the views expressed by the anti-Ethiopian wing following the Fascists' final triumph in Ethiopia and their occupation of the country. A lifelong friend of Shakib Arslan, he also shared his support for Ibn Sa'ud as ideally embodying the Arab-Islamic national identity. (He called his newspaper *al-Jazira* [the Peninsula], to emphasize the centrality of Arabia in Islam.) As Arslan's friend, Zabiyan was well informed and interested in the cause of Islam in Ethiopia.

In October 1937, Zabiyan's book *Muslim Ethiopia: My Experiences in Islamic Lands* appeared in Damascus.[46] It was an account of his visit to Ethiopia in June 1936. The idea to go there was conceived in Mecca during the hajj of 1935, he wrote.[47] There he met with pilgrims from Ethiopia who told him at length about the plight of Muslims in their country and testified to the deprivation—economic, social, and cultural—they had suffered in the now crumbling Christian empire. Without mentioning him by name, Zabiyan repeated the ideas found in 'Abd al-Rahman al-Kawakibi's 1901 book, *'Umm al-Qura* (Mecca), considered the first expression of modern Arab-Islamic identity. Kawakibi described a meeting of Muslims in Mecca complaining about the weakness of Islam when one of them suggested that the Arabs should resume their initial leadership. On the strong recommendation of one of the Ethiopian pilgrims, Zabiyan decided to go to Ethiopia to see how the Italians could help the cause of Islam and Arabism. He crossed the Red Sea, but because in early 1936 the war was in full swing, the Italians would not let him in. He returned to Damascus and on May 12, 1936, celebrated the fall of Haile Selassie with an article in *al-Jazira*, stating that it was fitting punishment for what the emperor had done to Islam. On June 5, 1936, *al-Jazira* accused the British of saving the emperor's skin. Meanwhile, on June 4, Zabiyan arrived in Addis Ababa.

Zabiyan's book recorded the state of Islam in the newly occupied country. His visit began with a long interview with the Italian governor, Marshal R. Graziani,[48] the Fascist warrior and administrator who, more than anyone else, had been identified with the massacre of the Sanusis in Libya. Now, in occupied Addis Ababa, Zabiyan could hardly conceal his admiration for the Italian general and his gratitude for his promises to restore Islam, build mosques, spread Arabic, implement the sharia, and change the whole administrative construction of the Horn. By the time Zabiyan wrote his book in 1937, most of these developments had indeed occurred under the Italians. Zabiyan praised Graziani's knowledge of Arabic and quoted him as presenting himself as a born friend of Islam.

The main parts of the book consist of descriptions of the situation under the Italians and are not our direct concern here. Zabiyan was disillusioned with Ethiopia's Muslims. He said that their Islam was shallow, full of superstitions and ignorance, and contained too many Sufi influences of the worst kind. His visit culminated in Harar, now no longer a Christian-dominated town but a restored center of Islamic life and Arab studies. This new Arab-Islamic freedom in a Muslim Ethiopia, he repeated his main message time and again, was achieved thanks to the benevolence of the Fascists.

Before publishing his book, Zabiyan wanted to interview Mussolini himself. When Il Duce came to Libya in March 1937 to wave "the sword of Islam" and to proclaim himself its defender, Zabiyan hurried there from Damascus. He was granted an interview during which Mussolini repeated his promise to liberate the Muslims of Ethiopia and enhance Islam there:

"We granted the Muslims of Ethiopia full religious freedom," he quoted Mussolini. "We made Arabic the official language, built Mosques all over, and replaced non-Muslim functionaries in the Muslim-inhabited regions with Muslims. For that we have received the gratitude of the Muslims."[49] Mussolini also assured Zabiyan that he had no plans to invade Yemen or to penetrate the Arab Peninsula, and the grateful Zabiyan included the interview at the beginning of the book.[50]

For Zabiyan, it seems, everything had to be measured against what he saw as the interests of Islam. Because Mussolini promised not to invade the land of Islam, his destruction of Ethiopia, for Zabiyan, was hardly the worst of all evils. Under a section titled "Opposing Imperialism but Supporting Slavery," he condemned the Arab and Islamic supporters of Ethiopia:

There are those who would not like this book, for they are short-sighted and they are not interested in the truth. They speak of humanism and use such terms as national independence, liberty, sovereignty. But they preferred to ignore the barbaric crimes of the Ethiopians who sought to destroy six million Muslims through suppression and Christianization. Where is humanity there? These [supporters of Ethiopia] rather served the cause of imperialism when they created a storm over the issue of Ethiopia. We share with them the opposition to any form of imperialism, whatever the case, but it is hard for us to see no voice raised in the entire Islamic world in protest of *actions that were far worse than imperialism and conquest.*[51]

Shakib Arslan, he wrote, was the true hero of the Ethiopian war. Arslan was the man who, from the start, had foreseen where history was going—he was right about Ethiopia and about the Italians. There were times when Arslan stood alone against all those who were misled into thinking that in the name of humanity, Ethiopia had to be supported. Indeed, Arslan himself wrote the preface to Zabiyan's book, and in late 1937 he seemed to be in a position to celebrate his victory:

The blind Muslims who fell for British propaganda forgot what the Ethiopians had done to the Muslims in their country and in neighboring countries. What indescribable atrocities, generation after generation, what enslavement, land confiscations, and forced Christianization! . . . Oh you Muslims who blame Italy for occupying Ethiopia, would you not

remember . . . the tens of thousands of slaves, the majority of them Muslims, and that [Haile Selassie] personally owned one thousand of them?
. . . Two years ago, the distinguished author Yusuf Ahmad wrote a book
based on Arabic and European sources and documented all that. And
now the distinguished author Tayasir Zabiyan al-Kaylani of Damascus
himself went to Ethiopia and confirmed all we knew. You should all read
it so that you will know the truth.[52]

It seems that the "truth" for Arslan and Zabiyan was not that the Fascist
formula for rebuilding a nation had to be adopted, nor that the Fascists'
imperialist aspirations in this part of the world were only a blessing. Perhaps the best illustration of their conceptualization of the "truth" was
provided by Zabiyan:

I want to end this introduction by asking that in publishing the declarations of Mussolini or of Graziani or other Italians, I shall not be considered as agreeing to all that they say, and that I support Italian policy
in the lands of Islam [namely, in the colonies of Libya, Eritrea, Somalia,
and now in "Islamic Ethiopia"]. I published them as a service to factual
historical truth and as proof that *in every situation, I put the interests
of Islam and Arabism above all other considerations.*[53]

In 1937 Zabiyyan's eyes, like all others' in the Middle East, were already
focused on Palestine. His new book, *Bleeding Palestine*, came out as the
Arab Revolt of 1936–1939 was culminating. Mussolini's declaration in
Libya in March that he was the champion and defender of Islam was received with mixed feelings. Many Arab nationalists resented the pompous
paternalism of the Duce, whereas others, like Arslan and Zabiyan, welcomed his growing strength. They wanted to believe that the Fascists were
not aiming to replace the British and the French as occupiers, but aimed
to ally with Islam and help the Arab cause. Mussolini, they hoped, who
had kept his promise to destroy the Christian establishment in Ethiopia,
would, in a different way, help to destroy the enemies of Arabs and Muslims in Palestine.

By separating "the interests of Islam and Arabism" from universal
values, and by portraying Ethiopia as a demonic "other," the supporters
of Mussolini in the Middle East positioned themselves as polar opposites
of the supporters of Haile Selassie and their different interpretation of
Islamic and Arab "self." Moreover, the idea that supporting the Fascists
would serve Arab interests was to prove illusionary and self-destructive.

Conclusion

It is important to put the picture of conceptual polarization into perspective. Although the strategic options were quite clear, the period was of acute uncertainty. Between the dual conceptualizations of Ethiopia, on the one hand, and Fascist Italy, on the other, only a few dared to make a clear choice. Taking a side about one of these "others" meant also defining the identity of the national "self," a nuanced matter during the crises and transformations of the 1930s. After all, the ultimate goal was consensual: Arab and Islamic liberation from Western domination and occupation. A good example of this complexity was the fact that two of the leading polar opposites in our Ethiopian-Italian equation, Muhammad Rashid Rida and Shakib Arslan, remained good friends, personally and ideologically.[54]

It is also important to note that those who defended Ethiopia at that time were not blind to its medieval systems or to its record of oppressing Muslims. Reading their texts also leaves the impression that many in the Middle East were not actually sorry to see that the Ethiopians were not invincible after all and that their ability to retain independence would no longer shame those who fell to the Europeans. On the other hand, those who pinned their hopes on Italian success were not unaware of the aggressive, imperialist, and indeed overt racist dimensions of Fascism. Arslan stated at least once that he wanted Ethiopia to be punished and Italy to have dominant influence in the entire region, but that did not mean that he justified Ethiopia's falling to Italy and being conquered by Europeans.[55] Zabiyan al-Kaylani, who was so pleased about the victory of Islam in Ethiopia, did have, as quoted above, some reservations about imperialism, of whatever form.

By the time Zabiyan's book was published in 1937, the Ethiopian issue ceased to attract attention. The Italians completed their occupation of Ethiopia in May 1936, but the propaganda about favoring Islam and Arabism in their new Africa Orientale Italiana (they erased the name "Ethiopia") had little impact in the Middle East. In May 1941, when the British defeated the Italians and restored Ethiopia to Haile Selassie's rule, their victory as well made little impression. Other major developments in the Middle East, the Mediterranean, and Europe pushed Ethiopia and its historical meaning for Muslims to the sidelines.

Our chief protagonists and their arguments were also sidelined. Muhammad Rashid Rida died in 1935, and the leadership of political Islam was inherited by Hasan al-Banna, with his different set of concepts. Ahmad Lutfi Jum'a continued publishing, but gradually abandoned his emphasis on regional intrareligious solidarity and diverted his thoughts to Islam in history. Zabiyan al-Kaylani and his newspaper moved to Transjordan, where he continued writing histories of the Saudis and the Hashemites. By the time he died in 1946, Shakib Arslan, arguably the most prominent advocate of Arabism entwined with Islam in the interwar period, had long since lost his position as *al-mujahid al-kabir*. It seems indeed that their ideological messages no longer appealed to the new "political generation" that appeared during those years of crisis. The pluralist liberalism of Jum'a, the flexible Islam of Rida, and the Arabism and Islam of Arslan and Zabiyan al-Kaylani centering on traditional figures such as Ibn Sa'ud proved less meaningful to the frustrated, expanding educated Arab middle class. The ideas of the previous generation, which largely failed to address the social dimension and were less militant toward the British and the French, lost much of their appeal for the young people on the campuses and streets of the main Arab capitals. The emergence in 1936 of various youth organizations in the major urban centers signified the beginning of a new chapter in the history of Arab and Islamic political cultures. Members of the new political generation would continue to respond to Fascism, inspired by their new concepts, redefinitions, and goals. As for Ethiopia, for a while it was forgotten as a meaningful other. It would be addressed again as such in the era of Nasserite Arabism, and again today, when militant Islamic organizations aim to turn the Horn of Africa into one of their bases.

Notes

Note to Preface

1. See Ulrike Freitag and Israel Gershoni, eds., special issue, "Arab Encounters with Fascist Propaganda, 1933–1945," *Geschichte und Gesellschaft*, 37, no. 3 (2011).

Introduction

1. George Kirk, *The Middle East in the War: Survey of International Affairs, 1939–1946*, vol. 2 (London, 1952).

2. See, for example, James P. Jankowski, *Egypt's Young Rebels: "Young Egypt," 1933–1952* (Stanford, CA, 1975), 85. He justifiably characterizes the authors of these postwar memoirs as "men whose postwar writings have been eager to stress their opposition to the British during the war."

3. Anwar al-Sadat, *Asrar al-Thawra al-Misriyya: Taqdim al-Ra'is Jamal Abd al-Nasir* (Cairo, 1957); the subtitle of the book in Arabic is "Its [the revolution's] secret incentives and its psychological causes." The quotation of 'Abd al-Nasir is from *Asrar al-Thawra al-Misriyya*, 11. See also Anwar El Sadat, *Revolt on the Nile* (London, 1957). President Nasir's foreword is on viii–x. These memoirs were first published in Arabic in a series of articles in *al-Jumhuriyya* during 1954 and appeared as a book, Anwar al-Sadat, *Safahat Majhula* (Cairo, 1954). Later, Sadat published another memoir, *Qissat al-Thawra Kamilatan* (Cairo, 1956). *Revolt on the Nile* was based on Sadat's three memoirs, particularly on *Asrar al-Thawra al-Misriyya* and *Safahat Majhula*. In the late 1970s, President Anwar al-Sadat reproduced the main stories concerning his activities as a young officer during the Second World War in his official autobiography, *Al-Bahth 'an al-Zhat — Qissat Hayati* (Cairo, 1978), 25–68. See also the English translation under the title *In Search of Identity: An Autobiography* (New York, 1978), 21–40. Another "Free Officer" whose "official memoirs" were taken as evidence by many scholars was 'Abd al-Latif Baghdadi. See 'Abd al-Latif Baghdadi, "Ma Qabla al-Dubat al-Ahrar," in *Hadhihi al-Thawra: Kitab al-'Am al-Awwal, 23 July 1952–23 July 1953* (Cairo, 1953), 188–189. See also

the memoirs and other works by Mohammed Neguib, *Egypt's Destiny* (London, 1955); Jamal ʿAbd al-Nasir, *Falsafat al-Thawra* (Cairo, 1953); Muhammad Najib, *Kalimati Li-al-Taʾrikh* (Cairo, 1981) and *Mudhakkirat Muhammad Najib: Kuntu Raʾisan li-Misr*, 6th ed. (1984; reprint, Cairo, 1993); Khalid Muhy al-Din, *Wa-al-An Atakalam* (Cairo, 1992); Khaled Mohi El-Din, *Memoirs of a Revolution: Egypt 1952* (Cairo, 1995); Ahmad Hamrush, *Thawrat 23 Yuliyu* (Cairo, 1992), 1:89–101; Muhammad al-Tabiʾi, *Misr Ma Qabla al-Thawra: Min Asrar al-Siyasa wa-al-Siyasiyyin* (Cairo, 1978), 114–125, 182–233; and Muhsayn Muhammad, *Al-Taʾrikh al-Sirri li-Misr, 1939–1945* (Cairo, 1979), 101–426. See also Muhammad Subayh's memoirs, *Min al-ʿAlamayn ila Sijn al-Ajanib: Safahat min al-Harb al-ʿAlamiyya al-Thaniya* (Cairo, 1963) and *Tariq al-Huriyya: Safahat min al-Harb al-ʿAlamiyya al-Thaniya* (Cairo, 1964).

4. For a recent extensive discussion regarding this issue, see Meir Litvak and Esther Webman, *From Empathy to Denial: Arab Responses to the Holocaust* (London, 2009); and the extensive response by Gilbert Achcar, *The Arabs and the Holocaust: The Arab-Israeli War of Narratives* (New York, 2009). Achcar convincingly highlights the intimate interactions between the ongoing Arab-Israeli, and in particular the Palestinian-Israeli, "war of Narratives," the mutual demonization between the two "sides," and the enduring interest in "Arab reactions to Nazism and anti-Semitism, 1933–1947." The Israeli-Jewish interest in al-Hajj Amin al-Husayni's collaboration with Nazi Germany and his active participation in the genocide of the European Jews had begun already during and immediately after the Second World War. See, for example, M. P. Waters, *Mufti over the Middle East* (London, 1942); Simon Wiesenthal, *Grossmufti: Grossagent der Achse* (Salzburg, 1947); and Maurice Perlman, *Mufti of Jerusalem: The Story of Haj Amin El Husseini* (London, 1947). According to Tom Segev's recent biography of Simon Wiesenthal, the latter collected source material for the Israeli authorities about the collaboration of the mufti with the Nazis during the war. Segev found out that during the late 1940s and early 1950s, Weisenthal served as a Mossad agent. See Tom Segev, *Simon Weisenthal: The Biography* (Tel Aviv, 2010), 99–103 (in Hebrew).

5. See the section "The Impact of September 11, 2001" later in the present review essay.

6. Some contributions to this early wave of scholarship also include journalistic and amateur scholarly literature from the 1940s and 1950s. See, for example, Jean Lugol, *Egypt and World War II: The Anti-Axis Campaigns in the Middle East* (Cairo, 1945); Kirk, *Middle East in the War*; J. Heyworth-Dunne, *Religious and Political Trends in Modern Egypt* (Washington, DC, 1950), 22–28, 36–45, 66–73, 103–105; Majid Khadduri, *Independent Iraq: A Study in Iraqi Politics since 1932* (London, 1951), 127–205; John Marlowe, *Anglo-Egyptian Relations, 1800–1956*, 2nd ed. (1954; reprint, London, 1965), 310–320; Jean Lacouture and Simon Lacouture, *Egypt in Transition* (New York, 1958), 97–104; Walter Z. Laqueur, *Nasser's Egypt* (London, 1956), 4–12; Elsa Marston, "Fascist Tendencies in Pre-war Arab Politics: A Study of Three Arab Political Movements," *Middle East Forum* 35, no. 5 (1959): 19–35; G. Vaucher, *Gamal Abdel Nasser et son équipe*, vols. 1–2 (Paris, 1959–1960), in particular 1:94–144; Robert St. John, *The Boss: The Story of Gamal Abdel Nasser* (New York, 1960), 35–57; and I. Sedar and H. J. Greenberg, *Behind the Egyptian Sphinx— Nasser's Strange Bedfellows: Prelude to World War III?* (New York, 1960), 3–33.

7. Lukasz Hirszowicz, *The Third Reich and the Arab East* (London, 1966). The book was first published in Warsaw, in Polish, in 1963. It was translated into Hebrew for the first time in 1965.

8. Ibid., 13 and, more broadly, 13–42, 62–249.

9. Ibid., 13–42, 62–249, 307–319.

10. Ibid., 13–268, 307–319.

11. Ibid., 69.

12. Ibid., 95–172, 250–268.

13. Ibid., 229–236.

14. Ibid., 241–243 and, more broadly, 236–249. In explaining "the officers' conspiracy," he employed Sadat's memoirs as evidence for strong, widespread pro-Axis moods in the army.

15. Ibid., 236 (Hebrew version, 244–245).

16. Ibid., 236–249.

17. Ibid., 170–172 and, more broadly, 134–172.

18. Ibid., 65–66, 188, and, more broadly, 173–192.

19. Ibid., 238 and, more broadly, 232–249.

20. Ibid., 236–248.

21. Ibid., 248–249, 269–306.

22. Ibid., 243.

23. Ibid., 315.

24. Ibid., 319 and, more broadly, 307–319.

25. Eliezer Be'eri, *The Officer Class in Politics and Society of the Arab East* (Tel Aviv, 1966). For the English version, which is slightly shorter than the original Hebrew, see *Army Officers in Arab Politics and Society* (Jerusalem, 1969).

26. Be'eri, *Army Officers*, 15–129.

27. Ibid., 39 and, more broadly, 15–40.

28. Ibid., 31–40.

29. Ibid., 35–40.

30. Ibid., 49.

31. Ibid., 44–45.

32. Ibid. Here Be'eri also uses Amin Sa'id, *Ta'rikh al-'Arab al-Hadith*, vol. 13, *al-Thawra* (Cairo, 1959), 26.

33. Be'eri, *Army Officers*, 45–47. See also 41–49, 76–96.

34. Ibid., 77. See also 76–80.

35. Ibid., 48. See also 41–49.

36. Ibid., 375 and, more broadly, 97–129, 373–400.

37. Ibid., 41–54, 76–129, 373–400.

38. Ibid., 49.

39. Sylvia G. Haim, *Arab Nationalism: An Anthology* (Berkeley, CA, 1962), 39–49; Bernard Lewis, *The Middle East and the West* (London, 1964), 82–83; Heinz Tillmann, *Deutschlands Araberpolitik im Zweiten Weltkrieg* (Berlin, 1965); Anouar Abdel-Malek, *Egypt: Military Society* (New York, 1968), 21–22; Elie Kedourie, "Egypt and the Caliphate, 1915-1952," in *The Chatham House Version and Other Middle Eastern Studies* (London, 1970), 199–207; Elie Kedourie, "Pan-Arabism and British Policy," in ibid., 213–235. The latter is a considerably expanded version of his article that appeared under the same title: see Elie Kedourie, "Pan Arabism

and British Policy," in *The Middle East in Transition*, edited by Walter Z. Laqueur (New York, 1958), 100–111. Tillmann's work is slightly different from that of the others in this grouping inasmuch as he extensively incorporated German archival materials.

40. See, for example, Kedourie, "Pan Arabism," 220–235; and Elie Kedourie, "The Kingdom of Iraq: A Retrospect," in his *Chatham House Version*, 271–282. See also Robert L. Melka, "The Axis and the Arab Middle East, 1933–1945" (PhD diss., University of Minnesota, 1966), 4–75, 114–389.

41. Melka, "Axis and the Arab Middle East," 398 and, more broadly, 390–399.

42. Ibid., 392.

43. Ibid., 390, 397.

44. Ibid., 397–398.

45. Ibid., 397–399.

46. See, for example, the works of Mohammad A. Tarbush, *The Role of the Military in Politics: A Case Study of Iraq to 1941* (London, 1982); Phebe Marr, *The Modern History of Iraq* (Boulder, CO, 1985), 55–93; Phebe Marr, "The Development of Nationalist Ideology in Iraq, 1921–1941," *Muslim World* 75, no. 2 (1985): 85–101; Reeva S. Simon, *Iraq between the Two World Wars: The Creation and Implementation of a Nationalist Ideology* (New York, 1986); Walid M. S. Hamdi, *Rashid Ali al-Gailani and the Nationalist Movement in Iraq, 1939–1941: A Political and Military Study of the British Campaign in Iraq and the National Revolution of May 1941* (London, 1987); Liora Lukitz, *Iraq: The Search for National Identity* (London, 1995), 72–103, 120–121; and Shmuel Moreh and Zvi Yehuda, eds., *Al-Farhud: The 1941 Pogrom in Iraq* (Jerusalem, 2010).

47. See, for example, A. L. Tibawi, *A Modern History of Syria Including Lebanon and Palestine* (London, 1969), 363–378; Labib Zuwiyya Yamak, *The Syrian Social Nationalist Party: An Ideological Analysis* (Cambridge, MA, 1969); Itamar Rabinovich, "Germany and the Syrian Political Scene in the Late 1930s," in *Germany and the Middle East, 1835–1939*, edited by Yehuda L. Wallach (Tel Aviv, 1975), 191–198; Philip S. Khoury, *Syria and the French Mandate* (London, 1987), 395–580, 626–630; Miloš Mendel and Zdenek Müller, "Fascist Tendencies in the Levant in the 1930s and 1940s," *Archív Oriéntální* 55 (1987): 1–7; Meir Zamir, *Lebanon's Quest: The Road to Statehood, 1926–1939* (London, 1997), 233–239; and Shafiq Jaha, *Al-Haraka al-'Arabia al-Siriyya: Jama'at al-Kitab al-Ahmar, 1935–1945* (Beirut, 2004).

48. See, for example, Eliyahu Eilat, *Haj Amin al-Husayni: The Previous Mufti of Jerusalem* (Tel Aviv, 1968), which focuses on the early career of Amin al-Husayni; David Yisraeli, *The Palestine Problem in German Politics, 1889–1945* (Ramat Gan, 1974) (in Hebrew), in particular 186–259; Anthony R. De Luca, "'Der Grossmufti' in Berlin: The Politics of Collaboration," *International Journal of Middle East Studies* 10 (1979): 125–138; 'Ali Muhafaza, *Al-'Alaqat al-Almaniyya al-Filastiniyya, 1841–1945* (Beirut, 1981), 227–271; Martin Kramer, "Congresses of Collaboration: Islam and the Axis, 1938–1945," in his *Islam Assembled: The Advent of the Muslim Congresses* (New York, 1986), 157–165; Bernard Lewis, "The Nazis and the Palestine Question," in his *Semites and Anti-Semites: An Inquiry into Conflict and Prejudice* (New York, 1986), 140–163; Yegal Karmon, "The Mufti of Jerusalem al-Hajj Amin al-Husayni and Nazi Germany during the Second World War" (master's thesis, Hebrew University of Jerusalem, 1987); Philip Mattar, *The*

Mufti of Jerusalem: Hajj Amin al-Husayni and the Palestinian National Movement (New York, 1988); Zvi Elpeleg, *The Grand Mufti: Haj Amin al-Hussaini, Founder of the Palestinian National Movement*, translated by David Harvey (London, 1993); 'Abd al-Rahman 'Abd al-Ghayni, *Almaniyya al-Naziyya wa-Filastin, 1933–1945* (Beirut, 1995), 187–405; Gerhard Höpp, ed., *Mufti-Papiere: Briefe, Memoranden, Reden und Aufrufe Amin al-Husaynis aus dem Exil, 1940–1945* (Berlin, 2002); and Klaus-Michael Mallmann and Martin Daniel Cüppers, *Halbmond und Hakenkreuz: Das Dritte Reich, die Araber und Palästina* (Darmstadt, 2006); cf. Klaus Gensicke, *Der Mufti von Jerusalem und die Nationalsozialisten: Eine Politische Biographie Amin el-Husseinis* (Darmstadt, 2007).

49. See, for example, Bernd Philipp Schröder, *Deutschland und der Mittlere Osten im Zweiten Weltkrieg* (Göttingen, 1975); Majid Khadduri, *Political Trends in the Arab World: The Role of Ideas and Ideals in Politics* (Baltimore, 1970), 176–179; Elie Kedourrie, "Arabic Political Memoirs," in his *Arabic Political Memoirs and Other Studies* (London, 1974), 189–192 and, more broadly, 177–205; Lewis, *Semites and Anti-Semites*, 140–163; Stefan Wild, "National Socialism in the Arab Near East between 1933 and 1939," *Die Welt des Islams* 25 (1985): 131–146; and Elie Kedourrie, *Democracy and Arab Political Culture* (London, 1994), 25–81, 103–105.

50. Kramer, *Islam Assembled*, 154–165.

51. Ibid., 155.

52. Ibid., 165.

53. Ibid., 154–165. For a slightly different interpretation of Shakib Arslan's pro-Axis tendencies, see William L. Cleveland, "Toward the Axis," in his *Islam against the West: Shakib Arslan and the Campaign for Islamic Nationalism* (London, 1985), 135–159. Nevertheless, in many ways, Cleveland reproduces themes of the established narrative. See, in particular, 138–149.

54. The oft-cited construct of the "crisis of liberalism" in 1930s Egypt was framed by historians already in the 1950s and 1960s and was reasserted from the 1970s onward. See, for example, Nadav Safran, *Egypt in Search of Political Community* (Cambridge, MA, 1961); Baber Johansen, *Muhammad Husayn Haikal: Europa und der Orient im Weltbild eines Ägyptischen Liberalen* (Beirut, 1967); Zaheer M. Quraishi, *Liberal Nationalism in Egypt: Rise and Fall of the Wafd Party* (Delhi, 1967); P. J. Vatikiotis, *The Modern History of Egypt* (London, 1969); Elie Kedourie, "Pan Arabism and British Policy," 215–235; Elie Kedourie, "The Fate of Constitutionalism in the Middle East," in his *Arabic Political Memoirs and Other Studies*, 1–27; Jacques Berque, *Egypt: Imperialism and Revolution* (London, 1972); Afaf Lutfi al-Sayyid Marsot, *Egypt's Liberal Experiment, 1922–1936* (Los Angeles, 1977); Marius Deeb, *Party Politics in Egypt: The Wafd and Its Rivals, 1919–1939* (London, 1979); Selma Botman, *The Rise of Egyptian Communism, 1939–1970* (Syracuse, NY, 1988); 'Abd al-Rahman al-Rafi'i, *Fi A'qab al-Thawra al-Misriyya—Thawrat Sanat 1919*, 3 vols. (Cairo, 1947–1951); 'Abd al-'Azim Ramadan, *Tatawwur al-Haraka al-Wataniyya fi Misr min Sanat 1937 ila Sanat 1948*, pts. 1–2 (Beirut, 1973–1974); Vernon Egger, *A Fabian in Egypt: Salamah Musa and the Rise of the Professional Classes in Egypt, 1909–1939* (New York, 1986), 194–201; and, more recently, Abdeslam M. Maghraoui, *Liberalism without Democracy: Nationhood and Citizenship in Egypt, 1922–1936* (Durham, NC, 2006).

55. See, for example, Richard P. Mitchell, *The Society of the Muslim Brothers*

(London, 1969); James P. Jankowski, "The Egyptian Blue Shirts and the Egyptian Wafd, 1935–1938," *Middle Eastern Studies* 6 (1970): 77–95; Jankowski, *Egypt's Young Rebels*; Shimon Shamir, "The Influence of German National Socialism on Radical Movements in Egypt," in *Germany and the Middle East*, edited by Wallach, 200–209; Israel Gershoni and James P. Jankowski, *Redefining the Egyptian Nation, 1930–1945* (Cambridge, 1995); Brynjar Lia, *The Society of the Muslim Brothers in Egypt: The Rise of an Islamic Mass Movement, 1928–1942* (London, 1998); Ramadan, *Tatawwur al-Haraka al-Wataniyya fi Misr min Sanat 1937 ila Sanat 1948*, pt. 1; 'Abd al-'Azim Ramadan, *Dirasat fi Ta'rikh Misr al-Mu'asir* (Cairo, 1981); Ramadan, *Al-Ikhwan al-Muslimun wa-al-Tanzim al-Sirri* (Cairo, 1982); 'Ali Shalabi, *Misr al-Fatah wa-Dawruha fi al-Siyasa al-Misriyya, 1933–1941* (Cairo, 1982); Abd al-Fattah Muhammad El-Awaisi, *The Muslim Brothers and the Palestine Question, 1928–1947* (London, 1998); Haggai Erlich, *Students and University in 20th Century Egyptian Politics* (London, 1989); Ahmad 'Abdalla, *The Student Movement and National Politics in Egypt, 1923–1973* (London, 1985); Lucie Ryzova, *L'effendiyya ou la modernité contestée* (Cairo, 1994); and Lucie Ryzova, "Egyptianizing Modernity: The 'New Effendiya': Social and Cultural Constructions of the Middle Class in Egypt under the Monarchy," in *Re-envisioning Egypt, 1919–1952*, edited by Arthur Goldschmidt, Amy J. Johnson, and Barak A. Salmoni (Cairo, 2005), 124–163.

56. See the early study of al-Rafi'i, *Fi A'qab al-Thawra al-Misriyya* (Cairo, 1951), 3:83–162; and the important memoirs of Muhammad Husayn Haykal, *Mudhakkirat fi al-Siyasa al-Misriyya*, 2nd ed. (1953; reprint, Cairo, 1977), 2:140–267. These two influential works carefully analyze Egypt during the Second World War, especially during the critical period of 1939–1942. They serve as an important source for many scholarly studies on Egypt during these years. In particular, al-Rafi'i and Haykal vehemently criticize the Wafd's "shameful behavior" throughout the crisis of February 4, 1942. One should remember that both al-Rafi'i, a Watanist and a prominent leader of al-Hizb al-Watani (the Nationalist Party), and Haykal, the leader of the Liberal Constitutionalist Party, penned these works while the Wafd held governmental power for the last time, 1950–1952. Their ardent opposition to the Wafd resonates throughout the works; al-Rafi'i's and Haykal's harsh critiques of the Wafd emanate from deep and traditional anti-Wafdist biases. Scholars who later used these two texts as crucial "documentary" sources for understanding Egypt during the Second World War often ignore this important context. See Kedourie, "Pan Arabism and British Policy," 213–235; Ramadan, *Tatawwur al-Haraka al-Wataniyya*, pt. 2; Gabriel Warburg, "Lampson's Ultimatum to Faruq, 4 February 1942," *Middle Eastern Studies* 11 (January 1975): 24–32; 'Asim al-Dasuqi, *Misr fi al-Harb al-'Alamiyya al-Thaniya, 1939–1945*, 2nd ed. (1976; reprint, Cairo, 1981); Ahmed M. Gomaa, *The Foundation of the League of Arab States: Wartime Diplomacy and Inter-Arab Politics, 1941 to 1945* (London, 1977); Mahmud Mutawali, *Hadith 4 Fabrayir 1942 fi al-Ta'rikh al-Misri al-Mu'asir* (Cairo, 1978); Muhsayn Muhammad, *Al-Ta'rikh al-Sirri li-Misr*; Charles D. Smith, "4 February 1942: Its Causes and Its Influence on Egyptian Politics and on the Future of Anglo-Egyptian Relations, 1937–1945," *International Journal of Middle East Studies* 10 (1979): 453–479; Muhammad Anis, *4 Fabrayir 1942 fi Ta'rikh Misr al-Siyasi* (Cairo, 1982); Thomas Mayer, *Egypt and the Palestine Question, 1936–1945* (Berlin, 1983), 138–208; Gabriel Warburg, "The 'Three-Legged Stool': Lampson, Faruq,

and Nahhas, 1936–1944," in his *Egypt and the Sudan: Studies in History and Politics* (London, 1985), 127–150 and, more broadly, 116–157; Yehoshua Porath, *In Search for Arab Unity, 1930–1945* (London, 1986), 197–319; 'Isam Diya' al-Din, *Hadith 17 Yuniyu 1940 fi al-Ta'rikh al-Misri al-Mu'asir* (Cairo, 1991); Charles Tripp, "Ali Mahir and the Politics of the Egyptian Army, 1936–1942," in his *Contemporary Egypt: Through Egyptian Eyes* (London, 1993), 45–71; Tewfik Aclimandos, "Revisiting the History of the Egyptian Army," in *Re-envisioning Egypt*, edited by Goldschmidt, Johnson, and Salmoni, 68–93, in particular 80–82. Tripp and Aclimandos demonstrate the shallowness and weakness of 'Aziz 'Ali al-Misri and "the Young Officers'" attempts to establish any subversive (anti-British and pro-Axis) organization. For more on British-Egyptian relations during the latter half of the 1930s and early 1940s and the domestic rivalries between the British, the king, and the Wafd under the shadow of the growing Nazi and fascist threats, see also Laila Morsy, "The Effect of Italy's Expansionist Policies on Anglo-Egyptian Relations in 1935," *Middle Eastern Studies* 20, no. 2 (1984): 206–231; Laila Morsy, "Farouk in British Policy," *Middle Eastern Studies* 20, no. 4 (1984): 193–211; Laila Morsy, "Indicative Cases of Britain's Wartime Policy in Egypt, 1942–1944," *Middle Eastern Studies* 30, no. 1 (1994): 91–122. For a comprehensive British view of Egypt in the war, see the diaries of Miles Lampson, the British ambassador in Egypt during this era, Lord Killearn (Sir Miles Lampson), *The Killearn Diaries, 1934–1946*, edited by Trefor Evans (London, 1972), 102–343.

57. Vatikiotis, *Modern History of Egypt*, 315 and, more broadly, 315–373.

58. P. J. Vatikiotis, *Nasser and His Generation* (London, 1978), 27. See also his earlier work, *The Egyptian Army in Politics* (Bloomington, IN, 1961), 21–68.

59. Vatikiotis, *Nasser and His Generation*, 23–97.

60. Ibid., 53.

61. Afaf Lutfi al-Sayyid Marsot, *A Short History of Modern Egypt* (Cambridge, 1985), 100 (quote), 98–101 and, more broadly, 82–106. Since the book first appeared in 1985, it was reprinted thirteen times, including new editions. In all of them, the author reproduced her descriptions of Egyptians' pro-Axis sympathies.

62. Ramadan, *Tatawwur al-Haraka al-Wataniyya Fi Misr min Sanat 1937 ila Sanat 1948*, pt. 1, 5–7 and, more broadly, 8–18 and 34–108.

63. Ibid., pt. 2, 207; pt. 1, 5–7.

64. Ibid., pt. 1, 6–14.

65. Ibid., pt. 2, 207 and, more broadly 125–229.

66. Ibid., pt. 2, 125–229 and, more broadly, 6–256.

67. Ibid., 207, 220.

68. Ibid., 220.

69. Ibid., 192–218 and, more broadly, 98–256. Ramadan reasserted some of these historical arguments in other works. See, for example, *Al-Sira' bayna al-Wafd wa-al-'Arsh* (Cairo, 1979) and *Dirasat fi Ta'rikh Misr al-Mu'asir* (Cairo, 1981).

70. Anis, 4 *Fabrayir 1942*, 88–89 and, more broadly, 81–94.

71. Al-Dasuqi, *Misr fi al-Harb al-'Alamiyya al-Thaniya, 1939–1945*, 27–104, 157–170.

72. Ibid., 104–121.

73. Ibid., 135–157.

74. Ibid., 173–325.

75. Ibid., 319.

76. Wajih 'Abd al-Sadiq 'Atiq, *Al-Malik Faruq wa-Almaniya al-Naziyya: Khams Sanawat min al-'Alaqa al-Siriyya* (Cairo, 1992); Wajih 'Abd al-Sadiq 'Atiq, *Al-Jaysh al-Misri wa-al-Alman fi Ithna al-Harb al-'Alamiyya al-Thaniya* (Cairo, 1993).

77. 'Atiq, *Al-Jaysh al-Misri*, 17.

78. 'Atiq, *Al-Malik Faruq*, 3–187.

79. 'Atiq, *Al-Jaysh al-Misri*, 38 and, more broadly, 34–66. 'Aziz 'Ali al-Misri remains an "idol" in some Egyptian memoirs and political circles. See, for example, Muhammad Subayh, *Batal La Nansahu: 'Aziz 'Ali al-Misri wa-'Asruhu* (Beirut, 1971); Muhammad 'Abd al-Rahman Burj, *'Aziz 'Ali al-Misri wa-al-Haraka al-Wataniyya al-Misriyya*, vols. 1–2 (Cairo, 1980). See also Muhammad Subayh, *Ayam wa-Ayam, 1882–1956* (Cairo, 1966), 257–279; and Majid Khadduri, "'Aziz 'Ali al-Misri and the Arab Nationalist Movement," in *Middle Eastern Affairs*, no. 4, edited by Albert Hourani (Oxford, 1965), 140–163.

80. 'Atiq, *Al-Jaysh al-Misri*, 38, 63–66, and, more broadly, 38–40, 52–66.

81. Ibid., 79–161.

82. Ibid., 104–153.

83. Ibid., 168.

84. Ibid., 7–66, 163–172; 'Atiq, *Al-Malik Faruq*, 3–30, 162–187. For other works on the Second World War by Egyptian historians, see Salah al-'Aqqad, *Al-Harb al-'Alamiyya al-Thaniya: Dirasa fi Ta'rikh al-'Alaqat al-Dawliyya* (Cairo, 1963); Salah al-'Aqqad, *Al-'Arab wa-al-Harb al-'Alamiyya al-Thaniya* (Cairo, 1966); Muhammad Kamal al-Dasuqi, *Al-Harb al-'Alamiyya al-Thaniya - Sira' Isti'mari* (Cairo, 1968); Mutawali, *Hadith 4 Fabrayir Sanat 1942 fi al-Ta'rikh al-Misri al-Mu'asir*; Muhammad Jamal al-Din Masadi, Yunan Labib Rizq, and 'Abd al-'Azim Ramadan, *Misr wa-al-Harb al-'Alamiyya al-Thaniya: Mu'assat al-Ahram* (Cairo 1979); and Latifa Muhammad Salim, *Faruq wa-Suqut al-Malakiyya fi Misr, 1936–1952* (Cairo, 1989), 249–390.

85. Francis Nicosia, "Arab Nationalism and National Socialist Germany, 1933–1939: Ideological and Strategic Incompatibility," *International Journal of Middle East Studies* 12 (1980): 366 and, more broadly, 351–367. See also Francis Nicosia, *The Third Reich and the Palestine Question* (London, 1985) and "Fritz Grobba and the Middle East Policy of the Third Reich," in *National and International Politics in the Middle East: Essays in Honour of Elie Kedourie*, edited by Edward Ingram (London, 1986), 206–228. For a similar line of interpretation, see Andreas Hillgruber, "The Third Reich and the Near and Middle East, 1933–1939," in *The Great Powers in the Middle East, 1919–1939*, edited by Uriel Dann (New York, 1988), 274–282.

86. Nicosia, "Arab Nationalism and National Socialist Germany," 366.

87. Wild, "National Socialism in the Arab Near East," 170, 131–138, and, more broadly, 126–173.

88. Ibid., 127–130, 139–147, 170.

89. Ibid., 170.

90. For a full discussion of anti-Hitler and anti-Nazi translated texts that were widespread in Egypt and the Arab world, see Israel Gershoni, *Dame and Devil: Egypt and Nazism, 1935–1940* (Tel Aviv, 2012), 2:229–243 (in Hebrew). Rauchning's *Hitler Speaks* was first published in London and Paris in 1939. In 1940 it was translated into Arabic and was published in Cairo, Alexandra, and Baghdad.

91. Lewis, "Nazis and the Palestine Question," 140–163.

92. Ibid., 140.

93. Ibid., 146–147.

94. Ibid., 154.

95. Ibid., 148–149.

96. Ibid., 159 (emphasis added).

97. Ibid., 147–148 and, more broadly, 146–160.

98. Ibid., 146–161.

99. Ibid., 159–160.

100. El Sadat, *Revolt on the Nile*, v. The formation and existence of a "real revolutionary conspiracy movement" are main themes in Sadat's narrative of events in Egypt during 1941–1942. This "reality" was first reproduced and popularized immediately after the publication of *Revolt on the Nile*, by pseudoacademic literature on intelligence and spies' activities in Egypt during the war. See, for example, L. Mosley, *The Cat and the Mice* (London, 1958); J. W. Eppler, *Rommel Ruft Kairo* (Bielefeld, 1959); H. V. Steffens, *Salaam* (Neckargemund, 1960); St. John, *The Boss*, 35–57; and A. W. Sansom, *I Spied Spies* (London, 1965). In some Egyptian memoirs and works on the war, Sadat's story was also accepted and institutionalized. See Subayh, *'Aziz 'Ali al-Misri*, 113–297; Husayn 'Id, *Mudhakkirat Hikmat Fahmi: Asrar al-'Alaqa bayn al-Sadat wa-al-Mukhabarat al-Almaniyya* (Cairo, 1990); al-Tabi'i, *Misr ma Qabla al-Thawra*, 148–233; and Muhammad, *Al-Ta'rikh al-Sirri li-Misr*. In 1975 James Jankowski presented the most authoritative and balanced portrayal of Sadat's story. He sought to determine to what extent an anti-British and pro-German revolutionary organization aimed at fomenting a "revolt/uprising" in Egypt in the spring of 1941 existed. He drew the correct conclusion that vague "talking" about a "revolt/uprising" never translated into real action. For details, see Jankowski, *Egypt's Young Rebels*, 81–87. Jankowski is convinced that "there is as yet no evidence indicating direct contact between the movement (Young Egypt/The Islamic Nationalist Party) and the Axis powers in this period [1941–1942]" (82).

101. Bernard Lewis, "Epilogue to a Period," in *Great Powers in the Middle East*, edited by Dann, 420 and, more broadly, 419–425.

102. Ibid., 425.

103. Ibid., 420. Lewis continued to express these views in his later publications. See, for example, *The Middle East: A Brief History of the Last 2,000 Years* (New York, 1995), 348–351. In a review article of this book, Basheer M. Nafi criticized Lewis's observations on positive Arab attitudes toward Nazi Germany. Nafi also characterized the pro-Fascist tendencies as expressions of pragmatism, not ideological affinities. Nafi, like others, adopted the common trope of "enemy of my enemy" and was unaware of the Arab anti-Fascist voices and forces that were also at play. See Basheer M. Nafi, "The Arabs and the Axis: 1933–1940," *Arab Studies Quarterly* 19, no. 2 (1997): 1–24.

104. See, for example, Chuck Morse, *The Nazi Connection to Islamic Terrorism: Adolf Hitler and Haj Amin al-Husseini* (New York, 2003); Paul Berman, *Terror and Liberalism* (New York, 2003); and Christopher Hitchens, "Defending Islamo-fascism," *Slate*, October 22, 2007.

105. Matthias Küntzel, *Jihad and Jew-Hatred: Islamism, Nazism, and the Roots*

of 9/11 (New York, 2007). The book was first published in German (Freiburg, 2002), and in 2008 it was translated into Hebrew with slight changes in the title: *Jihad and Jew-Hatred: The Nazi Origins of the 11 September Attack*. Its content was covered with great enthusiasm within the Western media. See, for example, Jeffrey Goldberg, "Seeds of Hate," *New York Times*, January 6, 2008; Stephen Schwartz's review in *Weekly Stanford*, April 28, 2008; and Russell A. Berman, "Islamofascism, Q.E.D.," *Telos* 141 (Winter 2007): 191–192.

106. Küntzel, *Jihad and Jew-Hatred*, xxiii.

107. Ibid., 3 and, more broadly, 6–37.

108. Ibid., 7–20.

109. Ibid., 20–60.

110. See the works of Mitchell, Lia, El-Awaisi, and, more recently, Gudrun Krämer, *Hasan al-Banna* (Oxford, 2010). See also Israel Gershoni, "The Muslim Brothers and the Arab Revolt in Palestine, 1936-1939," *Middle Eastern Studies* 22 (1986): 367–397.

111. Küntzel, *Jihad and Jew-Hatred*, 27.

112. Küntzel relied on a 2002 "intelligence report" from a journalistic publication produced by an activist center dedicated to "fighting hate and bigotry." See the official website: http://www.splcenter.org/who-we-are. Martin A. Lee, the author of this "intelligence report," based his findings about the war on a recent interview with someone who presents himself as a former Muslim Brother.

113. Küntzel, *Jihad and Jew-Hatred*, 27–28. For a general systematic critique of Islamofascism, see "Islamofascism," edited by Stefan Wild, special issue, *Die Welt des Islams* 12, nos. 3–4 (2012).

114. Ami Ayalon, "Egyptian Intellectuals versus Fascism and Nazism in the 1930s," in *Great Powers in the Middle East*, edited by Dann, 391–404.

115. Ibid., 395.

116. Ibid., 400.

117. Ibid., 402. For a slightly different interpretation, see Edmond Cao-Van-Hoa, *"Der Feind Meines Feindes . . .": Darstellungen des National-Sozialistischen Deutschland in Ägyptischen Schriften* (Frankfurt, 1990). It should be noted, however, that the major argument of this book remains "traditional," that is, that Egyptian support for the Axis and for Nazi Germany emanated from "the enemy of my enemy" syndrome.

118. Israel Gershoni, "Rejecting the West: The Image of the West in the Teachings of the Muslim Brothers, 1928-1939," in *Great Powers in the Middle East*, edited by Dann, 370–390. The characterization of the Muslim Brothers as an anti-imperialist and decolonizing force, which also rejected Nazism and Fascism as Western systems of rule and expansion, was also discussed briefly in the classic work of Mitchell, *Society of the Muslim Brothers*, 224–231, particularly 264–267. It is important to emphasize that Mitchell's, Lia's, and El-Awaisi's comprehensive and systematic works on the ideology and activities of the Muslim Brothers and Hasan al-Banna during the 1930s and early 1940s did not define the organization as Fascist, semi-Fascist, or pro-Nazi. On the contrary, they all demonstrate how this Islamic-Salafite organization leveled harsh criticism against Fascist and Nazi ideas and practices.

119. Israel Gershoni, *Light in the Shade: Egypt and Fascism, 1922–1937* (Tel Aviv, 1999) (in Hebrew). See also Israel Gershoni and Götz Nordbruch, *Sympathie und Schrecken: Begegnungen mit Faschismus und Nationalsozialismus in Ägypten, 1922–1937* (Berlin, 2011); and Gershoni, *Dame and Devil*.

120. For works of a similar vein, see Christoph Schumann, *Radikalnationalismus in Syrien und Libanon: Politische Sozialisation und Elitenbildung, 1930–1958* (Hamburg, 2001); Christoph Schumann, "The Generation of Broad Expectations: Nationalism, Education, and Autobiography in Syria and Lebanon, 1930–1958," *Die Welt des Islams* 41 (2001): 174–205; Christoph Schumann, "The Experience of Organized Nationalism: Radical Discourse and Political Socialization in Syria and Lebanon, 1930–1958," in *From the Syrian Land to the State of Syria*, edited by Thomas Philipp and Christoph Schumann (Würzburg, 2004), 343–358; Elizabeth Thompson, *Colonial Citizens: Republican Rights, Paternal Privilege, and Gender in French Syria and Lebanon* (New York, 1999), 191–196; Keith David Watenpaugh, "Steel Shirts, White Badges, and the Last Qabaday: Fascism, Urban Violence, and Civil Identity in Aleppo under French Rule," in *France, Syrie et Liban, 1918–1946: Les Ambiguïtés et les dynamiques de la relation mandataire*, edited by Nadine Méouchy (Damascus, 2002), 325–347; and Keith David Watenpaugh, *Being Modern in the Middle East: Revolution, Nationalism, Colonialism, and the Arab Middle Class* (Princeton, NJ, 2006), 255–278. For a more general discussion of the place of Fascism in non-European cultures and societies, see Stein U. Larsen, ed., *Fascism Outside Europe: The European Impulse against Domestic Conditions in the Diffusion of Global Fascism* (New York, 2001), particularly the editor's concluding article, "Was There Fascism Outside Europe?," 705–818.

121. See Peter Wien, *Iraqi Arab Nationalism: Authoritarian, Totalitarian, and Pro-Fascist Inclinations, 1932–1941* (London, 2006); Orit Bashkin, *The Other Iraq: Pluralism and Culture in Hashemite Iraq* (Stanford, CA, 2009); Orit Bashkin, "The Barbarism from Within: Discourses about Fascism amongst Iraqi and Iraqi-Jewish Communists, 1942–1955," *Die Welt des Islams* 52 (2012): 400–429.

122. See Götz Nordbruch, *Nazism in Syria and Lebanon: The Ambivalence of the German Option, 1933–1945* (London, 2009); Götz Nordbruch, "Defending the French Revolution during World War II: Raif Khury and the Intellectual Challenge of Nazism in the Levant," *Mediterranean Historical Review* 21, no. 2 (2006): 219–238; Götz Nordbruch, "Bread, Freedom, Independence: Opposition to Nazi Germany in Lebanon and Syria and the Struggle for a Just Order," special issue, edited by Amy Singer and Israel Gershoni, *Comparative Studies in South Asia, Africa, and the Middle East* 28, no. 3 (2008): 416–422; Eyal Zisser, "Writing a Constitution: Constitutional Debates in Syria and Lebanon in the Mandate Period," in *Liberal Thought in the Eastern Mediterranean: Late 19th Century until the 1960s*, edited by Christoph Schumann (Leiden and Boston, 2008), 195–215; Manfred Sing, "Between Lights and Hurricanes: Sami al-Kayyali's Review al-Hadith as a Forum of Modern Arabic Literature and Liberal Islam," in *The Middle Eastern Press as a Forum for Literature*, edited by Horst Unbehaun (Frankfurt, 2004), 119–141; Manfred Sing, "Illiberal Metamorphoses of a Liberal Discourse: The Case of Syrian Intellectual Sami al-Kayyali (1898–1972)," in *Liberal Thought in the Eastern Mediterranean*, edited by Schumann, 293–322.

123. René Wildangel, *Zwischen Achse und Mandatsmacht: Palästina und der Nationalsozialismus* (Berlin, 2007); Mustafa Kabha, "'My Enemy's Enemy—a Friend': Attitudes of the Palestinian National Movement towards Fascism and Nazism, 1925–1945," *Zmanim* 17 (1999): 79–86 (in Hebrew); Mustafa Kabha, *The Palestinian Press as Shaper of Public Opinion, 1929–1939: Writing Up a Storm* (London, 2007), 141–154, 252–254.

124. See Israel Gershoni and James Jankowski, *Confronting Fascism in Egypt: Dictatorship versus Democracy in the 1930s* (Stanford, CA, 2010). See also the following works of Israel Gershoni: "Confronting Nazism in Egypt: Tawfiq al-Hakim's Anti-totalitarianism, 1938–1945," *Tel Aviver Jahrbuch für Deutsche Geschichte* 26 (1997): 120–150; "Egyptian Liberalism Reassessed: Muhammad 'Abdalla 'Inan's Response to German Nazism, 1933–1935," *Jama'a* 4 (1999): 31–68 (in Hebrew); "Egyptian Liberalism in an Age of 'Crisis of Orientation': *Al-Risala*'s Reaction to Fascism and Nazism, 1933–1939," *International Journal of Middle East Studies* 31, no. 4 (1999): 551–576; "Beyond Anti-Semitism: Egyptian Responses to German Nazism and Italian Fascism in the 1930s," EUI Working Papers, *Mediterranean Programme Series*, RSC no. 2001/32 (2001): 1–26; "'Der Verfolgte Jude': Al-Hilals Reaktionen auf den Antisemitismus in Europa und Hitlers Machtergreifung," in *Blind für die Geschichte? Arabische Begegnungen mit dem Nationalsozialismus*, edited by Gerhard Höpp, Peter Wien, and René Wildangel (Berlin, 2004), 39–72; and "Liberal Democracy versus Fascist Totalitarianism in the Egyptian Intellectual Discourse: The Case of Salama Musa and *al-Majalla al-Jadida*," in *Nationalism and Liberal Thought in the Arab Middle East: Ideology and Practice*, edited by Christoph Schumann (London, 2010), 145–172. Additional contributions to the revised narrative concerning the entire Middle East can be found in Höpp, Vein, and Wildangel, *Blind für die Geschichte?*; Robert B. Satloff, *Among the Righteous: Lost Stories from the Holocaust's Long Reach into Arab Lands* (New York, 2006); and Nir Arielli, *Fascist Italy and the Middle East, 1933–1940* (London, 2010). Similar conclusions concerning Fascist Italy's failure in the Middle East can be found in early scholarly works on the topic. See, for example, Cladio G. Segrè, "Liberal and Fascist Italy in the Middle East, 1919–1939: The Elusive White Stallion," in *Great Powers in the Middle East*, edited by Dann, 199–212; and Manuela A. Williams, *Mussolini's Propaganda Abroad: Subversion in the Mediterranean and the Middle East, 1935–1940* (London, 2006). See also Callum A. MacDonald, "Radio Bari: Italian Wireless Propaganda in the Middle East and British Countermeasures, 1934–38," *Middle Eastern Studies* 13, no. 2 (1977): 195–207. For two recent perceptive review articles on this topic, see Peter Wien, "Coming to Terms with the Past: German Academia and Historical Relations between the Arab Lands and Nazi Germany," *International Journal of Middle East Studies* 42 (May 2010): 311–321; and Götz Nordbruch, "'Cultural Fusion' of Thought and Ambitions? Memory, Politics, and the History of Arab-Nazi German Encounters," *Middle Eastern Studies* 47, no. 1 (2011): 183–194.

125. In his book, *Nazi Propaganda for the Arab World* (New Haven, CT, 2009), Jeffrey Herf systematically and rigorously examines Nazi propagandist efforts in the Arab Middle East, particularly at the end of the 1930s and during the war. His important contribution to the discourse both revises conventional wisdom and

reasserts some aspects of the established narrative. Herf positions al-Hajj Amin al-Husayni at the center of this Nazi-Arab collaboration. He shows that despite the definitive defeat of Nazism, Husayni maintained his anti-Semitic convictions, received a celebrity's welcome in Egypt, and continued to lead the Palestinian national movement, all of which is proof of enduring Nazi anti-Semitic inspiration in the Arab-Islamic world.

Chapter One

1. See Olaf Farschid, "The First World War as a Factor of Political and Social Transformation," in *The First World War as Remembered in the Countries of the Eastern Mediterranean*, edited by Manfred Kropp and Stephan Dähne (Würzburg, 2006), 1–19; and Elisabeth Thompson, *Colonial Citizens: Republican Rights, Paternal Privilege, and Gender in French Syria and Lebanon* (New York, 1999), 23.

2. See Leyla Dakhli, *Une génération d'intellectuels arabes: Syrie et Liban (1908–1940)* (Paris, 2009), 155–195; and Keith David Watenpaugh, *Being Modern in the Middle East: Revolution, Nationalism, Colonialism, and the Arab Middle Class* (Princeton, NJ, 2006), 1–30.

3. Nadine Méouchy, "La presse de Syrie et du Liban entre les deux guerres, 1918-1939," in *Débats intellectuels au Moyen-Orient dans l'Entre-Deux-Guerres, Revue des Mondes Musulmans et de la Méditerranée 95–98* (Aix-en-Provence, 2002), 55–70. See also Thompson, *Colonial Citizens*, 211–223; Manfred Sing, "Between Lights and Hurricanes: Sami al-Kayyali's Review of al-Hadith as a Forum of Modern Arab Literature and Liberal Islam," in *The Middle Eastern Press as a Forum for Literature*, edited by Horst Unbehaun (Frankfurt, 2004), 119–141; and Sabrina Mervin, "Le Liban-Sud entre deux generations de reformistes," in *Débats intellectuels*, 257–266. The active involvement of the press in political events during the period prior to World War I is highlighted in Eliezer Tauber, "The Press and the Journalist as a Vehicle in Spreading National Ideas in Syria in the Late Ottoman Empire," *Die Welt des Islams*, n.s., 30, no. 1/4 (1990): 163–177.

4. Thompson, *Colonial Citizens*, 213.

5. "Intikhab al-Marshal Hindinburgh," *al-Insaniyya*, May 15, 1925.

6. Munir 'Ajlani, "Hal Bada'at al-Thawra fi Almaniya," *al-Qabas*, July 16, 1934.

7. Mishal Zakkur, "Al-Mayadin al-Hamra," *al-Ma'rid*, August 5, 1935. See also Mishal Zakkur, "Al-Daght al-Maddi wa-l-Siyasi," *al-Ma'rid*, July 25, 1935; and Mishal Zakkur, "Niza' al-Diktaturiyya," *al-Ma'rid*, October 19, 1935.

8. See Olivier Meier, *Al-muqtataf et le débat sur le Darwinisme: Beyrouth, 1876–1885* (Cairo, 1994), 8–10; and Georges Haroun, *Shibli Shumayyil: Une pensée évolutionniste arabe à l'époque d'an-nahda* (Beirut, 1985), 5–11. For similar debates in other Arab countries, and particularly in Egypt, see Omnia El Shakry, *The Great Social Laboratory: Subjects of Knowledge in Colonial and Postcolonial Egypt* (Stanford, CA, 2007), 170–173; and Israel Gershoni and James Jankowski, *Confronting Fascism in Egypt: Dictatorship versus Democracy in the 1930s* (Stanford, CA, 2010), 147–165.

9. See Stefan Wild, "National Socialism in the Arab Near East between 1933 and 1939," *Die Welt des Islams*, no. 25 (1985): 147–148.

10. Karim Muruwa, introduction to "Kifahi," by Adolf Hitler, *al-Nida'*, January 20, 1934.

11. Kazim al-Sulh, "Li-Madha 'Arrabna wa Nasharna Kitab Hitlir 'Kifahi,'" *al-Nida'*, May 22, 1934. See also Kazim al-Sulh, "Al-Sha'b al-'Arabi Huwa Ahatt min al-Zunuj," *al-Nida'*, April 20, 1934.

12. See "Hitlir wa-l-Yahud fi Almaniya," *al-Ma'rid*, February 7, 1932.

13. In the nineteenth and early twentieth centuries, anti-Jewish stereotypes originated mostly from within the Christian communities. See Kirsten E. Schulze, *Jews of Lebanon: Between Coexistence and Conflict* (Brighton, 2001), 18–20, 37. A French report from the early 1930s emphasized the lack of any equivalent anti-Jewish hostility among the Muslim community: "La population musulmane ne manifeste à l'égard de ces anciens juifs aucune hostilité particulière. Aucun problème anti-sémite ne se pose actuellement dans la politique syrienne. La question de l'immigration juive se présente sur un plan tout différent." Ministère des Affaires Etrangères, Archives diplomatiques, Nantes 615, "Note sur la question juive en Syrie," probably late 1933, 2. This note argues that recent tensions between Muslims and Jews were nearly exclusively due to Zionist immigration, which had gained momentum with the takeover by Hitler's regime in Germany.

14. See, for instance, Jibran Tuwayni, "Al-Nahiyya al-Qawmiyya," *al-Nahar*, April 9, 1934; and Jibran Tuwayni, "Hijrat al-Yahud ila Suriya wa-Lubnan," *al-Nahar*, April 6, 1934. In another context, *al-Nida'* claimed that Jewish immigration posed a threat to the very essence of Arab nationalism. If the strong German nation perceives Zionism as a threat to its national basis, the paper argued, should the weak Arab nation stay put? "Qad Yanju al-'Alam Kulluhu," *al-Nida'*, January 4, 1935. Antun Sa'ada, the founder of the then clandestine Syrian Nationalist Party, also highlighted in his edited journal the supposedly destructive influence of immigration to the national interest. With regard to the territories under French mandate, his focus was on Armenian immigration and its supposedly negative impact. See Antun Sa'ada, "Azmatuna al-Iqtisadiyya," *al-Majalla*, May 1933. It is noteworthy again that both Sa'ada and Tuwayni had a Christian background.

15. "Ya Shabab al-'Arab!," *al-Qabas*, May 5, 1935. See also "Al-Nitham al-Riyadi," *al-Nida'*, January 31, 1934; and "Al-Shabab fi Almaniya," *al-Qabas*, September 3, 1935. With regard to related debates in the Iraqi press, see Peter Wien, *Iraqi Arab Nationalism: Authoritarian, Totalitarian, and Pro-Fascist Inclinations, 1932–1941* (London, 2006), 88–112.

16. Sami al-Kayyali, "Mawqif al-Shabab min al-Naza'at al-Tajdidiyya," *al-Hadith*, February 1933, 134–150.

17. For one example of these articles, see Mari 'Ajami, "Al-Mar'a bayn al-Sharq wa-l-Gharb," *al-Insaniyya*, February 1935, 49–51.

18. See "Almaniya Turid Zawjat Ummahat," *al-Sahafi al-Ta'ih*, August 18, 1933; "Rai Musulini fi l-Mar'a," *al-Ma'rid*, July 10, 1932; "Markaz al-Mar'a al-Iqtisadi fi Almaniya wa Rusiya," *al-Ahrar*, August 10, 1933; and "Al-Haraka al-Nisawiyya al-Jadida fi Almaniya," *al-Ahrar*, July 19, 1933.

19. See, for instance, "Al-Diktaturiyya wa-l-Mar'a," *al-Sahafi al-Taih*, December 1, 1934.

20. Kazim al-Sulh, "Junuh al-Mar'a 'Indana," *al-Nida'*, March 11, 1934.

21. See Shams al-Din al-Kaylani, *Al-Hizb al-Shuyu'i al-Suri* (Damascus, 2003), 37–38, 43–44. For early Communist responses to Fascism and Nazism, see Husayn Muruwa, "Al-Udaba' wa-l-Mufakkirun al-Lubnayniyyun fi-l-Nidal didd al-Fashistiya wa-min ajil al-Sadaqa ma' al-Ittihad al-Sufiyati," *al-Tariq*, no. 4 (September 1985): 165–178; and 'Abdallah Hanna, *Al-haraka al-munahida li-l-fashiyya fi suriya wa lubnan 1933–45* (Beirut, 1974).

22. "Khamsat Ashur fi Isbaniya al-Jumhuriyya," *al-Tali'a*, no. 9 (November 1937): 793.

23. *Al-Duhur* was edited since 1930 by Ibrahim Haddad, a reputed Lebanese socialist intellectual. From January until December 1934, the Lebanese Marxist and member of the CP Salim Khayyata served as its editor. Regular contributors to the journal were such different writers as the liberal nationalist Amin al-Rihani, the future founder of the Ba'th Party Michel 'Aflaq, and the Marxist thinker Raif Khuri. See Muhammad Dakrub, "'Fi Masirat al-Tariq'—Tarikh wa Marahil," *al-Tariq*, no. 1 (January–February 2002): 261.

24. Walter Z. Laqueur, *Communism and Nationalism in the Middle East* (London, 1956), 145.

25. Tareq Y. Ismael and Jacqueline S. Ismael, *The Communist Movement in Syria and Lebanon* (Gainesville, FL, 1998), 29.

26. Ra'if Khuri, "Taqrir al-Lajna al-Tahdiriyya fi Mu'tamar Mukafahat al-Fashistiyya," *al-Tali'a*, no. 5 (May 1939): 358.

27. Kamil 'Ayyad was an alumnus of the Friedrich-Wilhelm University in Berlin where he studied sociology in the early 1920s. He was actively engaged in local student activities and was involved in Marxist circles and politics. This interest persisted following his return to Syria, where he was an active contributor to the anti-Fascist league.

28. Ibrahim Kaylani, "Nahdatuna al-Haditha: Al-Shabab al-Suri," *Majallat al-Mu'allimin wa-l-Mu'allimat*, no. 1 (October 1935): 29.

29. See, for example, "Al-Jil al-Muqbil fi Almaniya," *al-Hadith*, no. 1 (January 1936): 41–43; "Kayfa Naththama al-Mustashar Hitlir al-Shabab al-Almani?," *al-Musawwar*, July 1, 1936, 12; and "Harakat al-Shabab al-Almani," *al-Amali*, February 10, 1939, 8–12.

30. Sharif al-Kaylani, "Risalat al-Shabab," *al-Tamaddun al-Islami*, no. 5 (Rajab 1357h [September 1938]), 137.

31. See, for instance, the widely noted book *A Month in Europe*, by Sami al-Kayyali, the editor of *al-Hadith*. Kayyali drew on impressions he had gained during a visit that took him in 1935 to France, Switzerland, Italy, and Britain. See Sami al-Kayyali, "Dhahirat Urubbiyya," *al-Hadith*, no. 8 (August 1935): 578–581. The book was published as *Shahr fi Urubba* (Cairo, 1935).

32. See Salim 'Abd Salim, "Hakadha Takallama Zaradasht," *al-'Urwa al-Wuthqa*, May 1936, 3–6; and Nakhla Ward, "Insan nitsha," *al-Tali'a*, no. 1 (March 1936): 84–86. For the ambivalent place of Nietzsche in the thinking of Lebanese thinker Farah Antun (1874–1922), see, for instance, Alexander Flores, "Modernity, Romanticism, and Religion: Contradictions in the Writings of Farah Antun," in *Nationalism and Liberal Thought in the Arab East*, edited by Christoph Schumann (London, 2010), 121–122.

33. Filiks Faris, *Hakadha Takallama Zaradasht* (Beirut, 1970).

34. Munir al-Husami, "Falsafsat Nitsha wa-l-Subarman," *al-Amali*, October 28, 1938, 10.

35. See 'Umar Farrukh, "Hakadha Takallama Zaradasht," *al-Amali*, February 3, 1939, 29–30.

36. See Filiks Faris, "Al-Nabi Muhammad Asad al-Sahra," *al-Amali*, August 4, 1939, 2–3.

37. Khalil Hindawi, "Hakadha Takallama Zaradasht li-l-Filusuf al-Almani Nitsha," *al-Amali*, July 7, 1939, 8.

38. 'Umar Farrukh, "Harakat al-Iman al-Almani," *al-Amali*, October 7, 1938, 24–26.

39. Ibid., 25.

40. Here again it is noteworthy that similar influences were visible in other countries of the region. With regard to Egypt, Timothy Mitchell describes Le Bon as "probably the strongest individual European influence in turn-of-the-century Cairo on the political thought of Egypt's emergent bourgeoisie." Timothy Mitchell, *Colonising Egypt* (Berkeley, CA, 1997), 123. See also Charles Wendell, *The Evolution of the Egyptian National Image: From Its Origins to Ahmad Lutfi al-Sayyid* (Berkeley, CA, 1972), 251.

41. Thompson, *Colonial Citizens*, 48–49. I thank the anonymous reader of this article for pointing me to this aspect.

42. Shakib Arslan, "Le problème Palestinien et l'Islam," *La Nation Arabe*, nos. 20–21 (September–December): 1150.

43. Salah al-Din al-Tarzi, "Al-Fashiyya," *al-Hadith*, no. 7 (July 1937): 519.

44. See Götz Nordbruch, "Bread, Freedom, Independence: Opposition to Nazi Germany in Lebanon and Syria and the Struggle for a Just Order," *Comparative Studies of South Asia, Africa, and the Middle East* 28, no. 3 (2008): 416–427.

45. 'Ali 'Abd al-Mun'im Sha'ib, *Al-Tadakhkhul al-Ajnabi w-Azmat al-Hukm fi Tarikh al-'Arab al-Hadith wa-l-Mu'asir* (Beirut, 2005), 251.

46. Höpp papers, Zentrum Moderner Orient, Berlin, Auswärtiges Amt, Pol VII, note concerning report "Zur Frage eines Funks in arabischer Sprache durch deutsche Sender," January 8, 1938.

47. On Nazi propaganda toward the Arab Middle East, see Jeffrey Herf, *Nazi Propaganda for the Arab World* (New Haven, CT, 2009); and Chantal Metzger, *L'empire colonial Français dans la stratégie du Troisième Reich, 1936–1945* (Brussels, 2002), 1:191–193.

48. Ministère des Affaires Etrangères, Archives diplomatiques, Nantes 912, Service de la Presse et de la Propagande, "Compte Rendu de l'activité du Service de la Propagande (Mois de Novembre 1939)," December 1, 1939, 1.

49. Ibid., 2, and January 2, 1940, 2.

50. Ahmad Dimashqiyya, *Lisan al-Hal*, October 13, 1939, quoted in CAOM 909, Ministère des Colonies, "Revue de la Presse et des Questions Musulmanes," no. 13/1939, 197.

51. Salah al-Asir, "Al-Dimuqratiyya wa-l-'Arab," *al-Hadith*, no. 9 (September 1939): 748.

52. "Al-Harb, al-'Arab wa-l-Islam," *al-'Irfan*, no. 9 (November 1939): 1–2.

53. *Al-Dabbur*, May 1, 1939.

54. "Madha Jatarattab 'ala al-Lubnaniyyin," *al-Dabbur*, September 11, 1939, 3.

55. Ministère des Affaires Etrangères, Archives diplomatiques, Nantes 20, SG (Beirut), "Détenus politiques," August 13, 1941, 2.

56. Editorials by Faraj Allah al-Hilu are reproduced in Faraj Allah al-Hilu, *Kitabat Mukhtara* (Beirut, 1999).

57. Khalid Bakdash, *Sawt al-Sha'b*, January 20, 1942, quoted in Nazir Jazmati, *Al-Hizb al-Shuyu'i al-Suri, 1924–1958* (Damascus, 1990), 148.

58. See Karim Muruwa, "Majallatuna al-Thaqafa Tharwatuna al-Qawmiyya," *al-Tariq* (January–February 2002): 231–237.

59. Qadri Qala'aji, "Risalat al-'Usba," *al-Tariq*, December 20, 1941, 2.

60. Thompson, *Colonial Citizens*, 244.

61. Jibran Tuwayni, "Li-Madha Nahnu ma' al-Dimuqratiyyat?," *al-Adib*, January 1942, 5.

62. Jamil Saliba, "Al-Tarbiyya al-Qawmiyya," *al-Adib*, November 1942, 7–8.

63. See, for example, Qadri Qala'aji, "Al-'Unsuriyya wa-l-Isti'mar al-Almani," *al-Adib*, September 1942, 16–17; Qadri Qala'aji, "Tawazun al-Ijtima'i," *al-Adib*, October 1942, 3–4; Niqula Qiyyad, "Fridrik Nitsha wa-Din al-Quwwa," *al-Adib*, December 1942, 29–32; Iliyas Abu Shabka, "Irnst Rinan," *al-Adib*, December 1942, 38–40.

64. Nazi ideology was central to the coverage of the journal. See, for instance, Munir Sulayman, "Haqiqa al-Ishtirakiyya al-Wataniyya al-Almaniyya," *al-Tariq*, no. 4 (February 20, 1942): 2, 20–22; Qadri Qala'aji, "Ustura al-Dam al-Almani," *al-Tariq*, no. 17 (October 1, 1942): 2–6.

65. Ministère des Affaires Etrangères, Archives diplomatiques, Nantes 2396, SGA, Information "Communistes et Parti Populaire Syrien," June 27, 1944.

66. For public reactions to the liberation of Paris, see Ministère des Affaires Etrangères, Archives diplomatiques, Nantes 74, SGA, Information Spéciale 2094 "La libération de Paris," August 30, 1944.

67. "Ba'd Ikhtiyyar Wafdina li-l-Mu'tamar," *al-Kifah*, April 13, 1945.

68. See, for instance, Farajallah al-Hilu, "Ijtima' Butsdam wa-l-Qadiyya al-Lubnaniyya al-Suriyya," *Sawt al-Sha'b*, July 20, 1945.

69. Kamal Jumblatt in *Cahiers de l'Orient contemporain*, November 20, 1945, 7, quoted in Kamal Jumblatt, *Nahwa Sigha Jadida li-l-Dimuqratiyya al-Ijtima'iyya al-Isaniyya 1945* (al-Mukhtara, 2004), 5.

70. Bishara Khalil al-Khuri, *Majmu'at al-Khutab: Aylul 1943—Kanun al-Awwal 1951* (Beirut, 1951), 23.

Chapter Two

1. Eliyahu Sasson, "From my Memoirs—Iraq's Loyalty to the Allies," Jerusalem, December 5, 1941. A copy of this document, from his private papers, was given to the author by Eliyahu Sasson's daughter. Sasson was born in Damascus and served as the head of the Arab section in the Political Department in the Jewish Agency. From June 1940 until June 1941, he visited Vichy Syria and Lebanon

several times to gather intelligence for the British. For a summary of Nuri al-Sa'id's letter, see Lukasz Hirszowicz, *The Third Reich and the Arab East* (Tel Aviv, 1965), 114 (in Hebrew).

2. Riad al-Sulh is defined in this chapter as a member of the Syrian National Bloc, although he was a known Lebanese Arab nationalist leader. In fact, he was one of the founders of the National Bloc and in the 1930s and 1940s closely coordinated his stand toward the Lebanese state with his colleagues in Syria. See M. Zamir, "An Intimate Alliance: The Joint Struggle of General Edward Spears and Riad al-Sulh to Oust France from Lebanon, 1942–1944," *Middle Eastern Studies* 41, no. 6 (2005): 817–818.

3. Britain's use of covert action to control the Middle East during the war and to evict France from Syria and Lebanon was examined in M. Zamir, "The 'Missing Dimension': Britain's Secret War against France in Syria and Lebanon, 1942–1945," *Middle Eastern Studies* 46, no. 6 (2010): 791–899. The article is based on secret British and Syrian documents obtained by the French intelligence, uncovered by the author. In retaliation for their eviction by the British from Syria and Lebanon, the French secretly collaborated with the Zionist movement against Britain. See Zamir, "Bid for Altalena: France's Covert Action in the 1948 War in Palestine," *Middle Eastern Studies* 46, no. 1 (2010): 17–58.

4. Archives du Ministère des Affaires Etrangères (MAE), Nantes, Syrie et Liban, carton 1086, Bulletin d'Information Spécial, no. 707, June 24; no. 743, June 26; no. 837, Beirut, July 4, 1942; Information no. 152, Damascus, July 1, 1942; carton 1094, French Directive, September 4, 1942. For Anglo-French rivalry in the Levant from 1940 to 1942, see M. Zamir, "De Gaulle and the Question of Syria and Lebanon during the Second World War," *Middle Eastern Studies* 43, no. 5 (2007): 675–708.

5. Zamir, "'Missing Dimension,'" documents nos. 1–6, 820–824. On the ambivalent attitude of Syrian and Lebanese nationalists toward Nazi Germany before and during World War II, see Götz Nordbruch, *Nazism in Syria and Lebanon: The Ambivalence of the German Option, 1933–1945* (London, 2009).

6. Service Historique de l'Armée de Terre, Vincennes (SHAT), box 4H322, Note, Beirut, March 22, 1942, report of a high-ranking French official on his conversation with Jamil Mardam. See H. O. Dovey, "Security in Syria, 1941–45," *Intelligence and National Security* 6, no. 2 (1991): 422–423. See also Nordbruch, *Nazism in Syria and Lebanon*, 90.

7. Zamir, "Intimate Alliance," 816–818. See also Dovey, "Security in Syria," 419.

8. Albert Hourani, *Syria and Lebanon* (London, 1946), 230–231.

9. MAE, Nantes, Syrie et Liban, carton 2135, no. 4, Beirut, "Résumé des événements politiques de la quinzaine du 12 au 25 février," and no. 12, June 3–16, 1940.

10. MAE, Nantes, Syrie et Liban, carton 2135, no. 13, Beirut, "Résumé des événements politiques de la quinzaine du 17 au 30 juin," and no. 18, August 26–September 8, 1940. Ben-Gurion Archives, Sede Boqer (BGA), Correspondence, "A Report from Damascus," June 9, 1940, by Sasson, and a report by Eliyahu Epstein (Eilat) to Moshe Shertok, Beirut, June 29, 1940. Epstein, who had served as the Jewish Agency's emissary in Beirut during the 1930s and early 1940s, carried out several missions for the British intelligence in 1940–1942, including in Lebanon, Syria, Turkey, and Iran.

11. MAE, Nantes, Syrie et Liban, carton 2135, no. 18, Beirut, "Résumé des événements politiques de la quinzaine du 26 août au 8 septembre 1940"; carton 461, Note, Beirut, April 9, 1940; BGA, Correspondence, Sasson's report, August 14, 1940; Hourani, *Syria and Lebanon*, 234. The Hashemite-Saudi rivalry in Syria, whose secret aspects are yet to be studied, was a dominant feature in inter-Arab relations during the 1940s. See Zamir, "'Missing Dimension,'" document no. 1, 820–821; nos. 7–8, 824–826.

12. MAE, Nantes, Syrie et Liban, carton 2135, no. 184, Information, Beirut, June 5, 1941; BGA, Correspondence, Sasson's reports on his visit to Damascus, July 9 and 12 1940. See also S. Mardam, *Syria's Quest for Independence* (Reading, 1994), 18–22.

13. SHAT, box 4H394, no. 1116, "Activités allemandes en Syrie entre le 25/6/40 et 14/7/41," Beirut, June 4, 1942; France Combattante "les allemands en Syrie sous le gouvernement de Vichy," London, 1942; MAE, Nantes, Syrie et Liban, carton 2135, no. 5, "Résumé des événements politiques de la quinzaine du 4 février au 16 mars, 1941." One of the films was *Sieg im Westen* (Victory in the West). See United States, Office of Strategic Services, Report no. 1264, "Enemy Espionage in the Levant States," September 27, 1943. See also Jeffrey Herf, *Nazi Propaganda for the Arab World* (New Haven, CT, 2009).

14. On the activities of German agents in youth movements in Syria and Lebanon, see SHAT, box 4H394, no. 1116, "Activités allemandes en Syrie entre le 25/6/40 et 14/7/41," Beirut, June 4, 1942. See also the National Archives, Kew (TNA), FO 226, vol. 239, 159/5/42, "Arab Youth and the War," report prepared by Bayard Dodge, president of the American University of Beirut, December 30, 1942.

15. SHAT, box 4H394, Dossier 4, "Tracts de propagande allemande et italienne au Levant"; BGA, Correspondence, Sasson's report on his visit to Damascus, July 12, 1940.

16. SHAT, box 4H394, Dossier 4, "Tracts de propagande allemande et italienne au Levant," leaflet entitled "O anglais," translated from Arabic, October 22, 1942.

17. Ibid.

18. MAE, Nantes, Syrie et Liban, carton 2135, "Comment Répondre aux Diverses Propagandes Anti-Françaises," Beirut, April 8, 1941. The report illustrates the propaganda war between Vichy and Britain in Syria and Lebanon. See a copy of a report by the Iraqi consulate in Beirut in FO 371/27321 1483/76, no. 244, "Political Situation," Cairo, Lampson to Eden, March 18, 1941; and FO 371/31473 3571/207, Weekly Report no. 10, June 11, 1942. See also a British comparison between Churchill's speech from May 10, 1942, and Hitler's speech from April 26, 1942, and their impact on Arab public opinion in MAE, Nantes, Syrie et Liban, carton 1094, Middle East Fortnightly Guidance no. 2, May 20, 1942.

19. Middle East Center, St. Antony's College, Oxford, Spears Papers, box I, no. 26, Cairo, August 1, no. 2460, August 7, 1941, Minister of State to FO; FO 371/35177 2484/27 no. 274, Weekly Report no. 56, April 23, 1943; BGA, Correspondence, Sasson's report on "Nazi activities in the Middle East," Beirut, February 9, 1942. The British followed closely the German intelligence activities in Turkey and Syria. See H. O. Dovey, "The Intelligence War in Turkey," *Intelligence and National Security* 9, no. 1 (1994): 59–87.

20. BGA, Correspondence, Epstein's report on his visit to Turkey, Jerusalem, January 25, 1942. See the conflicting British intelligence information concerning Quwatli's ties with the Axis in Dovey, "Security in Syria," 422. 'Adil Arslan, Shekib's cousin, was high on the French and British lists of suspected Arab nationalist leaders who had collaborated with the Axis powers. On German activities among the Druze in Lebanon, especially their ties with 'Adil Arslan, see BGA, Correspondence, Epstein's report, August 16, 1940, and his report to J. P. Wallis, British Embassy, Ankara, May 5, 1941.

21. For British officials' messages to the Syrian leaders, see Spears Papers, box I, no. 2460, Cairo, August 7, 1941, Minister of State to FO; and SHAT, box 4H382, a circular by the commander in chief entitled "Political Aspect of the War." See also Zamir, "Intimate Alliance," 813.

22. Spears Papers, box I, no. 2460, Cairo, August 7, 1941, Minister of State to FO; BGA, Correspondence, Epstein's report, August 16, 1940, and his report to Wallis, British Embassy, Ankara, May 5, 1941.

23. On the Syrian nationalists' belief that they would be able to realize their national goals whether Germany or Great Britain won the war, see Sa'adallah al-Jabiri's statement in MAE, Nantes, Syrie et Liban, carton 2455, no. 615, Information, Beirut, August 8, 1942. Sasson recounted a similar attitude among the National Bloc leaders in his reports from Damascus. See his report from February 9, 1942.

24. FO 371/31473 3571/207, Weekly Report, June 11, 1942, German propaganda exploiting the Abadin incident in Egypt; and FO 371/31473 3571/207, no. 208, Weekly Report, June 11, 1942. See also M. Kolinsky, "Lampson and the Wartime Control of Egypt," in *Demise of the British Empire in the Middle East*, edited by M. Cohen and M. Kolinsky (London, 1998), 95–111.

25. For Sulh's collaboration with Roser, see SHAT, box 4H394, no. 1116, "Activités allemandes en Syrie entre le 25/6/40 et 14/7/41." For Sulh's ties with Tahsin al-Kadri, the Iraqi consul in Beirut, see box 4H319, Information no. 43, Beirut, July 28, 1941. On Anglo-Iraqi intelligence cooperation in Vichy Syria and Lebanon, see report prepared by the Iraqi consulate in Beirut, in FO 371/27321 1483/76, no. 244, "Political Situation," Cairo, Lampson to Eden, March 18, 1941. For Sulh's collaboration with Spears, see Zamir, "Intimate Alliance," 816–817.

26. In March–April 1941, the British intelligence sought information on Sulh, Quwatli, and other National Bloc leaders. See SHAT, box 4H311, report by a British agent in Vichy Syria and Lebanon, code name Romulus, Jerusalem, April 5, 1941. On Mardam's activities in Baghdad, see Mardam, *Syria's Quest for Independence*, 27–30. On May 9, 1941, Jamil Mardam arrived in Aleppo and took a train to Baghdad. The purpose of his trip at the height of the crisis in Iraq is unclear.

27. Spears Papers, box IA, Cairo, June 5, 1941, Spears to Churchill; no. 27, Cairo, August 1, 1941, Minister of State to the Prime Minister; MAE, Nantes, Syrie et Liban, carton 2135, no. 10, Beirut, "Résumé des événements politiques de la quinzaine du 12 au 25 mai 1941"; G. Catroux, *Dans la Bataille de Méditerranée* (Paris, 1949), 128, 137–140; Zamir, "De Gaulle and the Question of Syria and Lebanon," 682–683; Mardam, *Syria's Quest for Independence*, 44–48; Hourani, *Syria and Lebanon*, 192.

28. Spears Papers, box IA, Cairo, June 5, 1941, Spears to Churchill; no. 27,

Cairo, August 1, 1941, Minister of State to Churchill; no. 3387, Cairo, October 28, 1941, Minister of State to FO; no. 707, Beirut, March 7, 1942, Spears to FO; MAE, Nantes, Syrie et Liban, carton 2986, Spears to Catroux, Beirut, August 31, 1941.

29. Spears Papers, box IA, no. 26, Cairo, August 1, 1941, Minister of State to FO; no. 3387, Cairo, October 28, 1941, Minister of State to FO; MAE Nantes, Syrie et Liban, carton 2986, Beirut, August 30, 1941, Spears to Catroux; Sasson's report, February 9, 1942; Zamir, "Intimate Alliance," 816–817.

30. Spears Papers, no. 707, Beirut, March 7, 1942, Spears to FO; SHAT, box 4H322, no. 10367, Beirut, December 4, 1942, "A/S les Nationalistes Syriens et les Américains," memorandum from Jamil Mardam to George Wadsworth, the American consul-general in Beirut; BGA, Correspondence, Sasson's report "Conditions in Syria," Beirut, February 9, 1942.

31. BGA, Correspondence, Epstein's report on his conversation with the Egyptian consul upon his return from Damascus, Ankara, November 12, 1941; Sasson's report "Conditions in Syria," Beirut, February 9, 1942.

32. Spears Papers, box I, no. 18, Jedda, January 11, 1942, Stonehewer-Bird to FO; MAE, Nantes, Syrie et Liban, carton 768, "Note sur les relations Franco-Britanniques au Levant," Beirut, November 1943; BGA, Correspondence, Epstein's report from Ankara, January 15, 1942.

33. BGA, Correspondence, report "In the Country and the Neighboring States," Jerusalem, January 15, 1942. For Cornwallis's pressure on Quwatli to acquiesce to Syria's incorporation within a Hashemite federation, see his three days of conversations with Quwatli in September 1944 in Zamir, "'Missing Dimension,'" documents nos. 24–26, 834–838.

34. Zamir, "'Missing Dimension,'" document no. 1, 820–821.

35. FO 371/31472 2555/207, Weekly Report, April 23, 1943.

36. FO 226/233 31/106, no. 178, Beirut, June 29, 1942, Spears to Minister of State; MAE, Nantes, Syrie et Liban, carton 2207, Information no. 106, Beirut, March 3, 1942; BGA, Correspondence, Epstein's report on a visit to Beirut, Jerusalem, November 10, 1942; Mardam, *Syria's Quest for Independence*, 56–60.

37. MAE, Nantes, Syrie et Liban, carton 2455, no. 615, Information, Beirut, August 8, 1942.

38. W. M. Louis, *The British Empire in the Middle East, 1945–1951* (Oxford, 1984), 168; A. Hourani, book review on *The Anglo-French Clash in Lebanon and Syria, 1940–45* by A. B. Gaunson, *English Historical Review* 105, no. 414 (1990): 261–262.

Chapter Three

1. See Sami Moubayed, *Steel and Silk: Men and Women Who Shaped Syria, 1900–2000* (Seattle, 2006), 476.

2. Nassuh Babil, *Sihafa Wa Siyasa, Suriyya fi al-Qarn al-'Ishrin* (London, 1987), 121.

3. Mustafa Talas, *Mir'at Hayati* (Damascus, 1992), 1:48.

4. Ibid.

5. Mustafa Talas, *Fatir Sahyun* (Damascus, 2002).

6. Götz Nordbruch, *Nazism in Syria and Lebanon: The Ambivalence of the German Option, 1933–1945* (New York, 2008).

7. For more, see Patrick Seale, *The Struggle for Syria* (London, 1965). See also Raymond Hinnebusch, *Syria: Revolution from Above* (New York, 2001).

8. See Labib Zuwiyya Yamak, *The Syrian Social Nationalist Party: An Ideological Analysis* (Cambridge, MA, 1966).

9. See "The Syrian Phoenix: The Revival of the Syrian Social National Party in Syria," *Die Welt des Islams* 47, no. 2 (2007): 188–206. See also Kamel S. Abu Jaber, *The Arab Ba'th Socialist Party: History, Ideology, and Organization* (Syracuse, NY, 1966); Michael W. Suleiman, *Political Parties in Lebanon* (Ithaca, NY, 1967), 113–119.

10. See Albert Hourani, *Arabic Thought in the Liberal Age, 1798–1939* (Cambridge, 1984); David Dean Commins, *Islamic Reform: Politics and Social Change in Late Ottoman Syria* (Oxford, 1990); Marwan R. Buheiry, ed., *Intellectual Life in the Arab East, 1890–1939* (Beirut, 1981).

11. For more, see Philip S. Khoury, *Syria and the French Mandate* (Princeton, NJ, 1987).

12. See Eyal Zisser, *Lebanon: The Challenge of Independence* (London, 2000), 211–212.

13. Keith David Watenpaugh, *Being Modern in the Middle East: Revolution, Nationalism, Colonialism, and the Arab Middle Class* (Princeton, NJ, 2006), 121–122.

14. Sami al-Jundi, *Al-B'ath* (Beirut, 1969), 27.

15. Ibid., 25.

16. See Moubayed, *Steel and Silk*, 61, 264. See also Hanna Batatu, *Syria's Peasantry, the Descendants of Its Lesser Rural Notables, and Their Politics* (Princeton, NJ, 1999), 38, 60.

17. Al-Jundi, *Al-B'ath*, 25.

18. Ibid., 27.

19. See Batatu, *Syria's Peasantry.*

20. See Moubayed, *Steel and Silk*, 476.

21. Babil, *Sihafa Wa Siyasa*, 121.

22. Moubayed, *Steel and Silk*, 186–190.

23. Khalid al-'Azm, *Mudhdhakkirat Khalid al-'Azm* (Beirut, 1973), 2:326.

24. Moubayed, *Steel and Silk*, 140–142.

25. 'Adil Arsalan, *Mudhakkirat al-Amir 'Adil Arsalan* (Beirut, 1983), 1:30.

26. Ibid., 34.

27. Ibid., 97.

28. Ibid., 238.

29. Ibid., 281.

30. Ibid., 504.

31. Moubayed, *Steel and Silk*, 245–247.

32. Akram al-Hawrani, *Mudhakkirat Akram al-Hawrani* (Cairo, 2000), 1:192.

33. See Khoury, *Syria and the French Mandate*, 113–245.

34. Khoury, *Syria and the French Mandate*; Elizabeth F. Thompson, *Colonial Citizens: Republican Rights, Paternal Privilege, and Gender in French Syria and Lebanon* (New York, 2000).

35. For more, see Salma Mardam Bey, *Syria's Quest for Independence, 1939–1945* (Reading, 1994).

36. Moubayed, *Steel and Silk*, 192–193.

37. Khayriyya Qasimiyya, *Al-Ra'il al-'Arabi al-Awwal, Hayat wa Awrq Nabih wa 'Adil al-Azma* (London, 1991), 105.

Chapter Four

1. Matthias Küntzel, *Islamist Terrorism and Antisemitism: The Mission against Modernity* (n.p., 2008).

2. See Stefan Wild's study on the perception of anti-Semitic publications as the "Protocols of the Elders of Zion." Stefan Wild, "Die Protokolle der Weisen von Zion," in *Islamstudien ohne Ende: Festschrift für Werner Ende zum 65. Geburtstag* (Würzburg, 2002), 517–526.

3. For a bibliographic overview, see Gerhard Höpp, "Der Gefangene im Dreieck: Zum Bild Amin al-Husseinis in Wissenschaft und Publizistik seit 1941; Ein bio-bibliographischer Abriß," in *Eine umstrittene Figur: Hadj Amin al-Husseini—Mufti von Jerusalem*, edited by Rainer Zimmer-Winkel (Trier, 1999), 5–23. See also the revised version of Klaus Gensicke, *Der Mufti von Jerusalem und die Nationalsozialisten: Eine politische Biografie Amin el-Husseinis* (Darmstadt, 2008).

4. Some exceptions: the works of Rashid Khalidi, such as *The Iron Cage: The Story of the Palestinian Struggle for Statehood* (Boston, 2006); Zachary Lockman, *Comrades and Enemies: Arab and Jewish Workers in Palestine, 1906–1948* (Berkeley, CA, 1996); and Ted Swedenburg, *Memories of Revolt: The 1936–1939 Rebellion and the Palestinian National Past* (Minneapolis, 1995).

5. See Israel Gutman, ed., *Encyclopedia of the Holocaust* (New York, 1990).

6. Dan Diner, *Gedächniszeiten: Über jüdische und andere Geschichten* (Munich, 2003), 222.

7. Robert Satloff, *Among the Righteous: Lost Stories from the Holocaust's Long Reach into Arab Lands* (New York, 2006).

8. Ibid., 170.

9. Jeffrey Herf, *Nazi Propaganda for the Arab World*, 14 (New Haven, CT, 2009).

10. George Antonius, *The Arab Awakening: The Story of the Arab National Movement* (London, 1938), 388.

11. Some examples of studies that disregard Arab sources but make far-reaching conclusions on Arab and Islamic perception and responses to the Nazis: the early Simon Wiesenthal, *Großmufti—Großagent der Achse* (Wien, 1947); or recently Matthias Küntzel, *Jihad and Jew-Hatred: Islamism, Nazism and the Roots of 9/11* (New York, 2007).

12. This quote, which is often reproduced in this context, is from Sami al-Jundi. See Robert Wistrich, "The Old-New Anti-Semitism," *National Interest* 72 (2003): 60.

13. Hannah Arendt, *Eichmann in Jerusalem: A Report on the Banality of Evil*, rev. ed. (New York, 1965), 13.

14. See Tom Segev, *The Seventh Million: The Israelis and the Holocaust* (New York, 2000).

15. See, for example, Christopher Hitchens, "Defending 'Islamofascism,'" *Slate*, 2007, http://www.slate.com/id/2176389/nav/tap2/.

16. See "President Discusses War on Terror at National Endowment for Democracy," http://www.whitehouse.gov/news/releases/2005/10/20051006-3.html.

17. Ernst Nolte, *Die dritte radikale Widerstandsbewegung: Der Islamismus* (Berlin, 2009).

18. See Israel Gershoni's review essay in this volume; the recent issue "Arab Encounters with Fascist Propaganda, 1933-1945," *Geschichte und Gesellschaft* 37 (2011): 3; Götz Nordbruch, "Cultural Fusion of Thought and Ambitions? Memory, Politics, and the History of Arab-Nazi German Encounters," *Middle Eastern Studies* 47, no. 1 (2011): 183-194; and Peter Wien, "Coming to Terms with the Past: German Academia and Historical Relations between the Arab Lands and Nazi Germany," *International Journal of Middle Eastern Studies* 42, no. 2 (2010): 311-321. See also Gerhard Höpp, Peter Wien, and René Wildangel, eds., *Blind für die Geschichte? Arabische Begegnungen mit dem Nationalsozialismus* (Berlin, 2004); Israel Gershoni and James Jankowski, *Confronting Fascism in Egypt: Dictatorship versus Democracy in the 1930s* (Stanford, CA, 2010); Israel Gershoni and Götz Nordbruch, *Sympathie und Schrecken: Begegnungen mit Faschismus und Nationalsozialismus in Ägypten, 1922-1937* (Berlin, 2011); Götz Nordbruch, *Nazism in Syria and Lebanon: The Ambivalence of the German Option, 1933-1945* (New York, 2009); and the recent studies on Arab perception of the Holocaust: Gilbert Achcar, *The Arabs and the Holocaust: The Arab-Israeli War of Narratives* (New York, 2010); Meir Litvak and Ester Webman, *From Empathy to Denial: Arab Responses to the Holocaust* (New York, 2009).

19. See René Wildangel, *Zwischen Achse und Mandatsmacht: Palästina und der Nationalsozislismus* (Berlin, 2007).

20. The Arab population rose about 120 percent between 1922 and 1945 to approximately 1.2 million. See Joel S. Migdal, *Palestinian Society and Politics* (Princeton, NJ, 1980), 23.

21. Ami Ayalon, *Reading Palestine: Printing and Literacy, 1900-1948* (Austin, TX, 2004), 16 ff.

22. See Ayalon's excellent study on the subject, ibid.

23. For an extensive history of the Palestinian Arab press in this period, see Mustafa Kabha, *The Palestinian Press as Shaper of Public Opinion, 1929-1939* (London, 2007).

24. Ibid., 4-12.

25. Public Record Office (PRO) CO 323 346/10 Circulation of Palestinian newspapers.

26. See my publication on Palestine and National Socialism with an extensive discussion of pro-Nazi articles and the adaptation of German propaganda in the Arab press: Wildangel, *Zwischen Achse und Mandatsmacht*.

27. For example, see *Filastin*, September 2, 1933, 4.

28. *Al-Jami'a al-Islamiyyya*, March 8, 1933, 8.

29. See Wildangel, *Zwischen Achse und Mandatsmacht*, 129-139.

30. *Al-Difaʿ*, July 30, 1936, 3.

31. *Filastin*, June 14, 1934, 3.

32. *Al-Jamia al-Islamiyya*, February 27–April 30, 1935.

33. *Filastin*, April 21, 1933, 1.

34. *Filastin*, April 13, 1933, 3.

35. *Filastin*, April 21, 1933, 8.

36. 6 Adolf Hitler, *Mein Kampf* (Munich, 1939), 744. See Stefan Wild, "'Mein Kampf' in arabischer Übersetzung," *Die Welt des Islams* 9 (1964): 207–211.

37. *Filastin*, June 7, 1934. Quoted from Nezam al-Abbasi, *Die palästinensische Freiheitsbewegung im Spiegel ihrer Presse von 1929 bis 1945* (Freiburg, 1981), 172.

38. German Federal Archives (Bundesarchiv), B-R 58/954.

39. See, for example, the report on the Nabi Musa festival: "Near the Jaffa Gate, a café facing the tower of David displayed pictures of King Ghazi of Iraq, the son and political heir of Feysal, the impassioned 'upholder of the independence and unity of his co-religionists,' of Mussolini on the right, and of Hitler on the left." PRO CO 733−341/15, "Alleged Italian Activities in Palestine," May 28, 1937.

40. Matthias Küntzel, *Islamic Antisemitism and Its Nazi Roots* (2003), http://www.matthiaskuentzel.de/contents/islamic-antisemitism-and-its-nazi-roots.

41. PRO CO 733−341/15, "Alleged Italian Activities in Palestine," answer by High Commissioner Arthur Wauchope on August 23, 1937.

42. PRO WO 106−1594C, Palestine Historical; German Propaganda 1938–1939.

43. Ibid.

44. Klaus-Michael Mallmann and Martin Cüppers, *Halbmond und Hakenkreuz: Das Dritte Reich, die Araber und Palästina* (Darmstadt, 2006), 257.

45. Ibid.

46. George Antonius, *The Arab Awakening: The Story of the Arab National Movement* (London, 1938), 392.

47. For a detailed history of internal Palestinian politics, see Issa Khalaf, *Politics in Palestine: Arab Factionalism and Social Disintegration, 1939–1948* (New York, 1991); Manuel S. Hassassian, *Palestine: Factionalism in the National Movement, 1919–1939* (Jerusalem, 1990); and Yehoshua Porath, *The Palestinian Arab National Movement: From Riots to Rebellion, 1929–1939* (London, 1977).

48. CZA S 25/4131 report on the situation in Palestine (Hebrew), n.d., ca. 1939/1940.

49. Freya Stark, *The Arab Island: The Middle East, 1939–1943* (New York, 1945), 124.

50. PRO FO 371−24549 August 20, 1940, confidential telegram to B. Newton.

51. Reports between September 24, 1940, and October 15, 1942, by an author with the pseudonym "M. M.," in Hebrew: CZA S25/4135.

52. Ibid., report from March 27, 1941.

53. Ibid., report from May 8, 1941.

54. *Al-Ghad*, no. 5 (1939): 5.

55. Ibid.

56. *Filastin*, July 2, 1941, 1.

57. *Filastin*, July 15, 1941, 1.

58. *Filastin*, December 25, 1941, 1.

59. See Valerie Holman, "Kem's Cartoons in the Second World War," *History Today* 52, no. 3 (2002): 21–27.

60. *Al-Akhbar*, June 26, 1940, 2.

61. *Al-Akhbar*, May 24, 1940, 1.

62. *Al-Akhbar*, March 18, 1941, 4.

63. *Al-Akhbar*, January 27, 1942, 2.

64. *Al-Akhbar*, February 18, 1942, 1.

65. *Filastin*, December 23, 1941, 1.

66. *Filastin*, September 21, 1941, 4.

67. 'Ajaj Nuwayhid, *Mudhakkirat 'Ajaj Nuwayhid: Sittuna 'aman ma' al-qafila al-'arabiyya*, edited by Bayan Nuwayhid al-Hout (Beirut, 1993), 252–254.

68. PRO FO 371–23251, memorandum by the postmaster-general. There were 40,000 radio licenses in Palestine, of which 80 percent belonged to the Jewish community.

69. Stuart C. Dodd, *A Pioneer Radio Poll in Lebanon, Syria, and Palestine* (Palestine, 1943), 40.

70. Ibid., 4.

71. Herf, *Nazi Propaganda for the Arab World*, 9.

72. Dodd, *Pioneer Radio Poll*.

73. Ibid., 19.

74. Ibid., 26.

75. PRO FO 371–23251.

76. Stark, *Arab Island*, 107.

77. Al-Nuwayhid, *Mudhakkirat 'Ajaj Nuwayhid*.

78. Ibid., 257.

79. Ibid., 268.

80. For example, *Filastin*, May 22, 1941, 3; *al-Difa'*, July 1, 1941, 5.

81. *Al-Difa'*, July 1, 1941, 5.

82. Ibid.

83. *Al-Difa'*, September 20, 1940, and September 23, 1940, 1.

84. *Al-Difa'*, September 26, 1940, 1.

85. Valmar Cramer and Gustav Meinertz, eds., *Das Heilige Land in Vergangenheit und Gegenwart: Gesammelte Beiträge und Berichte zur Palästinaforschung* (Cologne, 1941), 3:326.

86. According to a Jewish Agency estimate in a Hebrew report evaluating the brochure (CZA, S 25/4131). An original copy of the brochure itself in Arabic can be found at the same file at the Central Zionist Archives in Jerusalem (CZA S25/4131).

87. CZA S 25/4131 letter from al-Jarkasi to the JA, September 9, 1940.

88. Ibid.

89. CZA S 25/4131, brochure 2.

90. Ibid.

91. Between 1940 and 1945, the number of Arabs who earned British education certificates increased from 228 to 1,261. A. L. Tibawi, *Arab Education in Mandatory Palestine: A Study of Three Decades of British Administration* (London 1956), 115.

92. PRO, CO 333/9 "Conduct of Arab Police," telegram from the Officer Ad-

ministering the Government of Palestine to the Secretary of State for the Colonies, November 4, 1937.

93. Morris Beckman, *The Jewish Brigade: An Army with Two Masters, 1944–1945* (Staplehurst, 1988), 24.

94. Ibid.

95. Ellen Fleischmann, *Nation and Its "New" Women: The Palestinian Women's Movement, 1920–1948* (Berkeley, CA, 2003), 192–193.

96. Haim Levenberg, *Military Preparations of the Arab Community in Palestine, 1945–1948* (London, 1993), 11.

97. P. J. Vatikiotis, *Politics and the Military in Jordan: A Study of the Arab Legion, 1921–1957* (New York, 1967).

98. Lockman, *Comrades and Enemies*, 267.

99. Migdal, *Palestinian Society and Politics*, 24.

100. Levenberg, *Military Preparations of the Arab Community*, 11.

101. CZA, S25/9334 "Nida ittihad hashumir hasair wal-usba al-ishtirakiyya fi filastin," May 1, 1943, 1.

102. Ibid., 2.

103. Dina Porat, *The Blue and Yellow Stars of David: The Zionist Leadership in Palestine and the Holocaust, 1939–1945* (Cambridge, MA, 1990).

104. Ibid., 23 ff.

105. Leila Kadi, *Arab Summit Conferences and the Palestine Problem, 1936–1950, 1964–1966* (Beirut, 1966).

106. CZA S25/3457 "An English Supplement of Al Ghad," issued by the Arab Students League at Bethlehem, Palestine, 5.

107. CZA, S25/3457, 6.

108. Yehoshua Porath, "*Usbat al-taharrur al-watani* (The National Liberation League), 1943–1948," *Asian and African Studies, Annual of the Israel Oriental Society* 4 (1968): 7.

109. CZA, S25/9334 "Nida' ila Sha'b al-'arabi al-karim," June 22, 1942, 2.

110. CZA, S25/9334 "Bayan ila al-sha'b al-'arabi al-karim," December 1942, 1.

111. CZA, S25/9351 "Usba al-taharrur al-watani," February 1, 1944, 1.

112. CZA, S25/9334 "Al-Ijtima' al-sha'bi al-kabir."

113. CZA, S25/9334 "Ila al-sha'b al-'arabi al-karim," October 10, 1942, 1.

114. Albert Habib Hourani (1915–1993), Middle East historian, Oxford, grew up in Great Britain and worked for the Palestinian government and the Arab Office. Ahmad Shuqayri (1908–1980) was the first chairman of the PLO (1964–1967).

115. Amikam Nachmani, "A Rare Testimony: Albert Hourani and the Anglo-American Committee, 1946," in *Middle Eastern Politics and Ideas: A History from Within*, edited by Moshe Maoz and Ilan Pappé (London, 1997), 113.

116. PRO, KV 2/401 and KV 2/402. For a more detailed account, see Wildangel, *Zwischen Achse und Mandatsmacht*, 350–357.

Chapter Five

1. On their involvement and particularly the personal experience of one of them (Najati Sidqi) in the propaganda mechanism of Spanish government forces, see

Hanna Abu Hanna, ed., *Muzakkarat Najati Sidqi: Muassat al-Dirasat al-Filastiniyya* (Beirut, 2001), 122–148.

2. *Filastin*: a Jaffa-based newspaper, established in 1911 by cousins 'Issa Dawoud al-'Issa and Yusuf Hanna al-'Issa. Initially appeared as a weekly and in 1929 began appearing as a daily until April 1948, when its publication was interrupted by the Palestinian Nakba. For more information, see Mustafa Kabha, *The Palestinian Press as Shaper of Public Opinion: Writing Up a Storm* (London, 2007), 4–73.

3. *Al-Difa'*: jointly established as a daily in Jaffa in 1934 by Palestinian journalist Ibrahim al-Shanti and Syrian journalists Khayr al-Din al-Zarkali and Sami al-Saraj. Later al-Shanti received full ownership of the newspaper. The paper had a national Arab orientation and continued appearing until April 1948. For more information, see Kabha, *Palestinian Press as Shaper of Public Opinion*, 3–73.

4. On this revolt, its character, validation, and location within Palestinian collective memory, see Mustafa Kabha, *Hapelestinim, 'Am Bifzurato* (Tel Aviv, 2010), 21–39 (in Hebrew).

5. *Al-Jabha al-Sha'biyya*, August 21, 1936.

6. *Al-Jabha al-Sha'biyya*, September 25, 1936.

7. Memorandum sent to Prime Minister Attlee on October 10, 1945. Cited in Maher al-Sharif, "Al-Shuyu'iyun al-'Arab wa al-nidal did al-fashiyya wa al-naziyya," http://www.palpeople.org.

8. *Filastin*, July 25, 1936.

9. Ibid.

10. Ibid.

11. *Filastin*, November 7, 1936.

12. *Filastin*, February 13, 1937.

13. Ibid.

14. *Filastin*, June 25, 1938.

15. Ibid.

16. *Filastin*, August 9, 1936.

17. *Filastin*, September 15, 1936.

18. *Al-difa'*.

19. Ibid.

20. *Al-difa'*, October 22, 1936.

21. Ibid.

22. Ibid.

23. *Al-difa'*, January 20, 1937.

24. *Al-difa'*, October 22, 1936.

25. *Al-difa'*, September 11, 1936.

26. *Al-difa'*, November 8, 1936.

27. *Al-difa'*, July 5, 1937.

28. For more information, see, for example, Latifa al-'Arsoni, "Al-Magharibah yanbishuna Qubur dahayahum fi al-Harb al-Ahaliyya al-Ispaniyya wa Markaz Maghribi yuqaddiru 'adadahum bi rub' Milyun," August 25, 2010, http://www.maghress.com.

29. Memoirs of Najati Sidqi, 127.

30. Ibid.

31. For more information, see the website of Nadi al-Fikr al-'Arabi, http:// www.nadyelfikr.com.

32. 'Abdallah Hanna, *Al-Haraka al-Munahida Lil Fashiyya fi Surya wa Lubnan* (Beirut, 1975).

33. Abdellatif Bensalem, "Los Voluntarios Arabes en las Brigadas internationals (Espana, 1936–1939)," *Revista International de Sociologia* 36 (1988).

34. For example, see *Filastin*, October 9, 1936.

35. Ibid.

36. *Filastin*, November 7, 1936.

37. *Filastin*, February 7, 1937.

38. *Filastin*, February 10, 1939.

39. *Filastin*, February 12, 1939.

40. Ibid.

41. *Filastin*, February 13, 1939.

42. *Al-difa'*, March 13, 1939.

43. *Al-difa'*, March 15, 1937.

44. *Al-Jami'a al-Islamiyya*, June 27, 1939.

45. *Al-Jami'a al-Islamiyya*, July 3, 1939.

46. *Al-difa'*, October 7, 1939.

47. *Filastin*, September 27, 1940.

48. "The Spanish War Fields Engulf the Best of Spain's Commanders and Youth," *Filastin*, February 9, 1939.

Chapter Six

AUTHOR'S NOTE: I thank Israel Gershoni, Peter Wien, Eve M. Troutt Powell, and Keith David Watenpaugh.

1. Khalid Kishtainy, *Tales from Old Baghdad: Grandmother and I* (London and New York, 1997), 14.

2. Ibid., 16.

3. Ibid., 16–17.

4. For a critique of these narratives, see the conclusions in Israel Gershoni and James Jankowski, *Confronting Fascism in Egypt: Dictatorship versus Democracy in the 1930s* (Stanford, CA, 2009). See also Peter Wien, "Coming to Terms with the Past: German Academia and Historical Relations between the Arab Lands and Nazi Germany," *International Journal of Middle Eastern Studies* 42, no. 2 (2010): 311–321; Götz Nordbruch, "'Cultural Fusion' of Thought and Ambitions? Memory, Politics and the History of Arab–Nazi German Encounters," *Middle Eastern Studies* 47, no. 1 (2011): 183–194; Joel Beinin, "Book Review"; Jeffrey Herf, *Nazi Propaganda for the Arab World*; and Meir Litvak and Esther Webman, "From Empathy to Denial: Arab Responses to the Holocaust," *International Journal of Middle East Studies* 42 (2010): 689–692.

5. For popular representations of these narratives, see Norman Podhoretz, *World War IV: The Long Struggle Against Islamofascism* (New York, 2007); Stephen

Schwartz, "What Is 'Islamofascism'?" August 16, 2006, http://www.ideasinaction tv.com/tcs_daily/2006/08/what-is-islamofascism.html; and Christopher Hitchens, "Defending *Islamofascism*: It's a Valid Term. Here's Why," October 22, 2007, http://www.slate.com/id/2176389/. On protests against Islamofascism in American universities organized by David Horowitz, see http://www.terrorismawareness .org/islamo-fascism-awareness-week/. See also http://www.youtube.com/watch ?v=gi6DY2E2w-Q and http://www.youtube.com/watch?v=4bh6-3v3hss&feature =related.

6. Fadhil al-Barrak, *Al-Madaris al-Yahudiyya wa'l Iraniyya fi'l 'Iraq: Dirasa muqarana* (Baghdad, 1985).

7. Kanan Makiya, *Republic of Fear: The Politics of Modern Iraq* (Berkeley, CA, 1989).

8. See, for example, Hazem Saghieh, "The Life and Death of De-Baathification," *Revue des mondes musulmans et de la Méditerranée* (July 2007): 117–118, http:// remmm.revues.org/index3451.html.

9. Peter Wien, *Iraqi Arab Nationalism: Authoritarian, Totalitarian, and Profascist Inclinations, 1932–1941* (London, 2006); Eric Davis, *Memories of the State: Politics, History, and Collective Identity in Modern Iraq* (Berkeley, CA, 2005); Sami Zubaida, "The Fragments Imagine the Nation: The Case of Iraq," *International Journal of Middle East Studies* 32, no. 2 (2002): 205–215.

10. Orit Bashkin, *New Babylonians: A History of Jews in Modern Iraq* (Stanford, CA, 2012), 106–107; Stefan Wild, "National Socialism in the Arab Near East between 1933 and 1939," *Die Welt des Islams* 1, no. 4 (1985): 126–173; Reeva Simon, *Iraq between Two World Wars: the Creation and Implementation of a Nationalist Ideology* (New York, 1986); Mohammad A. Tarbush, *The Role of the Military in Politics: A Case Study of Iraq to 1941* (Boston, 1982).

11. Foreign Office (FO) 371/23303, April 15, 1939, Mr. Houstoun-Boswall (Baghdad) to Baxter (Foreign Office, London); FO 371/23203, July 11, 1939, Sir Basil Newton (Baghdad) to Halifax (Foreign Office, London); FO 371/23203, July 18, 1939, Captain H. M. Merry, Air Ministry to Foreign Office; FO 371/37063, February 15, 1941, To: Embassy from C. J. Edmonds.

12. Bashkin, *New Babylonians*, 112; Tarbush, *Role of the Military in Politics*; Simon, *Iraq between the Two World Wars*, 135–155; Walid M. S. Hamdi, *Rashid Ali al-Gailani and the Nationalist Movement in Iraq, 1939–1941: A Political and Military Study of the British Campaign in Iraq and the National Revolution of May 1941* (London, 1987).

13. Bashkin, *New Babylonians*, 112–121; Hayyim J. Cohen, "The Anti Jewish Farhud in Baghdad, 1941," *Middle Eastern Studies* 3, no. 1 (1966): 2–17; Elie Kedourie, "The Sack of Basra and the Farhud in Baghdad," in *Arabic Political Memoirs and Other Studies* (London, 1974), 283–314.

14. This approach colors Makiya's book. See also Simon and Sylvia Haim, introduction in *Arab Nationalism: An Anthology* (Berkeley: University of California Press, 1976), edited by Sylvia G. Haim.

15. Reeva S. Simon, "The Teaching of History in Iraq before the Rashid 'Ali Coup of 1941," *Middle Eastern Studies* 22, no. 1 (1986): 43.

16. FO 371/24562/, no. 310, Personality File, August 1, 1940 [entry 82, 24]; Simon, *Iraq between Two World Wars*, 80.

17. Sylvia J. Haim, "Arabic Antisemitic Literature: Some Preliminary Notes,"

Jewish Social Studies 17, no. 4 (1955): 311. For a different view, see Wien, *Iraqi Arab Nationalism*, 101–102.

18. Sami Shawkat, *Hadhihi Ahdafuna* (Baghdad, 1939), 64.

19. Ibid., 75.

20. Ibid., 22.

21. Ibid., 100–101.

22. Ibid., 10, 61.

23. Ibid., 91.

24. Ibid., 35.

25. Ibid., 6.

26. Ibid., 39, 12.

27. Ibid., 15–16.

28. Ibid., 44.

29. Ibid., 3.

30. Ibid., 78.

31. Mark Mazower, *The Dark Continent: Europe's Twentieth Century* (New York, 1999), 71.

32. Yitzhak Nakash, *Shi'is of Iraq* (Princeton, NJ, 1994), 120–125; Frederic M. Wehrey, "The Insurgent State: Politics and Communal Dissent in Iraq, 1919–1936" (master's thesis, Princeton University, 2002); Nelida Fuccaro, "Ethnicity, State Formation, and Conscription in Postcolonial Iraq: The Case of the Yazidi Kurds of Jabal Sinjar in Creating National Identities," *Middle Eastern Studies* 29, no. 4 (1997): 559–580.

33. S25/3522 February 28, 1937, a report on a visit to Iraq by Zionist emissary Eliyahu Epstein, cited in Bashkin, *New Babylonians*, 105.

34. FO 406/77, April 8, 11, 1939, W. E. Houstoun-Boswall, British Embassy (Baghdad), to Lord Halifax, Foreign Secretary (London); FO 406/77, April 14, 1939, Lord Halifax to W. E. Houstoun-Boswall (Baghdad); Emile Marmorstein, "Fritz Grobba," *Middle Eastern Studies* 23, no. 3 (1987): 378; FO 371/23203, May 25, 1939, Sir Basil Newton (Baghdad) to Sir Oliphant (London). Newton reported that it was Nuri al-Sa'id who prevented the club from being opened; FO 371/23203, June 17, 1939, I. P. Domorle, Air Liaison officer, Baghdad, to Air Staff Intelligence, Habbaniyya.

35. FO 371/23203, June 17, 1939, I. P. Domorle, Air Liaison officer (Baghdad) to Air Staff Intelligence (Habbaniyya); FO 624/11/216, December 19, 1938, D. T. Brickell (consul in Basra) to Ambassador Maurice Petersen; FO 371/23203, July 18, 1939, Captain H. M. Merry, Air Ministry, to Foreign Office.

36. FO 371/20801, April 19, 1937, telegram from Sir Clark-Kerr, British Embassy (Baghdad) to Foreign Office (London); FO 371/20801, March 27, 1937, extract from local press.

37. Wien, *Iraqi-Arab Nationalism*.

38. *Habazbuz*, no. 248 (March 30, 1937): 2.

39. Ibid., 3.

40. *Habazbuz*, no. 207 (April 21, 1936): 7.

41. *Habazbuz*, no. 259 (June 29, 1937): 2–3.

42. *Habazbuz*, no. 247 (March 22, 1937): 2.

43. *Habazbuz*, no. 261 (July 13, 1937): 4.

44. On Turkish culture in Iraq, see Orit Bashkin, *The Other Iraq, Pluralism, and Culture in Hashemite Iraq* (Stanford, CA, 2009), 177–182.

45. *Habazbuz*, no. 266 (August 7, 1937): 2.

46. Ibid., 6.

47. *Habazbuz*, no. 269 (September 29, 1937): 6.

48. *Habazbuz*, no. 258 (June 22, 1937): 6.

49. *Habazbuz*, no. 248 (March 30, 1937): 5. In this article, one of the speakers in a dialogue says the descendants of Harun al-Rashid cannot take over al-Rashid's street, presently dominated by Jewish businessmen.

50. See his article on Karkhi's poetry in *Ha-Ilan ve-Ha-'anaf, Ha-safrut ha-'aravit ha-hadasha ve-yetziratam shel yehudi 'iraq* (Jerusalem, 1997), 191–215.

51. *Habazbuz*, no. 236 (December 19, 1936): 5.

52. *Al-Istiqlal*, October 8, 1936, quoted in *Sha'ul Sasun Khaduri, Ra'i wa-ri'aya, sirat hayat al-hakham Sasun Khaduri* (Jerusalem, 1999), 389.

53. Nissim Kazzaz, *He-Yehudim be-Iraq ba-ma'a he-'esrim* (Jerusalem, 1991), 68, 228–229.

54. See Husri's critique of Shawkat: Simon, *Iraq between Two World Wars*, 112–114. See also FO 371/23217, July 7–11, 1939, from Basil Newton to FO.

55. Hasan al-'Alawi, *Al-Ta'thirat al-Turkiyya fi al-Mashru' al-Qawmi al-'Arabi fi al 'Iraq* (London, 1988), 112–130; Wien, *Iraqi-Arab Nationalism*, 58–61.

56. FO 371/20801, extract from local press, April 19, 1937.

57. *Al-'Ilm*, no. 8 (1910): 374.

58. Orit Bashkin, "The Iraqi Afghanis and 'Abduhs: Debate over Reform among Shiite and Sunni 'Ulama' in Interwar Iraq," in *Guardians of Faith in Modern Times: 'Ulama' in the Middle East*, edited by Meir Hatina (Leiden, 2009), 141–170; Bashkin, *Other Iraq*, 59–60.

59. Rom Landau, *Search for Tomorrow* (London, 1938), 226–227.

60. David Sagiv, *Yahadut be-mifgash ha-nahariyim, Kehilat yehudey basra* (Jerusalem, 2004), 92–110; Jonah Cohen, *Hilla 'Al gedot ha-perat* (Carmiel, 2004), 121–122; Avraham Twena, *Golim u-Ge'ulim, Helek sesh: Me'ora'ot hagg ha-shavu'ot, juni 1941* (Ramla, 1979), 6:87–89; Shemu'el Moreh and Zvi Yehudah, eds., *Sin'at yehudim u-fera'ot be-'iraq* (Or Yehudah, 1992), 310–311.

61. Bashkin, *New Babylonians*, 125–130; Twena, *Golim u-Ge'ulim, Helek sesh*, 6:84.

62. Bashkin, *New Babylonians*, 106–109; Anwar Sha'ul, *Qissat hayati fi wadi al-Rafidayn* (Jerusalem, 1980), 216–219, 251–256; Bashkin, *Other Iraq*, 59.

63. Mir Basri, *Rihlat al-'umar: Min difaf dijla ila wadi al-tims* (Jerusalem, 1991), 74.

64. FO 371/20010, June 4, 1936. Sir A. Clark Kerr (Baghdad) to Eden, Foreign Office, London.

65. Fu'ad Husayn al-Wakil, *Jama'at al-Ahali fi'l 'Iraq, 1932–1937* (Baghdad, 1980), 265, 234; Bashkin, *Other Iraq*, 61–73.

66. *Al-Ahali*, no. 168 (May 15, 1933): 1. The original article is Sidney B. Fay, "Germany's Anti-Jewish Campaign," *Current History* (May 1933): 142–145.

67. *Al-Ahali*, no. 168 (May 15, 1933): 1.

68. *Al-Ahali*, no. 231 (July 27, 1933): 1.

69. *Al-Ahali*, no. 291 (November 25, 1933): 1; *al-Ahali*, no. 133 (June 8, 1932): 1.

70. Muzaffar 'Abd Allah al-Amin, *Jama'at al-Ahali: Munshu'ha, 'aqidatuha, wa-dawruha fi'l siyasa al-'iraqiyya, 1932–1946* (Beirut and Amman, 2001), 66–68, 172–177; Wakil, *Jama'at al-Ahali fi'l 'Iraq*, 172–189.

71. 'Abd al-Rahman al-Bazzaz, *Muhadarat 'an al-'iraq min al-ihtilal hatta al-istiqlal* (Cairo, 1954); 'Abd al-Razzaq al-Hasani, *Al-'Iraq fi zill al-mu'ahadat* (Sayda, 1947) and *Ta'rikh al-'iraq al-siyasai al-hadith* (Sayda, 1957); Nissim Rejwan, *The Last Jew in Baghdad: Remembering a Lost Homeland*, 147 (Austin, TX, 2004).

72. He based some of his arguments on the writings of Alexander Brady (1901–1963), especially *The Spirit and Structure of German Fascism*, to which Harold Laski wrote an introduction (1937). An American economist who wrote about technology, organization, business, and capitalism, Brady analyzed German decline from the heights of civilization to its debased conditions, by emphasizing how German militarism and expansionism were connected to the country's lack of resources and its problematic shift from a feudal to industrial society.

73. 'Abd al-Fattah Ibrahim, *Muqaddima fi'l ijtima'* (Baghdad, 1939), 45–59.

74. Ibid., 191–195.

75. Ibid., 197.

76. Ibid., 223. See also Bashkin, *Other Iraq*, 132–133.

77. The Central Committee of the Iraqi Communist Party, September 24, 1940, cited in Aziz Sibahi, *'Uqud min ta'rikh al-hizb al-shuyu'i al-'Iraqi* (Damascus, 2002), 197; letter written to Kaylani, May 7, 1941, quoted in Hanna Batatu, *The Old Social Classes and the Revolutionary Movements of Iraq* (Princeton, NJ, 1978), 442–445.

78. *Sawt al-Sha'b*, no. 1188 (June 22, 1940).

79. Batatu, *Old Social Classes*, 442–445.

80. On Jews in the ICP, see Yosef Me'ir, *Be'ikar ba-mahteret, yehudim u-politika be-'iraq* (Tel Aviv, 1993).

81. Bashkin, *Other Iraq*, 73–79.

82. Dhu Nun Ayyub, "Fi sabil majd al-'arab," in *al-Athar al-kamila li-athar Dhi al-Nun Ayyub*, 1:39–50 (Baghdad, 1978).

83. Ibid., 2:187.

84. Dhu Nun Ayyub, "Mu'amarat al-aghbiya'," in *al-Athar*, 1:9–50.

85. Ayyub, "Al-Nabi," in *al-Athar*, 1:321–333.

86. On Ayyub, see also Bashkin, *Other Iraq*, 80–84, 234; Orit Bashkin, "'Out of Place': Home and Empire in the Works of Mahmud Ahmad al-Sayyid and Dhu Nun Ayyub," *Comparative Studies of South Asia, Africa, and the Middle East* 28, no. 3 (2008): 428–442; Orit Bashkin, "When Mu'awiya Entered the Curriculum: Some Comments on the Iraqi Education System in the Interwar Period," *Comparative Education Review* 50, no. 3 (2006).

87. S25/10372, June 25, 1941, Eliyahu Epstein to Moshe Shertok.

88. Testimony given on August 2, 1941, reprinted in Moreh and Yehudah, *Sin'at yehudim u-fera'ot be-'iraq*, 233.

89. S6/4575, April 1942, report by Matilda Musseiri.

90. Sylvia G. Haim, "Aspects of Jewish Life in Baghdad under the Monarchy," *Middle Eastern Studies* 12, no. 2 (1976): 188–208, 194. Other testimonies, however, critique Sa'ib for his lack of care of the Jewish patients.

91. On the activities of the tribal leader Sheikh Bash-'Ayan that helped the Jews

of Basra, see S107/901, July 2, 1941, letter from the president of the Jewish community in Basra to the Jewish Agency.

92. FO 371/27079, July 25, 1941, Sir K. Cornwallis (Baghdad) to Foreign Office (Eden).

93. Bashkin, *New Babylonians*, 120–125.

94. Israel Gershoni, "Beyond Anti-Semitism: Egyptian Responses to German Nazism and Italian Fascism in the 1930s," EIU Working Papers, Mediterranean Programme Series, RSS 32, 2001; Orit Bashkin, "The Nile Valley at the Banks of the Euphrates and Tigris: Egyptian Intellectuals in Iraq during the Interwar Period," in *Narrating the Nile: Politics, Cultures, Identities*, edited by Israel Gershoni and Meir Hatina (Boulder, CO, 2008); Bashkin, *Other Iraq*, 59.

95. Ernest C. Dawn, "The Formation of Pan-Arab Ideology in the Inter-war Years," *International Journal of Middle East Studies* 20, no. 1 (1988): 67–91.

96. For the text of the investigation committee report, see 'Abd al-Razzak al-Hasani, *Al-Asrar al-khaffiyya fi harakat 1941 al-tahririyya* (Sayda, 1964), 246–256.

97. FO 371/23203, June 17, 1939, I. P. Domorle, Air Liaison officer (Baghdad) to Air Staff Intelligence (Habbaniyya).

98. On the *dukhala* debate, and Zu'aytar's role in it, see Bashkin, *Other Iraq*, 190–193.

99. Akram Zu'aytar, *Bawakir al-Nidal, min mudhakkirat Akram Zu'aytar, 1909–1935* (Beirut, 1994), diary entry: February 1, 1934, 616.

100. Ibid., February 4, 1934, 617–618.

101. Ibid., February 5, 1934, 619.

102. Ibid., January 26, 1935, 695–696.

103. Ibid., February 3, 1935, 702–705; February 5, 1935, 705–707.

104. On the importance of the Palestinian question in Iraq, see Michael Eppel, *The Palestine Conflict in the History of Modern Iraq: the Dynamics of Involvement, 1928–1948* (London, 1994).

105. Zu'aytar, *Bawakir al-Nidal*, January 27, 1935, 697.

106. Ibid.

107. Mustafa Kabha, *The Palestinian Press as Shaper of Public Opinion, 1929–39: Writing Up a Storm* (London and Portland, 2007); Weldon C. Matthews, *Confronting an Empire, Constructing a Nation: Arab Nationalists and Popular Politics in Mandate Palestine* (London and New York, 2006); Ellen L. Fleischmann, *The Nation and Its "New" Women: The Palestinian Women's Movement, 1920–1948* (Berkeley, CA, 2003); Zachary Lockman, *Comrades and Enemies: Arab and Jewish Workers in Palestine, 1906–1948* (Berkeley, CA, 1996).

108. Rena Barakat, "Thawrat al-Buraq in British mandate Palestine: Jerusalem, Mass Mobilization, and Colonial Politics, 1928–1930" (PhD thesis, University of Chicago, 2007).

Chapter Seven

1. Bateman to Halifax, June 12, 1941, Great Britain, Public Record Office, Foreign Office (FO) 371/27431, J1831/18/16.

2. Lampson to Eden, September 23, 1941, FO 407/225, 133.

3. Details concerning British demands for Egypt to enter the war as a formal belligerent and the probable reasons for the refusal of the Mahir ministry to do so are contained in FO 371/23368 and FO 371/23369. See also the discussion in 'Abd al-'Azim Muhammad Ramadan, *Tatawwur al-Haraka al-Wataniyya fi Misr, 1937–1948* (Beirut, 1973), 2:6–21.

4. Lampson to Halifax, November 8, 1939, FO 371/15871/43, J4594/1/16, as reprinted in *British Documents on Foreign Affairs: Reports and Papers from the Foreign Office Confidential Print (BDFA)*, edited by Kenneth Bourne, D. Cameron Watt, and Michael Partridge, pt. 2, Series G, *Africa, 1914–1939: Egypt and the Sudan*, edited by Peter Woodward, 19 vols. (Lanham, MD, 1994–1995), 19:256. Same view in Lampson to Halifax, October 2, 1939, FO 371/15871/33, J4046 (*BDFA*, 1914–1939, 19:248).

5. Lampson to Halifax, September 15, 1939, FO 371/23369, J3838/3369/16.

6. Lampson to Halifax, November 8, 1939, FO 371/15981/48, J4740/1/16 (*BDFA*, 1914–1939, 19:253).

7. Lampson to Halifax, November 8, 1939, FO 371/15871/43, J4594/1/16 (*BDFA*, 1914–1939, 19:253–258). Similar evaluation in Lampson to Halifax, January 20, 1940, FO 407/224, 21–22.

8. Lampson to Halifax, January 5, 1940, FO 407/224, 4–6.

9. Lampson to Halifax, March 8, 1940, FO 407/224, 39–41.

10. Lampson to Halifax, April 9, 1940, FO 407/224, 51. See also Lampson to Halifax, May 4, 1940, FO 407/224, 69–71.

11. Lampson to Halifax, May 3, 1940, FO 407/224, 51, 62–68.

12. "The Anglo-Egyptian Treaty," n.d., FO 403/468, 16814, J1407/16/1943, as reprinted in *BDFA*, edited by Paul Preston and Michael Partridge, pt. 3, Series G, *Africa, from 1940 through 1945*, edited by Peter Woodward, 5 vols. (Lanham, MD, 1998), 3:290–293. For an early discussion of the presumed impact of Axis propaganda during the period of the phony war, see Marcel Colombe, *L'évolution de l'Égypte, 1924–1950* (Paris, 1951), 82–83.

13. See FO 407/224, 26, 34, 52–53. See also Ramadan, *Tatawwur al-Haraka al-Wataniyya fi Misr*, 2:160–165; George Kirk, *The Middle East in the War*, vol. 2 of *Survey of International Affairs, 1939–1946* (London, 1952), 35–36.

14. Lampson to Halifax, February 7, 1940, FO 407/224, 24–29.

15. Lampson to Halifax, April 20, 1040, FO 407/224, 59–61.

16. Lampson to Halifax, May 3, 1940, FO 407/224, 62–68.

17. Lampson to Halifax, May 4, 1940, FO 407/224, 68–71. Similar comments in Lampson's retrospective report on the year 1940 in Lampson to Halifax, January 28, 1941, FO 407/225, 9–14.

18. Evidence not available to the British in 1940 confirms that 'Ali Mahir's policy as prime minister was directed at keeping Egypt out of the war. Prior to the Italian declaration of war, Italian archival materials indicate that Mahir assured the Italian minister in Egypt that Egypt would not declare war in case of Italian entry into the conflict. See Lukasz Hirszowicz, *The Third Reich and the Arab East* (London, 1966), 75. After the war, Mahir stated (in a court case) that "in 1940 he had firmly believed that Germany was going to win the war and therefore had worked to prevent Egypt from becoming involved." Lord Killearn to Bevin, July 30, 1945, FO 403/468, 17102, J2680/3/16, 12 (*BDFA*, 1940–1945, 5:186).

19. Lampson to Halifax, June 13, 1940, FO 407/224, 83–84. See also Lampson to Halifax, June 14, 1940, FO 407/224, 84–85.

20. For accounts of the crisis of June 1940, see Colombe, *L'évolution de l'Égypte*, 85–88; Kirk, *Middle East in the War*, 38–40; and Ramadan, *Tatawwur al-Haraka al-Wataniyya fi Misr*, 2:55–97. A recent study is 'Asam Diya' al-Din, *Hadith 17 Yunyu 1940 fi Ta'rikh Misr al-Mu'asir* (Cairo, 1991).

21. For Mahir's statement in parliament, see Lampson to Halifax, June 12, 1940, FO 407/224, 82–83.

22. FO 407/224, 101–102, 106–110, 113.

23. Lord Killearn, *The Killearn Diaries, 1939–1946*, edited by Trefor E. Evans (London, 1972), 136–137.

24. Lampson to Halifax, November 15, 1941, FO 407/224, 146. The degree to which Prime Minister Sirri was willing to follow British advice and instructions appears in a conversation of April 1941: when Lampson suggested a course of action intended to restrict the influence of 'Ali Mahir, Sirri is reported to have said, "Dictate to me roughly what you would like me to do." Lampson promptly did so. Cairo to Foreign Office, April 8, 1941, FO 371, J897/18/16.

25. See FO 407/224, 109–113. See also Kirk, *Middle East in the War*, 193–194.

26. Lampson to Halifax, August 23, 1940, FO 407/224, 116–117.

27. Lampson to Halifax, September 20, 1940, FO 407/224, 121.

28. The Sa'dist campaign was rejected by the Egyptian Parliament, which in August reaffirmed the stance of formal nonbelligerence taken by the 'Ali Mahir ministry in June; as a result, Ahmad Mahir and his fellow Sa'dist ministers resigned from the government in September 1940. For details, see FO 407/224, 116–124; and Ramadan, *Tatawwur al-Haraka al-Wataniyya fi Misr*, 2:100–124.

29. Lampson to Halifax, October 19, 1940, FO 407/224, 140.

30. Lampson to Halifax, October 8, 1940, FO 407/224, 153–157. Similar views expressed in Lampson to Eden, January 28, 1941, FO 407/225, 9–14.

31. Lampson to Halifax, November 2, 1940, FO 407/224, 143.

32. Lampson to Halifax, June 14, 1940, FO 407/224, 84–85.

33. Lampson to Halifax, October 8, 1940, FO 407/224, 155.

34. Lampson to Halifax, October 12, 1940, FO 407/224, 135, 137. See also A. W. Sansom, *I Spied Spies*, 22–31; and Martin Kolinsky, *Britain's War in the Middle East: Strategy and Diplomacy, 1936–1942* (New York, 1999), 130–131.

35. Lampson to Halifax, January 28, 1941, FO 407/225, 13.

36. For Anwar al-Sadat's accounts of a possible army revolt, see his *Revolt on the Nile* (New York, 1957), 23–26, and *Anwar el-Sadat: In Search of Identity, an Autobiography* (New York, 1977), 26–27 (the two accounts date a projected revolt variously in late 1940 or the summer of 1941). See also Sansom, *I Spied Spies*, 61–76; Ramadan, *Tatawwur al-Haraka al-Wataniyya fi Misr*, 2:134–146; Charles Tripp, "Ali Mahir and the Politics of the Egyptian Army, 1936–1942," in *Contemporary Egypt through Egyptian Eyes*, edited by Charles Tripp (New York, 1993), 45–71, esp. 59–60.

37. Lampson to Halifax, December 14, 1940, FO 407/224, 164.

38. Lampson to Halifax, January 28, 1941, FO 407/225, 9–14.

39. Lampson to Halifax, January 28, 1941, FO 407/225, 14–17.

40. Lampson to Eden, January 28, 1941, FO 407/225, 14; similar view in Killearn, *Diaries*, 141.

41. Hare to Secretary of State, June 24, 1940; United States Government Printing Office, *Foreign Relations of the United States* (*FRUS*), 1940 (Washington, DC, 1958), 3:471.

42. Fish to Secretary of State, August 23, 1940, *FRUS*, 1940, 3:474.

43. Fish to Secretary of State, September 20, 1940, *FRUS*, 1940, 3:479.

44. Cairo to Foreign Office, April 7, 1941, FO 371/27429, J899/18/16.

45. Cairo to Foreign Office, April 12, 1941, FO 371/27429, J965/18/16.

46. Lampson to Eden, April 29, 1941, FO 407/225, 29–34.

47. Cairo to Foreign Office, June 7, 1941, FO 371/27431, J1808/18/16.

48. Cairo to Foreign Office, June 15, 1941, FO 371/27431, J1886/18/16.

49. Cairo to Foreign Office, March 16, 1941, FO 371/27429, J614/18/16.

50. Cairo to Foreign Office, April 26, 1941, FO 371/27431, J1115/1816.

51. Cairo to Foreign Office, May 26, 1941, FO 371/27431, J1655/18/16.

52. Lampson to Eden, April 29, 1941, FO 407/225, 29–34.

53. Cairo to Foreign Office, May 26, 1941, FO 371/27431, J1646/18/16.

54. See FO 371/27431, J1737/18/16; and FO 371/27431, J1846/18/16.

55. Lampson to Eden, April 29, 1941, FO 407/225, 29–34. For government action against the society in 1941, see Ramadan, *Tatawwur al-Haraka al-Wataniyya fi Misr*, 2:126–130; Richard P. Mitchell, *The Society of the Muslim Brothers* (Oxford and New York, 1993), 22–23; Brynjar Lia, *The Society of the Muslim Brothers in Egypt* (Reading, 1998), 261–268.

56. Cairo to Foreign Office, April 9, 1941, FO 371/27429, J898/18/16.

57. Misri's attempted flight (maladroitly encouraged by a British intelligence officer who hoped his presence in Iraq might moderate Iraqi opposition to Great Britain) is discussed in numerous works; among others, see Wajih 'Atiq, *Al-Malik Faruq wa Almaniya al-Naziyya: Khams Sanawat min al-'Alaqa al-Sirriyya* (Cairo, 1992), 56–66; Ramadan, *Tatawwur al-Haraka al-Wataniyya fi Misr*, 2:148–153; Killearn, *Diaries*, 171, 185–186; and Sansom, *I Spied Spies*, 70–75.

58. Lampson to Eden, June 17, 1941, FO 371/27431, J2157/18/16. See also FO 371/27431, J1646/18/16, J2418/18/16. See also Ramadan, *Tatawwur al-Haraka al-Wataniyya fi Misr*, 2:131–133.

59. Cairo to Foreign Office, June 15, 1941, FO 371/27431, J2136/18/16. See also Kirk, *Middle East in the War*, 199–200.

60. For a discussion of the attempt of Misri, in league with civilian politicians such as Muhammad Salih Harb and with the possible knowledge of King Faruq, to organize such an uprising in the spring of 1941, see 'Atiq, *al-Malik Faruq*, 49–61. Misri and Harb reportedly sought German financial support for a projected uprising, but the Germans were skeptical of the effort and declined assistance (55–56). See also James Jankowski, *Egypt's Young Rebels: "Young Egypt," 1933–1952* (Stanford, CA, 1975), 82–85; Abd Al-Fattah Muhammad El-Awaisi, *The Muslim Brothers and the Palestine Question, 1928–1947* (London, 1998), 111.

61. Kirk to Secretary of State, May 29, 1941, *FRUS*, 1941 (Washington, DC, 1959), 3:274–275.

62. Cairo to Foreign Office, June 15, 1941, FO 371/27431, J1886/18/16.

63. Cairo to Foreign Office, June 30, 1941, FO 371/27431, J2065/18/16.

64. Cairo to Foreign Office, July 7, 1941, FO 371/27431, J2108/18/16.

65. Lampson to Eden, September 23, 1941, FO 407/225, 133.

66. Reports in FO 371/27431, J2362/18/16, J2483/18/16, J2577/18/16, and J2586/18/16.

67. Lampson to Eden, September 23, 1941, FO 407/225, 133; Lampson to Eden, February 12, 1942, FO 403/466, 8 (*BDFA*, 1940–1945, 2:12).

68. Kirk to Secretary of State, September 18, 1941, *FRUS*, 1941, 3:293–294.

69. Kirk to Secretary of State, September 17, 1941, *FRUS*, 1941, 3:291. See also Kirk, *Middle East in the War*, 200–201.

70. Lampson to Eden, February 12, 1942, FO 403/466, 16237, 6–10 (*BDFA*, 1940–1945, 2:9–14).

71. Lampson to Eden, September 23, 1941, FO 407/225, 131–134.

72. See FO 407/225, 128–129, 132.

73. Lampson to Eden, September 23, 1941, FO 407/225, 131–134.

74. Lampson to Eden, February 12, 1942, FO 403/466, 16237, 6–10 (*BDFA*, 1940–1945, 2:9–14). The economic bottlenecks that developed in 1941 are analyzed in Kirk, *Middle East in the War*, 201–206; and Ramadan, *Tatawwur al-Haraka al-Wataniyya fi Misr*, 2:168–171.

75. For differing analyses of the incident of February 4, 1942, see Gabriel Warburg, "Lampson's Ultimatum to Faruq, 4 February, 1942," *Middle Eastern Studies* 11 (1975): 24–32; Charles D. Smith, "4 February 1942: Its Causes and Its Influence on the Future of Anglo-Egyptian Relations, 1937–1945," *International Journal of Middle East Studies* 10 (1979): 453–479; and Gabriel Warburg, "The 'Three-Legged Stool': Lampson, Faruq, and Nahhas, 1936–1944," in his *Egypt and the Sudan: Studies in History and Politics* (London, 1985), 116–157.

76. Lampson to Eden, March 12, 1942, FO 403/466, 16260, 1–6 (*BDFA*, 1940–1945, 2:53–58).

77. Lampson to Eden, July 4, 1942, FO 403/466, 16296, 16 (*BDFA*, 1940–1945, 2:134).

78. Lampson to Eden, March 12, 1942, FO 403/466, 16260, 1–6 (*BDFA*, 1940–1945, 2:53–58). See also Killearn, *Diaries*, 197, 209; and Ramadan, *Tatawwur al-Haraka al-Wataniyya fi Misr*, 2:172–191.

79. Lampson to Eden, March 12, 1942, FO 403/466, 16296, 1–6 (*BDFA*, 1940–1945, 2:53–58). See also Kirk, *Middle East in the War*, 212; Colombe, *L'évolution de l'Égypte, 1924–1950*, 104; and Janice J. Terry, *The Wafd, 1919–1952* (London, 1982), 253.

80. Speech of April 21, 1942, as translated in Lampson to Eden, April 22, 1942, FO 403/466, 16260, 8 (*BDFA*, 1940–1945, 2:60).

81. See Lampson to Eden, April 2, 1942, FO 403/466, 16260, 14–15 (*BDFA*, 1940–1945, 2:66–67).

82. Lampson to Eden, July 19, 1942, FO 403/466, 16296, 17 (*BDFA*, 1940–1945, 2:135).

83. Lampson to Eden, July 4, 1942, FO 403/466, 16296, 16 (*BDFA*, 1940–1945, 2:134).

84. Lampson to Eden, September 28, 1942, FO 403/466, 16372, 22–27 (*BDFA*, 1940–1945, 2:188–193). Additional information in Killearn, *Diaries*, 226–227.

85. Lampson to Eden, September 28, 1942, FO 403/466, 16372, 22–27 (*BDFA*, 1940–1945, 2:188–193). On March 13, 1942, *al-Ahram* published a statement by Hasan al-Banna pledging his movement's support to the new Wafdist ministry and announcing that he would not be a candidate in the elections. (I thank Professor Israel Gershoni for this reference.) The rapprochement was a fragile one: in early 1943 the Ministry of Interior ordered the closure of all of the society's branches other than its Cairo headquarters. Lampson to Eden, February 8, 1943, FO 403/466, 16372, 91 (*BDFA*, 1940–1945, 2:351). The rupture was not total; in mid-1943, the government was reportedly still "patronizing and subsidizing this society, which professes to be prepared to co-operate with both the Wafd and the British." Lord Killearn to Eden, June 16, 1943, FO 403/467, 16446, 63–68 (*BDFA*, 1940–1945, 3:73–78). On the relationship between the Wafdist ministry and the Muslim Brothers in 1942–1944, see also James Heyworth-Dunn, *Religious and Political Trends in Modern Egypt* (Washington, DC, 1950), 38–41; Mitchell, *Society of the Muslim Brothers*, 27; Lia, *Society of the Muslim Brothers in Egypt*, 223, 268–269.

86. Lampson to Eden, July 26, 1942, FO 403/466, 16296, 17–18 (*BDFA*, 1940–1945, 2:136–137).

87. Lampson to Eden, September 28, 1942, FO 403/466, 16362, 22–27 (*BDFA*, 1940–1945, 2:188–193). The same points are reiterated in the ambassador's overall review of the year 1942. See Lord Killearn to Eden, December 22, 1943, FO 403/468, 16609, 4–9 (*BDFA*, 1940–1945, 4:12–17).

88. Lampson to Eden, September 28, 1942, FO 403/466, 16372, 22–27 (*BDFA*, 1940–1945, 2:188–193). The Germans appear to have missed the shift in the Wafd's attitude toward Great Britain by 1942. Apparently relying on the Wafd's previous nationalist and hence anti-British stance, through much of 1942 the German Foreign Office is reported to have believed that it would be able to reach an understanding with the Wafd in case of a German occupation of Egypt and hence refrained from anti-Wafdist propaganda. See 'Atiq, *al-Malik Faruq*, 168; and Hirszowicz, *Third Reich and the Arab East*, 282–283. The Wafd may also have been hedging its bets in 1942. For information concerning the Wafd's (limited) efforts to contact the Germans in 1942 in order to mitigate the effects of a successful Axis invasion of the Nile Valley, see Ramadan, *Tatawwur al-Haraka al-Wataniyya fi Misr*, 2:241–243; and Kolinsky, *Britain's War in the Middle East*, 181.

89. Lampson to Eden, September 30, 1942, FO 403/466, 16296, 14–15 (*BDFA*, 1940–1945, 2:133–134).

90. Lord Killearn to Eden, December 22, 1943, FO 403/468, 16609, 4–9 (*BDFA*, 1940–1945, 4:12–17).

91. For firsthand accounts of the episode from different perspectives, see Sadat, *Revolt on the Nile*, 51–63; Sadat, *In Search of Identity*, 33–40; Sansom, *I Spied Spies*, 108–132; and John W. Eppler, *Rommel Ruft Kairo: Aus dem Tagebuch eines Spions* (Gütersloh, 1959).

92. One pilot was mistakenly shot down by the Germans; the other reached Rommel's lines, from which he was taken to Berlin and advised the Germans on their propaganda efforts. See Wajih 'Atiq, *Al-Jaysh al-Misri wa Al-Alman fi Ithna' al-Harb al-'Alamiyya al-Thaniyya* (Cairo, 1993), 70–161.

93. Lampson to Eden, August 10, 1952, FO 403/466, 16296, 6–7 (*BDFA*, 1940–1945, 2:124–125).

94. Lampson to Eden, October 11, 1942, FO 403/466, 16372, 9–10 (*BDFA*, 1940–1945, 2:175–176).

95. Lampson to Eden, October 21, 1942, FO 403/466, 16372, 13–14 (*BDFA*, 1942–1943, 2:179–180). The officers in question were eventually dismissed from active service. Lampson to Eden, October 30, 1942, FO 403/466, 16372, 28–29 (*BDFA*, 1940–1945, 2:194–195). Wafdist measures to counter military discontent are discussed in Tripp, "Politics of the Egyptian Army," 65–66; Warburg, "'Three-Legged Stool,'" 138–139.

96. Lampson to Eden, July 12, 1942, FO 403/466, 16296, 16 (*BDFA*, 1940–1945, 2:134).

97. Lampson to Eden, September 13, 1942, FO 403/466, 16296, 21 (*BDFA*, 1940–1945, 2:139).

98. Lampson to Eden, November 9, 1942, FO 403/466, 16372, 29 (*BDFA*, 1940–1945, 2:195).

99. Lampson to Eden, February 1, 1943, FO 403/467, 16400, 10 (*BDFA*, 1940–1945, 2:270).

100. Lampson to Eden, January 31, 1943, FO 403/467, 16400, 98–102 (*BDFA*, 1940–1945, 2:358–362).

101. Lord Killearn to Eden, December 22, 1943, FO 403/468, 16609, 4–9 (*BDFA*, 1940–1945, 2:12–17).

102. Lampson to Eden, March 12, 1942, FO 403/466, 16260, 1–6 (*BDFA*, 1940–1945, 2:53–58). See also Kirk, *Middle East in the War*, 211–212.

103. Lampson to Eden, January 31, 1943, FO 403/467, 16400, 98–102 (*BDFA*, 1940–1945, 2:358–362). The Egyptian cost-of-living index increased from 131 in 1939 to 195 in 1941 and 276 by December 1942. See Joel Beinin and Zachary Lockman, *Workers on the Nile: Nationalism, Communism, Islam, and the Egyptian Working Class, 1882–1954* (Princeton, NJ, 1987), 237.

104. Lord Killearn to Eden, November 29, 1943, FO 403/467, 16574, 21–25 (*BDFA*, 1940–1945, 3:317–321).

105. Lord Killearn to Eden, February 25, 1944, FO 403/468, 16609, 28–35 (*BDFA*, 1940–1945, 4:36–42).

106. Lampson to Eden, May 15, 1943, FO 403/467, 16446, 46 (*BDFA*, 1940–1945, 3:56).

107. Lord Killearn to Eden, July 15, 1943, FO 371/35536, J3175/2/16.

108. For examples, see Shone to Eden, November 3, 1944, FO 371/41319, J4031/14/16; Weekly Political and Economic Report, November 30–December 6, 1944, FO 371/41319, 218/49/44.

109. Lampson to Eden, February 1, 1943, FO 403/467, 16400, 10 (*BDFA*, 1940–1945, 2:270).

110. Lampson to Eden, January 31, 1943, FO 403/467, 16400, 98–102 (*BDFA*, 1940–1945, 2:358–362). Similar views expressed in Lord Killearn to Eden, February 25, 1944, FO 403/468, 16609, 28–34 (*BDFA*, 1940–1945, 4:36–42).

111. For example, see Lord Killearn to Eden, August 24, 1943, FO 403/467, 16526, 20 (*BDFA*, 1940–1945, 3:194); Shone to Eden, September 13, 1943, FO 403/467, 16526, 43–44 (*BDFA*, 1940–1945, 3:217–218); Lord Killearn to Eden, February 25, 1944, FO 403/468, 16609, 28–34 (*BDFA*, 1940–1945, 4:36–40); and

Lord Killearn to Eden, June 26, 1944, FO 403/468, 16814, 1–2 (*BDFA*, 1940–1945, 4:279–280).

112. Lord Killearn to Eden, June 27, 1944, FO 403/468, 16748, 2–7 (*BDFA*, 1940–1945, 4:280–285).

113. Shone to Eden, September 13, 1943, FO 403/467, 16526, 43–44 (*BDFA*, 1940–1945, 3:217–219).

114. Shone to Eden, September 13, 1943, FO 403/467, 16526, 43–44 (*BDFA*, 1940–1945, 3:217–219).

115. As cited in Shone to Eden, November 16, 1943, FO 403/467, 16574, 10–11 (*BDFA*, 1940–1945, 3:306–307).

116. As cited in Lord Killearn to Eden, November 21, 1943, FO 403/467, 16574, 11–12 (*BDFA*, 1940–1945, 3:307–308).

117. As quoted in Lord Killearn to Eden, August 29, 1944, FO 403/468, 16814, 11–12 (*BDFA*, 1940–1945, 4:290–291).

Chapter Eight

AUTHOR'S NOTE: This chapter sprouted out of my research work *A History of Egyptian Communism: Jews and Their Compatriots in Quest of Revolution* (Boulder, CO, 2011) and my current research project entitled *Representing the Unity of the Nile Valley: Politics and Public Discourse in Egypt, 1943–1953*. I would like to express my deep appreciation to the Israel Science Foundation for their generous research grants, which helped in pursuing these studies.

1. See, for instance, James Jankowski, "The Egyptian Blue Shirts and the Egyptian Wafd, 1935–1938," *Middle Eastern Studies* 6 (1970): 77–95, and Jankowski, *Egypt's Young Rebels: "Young Egypt," 1933–1952* (Stanford, CA, 1975). On the new *effendiyya*, see Israel Gershoni, *Light in the Shade: Egypt and Fascism, 1922–1937* (Tel Aviv, 1999), 84–106, 130–143, 180–189. (In Hebrew.)

2. Manfred Halpern, *The Politics of Social Change in the Middle East and North Africa* (Princeton, NJ, 1963), 159–160; Roel Meijer, *The Quest for Modernity* (London, 2002), 96–97.

3. Joel Beinin and Zachary Lockman, *Workers on the Nile: Nationalism, Communism, Islam, and the Egyptian Working Class, 1882–1954* (Princeton, NJ, 1987), 313–314. See also Rif'at al-Sa'id, *Ta'rikh al-Munazzamat al-Yasariyya al-Misriyya, 1940–1950* (Cairo, 1976), 104–119.

4. See, for instance, P. J. Vatikiotis, *The History of Modern Egypt* (Jerusalem, 1983), 311–325 (in Hebrew); Selma Botman, *The Rise of Egyptian Communism, 1939–1970* (Syracuse, NY, 1988), 20; Donald M. Reid, *Cairo University and the Making of Modern Egypt* (Cambridge, 1990), 128; Elie Kedourie, *Politics in the Middle East* (Oxford, 1992), 186–7; Beinin and Lockman, *Workers on the Nile*, 313; and Rif'at al-Sa'id, *Al-Yasar al-Misri, 1925–1940* (Beirut, 1972), 49–53.

5. DMNL (Hadetu) was founded in mid-1947 as an attempt to unify the main communist groups. On the DMNL, see, in detail, Rami Ginat, "Ephemeral Unity," chap. 10 in *A History of Egyptian Communism: Jews and Their Compatriots in Quest of Revolution* (Boulder, CO, in press).

6. Al-Sa'id, *Al-Yasar al-Misri*, 50.

7. Ibid., 51–53. See also al-Sa'id, *Ta'rikh al-Munazzamat*, 105.

8. Ginat, *History of Egyptian Communism*.

9. Rif'at al-Sa'id, "Al-Haraka al-Shuyu'iyya al-Misriyya 'Abr Sab'in 'Aman," *Qadaya Fikriyya*, July 1992, 21–37. See also Sa'ida Muhamad Husni, *Al-Yahud fi Misr Min 1882–1947* (Cairo, 1993), 156.

10. Al-Sa'id, *Ta'rikh al-Munazzamat*, 105–106.

11. Ibid., 116. Quote is taken from R. P. Mitchell, *The Society of the Muslim Brothers* (Oxford and New York, 1993), 232. See also Hasan al-Banna, "Islamuna — Risalat al-Mu'tamar al-Khamis," *Sawt al-Haqq* 5 (1977): 36; and Olivier Carré, "From Banna to Qutb and 'Qutbism': The Radicalization of Fundamentalist Thought under Three Regimes," in *Egypt: From Monarchy to Republic*, edited by S. Shamir (Boulder, CO, 1995), 181–185.

12. Al-Sa'id, *Ta'rikh al-Munazzamat*.

13. Ibid., 88–89.

14. Ibid., 23–24. See also Tariq al-Bishri, "Qira'ah Misriyya fi Awraq Henry Curiel," *al-Hilal*, April 1988, 19.

15. Al-Sa'id, *Ta'rikh al-Munazzamat*, 92–96.

16. See next section.

17. See, for instance, *Jaridat Misr al-Fatat*, October 6, 1938.

18. Ahmad Sadiq Sa'd, *Safahat min al-Yasar al-Misri fi A'qab al-Harb al-'Alamiyya al-Thaniyya* (Cairo, 1976), 39–43.

19. Muhammad Abu al-Ghar, *Yahud Misr min al-Izdihar ila al-Shatat* (Cairo, 2004), 63, 94; Joel Beinin, *The Dispersion of Egyptian Jewry* (Cairo, 2005), 34; Botman, *Rise of Egyptian Communism*, 6; al-Sa'id, *Ta'rikh al-Munazzamat*, 104. For a detailed account on Zionist press in Egypt, see, for instance, Hagar Hillel, *"Israel" in Cairo: A Zionist Newspaper in Nationalist Egypt, 1920–1939* (Tel Aviv, 2004).

20. Botman, *Rise of Egyptian Communism*, 6. See also interviews with Edward Levi, Eli Mizan, and Paul Jacot Descombes in al-Sa'id, *Al-Yasar al-Misri*, 238–239, 241, 247–250.

21. Al-Sa'id, *Ta'rikh al-Munazzamat*, 120–121.

22. Yusuf Abu Sayf, *Watha'iq wa-Mawaqif Min Ta'rikh al-Yasar al-Misri, 1941–1957* (Cairo, 2000), 44–45; al-Sa'id, *Al-Yasar al-Misri*, 243.

23. Ginat, *History of Egyptian Communism*, 209–210; Irmgard Schrand, *Jews in Egypt: Communists and Citizens* (Hamburg and London, 2004), 95.

24. Ginat, *History of Egyptian Communism*.

25. Ibid.

26. Marsil Shirizi (Israel), *Awraq Munadil Itali fi Misr* (Cairo, 2002), 18, 142.

27. "Mudhakkirat Yusuf Darwish" (1991), 1–9 (unpublished memoirs courtesy of Mr. Ovadya Yerushalmi). See also Ginat, *History of Egyptian Communism*, 213–214.

28. Henri Curiel, *Pages autobiographiques: Une contribution à l'histoire de la naissance du Parti Communiste Egyptien de 1940 à 1950* (Paris, 1977), 6–10, File 402, in Egyptian Communists in Exile (Rome Group) Archives, International Institute of Social History, Amsterdam; interview with Curiel, in al-Sa'id, *Ta'rikh al-Munazzamatt*, 283. See also Curiel, *Pages autobiographiques*, 23. Didar Fawzi-

Rossano emphasized the anti-Fascist and anti-Nazi character of this organization that attracted many young Jews, foreigners, educated Egyptians, and a few Muslims from large families. Didar Fawzi-Rossano, *Rasa'il ila' Haba'ibi—Misr* (Cairo, 2006), 45–47; Shirizi, *Awraq Munadil*, 77–48, 142–143.

29. Ra'uf 'Abbas, *Awraq Henri Curiel wa-al-Haraka al-Shuyu'iyya al-Misriyya* (Cairo, 1988), 21.

30. Curiel, *Pages autobiographiques*, 9–11, 53; interview with Curiel, in al-Sai'd, *Al-Yasar al-Misri*, 283.

31. George Pointée was an activist within IAS. Pointée, of Swiss origin, was a high school teacher of French. While in Egypt, he continued to be a member of the Swiss Communist Party and tried to persuade Descombes to use his connections in order to establish contacts with the Comintern. He joined the Free French Army following the French defeat, shortly after the outbreak of World War II. Pointée was killed in the battlefield in August 1944.

32. Gilles Perrault, *A Man Apart: The Life of Henry Curiel* (London, 1987), 67–68; Curiel, *Pages autobiographiques*, 9–10.

33. Curiel, *Pages autobiographiques*, 26; al-Sa'id, *Ta'rikh al-Munazzamat*, 329. See also Abbas, *Awraq Henri Curiel*, 24–26.

34. Curiel, *Pages autobiographiques*, 27.

35. Ibid., 28.

36. Ibid., 37; al-Sa'id, *Ta'rikh al-Munazzamat*, 333.

37. Faiza Rad, "Youssef Darwish: The Courage to Go On," *al-Ahram Weekly*, no. 719 (December 2–8, 2004).

38. Interview with Arie Albert, Cairo, February 18, 2007; Azza Khattab, "The Converts," *Egypt Today* 27, no. 3 (2006).

39. Ibid.

40. Interview with Arie Albert; Khattab, "The Converts."

41. Quote from Ginat, *History of Egyptian Communism*, 272n34. See also Sharif Hatata, *Al-Nawafidhu al-Maftuha: Mudhakkirat Duktur Sharif Hatata* (Cairo, 2006), 11–12.

42. Sharif Hatata, "Henri Curiel," in *Al-Haraka al-Shuyu'iyya wa-Haykal* (Cairo, 2006), 41–62.

43. Al-Bishri, a retired senior judge, a writer and philosopher, was born in 1933. In 1953 he graduated from the faculty of law at the Cairo University. Throughout, he published extensively on issues related to state and society, democracy, Islam, Nasirism, communism, and many others. In his youth he was active in leftist circles, and later in his life he shifted to liberal Islam and was also the legal adviser to Kifaya (founded in 2004), an anti-Mubarak opposition movement. In February 2011, several days after Mubarak was toppled, al-Bishri was appointed by the Supreme Council of the Armed Forces to head the committee designated to re-evaluate and propose modifications to the Egyptian constitution.

44. Al-Bishri, "Qira'a Misriyya," 18–19.

45. Ibid., 19–21.

46. Ibid., 21–23.

47. Ibid., 23–24.

48. Muhammad Sid Ahmad, *Mustaqbal al-Nizam al-hizbi fi Misr* (Cairo, 1984).

49. Ibid.

50. Sa'd Zahran, *Fi Usul al-Siyasa al-Misriyyah: Naqal Tahlili Naqdi fi al-Ta'rikh al-Siyasi* (Cairo, 1985), 138–139.

51. Ibid.

52. Muhammad Sid Ahmad, "Al-Yahud fi al-Haraka al-Shuyu'iyya al-Misriyya wa al-Sira' al-'Arabi al-Isra'ili," *al-Hilal*, June 1988, 21.

53. Ibid., 22–23.

54. Ibid., 23–24.

55. Interview with Muhammad Sid Ahmad, May 17, 1997, "Episode 17: Good Guys, Bad Guys," http://www.gwu.edu/~nsarchiv/coldwar/interviews/episode-17/ahmed1.html.

56. Sid Ahmad, "Al-Yahud fi al-Haraka," 23–24; Sid Ahmad, *Mustaqbal al-Nizam*, 114–145.

57. The famous Curiel bookstore in central Cairo served as a tool to advance Marxism rather than a profitable business. In fact, the bookstore served also as a library for those who could not afford to buy the reading material.

58. Muhammad Yusuf al-Jindi, "21 Fibrayir: Dawr Bariz lil-Shuyu'iyyun al-Misriyyin fi al-Haraka al-Wataniyya al-Misriyya," *Qadaya Fikriyya*, July 1992, 240–241; Muhammad Yusuf al-Jindi, "Al-Tayyarat al-Asasiyya fi al-Haraka al-Shuyu'iyya al-Misriyya," *Qadaya Fikriyya*, July 1992, 50–51; interview with Muhammad Yusuf al-Jindi, *Dar al-Thaqafa al-Jadida*, Cairo, February 22, 2007. See also Muhammad Yusuf al-Jindi, *Masirat Hayati* (Cairo, 2006), 36; and al-Jindi's introduction to Marcel Israel's memoirs in Shirizi, *Awraq Munadil*, 7–8.

59. Fawzi-Rossano, *Rasa'il ila' Haba'ibi*, 21–36, quote on 36.

60. Ibid., 46–47.

61. Ibid., 42.

62. Mustafa Tiba, "Matlub Taqwim Mawdu'i lil-Ta'rikh al-Hadith," *al-Hilal*, November 1988, 52–53.

63. Abu Sayf, *Watha'iq*, 16.

64. *Al-Mu'tamar*: a mouthpiece of the cultural committee of the young Wafdists in *awlila*, 1947, File 90, Collection of *Tali'at al-'Ummal* (*Al-Fajr al-Jadid*), International Institute of Social History, Amsterdam (hereafter cited as T/U).

65. An internal document of *Tali'at al-'Ummal*, December 14, 1947, File 89, T/U. See also a reference to the Muslim Brothers as a Fascist organization, in "Ayuha al-Shuyu'iyyun Itahhidu," August 15, 1947, File 7, T/U. Muhammad Amin (pseudonym of Raymond Duwayk), "Al-Dimuqratiyya al-Misriyya Baina Ansarha wa-A'da'iha," *al-Fajr al-Jadid*, July 16, 1945.

66. Amin, "Al-Dimuqratiyya al-Misriyya."

67. An inside document of *Tali'at al-'Ummal*, August 1951, File 53, T/U.

68. Ibid. See also Ahmad Sadiq Sa'd, "Wahadha Sawt Misr al-Fatat," *al-Fajr al-Jadid*, no. 9 (September 1945).

69. Fu'ad Mursi, *Tatawwur al-Ra'smaliyya wa-Kifah al-Tabaqat fi Misr* (Cairo, 1992), 32–33, 38, 42–43, 256–258.

70. Abu Sayf, *Watha'iq*, 265–266.

71. A pamphlet by Tali'at al-'Ummal, July 14, 1952, File 30, T/U; Ra'uf 'Abbas, "Al-Hukuma al-'Askariyya wa-al-Kifah al-Musallah Didd al-Isti'mar al-Muhtall,"

July 9, 1953, File 31, T/U. See also Mustafa Tiba, "Matlub Taqwim Mawdu'i lil-Ta'rikh al-Hadith," *al-Hilal*, November 1988, 57.

72. Ginat, "The New Communist Organizations," chap. 9 in *History of Egyptian Communism*.

Chapter Nine

AUTHOR'S NOTE: The research for this article was supported by the Israel Science Foundation (grant 623/10).

1. Charles D. Smith, "The 'Crisis of Orientation': The Shift of Egyptian Intellectuals to Islamic Subjects in the 1930's," *International Journal of Middle East Studies* 4 (October 1973): 382–410.

2. Nadav Safran, *Egypt in Search of Political Community* (Cambridge, MA, 1961), 165–180 and, more broadly, 181–244; P. J. Vatikiotis, *The Modern History of Egypt: From Muhammad Ali to Mubarak* (London, 1991), 323–324 and, more broadly, 315–339, 343–349.

3. Safran, *Egypt in Search of Political Community*, 191–193, 209–228; Vatikiotis, *Modern History of Egypt*, 315–316, 324–325, 339–354.

4. Charles D. Smith, *Islam and the Search for Social Order in Modern Egypt: A Biography of Muhammad Husayn Haykal* (Albany, NY, 1983), vii–ix, 89–157; Afaf Lutfi al-Sayyid-Marsot, *Egypt's Liberal Experiment, 1922–1936* (Berkeley, CA, 1977), 228–231.

5. Smith, *Islam and the Search for Social Order*, 145–180.

6. See, for example, al-Sayyid-Marsot, *Egypt's Liberal Experiment*, 229–230. See also Afaf Lutfi al-Sayyid-Marsot, *A Short History of Modern Egypt* (Cambridge, 1994), 99–100. For a critical treatment of these two narratives within a broader framework of the development intellectual history in Middle Eastern studies, see Israel Gershoni, "The Theory of Crisis and the Crisis in a Theory: Intellectual History in Twentieth-Century Middle Eastern Studies," in *Middle East Historiographies: Narrating the Twentieth Century*, edited by Israel Gershoni, Amy Singer, and Hakan Y. Erdem (Seattle, 2006), 131–182.

7. Joel Beinin and Zachary Lockman, *Workers on the Nile: Nationalism, Communism, Islam, and the Egyptian Working Class, 1882–1954* (Princeton, NJ, 1987), 286; see also 285–287. In a slightly different fashion, in his insightful work on Egyptian labor history, Ellis Goldberg stated that "during World War II, the Wafd came to power [through the famous incident of the February 4, 1942] because it was the only political force in Egypt willing to cooperate with the Allies in any way whatsoever." For Goldberg, it seems as though all the other national and social non-Wafdist forces demonstrated sympathy or support for the Axis. See Ellis Goldberg, *Tinker, Tailor, and Textile Worker: Class and Politics in Egypt, 1930–1952* (Berkeley, CA, 1986), 65. True, the syndrome of "the enemy of my enemy is my ally" was developed and reworked in early historiographies to explain the sympathy of Egyptian nationalists for Fascism and Nazism. See, for example, Anwar al-Sadat, *Revolt on the Nile* (London, 1957), 19–38; Anouar Abdel-Malek, *Egypt: Mili-*

tary Society (New York, 1968), 21–22; Gabriel Warburg, "Lampson's Ultimatum to Faruq, 4 February, 1942," *Middle Eastern Studies* 11 (1975): 26–28; and Bernard Lewis, "The Nazis and the Palestine Question," in his *Semites and Anti-Semites: An Inquiry into Conflict and Prejudice* (New York, 1986), 144–150, 157–160. This third narrative seems merely to contextualize the syndrome in its social context.

8. See, for example, Israel Gershoni and James Jankowski, *Confronting Fascism in Egypt: Dictatorship versus Democracy in the 1930s* (Stanford, CA, 2009).

9. For al-Zayyat's intellectual career, his ideas and activities, and his stewardship of *al-Risala*, see Muhammad Sayyid Muhammad, *Al-Zayyat wa-al-Risala* (Riyadh, 1982); Ni'mat Ahmad Fu'ad, *Qimam Adabiyya* (Cairo, 1966), 175–232; J. Brugman, *An Introduction to the History of Modern Arabic Literature in Egypt* (Leiden, 1984), 380–387; and Dennis Walker, "Egypt's Liberal Arabism: The Contribution of Ahmad Hasan al-Zayyat's Arabism," *Rocznik Orientalistyczny* 49 (1995): 61–97. See also Zayyat's self-narrative, Ahmad Hasan al-Zayyat, "al-Risala," *al-Risala* 1, no. 1 (1933): 1; and Ahmad Hasan al-Zayyat, *Wahy al-Risala* 4 (1958): 72–75.

10. See, in detail, Israel Gershoni, "Egyptian Liberalism in an Age of 'Crisis of Orientation': *Al-Risala*'s Reaction to Fascism and Nazism, 1933–39," *International Journal of Middle East Studies* 31, no. 4 (1999): 551–576; and Israel Gershoni, *Light in the Shade: Egypt and Fascism, 1922–1937* (Tel Aviv, 1999), 154–166, 299–329, 341–347 (in Hebrew).

11. Gershoni, *Light in the Shade*, 157–166, 300–311, 319–322; Israel Gershoni, "Egyptian Liberalism Reassessed: Muhammad 'Abdallah 'Inan's Response to German Nazism, 1933–1935," *Jama'a* 4 (1999): 31–68 (in Hebrew).

12. Gershoni, *Light in the Shade*, 155–161, 316–323.

13. Ahmad Hasan al-Zayyat, "Min Ahadith al-Shabab: Hawla al-Dimuqratiyya," *al-Risala*, April 26, 1937, 681–682.

14. Ibid., 682. See also Ahmad Hasan al-Zayyat, "Ila Ayna Yattajiha al-Shabab?," *al-Risala*, May 3, 1937, 746–747; and Ustadh Kabir [Misri], "Ila al-Shabab: Hawla al-Dimuqratiyya Aydan," *al-Risala*, May 3, 1937, 721–722.

15. Ahmad Hasan al-Zayyat, "Kalimah fi Awaniha," *al-Risala*, April 11, 1938, 601–602.

16. Ahmad Hasan al-Zayyat, "'Ala Dhikr Khutbat Hitlar fi Yawm al-Jum'a al-Madi: Hadha Rajul ! . . . ," *al-Risala*, May 1, 1939, 847–848.

17. Ibid., 848.

18. Ibid. See also Ahmad Hasan al-Zayyat, "Muhammad al-Za'im," *al-Risala*, March 4, 1940, 361–362.

19. Gershoni and Jankowski, *Confronting Fascism in Egypt*, 177–180, 187–188.

20. Ahmad Hasan al-Zayyat, "Bayna al-Dimuqratiyya wa-al-Diktaturiyya: Usbu' Mahmum . . . ," *al-Risala*, September 26, 1938, 1561–1562.

21. Ibid.

22. Ibid., 1562.

23. Ibid.

24. Ahmad Hasan al-Zayyat, "Maghazan Risalat al-Ra'is Ruzfalt: Uqtulu al-Ju' Taqtulu al-Harb," *al-Risala*, April 24, 1939, 799–800.

25. Ahmad Hasan al-Zayyat, "Jarirat al-Naziyya 'ala al-Insaniyya," *al-Risala*, October 9, 1939, 1927.

26. Ibid., 1927–1928.

27. Ibid., 1928.
28. Ibid.
29. Ibid.; Gershoni and Jankowski, *Confronting Fascism in Egypt*, 166–204.
30. Zayyat, "Jarirat al-Naziyya 'ala al-Insaniyya," 1928.
31. Ibid.
32. Ibid.
33. Ibid.
34. Ahmad Hasan al-Zayyat, "Al-Harb bayna al-Ams wa-al-Yawm," *al-Risala*, June 10, 1940, 961–962.
35. Ahmad Hasan al-Zayyat, "Al-Fikr wa-al-Hrab . . . ," *al-Risala*, May 27, 1940, 881–882.
36. Ahmad Hasan al-Zayyat, "Fransa Tanharu?!," *al-Risala*, June 24, 1940, 1037–1038.
37. Zayyat, "Jarirat al-Naziyya 'ala al-Insaniyya," 1928.
38. Ahmad Hasan al-Zayyat, "Siyasat al-Samak!," *al-Risala*, December 11, 1939, 2251–2252.
39. Ibid.
40. Ahmad Hasan al-Zayyat, "Ba'd Isdal al-Sitar 'ala Ma'sat Finlanda: Fashl al-'Aql . . . ," *al-Risala*, March 18, 1940, 481–482.
41. Zayyat, "Siyasat al-Samak," 2252.
42. Ibid.; Zayyat, "Fashl al-'Aql," 482; Zayyat, "Siyasat al-Samak!," 2252. For Zayyat's similar ideas and scenarios, see also his following articles: "Ummat al-Tawhid Tatahidu . . . ," *al-Risala*, November 11, 1940, 1673–1674; and "Injiltra hiya al-Mathal," *al-Risala*, November 25, 1940, 1729–1730.
43. For these intellectual attitudes, see Gershoni and Jankowski, *Confronting Fascism in Egypt*, 111–204. More specifically, for 'Aqqad's strong anti-Hitler views, see his important book *Hitlar fi al-Mizan* (Cairo, 1940). The book was published in early June 1940. For Taha Husayn's prodemocratic views, see, for example, "Al-Dimuqratiyya wa al-Ta'lim al-Awwali," *al-Hilal*, January 1939, 244–248; and Taha Husayn, *Mustaqbal al-Thaqafa fi Misr* (Cairo, 1938), 94–102. For Hakim's anti-Nazi position, see my "Confronting Nazism in Egypt: Tawfiq al-Hakim's Anti-Totalitarianism, 1938–1945," *Tel Aviver Jahrbuch für deutsche Geschichte* 26 (1997): 121–150. For Musa's anti-Nazism, see my "Liberal Democracy versus Fascist Totalitarianism in the Egyptian Intellectual Discourse: The Case of Salama Musa and *al-Majalla al-Jadida*," in *Nationalism and Liberal Thought in the Arab Middle East*, edited by Christoph Schumann (London, 2010), 145–172. For 'Inan's anti-Nazi stance, see my "Egyptian Liberalism Reassessed: Muhammad 'Abdallah 'Inan's Response to German Nazism, 1933–1935," *Jama'a* 4 (1999): 31–68 (in Hebrew). For a slightly different German version, see my "Eine Stimme der Vernuunft: Muhammad Abdallah Inan und die Zeitschrift Al-Risala," in *Konstellationen Über Geschichte, Erfahrung und Erkenntnis, Festschrift for Dan Diner*, edited by Herausgegeben von Nicolas Berg et al. (Leipzig, 2011), 105–124. For Muhammad Lutfi Jum'a's anti-Fascist stance, see Haggai Erlich's article in this collection.

Chapter Ten

1. See James Jankowski, "The View from the Embassy: British Assessments of Egyptian Attitudes during World War II," a paper presented at TAU's workshop "Arab Responses to Fascism and Nazism, 1933–1945: Reappraisals and New Directions," May 23–26, 2010.

2. See, for example, Alistair Horne, *A Savage War of Peace: Algeria, 1954–1962* (New York, 1987), 23–28; Jean-Louis Planche, "Violence et nationalisme en Algérie (1942–1945)," *Les Temps Modernes*, no. 590 (1996): 112–134; Edward J. Hughes, "'Le prélude d'une sorte de fin de l'histoire': Underpinning Assimilation in Camus's *Chroniques algériennes*," *L'Esprit Créateur* 47, no. 1 (2007): 7–18.

3. Celia Britton, foreword to *L'Esprit Créateur* 47, no. 1 (2007): 4.

4. Ferhat Abbas, *Guerre et révolution d'Algérie*, vol. 1, *La nuit coloniale* (Paris, 1962), 110–11, as quoted in Jeremy F. Lane, "Ferhat Abbas, Vichy's National Revolution, and the Memory of the *Royaume arabe*," *L'Esprit Créateur* 47, no. 1 (2007): 2.

5. *El-Islah*, May 8, 1947.

6. In my PhD dissertation, "The Representation of the Holocaust in the Egyptian Public Discourse, 1945–1962" (in Hebrew) (Tel Aviv University, 2006), and then in the book with Meir Litvak, *From Empathy to Denial: Arab Responses to the Holocaust* (New York, 2009), the period is extended to the establishment of Israel and the 1948 war, but these two events were the culmination of processes that developed earlier.

7. 'Abd al-Rahman al-Rafi'i, *Fi A'qab al-Thawra al-Misriyya: Thawrat 1919* (Cairo, 1989), pt. 3, 183; Tariq al-Bishri, *Al-Haraka al-Siyasiyya fi Misr, 1945–1952* (Cairo, 1972), 26.

8. For a broad discussion of Holocaust representation, see Litvak and Webman, *From Empathy to Denial*; 'Azmi Bishara, "The Arabs and the Holocaust: The Analysis of a Problematic Conjunctive Letter," *Zmanim*, no. 53 (1995): 54–71 (in Hebrew); and Gilbert Achcar, *The Arabs and the Holocaust: The Arab-Israeli War of Narratives* (New York, 2010).

9. For a comprehensive discussion of Egyptian intellectuals' attitudes toward Nazism and Fascism, see Israel Gershoni, *Light in the Shade: Egypt and Fascism, 1922–1937* (Tel Aviv, 1999; in Hebrew) and "'The Crime of Nazism against Humanity': Ahmad Hasan al-Zayyat and the Outbreak of World War II," a paper submitted to TAU's workshop "Arab Responses to Fascism and Nazism, 1933–1945: Reappraisals and New Directions," May 23–26, 2010.

10. King Faruq and members of his entourage held secret contacts with the Nazis. See, for example, Wajih 'Abd al-Sadiq 'Atiq, *Al-Malik Faruq wa Almaniya al-Naziyya: Khams Sanawat min al-'Alaqa al-Sirriyya* (Cairo, 1992).

11. Ahmad Baha' al-Din, *Isra'iliyyat* (Cairo, 1965), 95–96.

12. George Kirk, *The Middle East in the War: Survey of International Affairs, 1939–1946* (London, 1952), 2:265–67; Lord Killearn, Cairo, to Foreign Office, February 25, 1945, PRO, FO 371/45918S.

13. For the Egyptian postwar political and social atmosphere, see James P. Jankowski, *Nasser's Egypt, Arab Nationalism, and the United Arab Republic* (Boulder, CO, 2001), 11–41; 'Izza Wahbi, *Tajribat al-Dimuqratiyya al-Libiraliyya fi misr*

(Cairo, 1985); P. J. Vatikiotis, *The History of Modern Egypt: From Muhammad Ali to Mubarak* (London, 1991), 345–374; Jacques Berque, *Egypt: Imperialism and Revolution* (London, 1972), 559–673.

14. Haykal wrote that in the "popular press" he was also nicknamed "*faqih al-qariya*," for he issued edicts that suited the needs of the person who asked for his opinion. Muhammad Hasanayn Haykal, *Suqut Nizam: Limadha Kanat Thawrat Yuliyu Lazima?* (Cairo, 2003), 180.

15. Ibid., 20–21; Berque, *Egypt: Imperialism and Revolution*, 565.

16. Haykal, *Suqut Nizam*, 180.

17. *Le Journal d'Egypte*, February 6, 1945, PRO, FO 371/45918.

18. Tawfiq al-Hakim, "Himari Qala li wa-Mu'tamar al-Sulh," in *Himari Qala Li* (Cairo, 1945), 50–58. For a discussion of Hakim's views on Hitler and Mussolini, see Israel Gershoni, "Kol'im ve-Rozhim: Tawfiq al-Hakim Neged Musolini ve-Hitler, 1925–1945," *Zmanim* 87 (Summer 1999): 62–78 (in Hebrew).

19. *Al-Ahram*, March 2, 5, 9, 1945. For another editorial on Egypt as part of Europe, see *al-Ahram*, February 20, 1948. See also Muhammad Khalaf Muhammad, "Misr wal-Tarbiya al-'Alamiyya ba'da al-Harb," *al-Thaqafa*, March 30, 1945, 17–19; Taha Husayn, "Bayna al-'Adl wal-Hurriyya," *al-Katib al-Misri*, July 4, 1946, 189–204; and al-Bishri, *Al-Haraka al-Siyasiyya fi Misr*, 26.

20. *Al-Ahram*, May 10, 15, 1945. Faruq repeats his words at the opening of the Egyptian Parliament on November 12. See *al-Ahram*, November 13, 1945. See also *al-Ahram*, February 22, 28, March 4, 19, April 10, May 8, 10, 13, 15, September 4, 18, 1945.

21. *Al-Ahram*, May 13, 1945.

22. *Al-Ahram*, May 3, 1946.

23. Tawfiq Muhammad al-Shawi, "Ahdafuna al-Qawmiyya wal-Qadaya al-'Arabiyya," *al-Risala*, September 24, 1945, 1023–24.

24. *Al-Ahram*, May 8, 1945.

25. For an analysis of al-Zayyat's views, see Gershoni, "Crime of Nazism against Humanity."

26. Ahmad Hasan al-Zayyat, "Nihayat Dictaturayn," *al-Risala*, May 7, 1945, 463–464.

27. 'Abbas Mahmud al-'Aqqad, "Al-Tarbiya al-Siyasiyya," *al-Risala*, May 15, 1945, 491–493. See also 'Abbas Mahmud al-'Aqqad, "Khamas Wasaya lil-Jil al-Jadid," *al-Hilal*, June 1947, 98–101.

28. See by 'Abbas Mahmud al-'Aqqad: *Al-Naziyya wal-Adiyan al-Samawiyya* (1941; reprint, Cairo, 1976), *Al-Harb al-'Alamiyya al-Thaniya: Dirasa fi Ta'rikh al-'Alaqat al-Duwaliyya* (Beirut, 1970) and *Hitler fi al-Mizan* (Beirut, 1971).

29. On 'Inan's views of Nazism, see Gershoni, *Light in the Shade*, 157–166, 305–309; and Israel Gershoni, "Egyptian Liberalism on Trial: Muhammad 'Abdallah 'Inan's Reaction to the Rise of Nazism to Power in Germany, 1933–1935," *Jama'a*, no. 4 (1999): 31–68 (in Hebrew).

30. Muhammad 'Abdallah 'Inan: "Nihayat Almaniya al-Naziyya wal-Mu'dila al-Almaniyya al-Haqiqiyya," *al-Thaqafa*, May 1, 1945, 1–3; "Ba'da Taslim Almaniya," *al-Thaqafa*, May 15, 1945, 1–3; and "'Asr al-Dimuqratiyya," *al-Thaqafa*, September 4, 1945, 1–3. For praise for democracy and the new world order, see also

'Abd al-Qadir al-Maghribi, "Al-Tatawwur al-Ijtima'i ba'da al-Harb," *al-Risala*, April 4, 1945, 443–445; Shafir Jabri, "Adab al-Nasr," *al-Thaqafa*, May 29, 1945, 4–6; and Baha' al-Din Barakat, "Ahdafuna al-Jadida," *al-Hilal*, January 1947, 7–9.

31. "Khitam al-Ma'asa," *al-Thaqafa*, May 8, 1945, 1–2.

32. Sami 'Azir Jubran, "Ma'rakat al-Salam," *al-Thaqafa*, February 27, 1945, 1–2; Muhammad Farid Abu Hadid, "Al-Mu'allim! al-Mu'allim," *al-Thaqafa*, May 15, 1945, 7–9. For further discussion of German philosophies and Nazism, see Khalil al-Salim, "Al-'Ilm al-Almani, Usulihi wa-Maramihi," *al-Muqtataf*, January 1946, 9–16, 26; and Majid Bahjat, "Nazariyyat al-Ajnas al-Bashariyya wal-Kunt di Ghubinu," *al-Risala*, April 29, 1946, 466–469.

33. Muhammad 'Awad Muhammad, "Shu'un al-Harb wa-Shu'un al-Siyasa," *al-Thaqafa*, February 13, 1945, 1–4. For a comprehensive discussion of his views on Nazism, see Gershoni, *Light in the Shade*, 155–57; and Israel Gershoni and James Jankowski, *Confronting Fascism in Egypt: Dictatorship versus Democracy in the 1930s* (Stanford, CA, 2009), 184, 186–87.

34. Muhammad 'Awad Muhammad, "'Ala bab 'am Jadid," *al-Thaqafa*, January 2, 1945, 3–6.

35. "Quwwad al-Ta'rikh Yahkamuna Hitler," *al-Hilal*, September 1945, 497–500.

36. Al-'Aqqad, *Al-Harb al-'Alamiyya al-Thaniya*, 9, 243–249.

37. Tawfiq al-Hakim, "Himari wa-Hitler," in *Himari Qala Li*, by al-Hakim, 26–39.

38. See by 'Ali Adham: "Al-Ta'rikh wal-Di'aya," *al-Thaqafa*, January 7, 1947, 8–11; "Al-Umam wal-Siyasa wal-Adab," *al-Thaqafa*, July 8, 1947, 11–14; and "Al-Ustura wal-Siyasa," *al-Thaqafa*, June 13, 1949, 6–9, 11. 'Ali Adham is another Egyptian intellectual whose views are discussed in Gershoni and Jankowski, *Confronting Fascism in Egypt*, 117–120, 123–125, 159–161, 201–202.

39. Muhammad Fu'ad Shukri, *Almaniya al-Naziyya: Dirasa fi al-Ta'rikh al-Urubi al-Mu'asir, 1939–1945* (Cairo, 1948), 9, 64.

40. See by Sami al-Jaridini: "Al-Harb ba'da Khamas Sanawat," *al-Hilal*, July–August 1944, 444–48; "Ma'rakat al-Salam," *al-Hilal*, September–October 1944, 587–89; and "Al-Wahsh al-Nazi," *al-Hilal*, July 1945, 343–47. Jaridini continued to praise internationalism (*'alamiyya*) and hoped that it would replace all kinds of nationalism. See his "Al-Tahawwul ila al-Nizam al-'Alami," *al-Hilal*, January 1946, 7–10.

41. Ahmad Amin, "Al-'Alam al-Jadid," *al-Thaqafa*, June 19, 1945, 1–3.

42. Amir Buqtor, "Hitler wa-Musolini fi Zimmat al-Ta'rikh," *al-Hilal*, July 1945, 327–332.

43. Gershoni, *Light in the Shade*, 120, 128–129, 147, 165, 205–207, 225–226, 238, 264–265.

44. Ibid., 215–216.

45. *Al-Ahram*, January 3, March 9, April 22, 1945. See also "Madha Yadda'un bi-Almaniya ba'da al-Harb," *al-Hilal*, August 1944, 462–466; and 'Abdallah 'Inan, "Jara'im al-Harb wa-Masir al-Mas'ulin 'Anha," *al-Thaqafa*, February 20, 1945, 221–212. The term *madhbaha* (massacre) appears numerous other times as well.

46. *Al-Ahram*, January 5, July 24, December 14, 1945.

47. *Al-Ahram*, March 15, 29, September 19, 1945.

48. *Al-Ahram*, March 15, April 8, May 8, 1945.

49. *Al-Ahram*, January 3, 12, March 9, 21, May 15, 31, June 27, 1945, February 27, 1946.

50. Jon Petrie, "The Secular Word 'Holocaust': Scholarly Sacralization, Twentieth Century Meanings," http://www.berkeleyinternet.com/holocaust.

51. *Al-Ahram*, May 23, July 13, August 6, 1945, May 24, 27, 29, 1946; Muhammad 'Awad Muhammad, "Mas'alat Filastin," *al-Thaqafa*, April 10, 1945, 391.

52. *Al-Ahram*, March 29, August 10, October 15, 28, 29, 30, November 15, 16, 1945, May 24, June 19, 1946.

53. Taha Husayn, "Min al-Qahira ila Bayrut," *al-Katib al-Misri*, June 3, 1946, 3–13.

54. Siham Nassar, *Al-Yahud al-Misriyyun, Suhufuhum wa-Majallatuhum, 1877–1950* (Cairo, 1981), 78–79.

55. *Al-Hilal*, January–February 1945, 16. See also Salah al-Zihni, "Hukm al-Mintaq fi Qadiyyat Filastin," *al-Thaqafa*, February 20, 1945, 197.

56. Michael R. Marrus, *The Holocaust in History* (Hanover, 1987), 6.

57. *Al-Ahram*, January 9, 11, 15, 17, 1946. Dönitz was commander of the German Navy and Hitler's successor as führer.

58. *Al-Ahram*, October 22, November 20, 24, December 14, 1945, January 3, 4, 11, October 2, 1946. See also *al-Misri*, December 16, 1945; and *al-Thaqafa*, March 12, 1946, 23.

59. *Al-Ahram*, February 3, 1946. The series was published on February 1, 3, 4, 7, 10, 15, 24, 26, 1946.

60. *Al-Ahram*, February 7, 1946.

61. *Al-Ahram*, February 4, 7, 1946.

62. *Al-Ahram*, September 4, 18, 1945; Ahmad Zaki, "'Araqil fi Sabil al-Nahda al-'Arabiyya," *al-Thaqafa*, November 13, 1945, 1282–1283.

63. Berque, *Egypt: Imperialism and Revolution*, 583.

64. *Al-Ahram*, August 14, 1946, August 12, 14, 1947. Nahhas as well issued a communication following the security council's meeting, reiterating that Britain ignores international treaties despite Egypt's stand on the side of the democracies during the war and the suffering caused to her as a result. See *al-Ahram*, September 21, 1947. For articles in the same vein, see Amin, "Al-'Alam al-Jadid," 1–3; and "Al-Harb bayna al-Khayr wal-Sharr," *al-Thaqafa*, August 7, 1945, 15–16.

65. Muhammad 'Awad Muhammad, "Bayna al-Raja' wal-Ya's," *al-Thaqafa*, October 23, 1945, 1–4.

66. See by Muhammad 'Abdallah 'Inan: "Ittijahat al-Siyasa al-Urubbiyya al-Jadida wa-Silatiha bi-Isabat al-Qalaq al-Hadhir," *al-Thaqafa*, June 5, 1945, 1–3; "Ba'da 'Am," *al-Thaqafa*, May 28, 1946, 1–3; and "Qalaq Ijtima'i wa-Iqtisadi," *al-Thaqafa*, October 1, 1946, 1–4.

67. "Al-Jil al-Jadid Yabdi Ra'yahu fi Mashakil al-Yawm," *al-Hilal*, June 1947, 124. See also *al-Ahram*, May 3, 1946, September 18, 1947.

68. This corroborates British assessments of Egyptian attitudes toward the war, "as overwhelmingly shaped by considerations of the war consequences for Egypt," according to Jankowski's presentation to the workshop.

69. *Al-Ahram*, November 2, 1947.

70. 'Abd al-Majid Nafi', *Britaniya al-Naziyya* (Cairo, 1947), 52.

71. Ibid., 32–33.

72. Ibid., 35. 'Abbas Mahmud al-'Aqqad, who welcomed in principle the trials, believed that independent courts should be established in the victorious states to examine their war crimes. Only then, he said, humanity will rise to a higher level until wars will be totally prohibited. 'Abbas Mahmud al-'Aqqad, "Al-'Adl al-Insani fi Jara'im al-Hurub," *al-Risala*, October 29, 1945, 1163–1164. 'Abdallah 'Inan as well assumed that no justice can be made in them without the participation of neutral judges who do not belong to the victorious camp. Muhammad 'Abdallah 'Inan, "Jara'im al-Harb," *al-Katib al-Misri*, August 3, 1946, 390–401. Historian Salah al-'Aqqad considers the Nuremberg trials as political trials that did not stem out of international criminal law. Salah al-'Aqqad, *Al-Harb al-'Alamiyya al-Thaniya*, 404.

73. 'Ali Adham, "Al-Umam wal-Siyasa wal-Adab," *al-Thaqafa*, July 8, 1947, 11–14; "Haza al-'Alam al-Qalaq," *al-Thaqafa*, June 18, 1946, 1–2.

74. Sami 'Azir Jubran, "Mas'uliyyat al-Shu'ub wa-Tab'i'iha," *al-Thaqafa*, April 23, 1945, 1–3; 'Abd al-Rahman al-Rafi'i, "Al-Mushkila al-Almaniyya," *al-Risala*, March 31, 1947, 379–380.

75. See Gershoni, *Light in the Shade*, 302–304, 321.

76. Ahmad Hasan al-Zayyat, "Rahima Allah Adulf Hitler," *al-Risala*, January 27, 1947, 1.

77. Al-'Aqqad, *Hitler fi al-Mizan*, 237. See also 'Atiq, *Al-Malik Faruq*, 4.

78. *Al-Misri*, August 24, 1946. For the British accusations in the UN, see *al-Ahram*, August 12, 14, 1947.

79. *Al-Ahram*, November 1, 1947.

80. The issue became increasingly important following President Truman's proposal on August 16, 1945, to allow the immigration of one hundred thousand displaced Jews to Palestine, the establishment of the Anglo-American Committee on November 13, 1945, and its subsequent recommendations, as well as the formation of the United Nations Special Committee on Palestine (UNSCOP) on May 15, 1947, which led to the UN resolution on the partition of Palestine on November 29 that year and the establishment of the State of Israel on May 14, 1948. See Martin Gilbert, *Exile and Return: The Emergence of Jewish Statehood* (London, 1978), 258–309; and Michael J. Cohen, *Truman and Israel* (Berkeley, CA, 1990), 59 ff.

81. 'Awad Muhammad, "Mas'alat Filastin," 1–4.

82. *Al-Ahram*, June 21, 1946.

83. See by Sayyid Qutb: "Ayyuha al-'Arab . . . Ayqazu wa-Ihzaru," *al-Risala*, November 26, 1945, 1281–1282; "Shylock al-Jadid," *al-Risala*, January 21, 1946, 84; and "Al-Damir al-Amrikani . . . wa-Qadiyyat Filastin," *al-Risala*, October 21, 1946, 1155–1157. His views were adopted and quoted by 'Abd al-Ghaffar al-Jiyar in his book *Filastin lil-'Arab* (Cairo, 1947).

84. *Al-Ahram*, August 20, 24, 1945. See also Syrian president Shukri al-Quwatli to President Truman, *al-Ahram*, November 13, 1945.

85. *Al-Ahram*, July 3, 4, 5, 11, 12, 1946; 'Inan, "Ba'da 'Am," 2; 'Inan, "Hawadith Filastin," *al-Thaqafa*, July 9, 1946, 759–760; 'Inan, "Filastin fi al-Midan al-Dawli," *al-Thaqafa*, February 25, 1947, 2; Sayyid Qutb, "Wal-Aan Ayyuha al-'Arab: Imma Tazalun Tantazirun," *al-Risala*, February 17, 1947, 190–192.

86. *Al-Ahram*, May 15, 1946. See similar objections in the memorandum pre-

sented by the Egyptian Foreign Ministry: CO 733/463/17/1538, 1549, Ministere des Affaires Etrangères, Departement des Affaires Arabes, Observations et Remarques au Sujet des Recommandations de la Commission Anglo-Americaine, Le Caire, June 20, 1946.

87. See Gershoni, *Light in the Shade*, 340–341; Israel Gershoni, "Egyptian Liberalism in an Age of 'Crisis of Orientation': *Al-Risala*'s Reaction to Fascism and Nazism, 1933–1939," *International Journal of Middle East Studies* 31, no. 4 (1999): 562–568.

88. Ibrahim 'Abd al-Qadir al-Mazini, "Filastin bayna al-'Arab wal-Sahyuniyya," *al-Risala*, December 3, 1945, 1303–1304. See also his "Shu'un Filastiniyya," *al-Risala*, February 11, 1946, 150.

89. "Al-Malik Sulayman," *al-Thaqafa*, December 16, 1947, 1–2.

90. Al-'Aqqad, *Al-Harb al-'Alamiyya al-Thaniya*, 5. 'Aqqad published two more books on Zionism: *Al-Sahyuniyya wa-Qadiyyat Filastin* (Beirut, Sidon, n.d.), a compilation of articles broadcast and published during the war in Palestine in 1948; and *Al-Sahyuniyya al-'Alamiyya* (Cairo, 1956), as part of the government series Ikhtarna Laka.

91. Anwar Kamil, *Al-Sahyuniyya* (Cairo, 1944).

92. Subsequent to the publication of the Anglo-American Committee, the UN formed on May 15, 1947, the United Nations Special Committee on Palestine.

93. *Al-Ahram*, August 3, 29–31, September 1, 2, December 2, 1947; Ahmad Hamza, "Mihnat Filastin," *Liwa' al-Islam*, November 1947, 4.

94. Niqula al-Haddad, "Al-Talmud Yakhda' al-Yahud," *al-Risala*, December 22, 1947, 1395–1396.

95. *Al-Ahram*, August 3, 29, 30, 31, September 1, 2, 9, October 3, 5, 9, 29, November 25, 1947; *al-Misri*, 9, 10 September, November 25, 1947; *Arab News Bulletin*, nos. 43–44 (August 8, 22, 1947), CO 733/482/1/9, 11; *Arab News Bulletin*, no. 46 (September 19, 1947), CO 733/482/1/15; Ahmad Hamza, "Filastin Shahida," *Liwa' al-Islam*, November 1947, 4, and December 1947, 4.

96. See by Mahmud Muhammad Shakir: "Hadith al-Dawlatayn," *al-Risala*, October 20, 1947, 1140–1141; "La Hawada ba'da al-Yawm," *al-Risala*, October 6, 1947, 1085; and "Labayki ya Filastin," *al-Risala*, December 11, 1947, 1313–1315.

97. Baha' al-Din, *Isra'iliyyat*, 174, 202–204, 226.

98. Hamdi Hafiz, *Thawrat 23 Yuliu: al-Ahdath, al-Ahdaf, al-Injazat* (Cairo, 1964), 304.

99. Muhammad Kamal al-Dissuqi, *Al-Harb al-'Alamiyya al-Thaniya—sira' isti'mari* (Cairo, 1968), 249–250, 278.

100. Ibid., t-l (introduction), 281, 284.

101. Salah al-'Aqqad, *Al-'Arab wal-Harb al-'Alamiyya al-Thaniya*, 14; al-'Aqqad, *Al-Harb al-'Alamiyya al-Thaniya*, 211.

102. Only a handful of books were published in Egypt on the war or Nazism, among them: Salah al-'Aqqad, *Dirasa Muqarina lil-Harakat al-Qawmiyya fi Almaniya, Italiya' al-Wilayat al-Muttahida wa-Turkiya* (Cairo, 1957); 'Adil Muhammad Shukri, *Al-Naziyya bayna al-Idiulujiyya wal-Tatbiq* (Cairo, 1966); and Jalal Yahya, *Al-'Alam al-'Arabi al-Hadith mundhu al-Harb al-'Alamiyya al-Thaniya* (Cairo, 1967). See also a later group of publications: 'Isam Muhammad al-Dissuqi, *Misr fi al-Harb al-'Alamiyya al-Thaniya* (Cairo, 1976); Muhammad Jamal al-Din al-Masdi

et al., *Misr wal-Harb al-'Alamiyya al-Thaniya* (Cairo, 1978); and 'Atiq, *Al-Malik Faruq*.

Chapter Eleven

1. The section above is based on several of my studies: Haggai Erlich, "Youth and Arab Politics: The Political Generation of 1935–1936," in *Alienation or Integration of Arab Youth*, edited by Roel Meijer (London, 2000), 47–69; "Egypt, Ethiopia, and the Abyssinian Crisis, 1935–1936," in *The Nile: Histories, Cultures, Myths*, edited by Haggai Erlich and Israel Gershoni (Boulder, CO, 2000), 183–198; "The Arab Youth and the Challenge of Fascism," in *Fascism Outside Europe: The European Impulse against Domestic Conditions in the Diffusion of Global Fascism*, edited by Stein Larsen (New York, 2001), 393–423; "Mussolini and the Middle East in the 1920s: The Restrained Imperialist," in *The Great Powers in the Middle East, 1919–1939*, edited by U. Dann (New York, 1988), 213–221; and two Hebrew textbooks: *The Middle East between the World Wars*, vol. 4, *The 1930s: Crises and Revolt* (Tel Aviv, 1992–2003); and *Youth and Politics in the Middle East: Generations and Identity Crises* (Tel Aviv, 1998).

2. The section above is based on my studies: Haggai Erlich, "Tigrean Politics, 1930–1935, and the Approaching Italo-Ethiopian war," in *Proceedings of the Sixth International Conference of Ethiopian Studies*, edited by G. Goldenberg (Rotterdam, 1986), 101–131; *Ethiopia and the Middle East* (Boulder, CO, 1994), chaps. 8, 9; *The Cross and the River: Ethiopia, Egypt, and the Nile* (Boulder, CO, 2002), chap. 6; *Saudi Arabia and Ethiopia: Christianity, Islam, and Politics Entwined* (Boulder, CO, 2007), chap. 3. The sections below are mostly based on rereading sources and documents used in those studies.

3. *Filastin*, September 25, October 2, 1935.

4. *Al-Qabas*, December 1, 1935.

5. "The Ethiopian Virgin" was reproduced in Anwar Shawul's autobiography, *Qisat Hayyati fi Wadi al-Rafidin* (Jerusalem, 1980), 216–219.

6. See, for example, *Al-Ahram*, July 22, 1935.

7. 'Abdalla al-Husayn, *Al-Mas'ala al-Habashiyya, min al-Tarikh al-Qadim ila 'Am 1935* (Cairo, 1935).

8. Ibid., 18–19.

9. Ibid., 151–170.

10. Muhammad Lutfi Jum'a, *Bayna al-Asad al-Ifriqi wal-Nimr al-Itali, Bahth Tahlili wa Ta'rikhi wa Nafsani wa Ijtima'i fi al-Mushkilla al-Habashiyya al-Italiyya* (Cairo, 1935).

11. For a detailed study of his career, see Ahmad Husayn al-Timawi, *Muhammad Lutfi Jum'a fi Mawkib al-Hayyat wal-Adab* (Cairo 1993).

12. See Israel Gershoni, *Light in the Shade: Egypt and Fascism, 1922–1937* (Tel Aviv, 1999), 142 and passim (in Hebrew).

13. See Israel Gershoni and James Jankowski, "'Easternism' in Egypt in the 1920s," chap. 11 in *Egypt, Islam, and the Arabs: The Search for Egyptian Nationhood, 1900–1930* (New York, 1987).

14. Jum'a, *Bayna al-Asad*, 9.

15. Ibid., 13–18.

16. Ibid., 6–7.

17. Ibid., 18.

18. Ibid., 23–27.

19. Ibid., 79–80.

20. Ibid., 34.

21. Ibid., 84.

22. See more in Gershoni, *Light in the Shade*, 113–116.

23. Jum'a, *Bayna al-Asad*, 90.

24. Ibid., 91.

25. Ibid., 72.

26. Ibid., 9.

27. Ibid., 48.

28. Ibid., 108.

29. Ibid., 93–94.

30. Ibid., 78.

31. Ibid., 11, 13, 29, 78.

32. See the section "The Terminology and Literature of Eritrea's Arabism" in my *Ethiopia and the Middle East*, 157–164.

33. Jum'a, *Bayna al-Asad*, 11, 78.

34. Ibid., 114.

35. Ibid., 113.

36. See my book *The Cross and the River*, 90.

37. See my book *Saudi Arabia and Ethiopia*, 44–47, 50.

38. The above section is based on *Ethiopia and the Middle East*, chap. 9; and *Saudi Arabia and Ethiopia*, chap. 3. For Arslan and Mussolini, see also William Cleveland, *Islam against the West: Shakib Arslan and the Campaign for Islamic Nationalism* (Austin, TX, 1985), mainly 144–146.

39. *Al-Jami'a al-'Arabiyya*, March 4, 1935.

40. See a report on the conference in *al-Jazira*, September 16, 1935.

41. *Al-Jazira*, November 10, 1935.

42. *Al-Ayyam*, January 24, 1936.

43. For more, see *Ethiopia and the Middle East*, 104–109.

44. Yusuf Ahmad, *Islam in Ethiopia*, 4–5.

45. For his writings and career, see 'Usama Yusuf Shihab, *Muhammad Tayasir Zabiyan, 1901–1978: Mukhtarat min A'malihi al-Matbu'a wal-Makhtuta* (Riyadh, 2002).

46. Muhammad Tayasir Zabiyan, *Al-Habasha al-Muslima—Mushahadati fi Diyar al-Islam* (Damascus, 1937).

47. Ibid., 10–11.

48. Ibid., 39–45.

49. Ibid., 15.

50. Ibid., 13–16.

51. Ibid., 12.

52. Ibid., 4–7.

53. Ibid., 15.

54. On their friendship, see Shakib Arslan, *Al-Sayyid Rashid Rida, Aw Ikha Arba'in Sanah* (Beirut, 1937).

55. *Al-Jami'a al-'Arabiyya*, March 4, 1935.

Selected Bibliography

Newspapers and Periodicals

al-Adib
al-Ahali
al-Ahram
al-Ahrar
al-Akhbar
al-Amali
al-Ayyam
al-Dabbur
al-Difa'
Filastin
al-Ghad
Habazbuz
al-Hadith
al-Hilal
al-'Ilm
al-Insaniyya
al-Ithnayn wa-al-Dunya
al-'Irfan
al-Istiqlal
al-Jabha al-Sha'biyya
al-Jami'a al-'Arabiyya
al-Jami'a al-Islamiyyya
al-Jazira
al-Kifah

Lisan al-Hal
Liwa' al-Islam
al-Majalla
Majallatal-Mu'allimin wa-al-Mu'allimat
al-Ma'rid
al-Misri
al-Musawwar
al-Nahar
La Nation Arabe
al-Nida'
al-Nuwayhid
al-Qabas
Qadaya Fikriyya
Ruz al-Yusif
al-Sahafi al-Ta'ih
Sawt al-Haqq
Sawt al-Sha'b
al-Sirat al-Mustaqim
al-Tali'a
al-Tamaddun al-Islami
al-Tariq
al-Thaqafa
al-'Urwa al-Wuthqa
Die Welt des Islams

Arabic and Hebrew Sources

'Abbas, Ra'uf. *Awraq Henri Curiel wa-al-Haraka al-Shuyu'iyya al-Misriyya*. Cairo, 1988.

Abu al-Ghar, Muhammad. *Yahud Misr min al-Izdihar ila al-Shatat*. Cairo, 2004.

Abu Hanna, Hanna, ed. *Mudhakkirat Najati Sidqi: Muassasat al-Dirasat al-Filastiniyya*. Beirut, 2001.

Abu Sayf, Yusuf. *Watha'iq wa-Mawaqif Min Ta'rikh al-Yasar al-Misri, 1941–1957*. Cairo, 2000.

al-'Alawi, Hasan. *Al-Ta'thirat al-Turkiyya fi al-Mashru' al-Qawmi al-'Arabi fi al-'Iraq*. London, 1988.

al-Amin, Muzaffar 'Abd Allah. *Jama'at al-Ahali: Munsha'uha, 'Aqidatuha, wa-Dawruha fi al-Siyasa al-'Iraqiyya, 1932–1946*. Beirut and Amman, 2001.

al-'Aqqad, Salah. *Dirasa Muqarina lial-Harakat al-Qawmiyya fi Almaniya, Italiya al-Wilayat al-Muttahida wa-Turkiya*. Cairo, 1957.

———. *Al-Harb al-'Alamiyya al-Thaniya: Dirasa fi Ta'rikh al-'Alaqat al-Dawliyya*. Cairo, 1963–1966.

———. *Al-Sahyuniyya al-'Alamiyya*. Cairo, 1956.

Arslan, 'Adil. *Mudhakkirat al-Amir 'Adil Arsalan*. Vol. 1. Beirut, 1983.

Arslan, Shakib. *Al-Sayyid Rashid Rida, Aw Ikha Arba'in Sanah*. Beirut, 1937.

'Atiq, Wajih 'Abd al-Sadiq. *Al-Jaysh al-Misri wa-al-Alman fi Ithna al-Harb al-'Alamiyya al-Thaniyya*. Cairo, 1993.

———. *Al-Malik Faruq wa-Almaniya al-Naziyya: Khams Sanawat min al-'Alaqa al-Sirriyya*. Cairo, 1992.

Ayyub, Dhu Nun. "Fi Sabil Majd al-'Arab." In *Al-Athar al-Kamila li-Athar Dhi al-Nun Ayyub*, 1:39–50. Baghdad, 1978.

———. "Mu'amarat al-Aghbiya'." In *Al-Athar al-Kamila li-Athar Dhi al-Nun Ayyub*, 1:9–50. Baghdad, 1978.

al-'Azm, Khalid. *Mudhakkirat Khalid al-'Azm*. Vol. 2. Beirut, 1973.

Babil, Nassuh. *Sihafa wa-Siyasa, Suriyya fi al-Qarn al-'Ishrin*. London, 1987.

al-Barrak, Fadhil. *Al-Madaris al-Yahudiyya wa-al-Iraniyya fi al-'Iraq: Dirasa Muqarana*. Baghdad, 1985.

Basri, Mir. *Rihlat al-'Umar: Min Difaf Dijla ila Wadi al-Tims*. Jerusalem, 1991.

al-Bazzaz, 'Abd al-Rahman. *Muhadarat 'an al-'Iraq min al-Ihtilal hatta al-Istiqlal*. Cairo, 1954.

Cohen, Jonah. *Hilla 'al Gedot ha-Perat*. Carmiel, 2004.

al-Dissuqi, 'Isam Muhammad. *Misr fi al-Harb al-'Alamiyya al-Thaniya*. Cairo, 1976.

al-Dissuqi, Muhammad Kamal. *Al-Harb al-'Alamiyya al-Thaniya—Sira' Isti'mari*. Cairo, 1968.

Diya' al-Din, 'Isam. *Hadith 17 Yuniyu 1940 fi Ta'rikh Misr al-Mu'asir*. Cairo, 1991.

Faris, Filiks. *Hakadha Takallama Zaradasht*. Beirut, 1970.

Fawzi-Rossano, Didar. *Rasa'il ila' Haba'ibi—Misr*. Cairo, 2006.

Fu'ad, Ni'mat Ahmad. *Qimam Adabiyya*. Cairo, 1966.

Gershoni, Israel. *Light in the Shade: Egypt and Fascism, 1922–1937*. Tel Aviv, 1999.

Hafiz, Hamdi. *Thawrat 23 Yuliyu: Al-Ahdath, al-Ahdaf, al-Injazat*. Cairo, 1964.

Hanna, 'Abdallah. *Al-Haraka al-Munahida li-al-Fashiyya fi Suriya wa Lubnan, 1933–45*. Beirut, 1974.

al-Hasani, 'Abd al-Razzak. *Al-Asrar al-Khaffiyya fi Harakat 1941 al-Tahririyya*. Sayda, 1964.

———. *Al-'Iraq fi Zill al-Mu'ahadat*. Sayda, 1947.

————. *Ta'rikh al-'Iraq al-Siyasai al-Hadith.* Sayda, 1957.

Hatata, Sharif. *Al-Nawafidhu al-Maftuha: Mudhakkirat Duktur Sharif Hatata.* Cairo, 2006.

————. "Henri Curiel." In *Al-Haraka al-Shuyu'iyya wa-Haykal.* Cairo, 2006.

al-Hawrani, Akram. *Mudhakkirat Akram al-Hawrani.* Vol. 1. Cairo, 2000.

Hilu, Faraj Allah. *Kitabat Mukhtara.* Beirut, 1999.

Hirszowicz, Lukasz. *The Third Reich and the Arab East.* Tel Aviv, 1965.

al-Husayn, 'Abdalla. *Al-Mas'ala al-Habashiyya, min al-Tarikh al-Qadim ila 'Am 1935.* Cairo, 1935.

Husni, Sa'ida Muhamad. *Al-Yahud fi Misr Min 1882–1947.* Cairo, 1993.

Ibrahim, 'Abd al-Fattah. *Muqaddima fi-al-Ijtima'.* Baghdad, 1939.

Jazmati, Nazir. *Al-Hizb al-Shuyu'i al-Suri, 1924–1958.* Damascus, 1990.

Jumblatt, Kamal. *Nahwa Sigha Jadida li-al-Dimuqratiyya al-Ijtima'iyya al-Iusaniyya 1945.* Al-Mukhtara, 2004.

al-Jundi, Sami. *Al-B'ath.* Beirut, 1969.

Kabha, Mustafa. *Hapelestinim, 'Am Bifzurato.* Tel Aviv, 2010.

Kamil, Anwar. *Al-Sahyuniyya.* Cairo, 1944.

al-Kaylani, Shams al-Din. *Al-Hizb al-Shuyu'i al-Suri.* Damascus, 2003.

al-Kayyali, Sami. *Shahr fi Urubba.* Cairo, 1935.

Kazzaz, Nissim. *He-Yehudim be-Iraq ba-Ma'ahe-'Esrim.* Jerusalem, 1991.

al-Khuri, Bishara Khalil. *Majmu'at al-Khutab: Aylul 1943 — Kanun al-Awwal 1951.* Beirut, 1951.

Lutfi Jum'a, Muhammad. *Bayna al-Asad al-Ifriqi wa-al-Nimr al-Itali, Bahth Tah- lili wa Ta'rikhi wa Nafsani wa 'Ijtima'i fi al-Mushkilla al-Habashiyya al-Italiyya.* Cairo, 1935.

al-Masdi, Muhammad Jamal al-Din, et al. *Misr wa-al-Harb al-'Alamiyya al- Thaniya.* Cairo, 1978.

Me'ir, Yosef. *Be'ikar ba-Mahteret, Yehudim u-Politika be-'Iraq.* Tel Aviv, 1993.

Moreh, Shemu'el, and Zvi Yehudah, eds. *Sin'atyyehudim u-Fera'ot be-'Iraq.* Or- Yehudah, 1992.

Muhammad 'Awad Muhammad. "Mas'alat Filastin." *Al-Thaqafa,* April 10, 1945.

Muhammad, Muhammad Sayyid. *Al-Zayyat wa-al-Risala.* Riyadh, 1982.

Mursi, Fu'ad. *Tatawwur al-Ra'smaliyya wa-Kifah al-Tabaqat fi Misr.* Cairo, 1992.

Nafi', 'Abd al-Majid. *Britaniya al-Naziyya.* Cairo, 1947.

Nassar, Siham. *Al-Yahud al-Misriyyun, Suhufuhum wa-Majallatuhum, 1877–1950.* Cairo, 1981.

Nuwayhid, 'Ajaj. *Mudhakkirat 'Ajaj Nuwayhid: Sittuna 'Aman ma' al-Qafila al- 'Arabiyya.* Edited by Bayan Nuwayhid al-Hout. Beirut, 1993.

Qasimiyya, Khayriyya. *Al-Ra'il al-'Arabi al-Awwal, Hayat wa Awraq Nabih wa-'Adil al-Azma.* London, 1991.

Ramadan, 'Abd al-'Azim Muhammad. *Tatawwur al-Haraka al-Wataniyya fi Misr, 1937–1948.* Vol. 2. Beirut, 1973.

Sagiv, David. *Yahadut be-Mifgash ha-Nahariyim, Kehilatyyehudey Basra.* Jerusalem, 2004.

al-Sa'id, Rif'at. "Al-Haraka al-Shuyu'iyya al-Misriyya 'Abr Sab'in 'Aman." *Qadaya Fikriyya,* July 1992.

————. *Ta'rikh al-Munazzamat al-Yasariyya al-Misriyya, 1940–1950*. Cairo, 1976.

Sha'ib, 'Ali 'Abd al-Mun'im. *Al-Tadakhkhul al-Ajnabi wa-al-Azmat al-Hukm fi Tarikh al-'Arab al-Hadith wa-l-Mu'asir*. Beirut, 2005.

Shawkat, Sami. *Hadhihi Ahdafuna*. Baghdad, 1939.

Shawul, Anwar. *Qissat Hayati fi Wadi al-Rafidin*. Jerusalem, 1980.

Shihab, 'Usama Yusuf. *Muhammad Tayasir Zabiyan, 1901–1978: Mukhtarat min A'malihi al-Matbu'a wal-Makhtuta*. Riyadh, 2002.

Shirizi, Marsil. *Awraq Munadil Itali fi Misr*. Cairo, 2002.

Shukri, 'Adil Muhammad. *Al-Naziyya bayna al-Idiulujiyya wa-al-Tatbiq*. Cairo, 1966.

Shukri, Muhammad Fu'ad. *Almaniya al-Naziyya: Dirasa fi al-Ta'rikh al-Urubbi al-Mu'asir, 1939–1945*. Cairo, 1948.

Sibahi, Aziz. *'Uqud min Ta'rikh al-Hizb al-Shuyu'i al-'Iraqi*. Damascus, 2002.

Sid Ahmad, Muhammad. *Mustaqbal al-Nizam al-Hizbi fi Misr*. Cairo, 1984.

Talas, Mustafa. *Fatir Sahyun*. Damascus, 2002.

————. *Mir'at Hayyati*. Vol. 1. Damascus, 1992.

Twena, Avraham. *Golim u-Ge'ulim, Heleksesh: Me'ora'o Thagg ha-Shavu'ot, Juni 1941*. Ramla, 1979.

al-Wakil, Fu'ad Husayn. *Jama'at al-Ahali fi-al-'Iraq, 1932–1937*. Baghdad, 1980.

Yahya, Jalal. *Al-'Alam al-'Arabi al-Hadith mundhu al-Harb al-'Alamiyya al-Thaniya*. Cairo, 1967.

Zabiyan, Muhammad Tayasir. *Al-Habasha al-Muslima—Mushahadati fi Diyar al-Islam*. Damascus, 1937.

Zahran, Sa'd. *Fi Usul al-Siyasa al-Misriyyah: Naqal Tahlili Naqdi fi al-Ta'rikh al-Siyasi*. Cairo, 1985.

Other Sources

Abu Jaber, Kamel S. *The Arab Ba'th Socialist Party: History, Ideology, and Organization*. Syracuse, NY, 1966.

Achcar, Gilbert. *The Arabs and the Holocaust: The Arab-Israeli War of Narratives*. New York, 2009.

Ahmad, Yusuf. *Islam in Ethiopia*. Cairo, 1935.

Antonius, George. *The Arab Awakening: The Story of the Arab National Movement*. London, 1938.

Arendt, Hannah. *Eichmann in Jerusalem: A Report on the Banality of Evil*. Rev. ed. New York, 1965.

Ayalon, Ami. *Reading Palestine: Printing and Literacy, 1900–1948*. Austin, TX, 2004.

Barakat, Rena. "Thawrat al-Buraq in British Mandate Palestine: Jerusalem, Mass Mobilization, and Colonial Politics, 1928-1930." PhD thesis, University of Chicago, 2007.

Bashkin, Orit. *New Babylonians: A History of Jews in Modern Iraq*. Stanford, CA, 2012.

————. "The Nile Valley at the Banks of the Euphrates and Tigris: Egyptian Intellectuals in Iraq during the Interwar Period." In *Narrating the Nile: Politics, Cultures, Identities*. Boulder, CO, 2008.

———. *The Other Iraq: Pluralism and Culture in Hashemite Iraq*. Stanford, CA, 2009.

Batatu, Hanna. *Syria's Peasantry, the Descendants of Its Lesser Rural Notables, and Their Politics*. Princeton, NJ, 1999.

Beckman, Morris. *The Jewish Brigade: An Army with Two Masters, 1944–1945*. Staplehurst, 1988.

Beinin, Joel, and Zachary Lockman. *Workers on the Nile: Nationalism, Communism, Islam, and the Egyptian Working Class, 1882–1954*. Princeton, NJ, 1987.

Berque, Jacques. *Egypt: Imperialism and Revolution*. London, 1972.

Bey, Salma Mardam. *Syria's Quest for Independence, 1939–1945*. Reading, 1994.

Botman, Selma. *The Rise of Egyptian Communism, 1939–1970*. Syracuse, NY, 1988.

Brugman, J. *An Introduction to the History of Modern Arabic Literature in Egypt*. Leiden, 1984.

Buheiry, Marwan R., ed. *Intellectual Life in the Arab East, 1890–1939*. Beirut, 1981.

Cleveland, William. *Islam against the West: Shakib Arslan and the Campaign for Islamic Nationalism*. Austin, TX, 1985.

Cohen, M., and M. Kolinsky, eds. *Demise of the British Empire in the Middle East*. London, 1998.

Cohen, Michael J. *Truman and Israel*. Berkeley, CA, 1990.

Colombe, Marcel. *L'évolution de l'Égypte, 1924–1950*. Paris, 1951.

Commins, David Dean. *Islamic Reform: Politics and Social Change in Late Ottoman Syria*. Oxford, 1990.

Cramer, Valmar, and Gustav Meinertz, eds. *Das Heilige Land in Vergangenheit und Gegenwart: Gesammelte Beiträge und Berichte zur Palästinaforschung*. Vol. 3. Cologne, 1941.

Curiel, Henri. *Pages autobiographiques: Une contribution à l'histoire de la naissance du Parti Communiste Egyptien de 1940 à 1950*. Paris, 1977.

Dakhli, Leyla. *Une génération d'intellectuels arabes: Syrie et Liban (1908–1940)*. Paris, 2009.

Dann, U., ed. *The Great Powers in the Middle East, 1919–1939*. New York, 1988.

Davis, Eric. *Memories of the State: Politics, History, and Collective Identity in Modern Iraq*. Berkeley, CA, 2005.

Diner, Dan. *Gedächniszeiten: Über jüdische und andere Geschichten*. Munich, 2003.

Dodd, Stuart C. *A Pioneer Radio Poll in Lebanon, Syria, and Palestine*. Palestine, 1943.

Dovey, H. O. "The Intelligence War in Turkey." *Intelligence and National Security* 9, no. 1 (1994).

———. "Security in Syria, 1941–45." *Intelligence and National Security* 6, no. 2 (1991).

El-Awaisi, Abd al-Fattah Muhammad. *The Muslim Brothers and the Palestine Question, 1928–1947*. London, 1998.

El Shakry, Omnia. *The Great Social Laboratory: Subjects of Knowledge in Colonial and Postcolonial Egypt*. Stanford, CA, 2007.

Eppel, Michael. *The Palestine Conflict in the History of Modern Iraq: The Dynamics of Involvement, 1928–1948*. London, 1994.

Eppler, John W. *Rommel Ruft Kairo: Aus dem Tagebuch eines Spions*. Gütersloh, 1959.

Erlich, Haggai. "Tigrean Politics, 1930–1935, and the Approaching Italo-Ethiopian

War." In *Proceedings of the Sixth International Conference of Ethiopian Studies*, edited by G. Goldenberg. Rotterdam, 1986.

———. "Youth and Arab Politics: The Political Generation of 1935-1936." In *Alienation or Integration of Arab Youth*, edited by Roel Meijer. London, 2000.

Erlich, Haggai, and Israel Gershoni, eds. *The Nile: Histories, Cultures, Myths*. Boulder, CO, 2000.

Farschid, Olaf. "The First World War as a Factor of Political and Social Transformation." In *The First World War as Remembered in the Countries of the Eastern Mediterranean*, edited by Manfred Kropp and Stephan Dähne. Würzburg, 2006.

Fleischmann, Ellen L. *The Nation and Its "New" Women: The Palestinian Women's Movement, 1920-1948*. Berkeley, CA, 2003.

Flores, Alexander. "Modernity, Romanticism, and Religion: Contradictions in the Writings of Farah Antun." In *Nationalism and Liberal Thought in the Arab East*, edited by Christoph Schumann. London, 2010.

Gershoni, Israel. "Egyptian Liberalism in an Age of 'Crisis of Orientation': *Al-Risala*'s Reaction to Fascism and Nazism, 1933-1939." *International Journal of Middle East Studies* 31, no. 4 (1999): 551-576.

Gershoni, Israel, and Meir Hatina, eds. *Narrating the Nile: Politics, Cultures, Identities*. Boulder, CO, 2008.

Gershoni, Israel, and James Jankowski. *Confronting Fascism in Egypt: Dictatorship versus Democracy in the 1930s*. Stanford, CA, 2009.

———. *Egypt, Islam, and the Arabs: The Search for Egyptian Nationhood, 1900-1930*. New York, 1987.

Gershoni, Israel, and Götz Nordbruch. *Sympathie und Schrecken: Begegnungen mit Faschismus und Nationalsozialismus in Ägypten, 1922-1937*. Berlin, 2011.

Gershoni, Israel, Amy Singer, and Hakan Y. Erdem, eds. *Middle East Historiographies: Narrating the Twentieth Century*. Seattle, 2006.

Gilbert, Martin. *Exile and Return: The Emergence of Jewish Statehood*. London, 1978.

Ginat, Rami. *A History of Egyptian Communism: Jews and Their Compatriots in Quest of Revolution*. Boulder, CO, in press.

Goldberg, Ellis. *Tinker, Tailor, and Textile Worker: Class and Politics in Egypt, 1930-1952*. Berkeley, CA, 1986.

Gutman, Israel, ed. *Encyclopedia of the Holocaust*. New York, 1990.

Haim, Sylvia G. *Arab Nationalism: An Anthology*. Berkeley, CA, 1976.

Halpern, Manfred. *The Politics of Social Change in the Middle East and North Africa*. Princeton, NJ, 1963.

Hamdi, Walid M. S. *Rashid Ali al-Gailani and the Nationalist Movement in Iraq, 1939-1941: A Political and Military Study of the British Campaign in Iraq and the National Revolution of May 1941*. London, 1987.

Haroun, Georges. *Shibli Shumayyil: Une pensée évolutionniste arabe à l'époque d'an-nahda*. Beirut, 1985.

Hassassian, Manuel S. *Palestine: Factionalism in the National Movement, 1919-1939*. Jerusalem, 1990.

Herf, Jeffrey. *Nazi Propaganda for the Arab World*. New Haven, CT, 2009.

Hillel, Hagar. *"Israel" in Cairo: A Zionist Newspaper in Nationalist Egypt, 1920–1939*. Tel Aviv, 2004.

Hinnebusch, Raymond. *Syria: Revolution from Above*. New York, 2001.

Hirszowicz, Lukasz. *The Third Reich and the Arab East*. London, 1966.

Hitler, Adolf. *Mein Kampf*. Munich, 1939.

Höpp, Gerhard, Peter Wien, and René Wildangel, eds. *Blind für die Geschichte? Arabische Begegnungen mit dem Nationalsozialismus*. Berlin, 2004.

Hourani, Albert. *Arabic Thought in the Liberal Age, 1798–1939*. Cambridge, 1984.

———. *Syria and Lebanon*. London, 1946.

Ismael, Tareq Y., and Jacqueline S. Ismael. *The Communist Movement in Syria and Lebanon*. Gainesville, FL, 1998.

Jankowski, James. *Egypt's Young Rebels: "Young Egypt," 1933–1952*. Stanford, CA, 1975.

———. *Nasser's Egypt, Arab Nationalism, and the United Arab Republic*. Boulder, CO, 2001.

Kabha, Mustafa. *The Palestinian Press as Shaper of Public Opinion, 1929–39: Writing Up a Storm*. London and Portland, 2007.

Kadi, Leila. *Arab Summit Conferences and the Palestine Problem, 1936–1950, 1964–1966*. Beirut, 1966.

Kedourie, Elie. *Politics in the Middle East*. Oxford, 1992.

Khalaf, Issa. *Politics in Palestine: Arab Factionalism and Social Disintegration, 1939–1948*. New York, 1991.

Khoury, Philip S. *Syria and the French Mandate*. Princeton, NJ, 1987.

Kishtainy, Khalid. *Tales from Old Baghdad: Grandmother and I*. London and New York, 1997.

Kolinsky, Martin. *Britain's War in the Middle East: Strategy and Diplomacy, 1936–1942*. New York, 1999.

Kropp, Manfred, and Stephan Dähne, eds. *The First World War as Remembered in the Countries of the Eastern Mediterranean*. Würzburg, 2006.

Küntzel, Matthias. *Islamist Terrorism and Antisemitism: The Mission against Modernity*. 2008. http://www.matthiaskuentzel.de/contents/islamist-terrorism-and-antisemitism-the-mission-against-modernity.

———. *Jihad and Jew-Hatred: Islamism, Nazism, and the Roots of 9/11*. New York, 2007.

Landau, Rom. *Search for Tomorrow*. London, 1938.

Laqueur, Walter Z. *Communism and Nationalism in the Middle East*. London, 1956.

Larsen, Stein U., ed. *Fascism Outside Europe: The European Impulse against Domestic Conditions in the Diffusion of Global Fascism*. New York, 2001.

Levenberg, Haim. *Military Preparations of the Arab Community in Palestine, 1945–1948*. London, 1993.

Lia, Brynjar. *The Society of the Muslim Brothers in Egypt: The Rise of an Islamic Mass Movement, 1928–1942*. Reading, 1998.

Litvak, Meir, and Ester Webman. *From Empathy to Denial: Arab Responses to the Holocaust*. New York, 2009.

Lockman, Zachary. *Comrades and Enemies: Arab and Jewish Workers in Palestine, 1906–1948*. Berkeley, CA, 1996.

Louis, W. M. *The British Empire in the Middle East, 1945–1951*. Oxford, 1984.

Lutfi al-Sayyid-Marsot, Afaf. *Egypt's Liberal Experiment, 1922–1936*. Berkeley, CA, 1977.

———. *A Short History of Modern Egypt*. Cambridge, 1994.

Makiya, Kanan. *Republic of Fear: The Politics of Modern Iraq*. Berkeley, CA, 1989.

Mallmann, Klaus-Michael, and Martin Daniel Cüppers. *Halbmond und Hakenkreuz: Das Dritte Reich, die Araber und Palästina*. Darmstadt, 2006.

Maoz, Moshe, and Ilan Pappé, eds. *Middle Eastern Politics and Ideas: A History from Within*. London, 1997.

Mardam, S. *Syria's Quest for Independence*. Reading, 1994.

Marrus, Michael R. *The Holocaust in History*. Hanover, 1987.

Matthews, Weldon C. *Confronting an Empire, Constructing a Nation: Arab Nationalists and Popular Politics in Mandate Palestine*. London and New York, 2006.

Mazower, Mark. *The Dark Continent: Europe's Twentieth Century*. New York, 1999.

Meier, Olivier. *Al-muqtataf et le débat sur le Darwinisme: Beyrouth, 1876–1885*. Cairo, 1994.

Meijer, Roel. *The Quest for Modernity*. London, 2002.

Méouchy, Nadine. "La presse de Syrie et du Liban entre les deux guerres, 1918–1939." In *Débats intellectuels au Moyen-Orient dans l'Entre-Deux-Guerres: Revue des mondes Musulmans et de la Méditerranée 95–98*. Aix-en-Provence, 2002.

Mervin, Sabrina. "Le Liban-Sud entre deux generations de reformistes." In *Débats intellectuels au Moyen-Orient dans l'Entre-Deux-Guerres: Revue des mondes Musulmans et de la Méditerranée 95–98*. Aix-en-Provence, 2002.

Metzger, Chantal. *L'empire colonial Français dans la stratégie du Troisième Reich, 1936–1945*. Vol. 1. Brussels, 2002.

Migdal, Joel S. *Palestinian Society and Politics*. Princeton, NJ, 1980.

Mitchell, R. P. *The Society of the Muslim Brothers*. Oxford and New York, 1993.

Mitchell, Timothy. *Colonising Egypt*. Berkeley, CA, 1997.

Moubayed, Sami. *Steel and Silk: Men and Women Who Shaped Syria, 1900–2000*. Seattle, 2006.

Nordbruch, Götz. "Bread, Freedom, Independence: Opposition to Nazi Germany in Lebanon and Syria and the Struggle for a Just Order." *Comparative Studies of South Asia, Africa, and the Middle East* 28, no. 3 (2008): 416–427.

———. "Cultural Fusion of Thought and Ambitions? Memory, Politics, and the History of Arab–Nazi German Encounters." *Middle Eastern Studies* 47, no. 1 (2011).

———. *Nazism in Syria and Lebanon: The Ambivalence of the German Option, 1933–1945*. London, 2009.

Perrault, Gilles. *A Man Apart: The Life of Henry Curiel*. London, 1987.

Podhoretz, Norman. *World War IV: The Long Struggle against Islamofascism*. New York, 2007.

Porat, Dina. *The Blue and Yellow Stars of David: The Zionist Leadership in Palestine and the Holocaust, 1939–1945*. Cambridge, MA, 1990.

Porath, Yehoshua. *The Palestinian Arab National Movement: From Riots to Rebellion, 1929–1939*. London, 1977.

Reid, Donald M. *Cairo University and the Making of Modern Egypt*. Cambridge, 1990.

Rejwan, Nissim. *The Last Jew in Baghdad: Remembering a Lost Homeland*. Austin, TX, 2004.

Safran, Nadav. *Egypt in Search of Political Community*. Cambridge, MA, 1961.

Sansom, W. *I Spied Spies*. London, 1965.

Satloff, Robert. *Among the Righteous: Lost Stories from the Holocaust's Long Reach into Arab Lands*. New York, 2006.

Schulze, Kirsten E. *Jews of Lebanon: Between Coexistence and Conflict*. Brighton, 2001.

Seale, Patrick. *The Struggle for Syria*. London, 1965.

Segev, Tom. *The Seventh Million: The Israelis and the Holocaust*. New York, 2000.

Shamir, S., ed. *Egypt: From Monarchy to Republic*. Boulder, CO, 1995.

Simon, Reeva S. *Iraq between the Two World Wars: The Creation and Implementation of a Nationalist Ideology*. New York, 1986.

Sing, Manfred. "Between Lights and Hurricanes: Sami al-Kayyali's Review al-Hadith as a Forum of Modern Arab Literature and Liberal Islam." In *The Middle Eastern Press as a Forum for Literature*, edited by Horst Unbehaun. Frankfurt, 2004.

Smith, Charles D. *Islam and the Search for Social Order in Modern Egypt: A Biography of Muhammad Husayn Haykal*. Albany, NY, 1983.

Stark, Freya. *The Arab Island: The Middle East, 1939–1943*. New York, 1945.

Suleiman, Michael W. *Political Parties in Lebanon*. Ithaca, NY, 1967.

Tarbush, Mohammad A. *The Role of the Military in Politics: A Case Study of Iraq to 1941*. Boston, 1982.

Tauber, Eliezer. "The Press and the Journalist as a Vehicle in Spreading National Ideas in Syria in the Late Ottoman Empire." *Die Welt des Islams*, n.s., 30 (1990).

Thompson, Elizabeth. *Colonial Citizens: Republican Rights, Paternal Privilege, and Gender in French Syria and Lebanon*. New York, 1999.

Tibawi, A. L. *Arab Education in Mandatory Palestine: A Study of Three Decades of British Administration*. London, 1956.

Tripp, Charles. "Ali Mahir and the Politics of the Egyptian Army, 1936–1942." In *Contemporary Egypt through Egyptian Eyes*, edited by Charles Tripp. New York, 1993.

Vatikiotis, P. J. *The History of Modern Egypt: From Muhammad Ali to Mubarak*. London, 1991.

———. *Politics and the Military in Jordan: A Study of the Arab Legion, 1921–1957*. New York, 1967.

Warburg, Gabriel. *Egypt and the Sudan: Studies in History and Politics*. London, 1985.

Watenpaugh, Keith David. *Being Modern in the Middle East: Revolution, Nationalism, Colonialism, and the Arab Middle Class*. Princeton, NJ, 2006.

Wehrey, Frederic M. "The Insurgent State: Politics and Communal Dissent in Iraq, 1919–1936." Master's thesis, Princeton University, 2002.

Wendell, Charles. *The Evolution of the Egyptian National Image: From Its Origins to Ahmad Lutfi al-Sayyid*. Berkeley, CA, 1972.

Wien, Peter. "Coming to Terms with the Past: German Academia and Historical Relations between the Arab Lands and Nazi Germany." *International Journal of Middle Eastern Studies* 42, no. 2 (2010).

———. *Iraqi Arab Nationalism: Authoritarian, Totalitarian, and Pro-Fascist Inclinations, 1932–1941*. London, 2006.

Wild, Stefan. "Die arabische Rezeption der Protokolle der Weisen von Zion." In *Islamstudien ohne Ende: Festschrift für Werner Ende zum 65. Geburtstag*. Würzburg, 2002.

Wildangel, René. *Zwischen Achse und Mandatsmacht: Palästina und der Nationalsozislismus*. Berlin, 2007.

Wistrich, Robert. "The Old-New Anti-Semitism." *National Interest* 72 (2003).

Yamak, Labib Zuwiyya. *The Syrian Social Nationalist Party: An Ideological Analysis*. Cambridge, MA, 1966.

Zamir, M. "Bid for Altalena: France's Covert Action in the 1948 War in Palestine." *Middle Eastern Studies* 46, no. 1 (2010): 17–58.

———. "De Gaulle and the Question of Syria and Lebanon during the Second World War." *Middle Eastern Studies* 43, no. 5 (2007): 675–708.

———. "An Intimate Alliance: The Joint Struggle of General Edward Spears and Riad al-Sulh to Oust France from Lebanon, 1942–1944." *Middle Eastern Studies* 41, no. 6 (2005).

———. "The 'Missing Dimension': Britain's Secret War against France in Syria and Lebanon, 1942–1945." *Middle Eastern Studies* 46, no. 6 (2010): 791–899.

Zisser, Eyal. *Lebanon: The Challenge of Independence*. London, 2000.

About the Contributors

ORIT BASHKIN got her PhD from Princeton University (2004) and her BA (1995) and MA (1999) from Tel Aviv University. Her publications include twenty book chapters and articles on the history of Arab Jews in Iraq, on Iraqi history, and on Arabic literature. She has edited a book, *Lefasel tarbut be-mitzrayim* (Sculpturing culture in Egypt), with Israel Gershoni and Liat Kozma, which includes translations into Hebrew of seminal works by Egyptian intellectuals. She is the author of the following books: *The Other Iraq: Pluralism, Intellectuals and Culture in Hashemite Iraq, 1921–1958* (2009) and *New Babylonians: A History of Jews in Modern Iraq* (2012).

HAGGAI ERLICH is a professor emeritus at the Department of Middle Eastern and African History, Tel-Aviv University, and an academic adviser at the Open University of Israel. His fields of research are Ethiopia's modern history and its relations with the Middle East, students and university in the politics of Middle Eastern societies, and modern histories of Egypt and the Nile countries. His recent studies include *Islam and Christianity in the Horn of Africa, Somalia, Ethiopia, Sudan* (2010); *Generations of Rage: University and Students in the Middle East* (2012, in Hebrew; an English version is forthcoming); and *Alliance and Alienation: Ethiopia and Israel during Haile Selassie's Time* (Hebrew and English versions forthcoming).

ISRAEL GERSHONI is a professor in the Department of Middle Eastern and African History, Tel Aviv University. Among his latest publications are *Narrating the Nile: Politics, Cultures, Identities* (2008), coedited with Meir Hatina; *Confronting Fascism in Egypt: Dictatorship versus Democ-*

racy in the 1930s (2010), coauthored with James Jankowski; and the two-volume *Dame and Devil: Egypt and Nazism, 1935–1940* (2012, in Hebrew).

RAMI GINAT is a professor of Middle Eastern studies in the Department of Political Studies, Bar-Ilan University, Israel. His books include *The Soviet Union and Egypt* (1993), *Egypt's Incomplete Revolution* (1997), and *Syria and the Doctrine of Arab Neutralism* (2005). His most recent books are *Egypt and the Second Palestinian Intifada* (2011) and *A History of Egyptian Communism: Jews and Their Compatriots in Quest of Revolution* (2011).

JAMES JANKOWSKI is professor emeritus at the University of Colorado, Boulder. A scholar interested in modern Egyptian history, his publications include *Egypt, Islam, and the Arabs* (1986), coauthored with Israel Gershoni; *Redefining the Egyptian Nation, 1930–1945* (1995), coauthored with Israel Gershoni; *Egypt: A Short History* (2000); and *Nasser's Egypt, Arab Nationalism, and the United Arab Republic* (2002).

MUSTAFA KABHA is chair of the Department of History, Philosophy, and Judaic Studies at the Open University of Israel. His fields of research are Middle East history in the modern era, the history of the Palestinian national movement, and the history of Arab mass communications. His last two books are *The Palestinian Press as Shaper of Public Opinion, 1929–1939: Writing Up a Storm* (2007) and *The Palestinian Arab In/Outsiders: Media and Conflict in Israel* (2011), coauthored with Dan Caspi.

GÖTZ NORDBRUCH is a research fellow at the Georg Eckert Institute for International Textbook Research in Brunswick, Germany. He has previously worked as assistant professor at the Centre for Contemporary Middle Eastern Studies at the University of Southern Denmark. His research is focused on the history of Arab-European encounters in the twentieth century.

ESTHER WEBMAN is a senior research fellow at the Dayan Center for Middle Eastern and African Studies and the Stephen Roth Institute for the Study of Antisemitism and Racism at Tel Aviv University. She is the head of the Zeev Vered Desk for the Study of Tolerance and Intolerance and an editorial board member of *Sharqiyya*, a journal of Middle Eastern and Islamic studies, and *Moreshet*, a journal for the study of the Holocaust and anti-Semitism. Her research is focused on Arab discourse analysis; modern Islamic movements; Muslim-Jewish relations, including Arab anti-Semitism and Arab perceptions of the Holocaust; and Muslims in the West. She is the editor of *The Global Impact of a Myth: The Protocols of the Elders of Zion* (2011). Her book *From Empathy to Denial: Arab Responses to the Holocaust,* coauthored with Meir Litvak, was the recipient of the Washington Institute for Near East Policy's book prize for 2010.

RENÉ WILDANGEL has been director of the Heinrich Böll Foundation in Ramallah since January 2012. He studied history in Cologne, Jerusalem, and Damascus. He was a researcher at the Berlin Centre for Modern Oriental Studies, where he completed his book on Palestine and Nazism. His served as an adviser to the Green Party in the German Parliament and in the German Federal Foreign Office. He is the author of *Zwischen Achse und Mandatsmacht: Palästina und der Nationalsozialismus.*

MEIR ZAMIR is a professor at the Department of Middle East Studies, Ben-Gurion University of the Negev. His research interests include intelligence studies, the modern history of Syria and Lebanon, and French and British colonialism in the Middle East.

EYAL ZISSER is the dean of the faculty of humanities at Tel Aviv University. He has written extensively on the history and modern politics of Syria and Lebanon and the Arab-Israeli conflict. Among his books are *Assad's Syria at a Crossroads* (1999), *Asad's Legacy: Syria in Transition* (2000), *Lebanon: The Challenge of Independence* (2000), *Faces of Syria* (2003), *Commanding Syria: Bashar al-Asad and the First Years in Power* (2006), and *The Bleeding Cedar* (2009).

Index

www.ingramcontent.com/pod-product-compliance
Lightning Source LLC
Chambersburg PA
CBHW020452270326
41926CB00008B/571